Thank you for picking up *Haikyu!!* volume 29! There are times when I really wish I hadn't used a line or a scene where I did. I can't rework the story that is already written, but boy do I sometimes wish I could write the chapters in large chunks instead of one a week. Of course, if I ever did get the time I'd need to do that, I'd probably just waste it by going out or something.

HARUICHI FURUDATE began his manga career when he was 25 years old with the one-shot *Ousama Kid* (King Kid), which won an honorable mention for the 14th Jump Treasure Newcomer Manga Prize. His first series, *Kiben Gakuha, Yotsuya Sensei no Kaidan* (Philosophy School, Yotsuya Sensei's Ghost Stories), was serialized in Weekly Shonen Jump in 2010. In 2012, he began serializing *Haikyu!!* in Weekly Shonen Jump, where it became his most popular work to date.

HAIKYU!!

VOLUME 29

SHONEN JUMP Manga Edition

Story and Art by

HARUICHI FURUDATE

Translation 1 **ADRIENNE BECK**
Touch-Up Art & Lettering 2 **ERIKA TERRIQUEZ**
Design 3 **JULIAN [JR] ROBINSON**
Editor 4 **MARLENE FIRST**

First published in Japan in 2012 by SHUEISHA Inc., Tokyo.
English translation rights arranged by SHUEISHA Inc.

Printed in the U.S.A.

Published by VIZ Media, LLC
P.O. Box 77010
San Francisco, CA 94107

10 9 8 7 6 5 4 3 2 1
First printing, November 2018

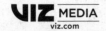

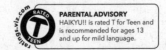

SHONENJUMP MANGA

Karasuno Taiko

HAIKYU!!

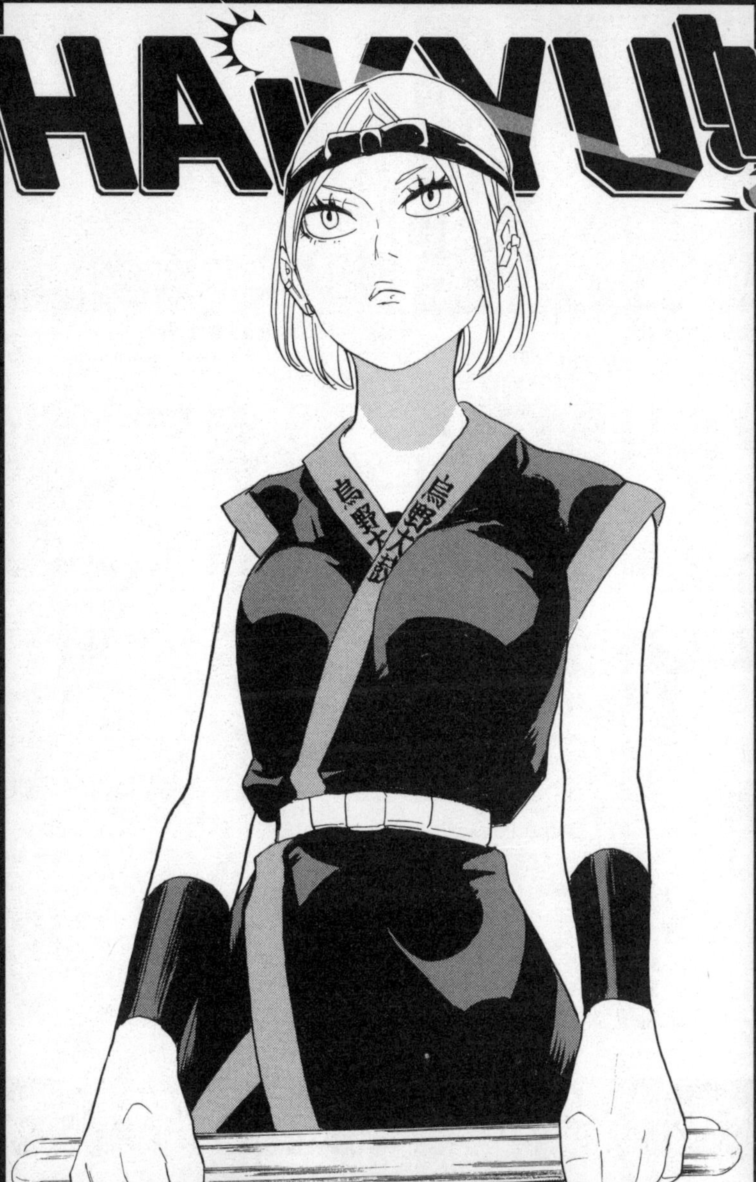

HARUICHI
FURUDATE

FOUND 29

Karasuno High School Volleyball Club

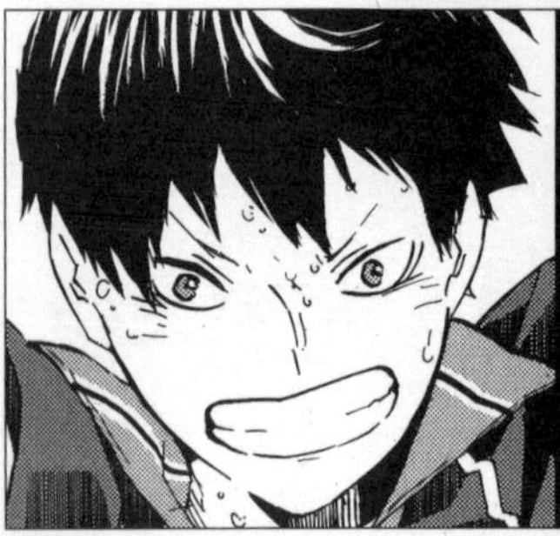

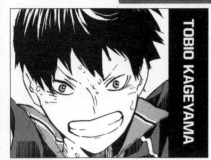

TOBIO KAGEYAMA

1ST YEAR / SETTER

His instincts and athletic talent are so good that he's like a "king" who rules the court. Demanding and egocentric.

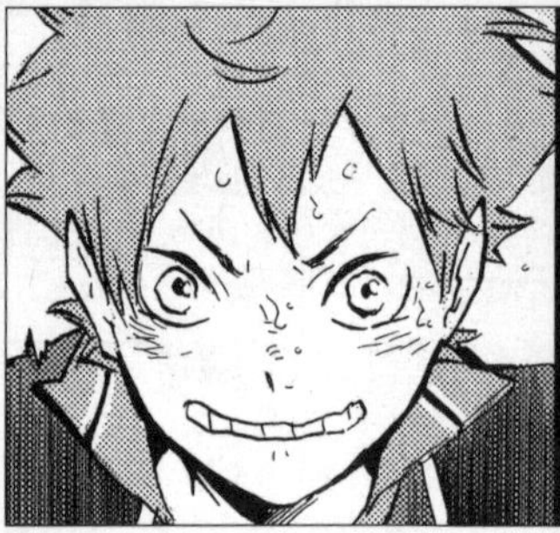

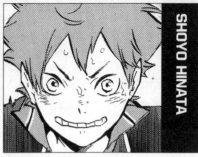

SHOYO HINATA

1ST YEAR / MIDDLE BLOCKER

Even though he doesn't have the best body type for volleyball, he is super athletic. Gets nervous easily.

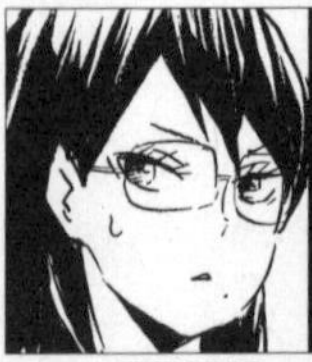

KIYOKO SHIMIZU

3RD YEAR
MANAGER

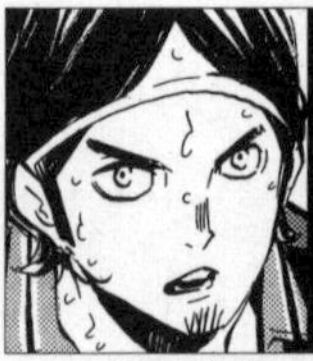

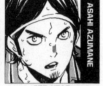

ASAHI AZUMANE

3RD YEAR
WING SPIKER

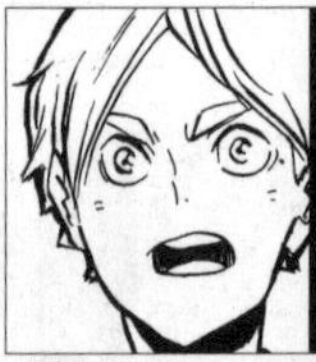

KOUSHI SUGAWARA

3RD YEAR (VICE CAPTAIN)
SETTER

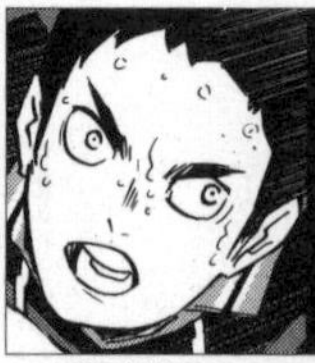

DAICHI SAWAMURA

3RD YEAR (CAPTAIN)
WING SPIKER

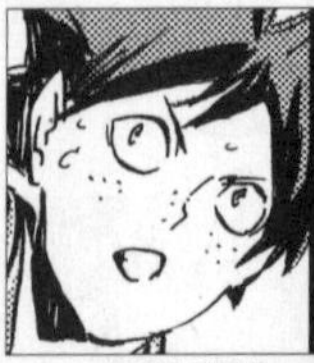

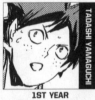

TADASHI YAMAGUCHI

1ST YEAR
MIDDLE BLOCKER

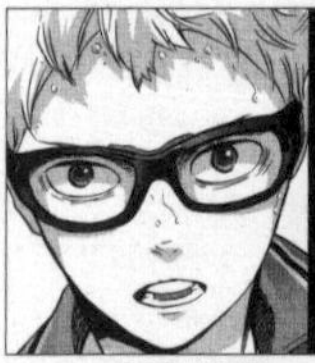

KEI TSUKISHIMA

1ST YEAR
MIDDLE BLOCKER

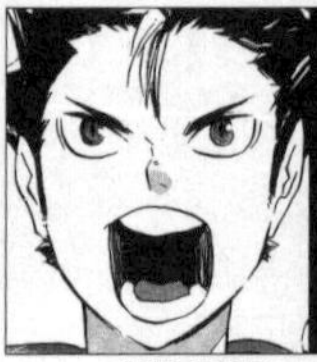

YU NISHINOYA

2ND YEAR
LIBERO

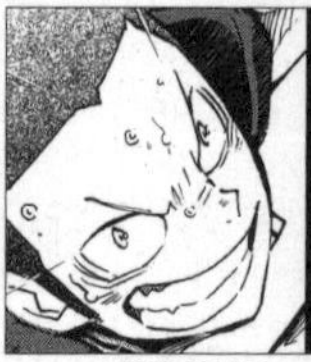

RYUNOSUKE TANAKA

2ND YEAR
WING SPIKER

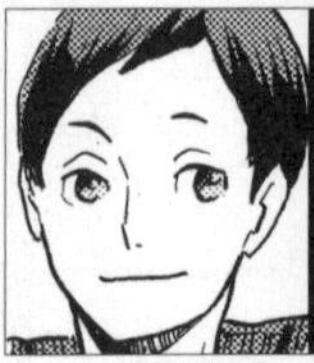

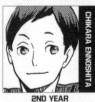

CHIKARA ENNOSHITA

2ND YEAR
WING SPIKER

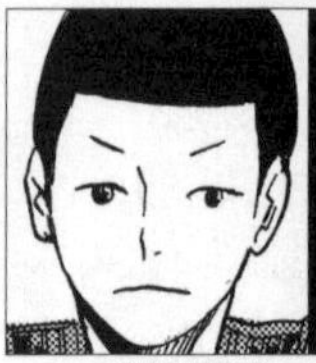

KAZUHITO NARITA

2ND YEAR
MIDDLE BLOCKER

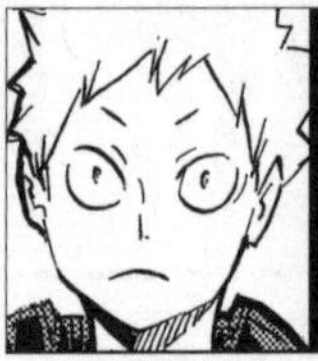

HISASHI KINOSHITA

2ND YEAR
WING SPIKER

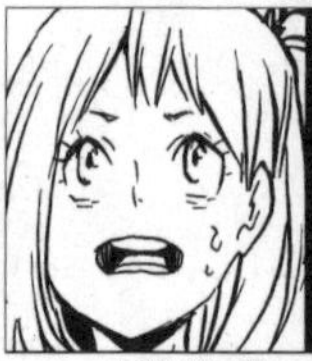

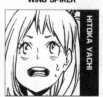

HITOKA YACHI

1ST YEAR
MANAGER

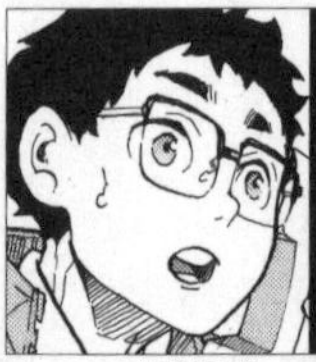

ITTETSU TAKEDA

ADVISER

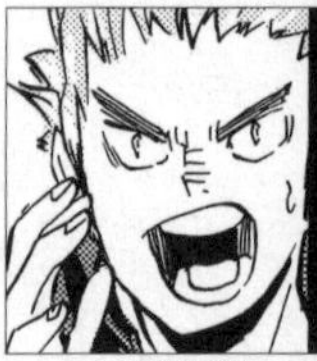

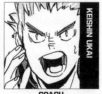

KEISHIN UKAI

COACH

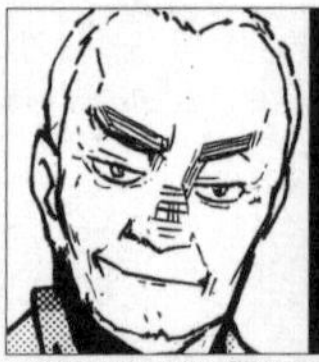

IKKEI UKAI

FORMER HEAD COACH

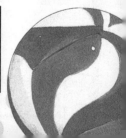

CHARACTERS

NATIONAL SPRING TOURNAMENT ARC

Inarizaki Volleyball Club

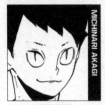

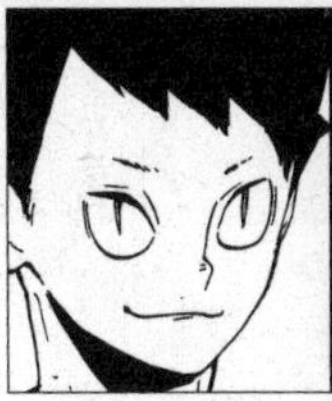
MICHINARI AKAGI
3RD YEAR
LIBERO

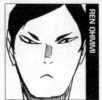

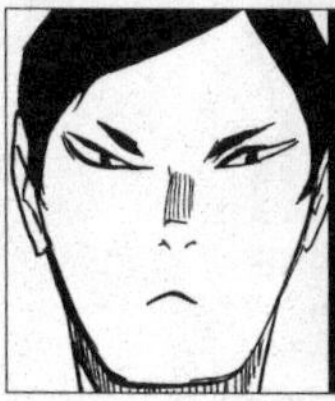
REN OHMIMI
3RD YEAR
MIDDLE BLOCKER

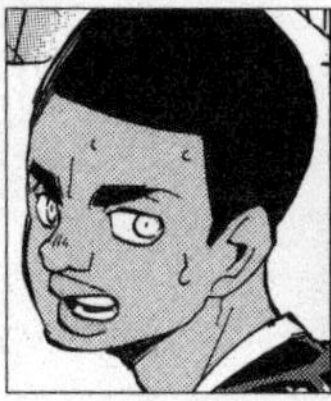
ARAN OJIRO
3RD YEAR
WING SPIKER

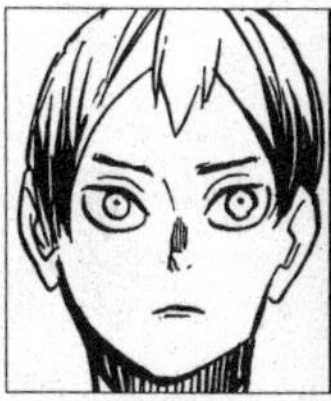
SHINSUKE KITA
3RD YEAR (CAPTAIN)
WING SPIKER

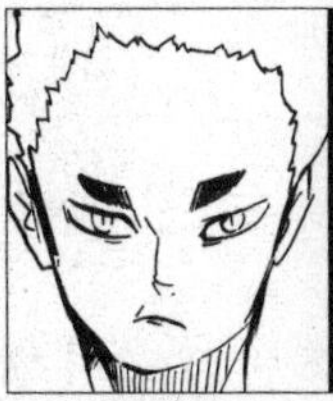
HITOSHI GINJIMA
2ND YEAR
WING SPIKER

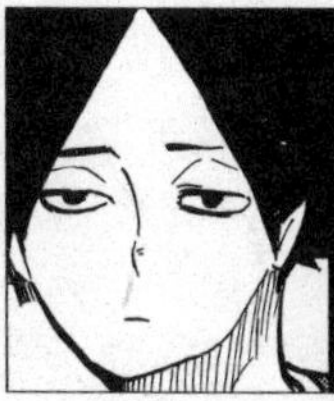
RINTARO SUNA
2ND YEAR
MIDDLE BLOCKER

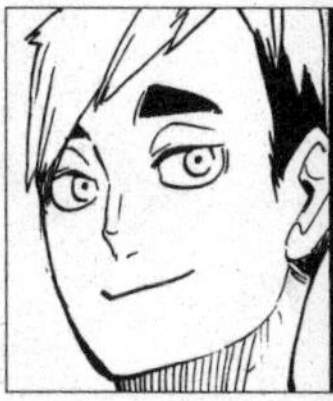
ATSUMU MIYA
2ND YEAR
SETTER

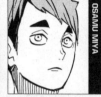

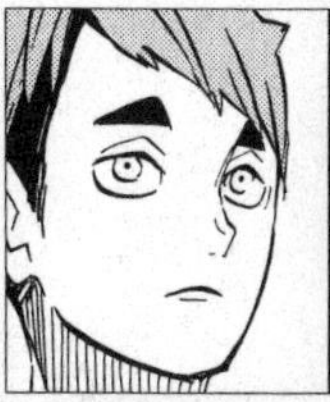
OSAMU MIYA
2ND YEAR
WING SPIKER

Fukurodani Academy

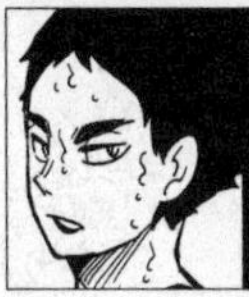
KEIJI AKAASHI
2ND YEAR
SETTER

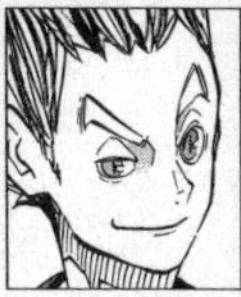
KOTARO BOKUTO
3RD YEAR (CAPTAIN)
WING SPIKER

Karasuno Cheer Section

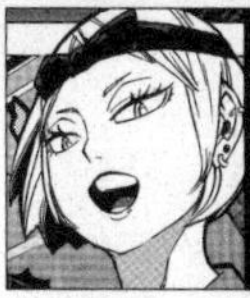
SAEKO TANAKA

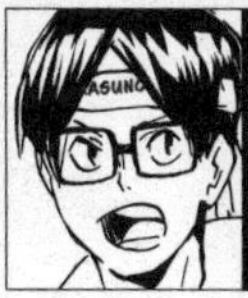
SHIMADA MART

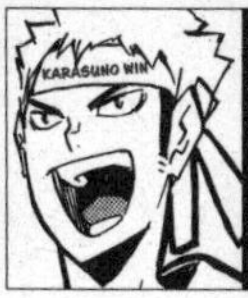
KARASUNO WIN
TAKINOUE APPLIANCE

Ever since he saw the legendary player known as "the Little Giant" compete at the national volleyball finals, Shoyo Hinata has been aiming to be the best volleyball player ever! He decides to join the volleyball club at his middle school and gets to play in an official tournament during his third year. His team is crushed by a team led by volleyball prodigy Tobio Kageyama, also known as "the King of the Court." Swearing revenge on Kageyama, Hinata graduates middle school and enters Karasuno High School, the school where the Little Giant played. However, upon joining the club, he finds out that Kageyama is there too! The two of them bicker constantly, but they bring out the best in each other's talents and become a powerful combo. Then the Spring Tournament begins! Both Karasuno and Nekoma secure victory in their round one matches. Free for the afternoon, Hinata gets excited to watch Kamomedai's Korai Hoshiumi play, because he is also known as a "Little Giant." That evening, the team learns who their next opponent is—Inarizaki High School, one of the favorites to win the whole tournament! With high school's greatest sibling duo, the Miya twins, on the court, and a top-class marching band for a cheering squad throwing off Karasuno's rhythm, it feels like Inarizaki is attacking Karasuno from every angle! But then Tanaka's sister, Saeko, arrives to save the day...

HAIKYU!!

29 FOUND

CHAPTER 252: Support System

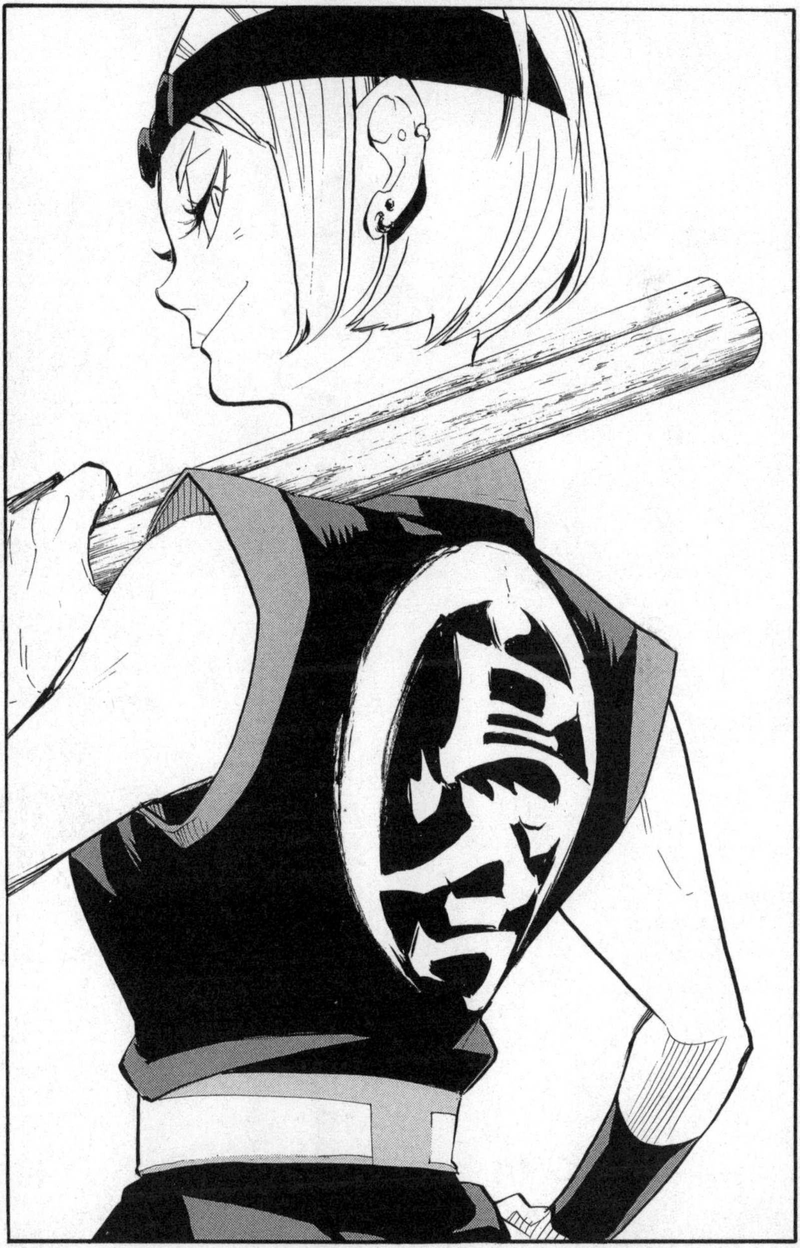

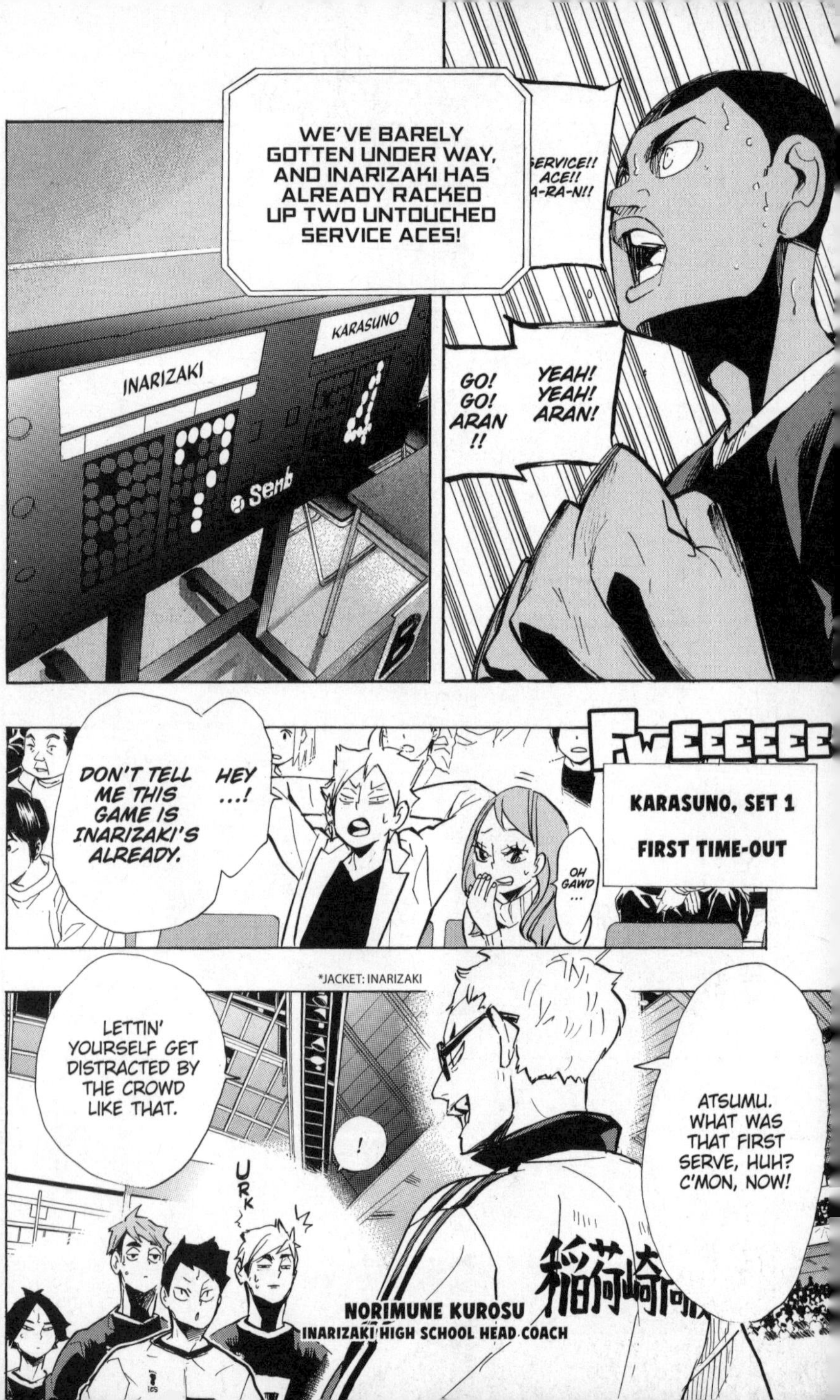
SERVICE!! ACE!! A-RA-N!!
YEAH! YEAH! ARAN!
GO! GO! ARAN !!
WE'VE BARELY GOTTEN UNDER WAY, AND INARIZAKI HAS ALREADY RACKED UP TWO UNTOUCHED SERVICE ACES!
KARASUNO
INARIZAKI
Senb
FWEEEEEE
KARASUNO, SET 1
FIRST TIME-OUT
OH GAWD ...
HEY ...!
DON'T TELL ME THIS GAME IS INARIZAKI'S ALREADY.
*JACKET: INARIZAKI
ATSUMU. WHAT WAS THAT FIRST SERVE, HUH? C'MON, NOW!
NORIMUNE KUROSU
INARIZAKI HIGH SCHOOL HEAD COACH
!
URK
LETTIN' YOURSELF GET DISTRACTED BY THE CROWD LIKE THAT.

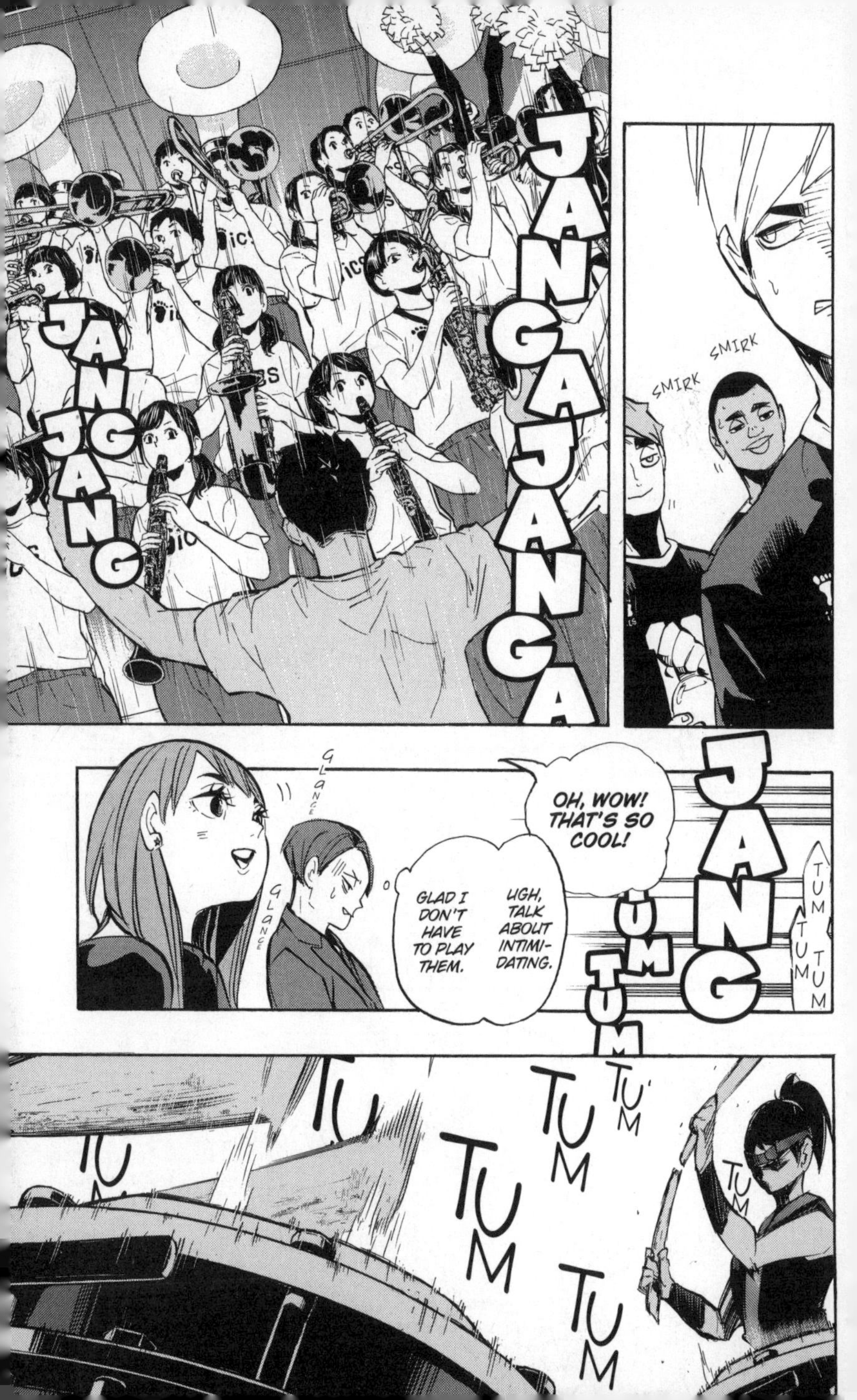
SMIRK
SMIRK
JANGAJANGA
JANGJANG
JANG
TUM TUM TUM TUM
OH, WOW! THAT'S SO COOL!
UGH, TALK ABOUT INTIMI-DATING.
GLAD I DON'T HAVE TO PLAY THEM.
GLANCE
GLANCE
TUM TUM
TUM
TUM TUM
TUM
TUM TUM
TUM
TU
TU

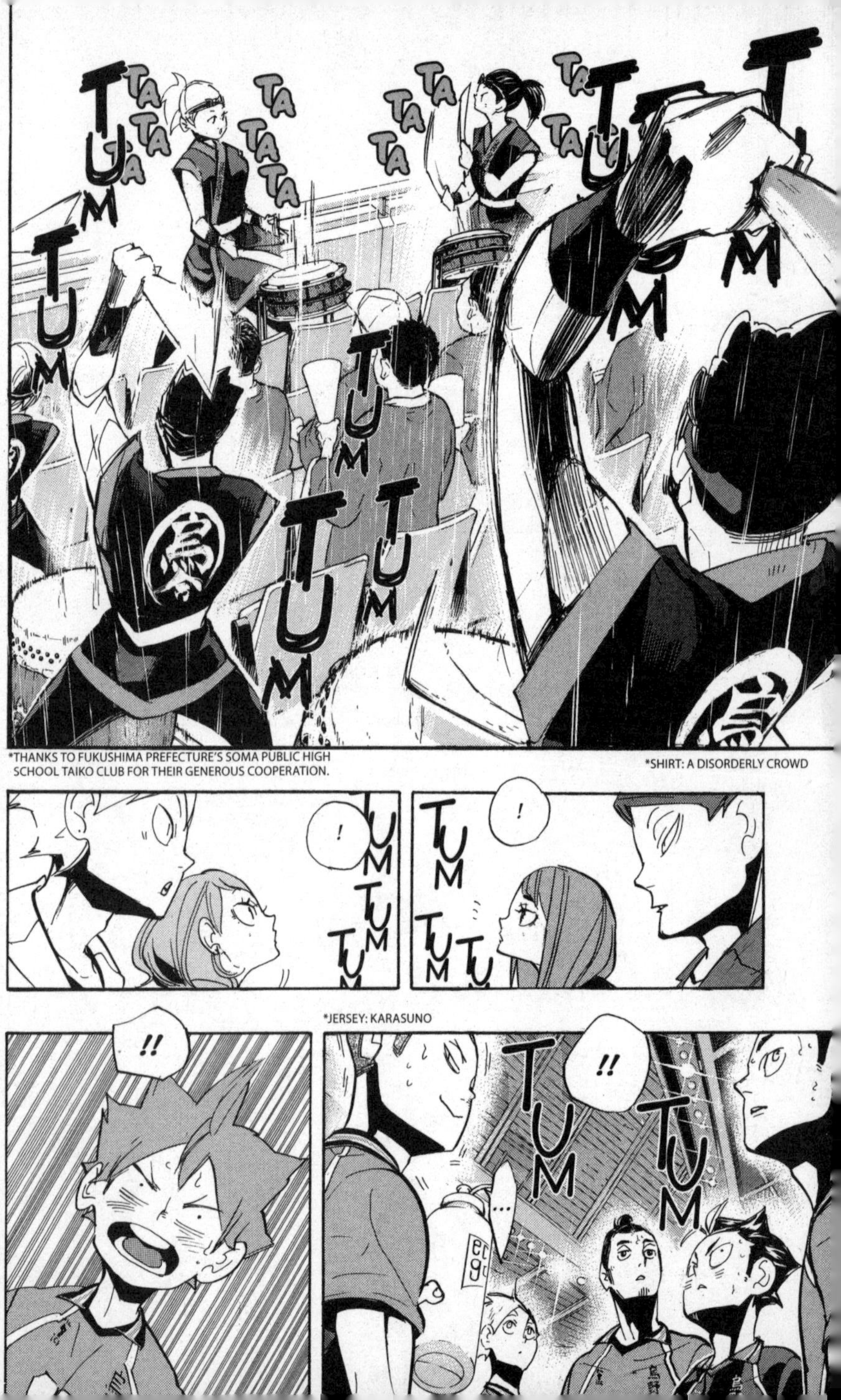
TA TA TA TA
TUM
TUM TUM TUM
TA TA TA TA TA TA
TUM TUM TUM
*SHIRT: A DISORDERLY CROWD
*THANKS TO FUKUSHIMA PREFECTURE'S SOMA PUBLIC HIGH SCHOOL TAIKO CLUB FOR THEIR GENEROUS COOPERATION.
!
TUM TUM
!
TUM TUM
*JERSEY: KARASUNO
!!
TUM TUM
...
!!

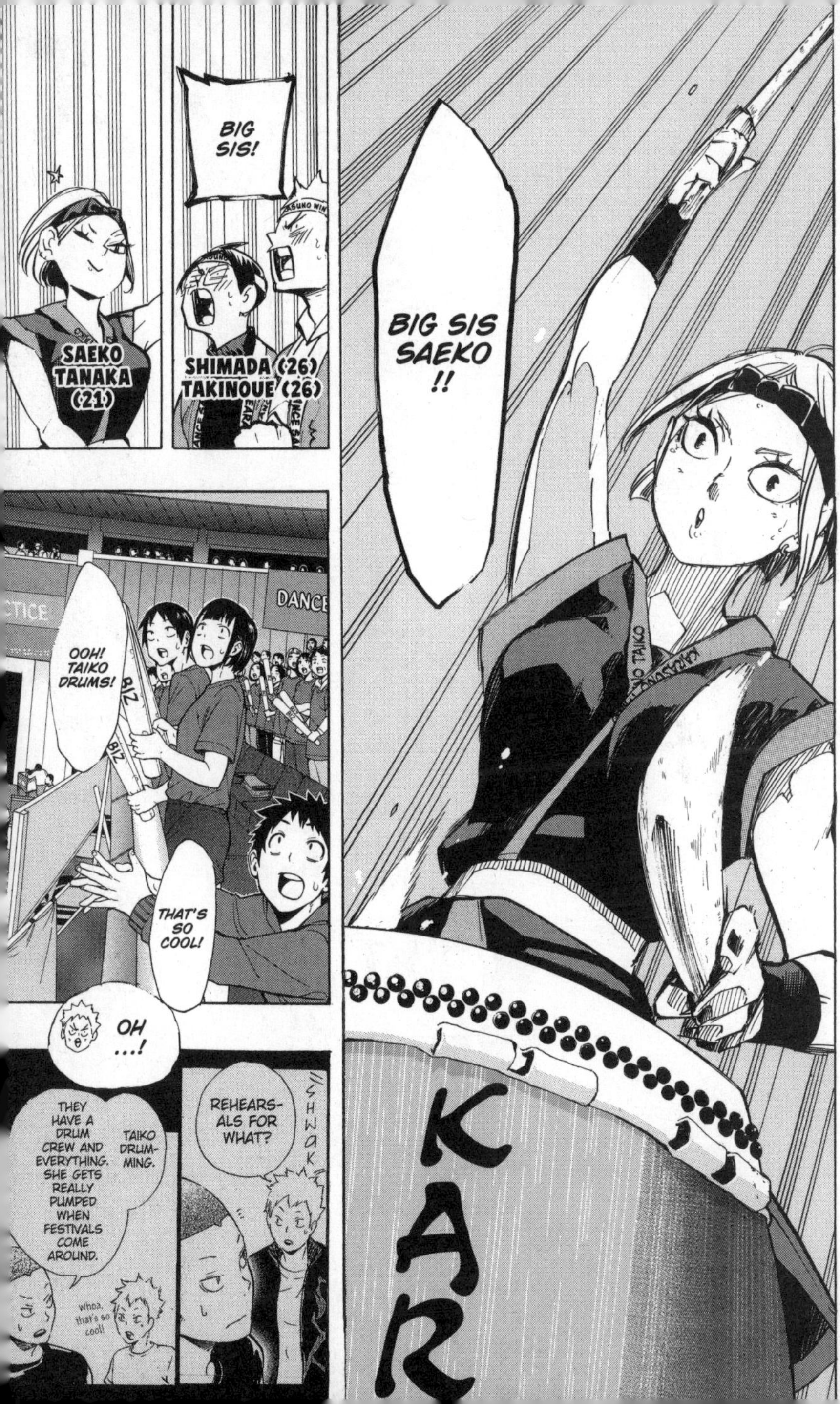
BIG SIS SAEKO !!
KAR
BIG SIS!
SHIMADA (26) TAKINOUE (26)
SAEKO TANAKA (21)
DANCE
OOH! TAIKO DRUMS!
THAT'S SO COOL!
OH ...!
REHEARS-ALS FOR WHAT?
SHWAK
TAIKO DRUM-MING.
THEY HAVE A DRUM CREW AND EVERYTHING. SHE GETS REALLY PUMPED WHEN FESTIVALS COME AROUND.
whoa, that's so cool!

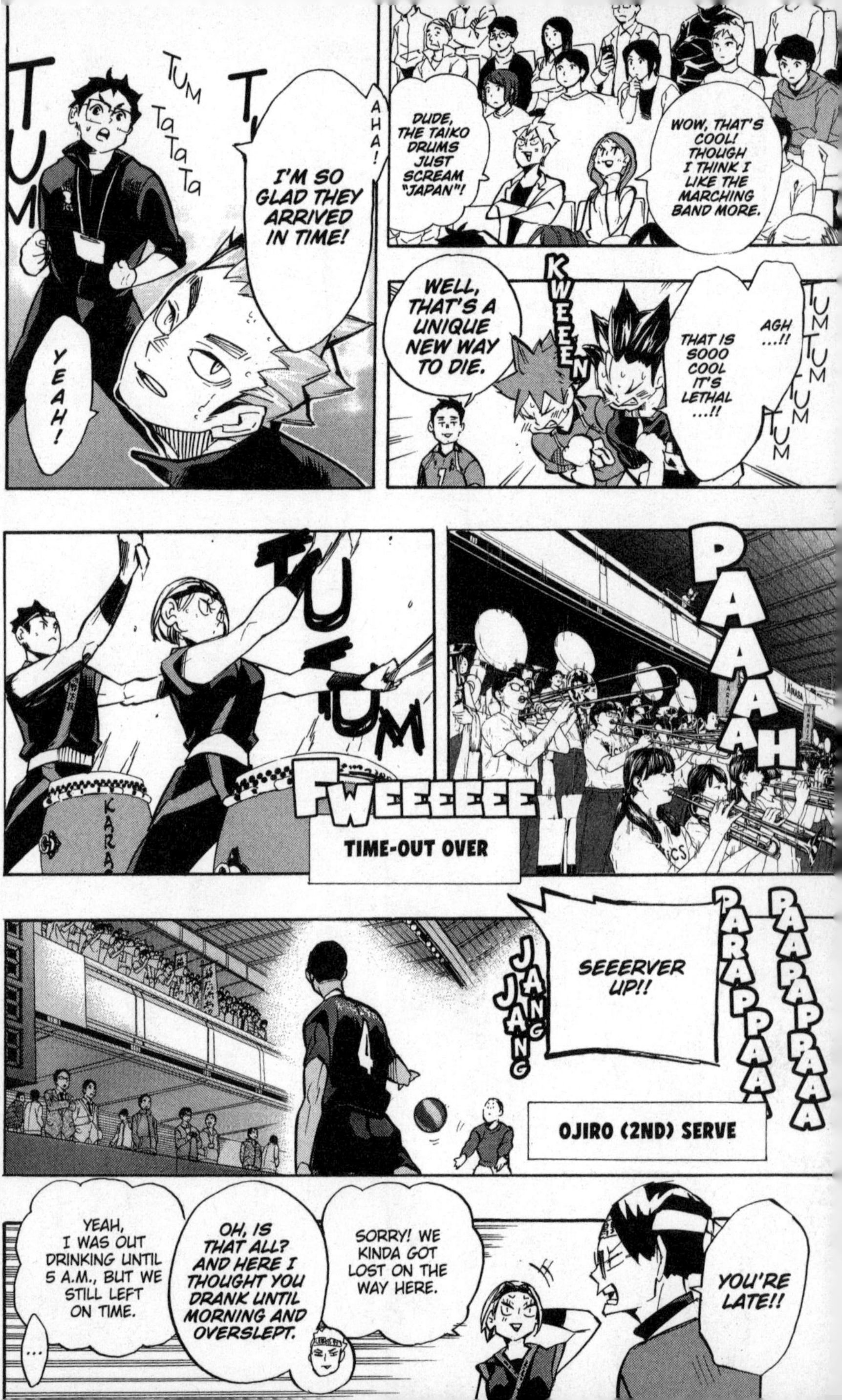
DUDE, THE TAIKO DRUMS JUST SCREAM "JAPAN"!
WOW, THAT'S COOL! THOUGH I THINK I LIKE THE MARCHING BAND MORE.
TUM TUM TUM TUM
AGH...!!
THAT IS SOOO COOL IT'S LETHAL...!!
KWEEEN
WELL, THAT'S A UNIQUE NEW WAY TO DIE.
AHA!
I'M SO GLAD THEY ARRIVED IN TIME!
TUM
TUM Ta Ta Ta
TUM
YEAH!
PAAAAAH
TUM TUM
FWEEEEEE
TIME-OUT OVER
PAAPAPPAAA
PARAPPAA
SEEERVER UP!!
JANG JANG
OJIRO (2ND) SERVE
YOU'RE LATE!!
SORRY! WE KINDA GOT LOST ON THE WAY HERE.
OH, IS THAT ALL? AND HERE I THOUGHT YOU DRANK UNTIL MORNING AND OVERSLEPT.
YEAH, I WAS OUT DRINKING UNTIL 5 A.M., BUT WE STILL LEFT ON TIME.
...

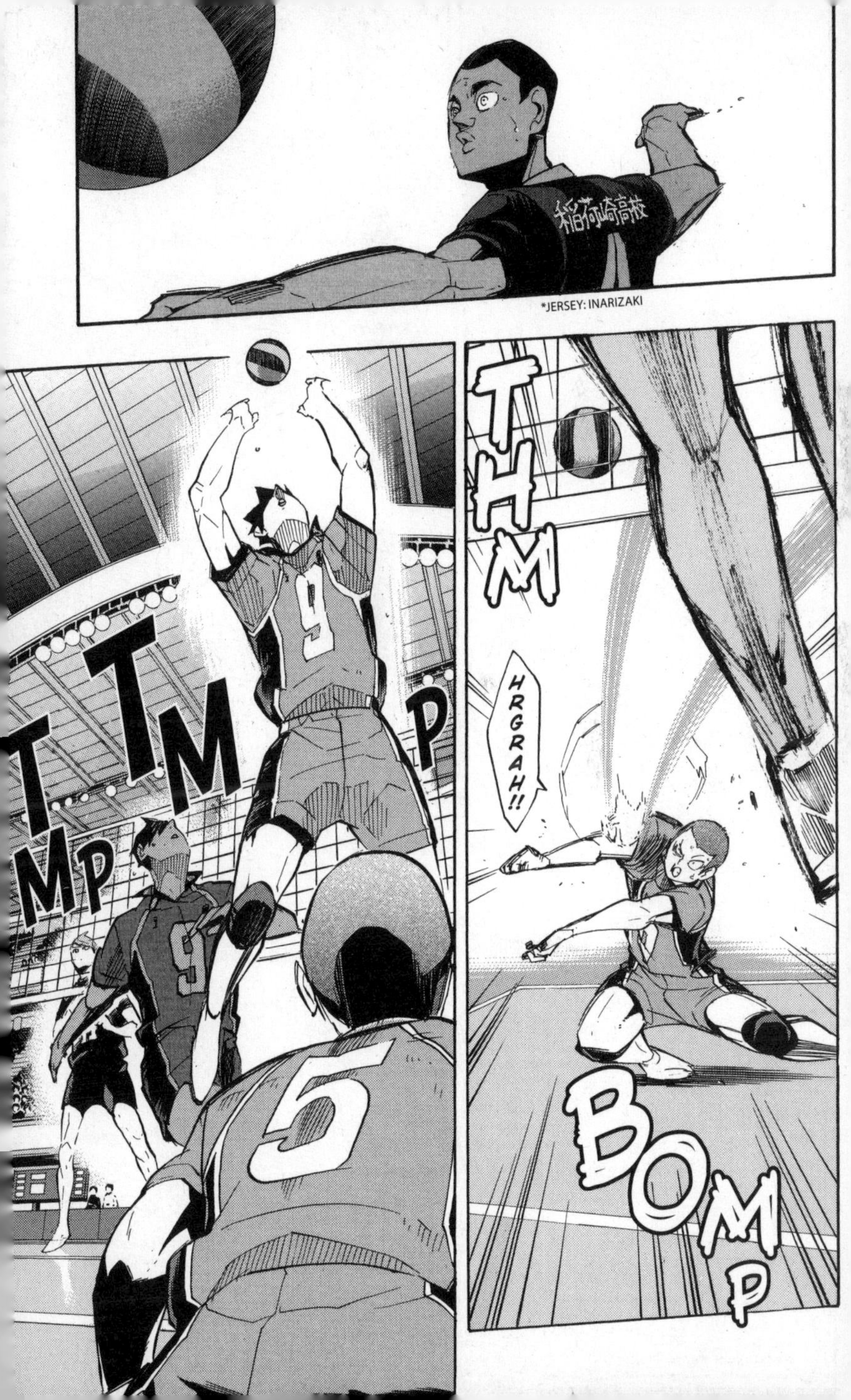
稲荷崎高校
*JERSEY: INARIZAKI
THM
HRGRAH!!
BOMP
TMP
TMP

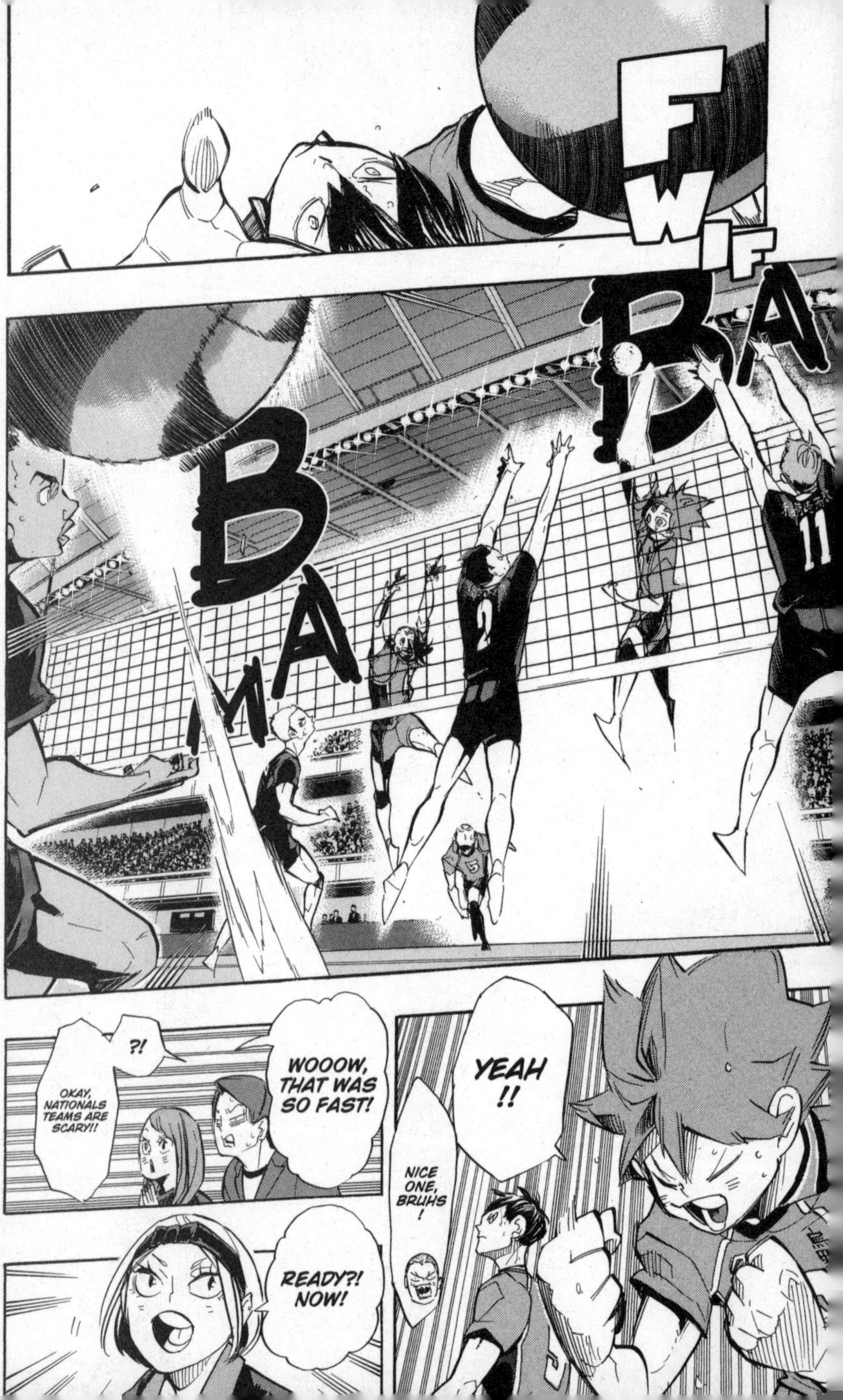
FWIF
BA
BAM
YEAH !!
NICE ONE, BRUHS !
WOOOW, THAT WAS SO FAST!
?!
OKAY, NATIONALS TEAMS ARE SCARY!!
READY?! NOW!

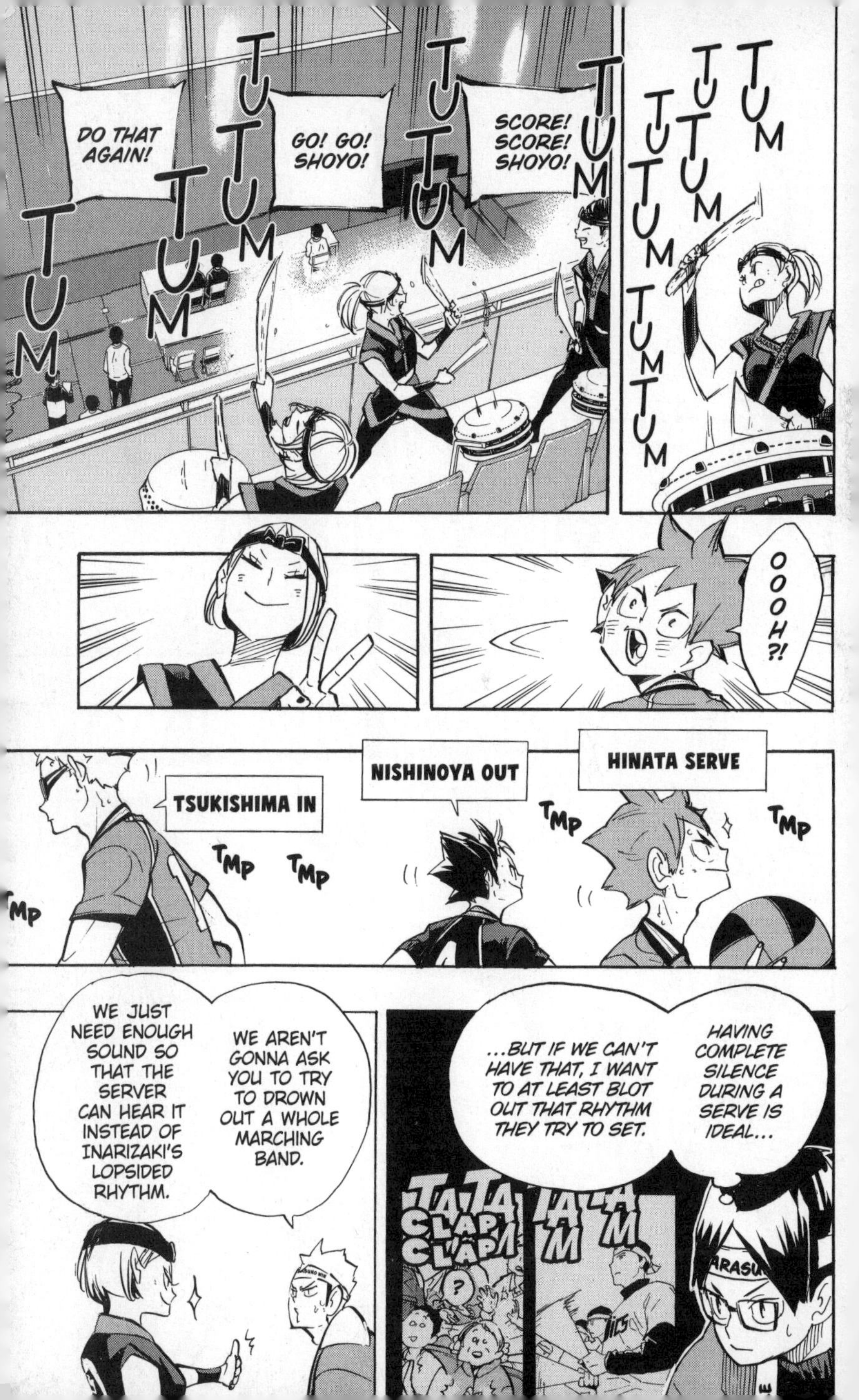
TUM TUM TUM TUM TUM TUM
TUM TUM
SCORE! SCORE! SHOYO!
TUM
GO! GO! SHOYO!
TUM TUM
DO THAT AGAIN!
TUM
OOOH?!
HINATA SERVE
TMP
NISHINOYA OUT
TMP
TSUKISHIMA IN
TMP TMP TMP
HAVING COMPLETE SILENCE DURING A SERVE IS IDEAL...
...BUT IF WE CAN'T HAVE THAT, I WANT TO AT LEAST BLOT OUT THAT RHYTHM THEY TRY TO SET.
TA TA
CLAP CLAP
WE AREN'T GONNA ASK YOU TO TRY TO DROWN OUT A WHOLE MARCHING BAND.
WE JUST NEED ENOUGH SOUND SO THAT THE SERVER CAN HEAR IT INSTEAD OF INARIZAKI'S LOPSIDED RHYTHM.

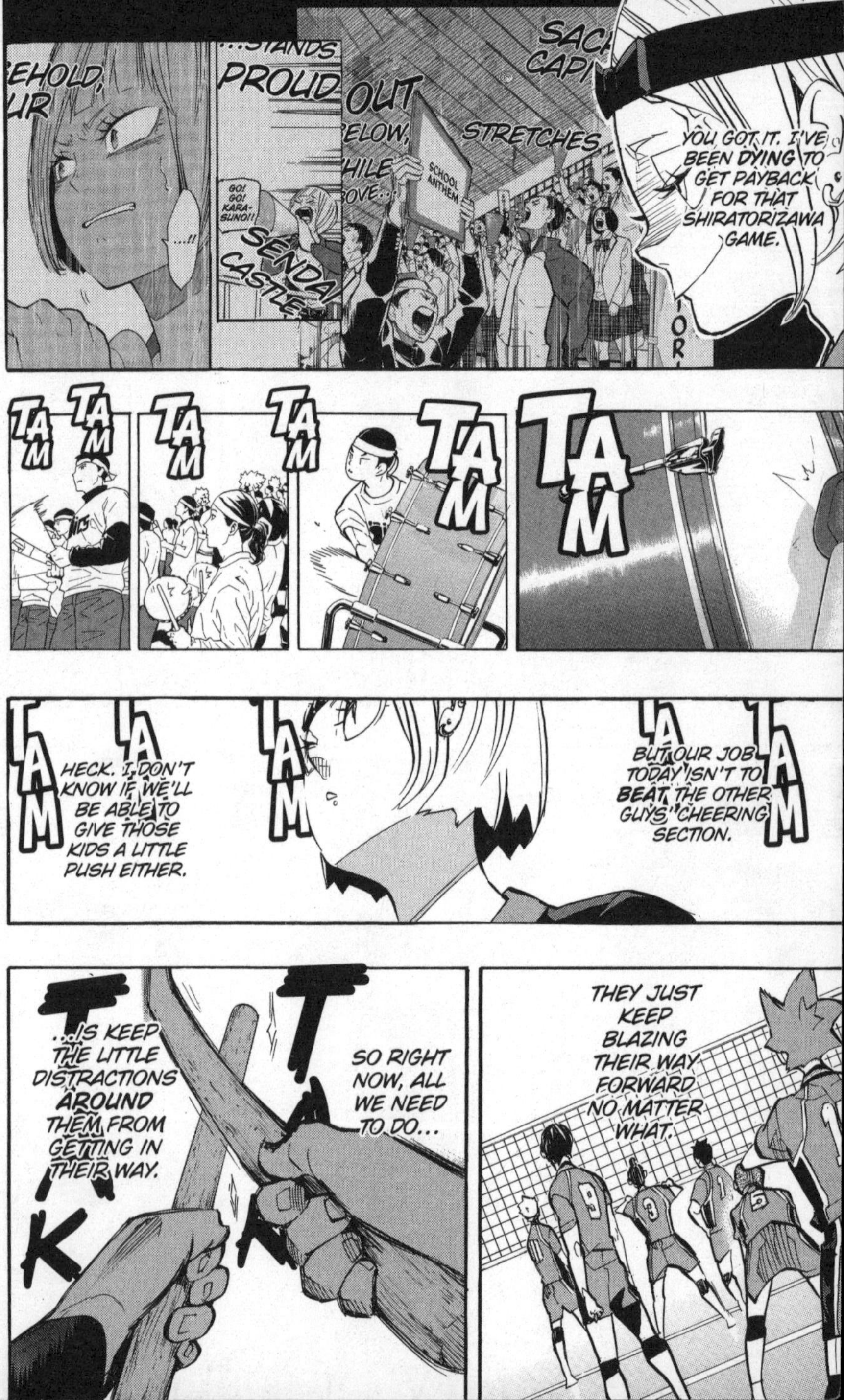
YOU GOT IT. I'VE BEEN DYING TO GET PAYBACK FOR THAT SHIRATORIZAWA GAME.
SACH
CAPI
STRETCHES
OUT
BELOW,
HILE
OVE...
SCHOOL ANTHEM
...STANDS
PROUD
GO! GO! KARA-SUNO!!
SENDAI CASTLE
EHOLD,
UR
...!!
TAM
TAM
TAM
TAM
TAM
TAM
BUT OUR JOB TODAY ISN'T TO BEAT THE OTHER GUYS' CHEERING SECTION.
TAM
TAM
TAM
TAM
HECK. I DON'T KNOW IF WE'LL BE ABLE TO GIVE THOSE KIDS A LITTLE PUSH EITHER.
TAM
THEY JUST KEEP BLAZING THEIR WAY FORWARD NO MATTER WHAT.
SO RIGHT NOW, ALL WE NEED TO DO...
T
...IS KEEP THE LITTLE DISTRACTIONS AROUND THEM FROM GETTING IN THEIR WAY.
TAK

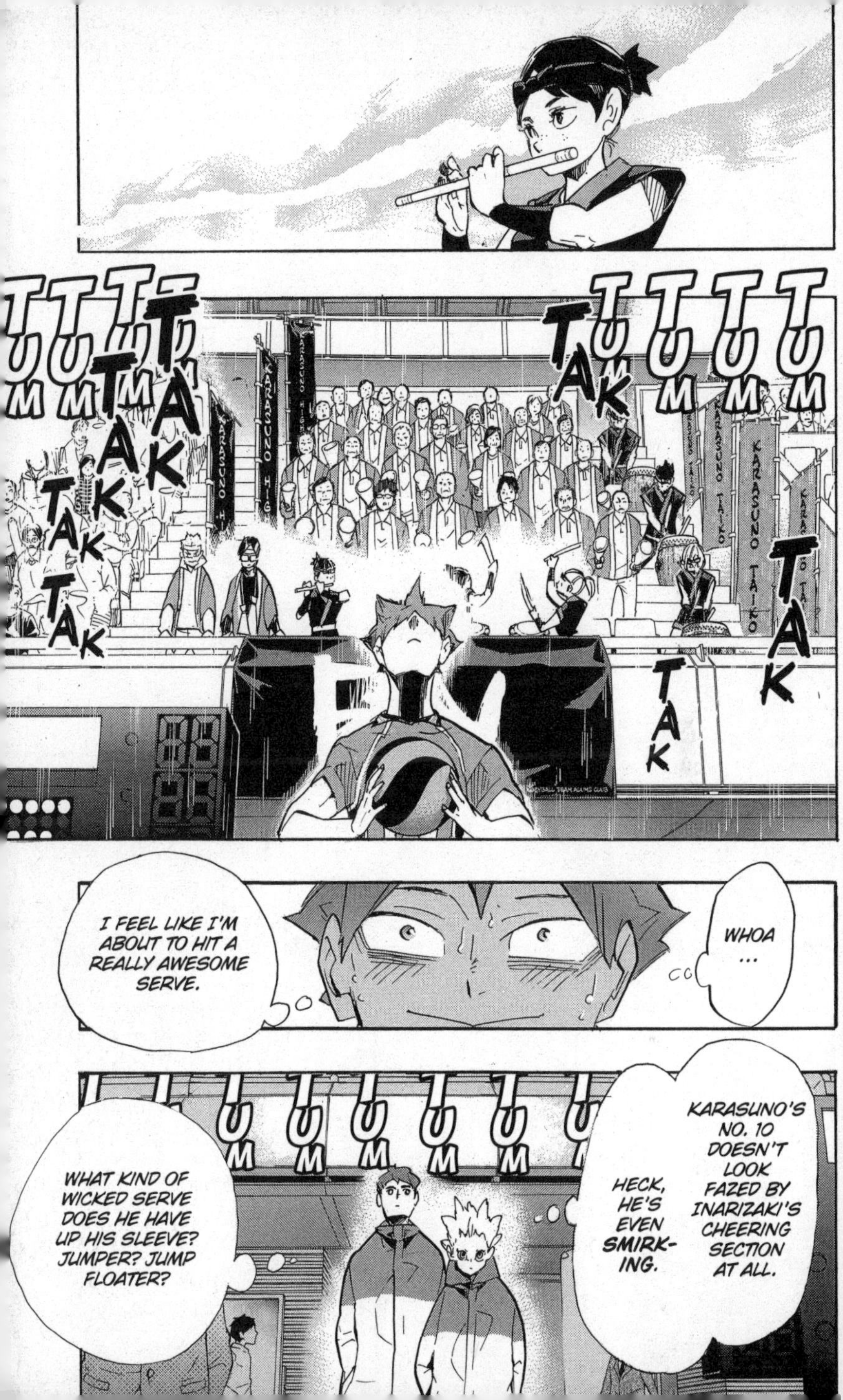
TUMM TUMM TUMM TUMM TUMM
TAK
TUMM TUMM TUMM TUMM
TAK TAK TAK TAK
TAK TAK
WHOA ...
I FEEL LIKE I'M ABOUT TO HIT A REALLY AWESOME SERVE.
TUMM TUMM TUMM TUMM TUMM TUMM TUMM
KARASUNO'S NO. 10 DOESN'T LOOK FAZED BY INARIZAKI'S CHEERING SECTION AT ALL.
HECK, HE'S EVEN SMIRKING.
WHAT KIND OF WICKED SERVE DOES HE HAVE UP HIS SLEEVE? JUMPER? JUMP FLOATER?

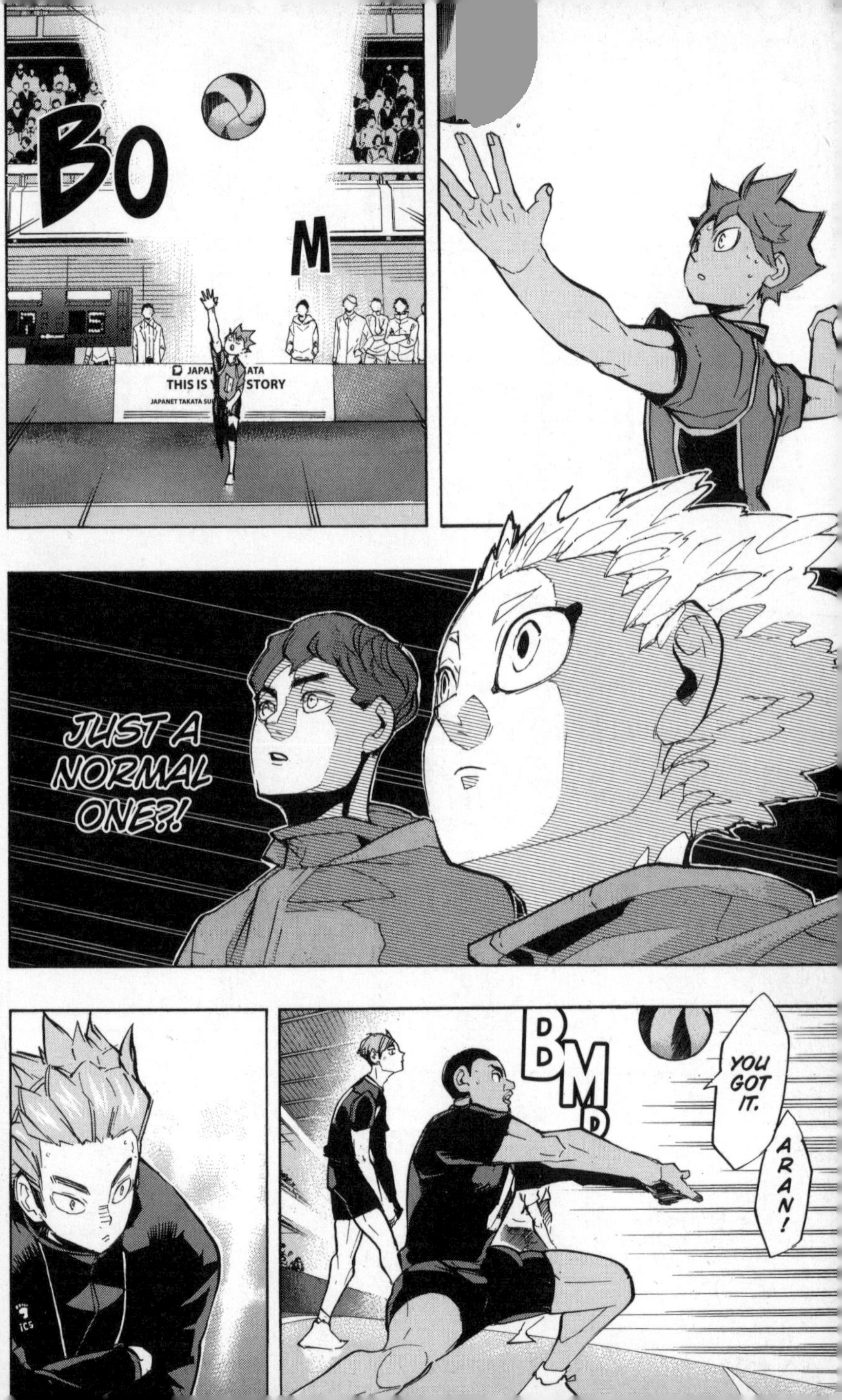
BO
M
THIS IS
STORY
JUST A NORMAL ONE?!
BMP
YOU GOT IT.
ARAN!

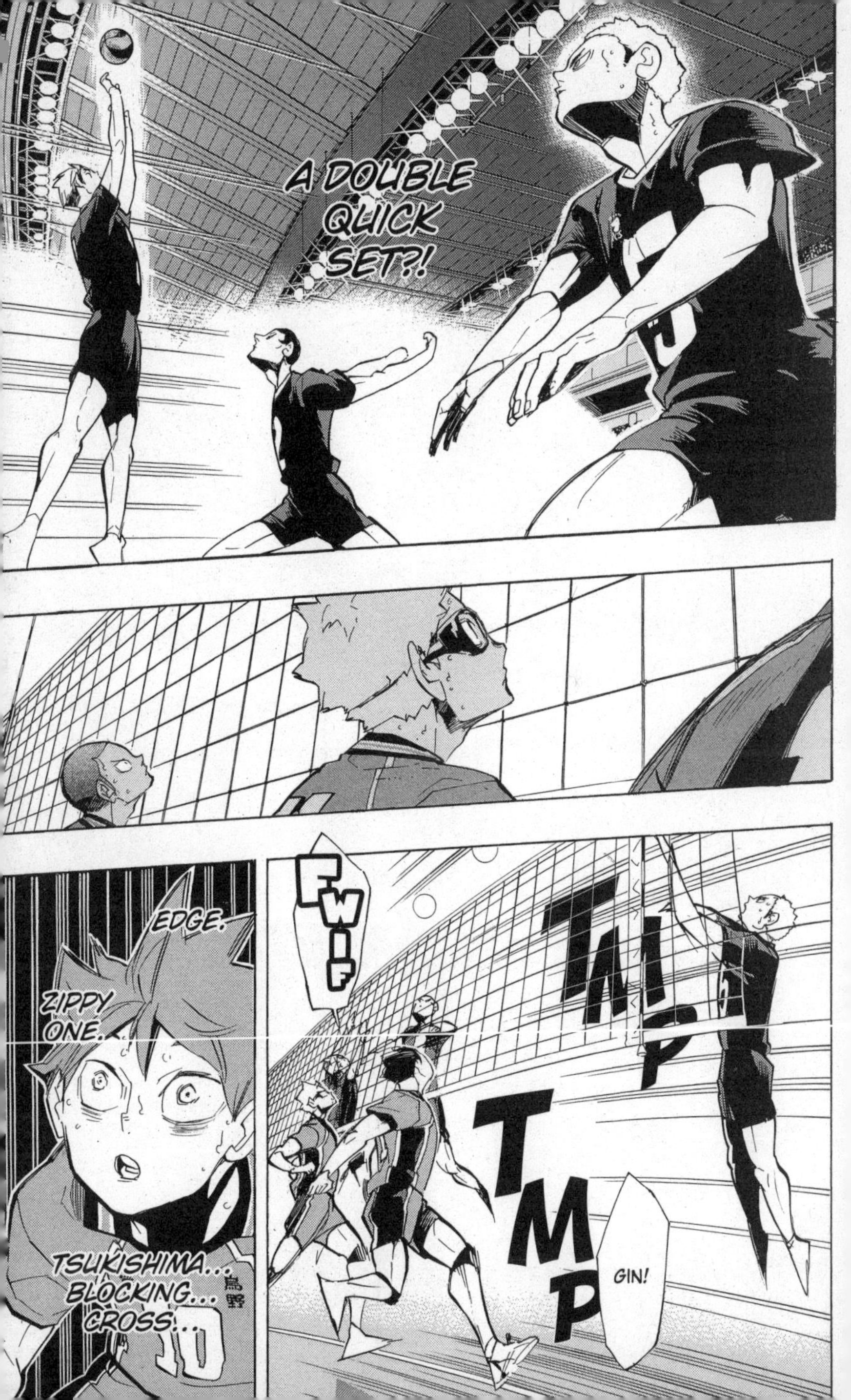
A DOUBLE QUICK SET?!
TMP
FWIF
TMP
GIN!
EDGE.
ZIPPY ONE.
TSUKISHIMA... BLOCKING... CROSS...

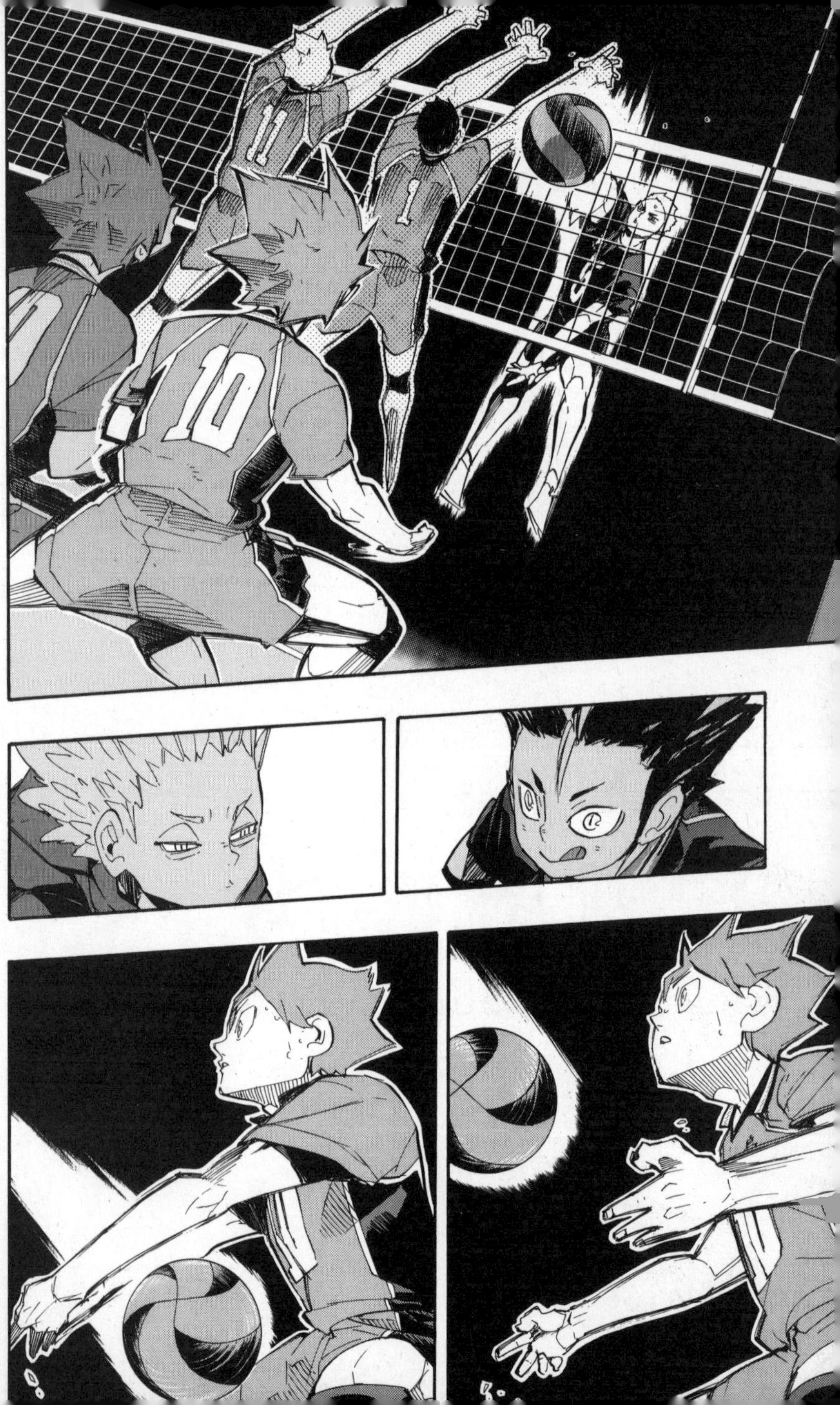

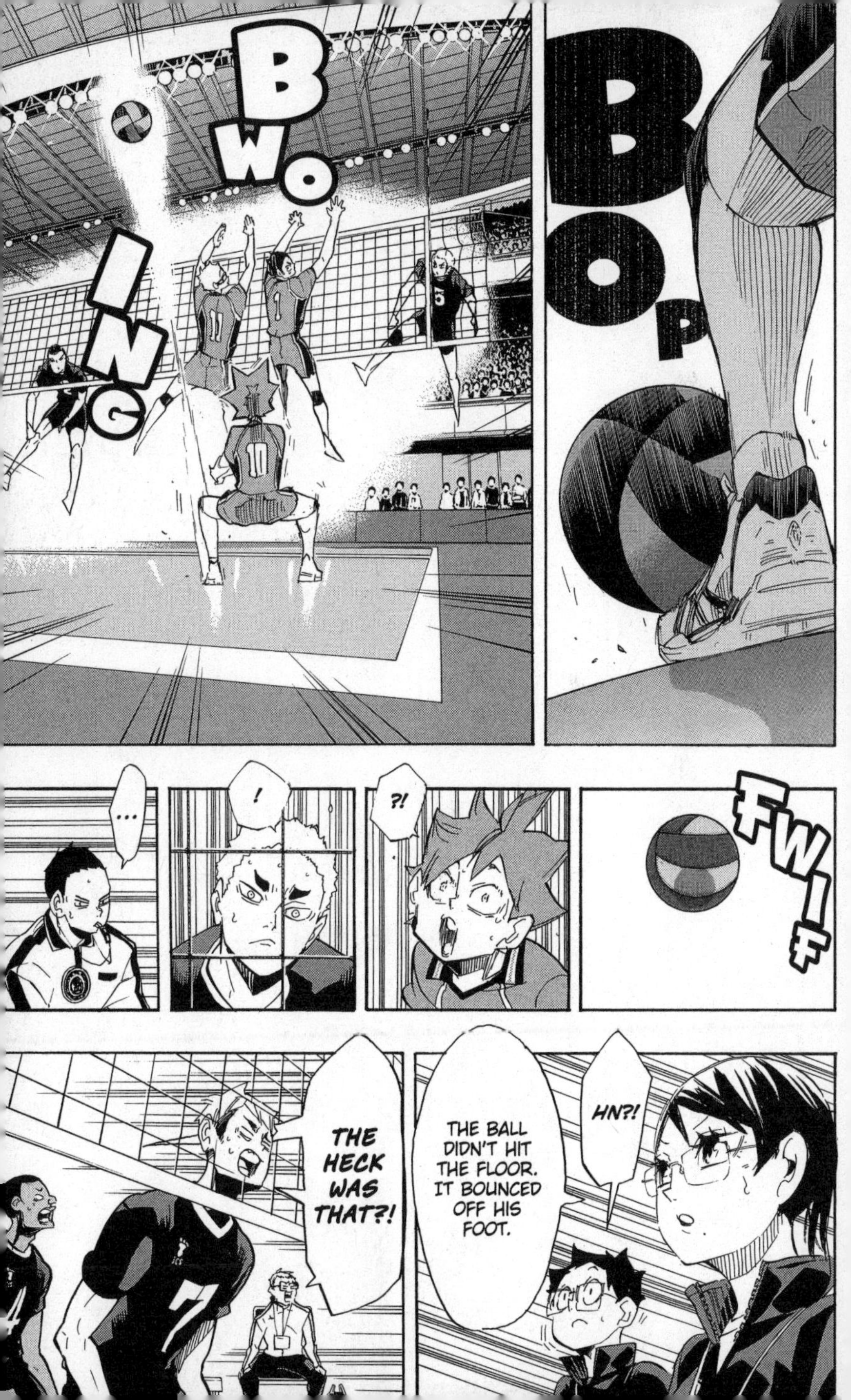
BOOP
BWOING
FWIF
?!
!
...
HN?!
THE BALL DIDN'T HIT THE FLOOR. IT BOUNCED OFF HIS FOOT.
THE HECK WAS THAT?!

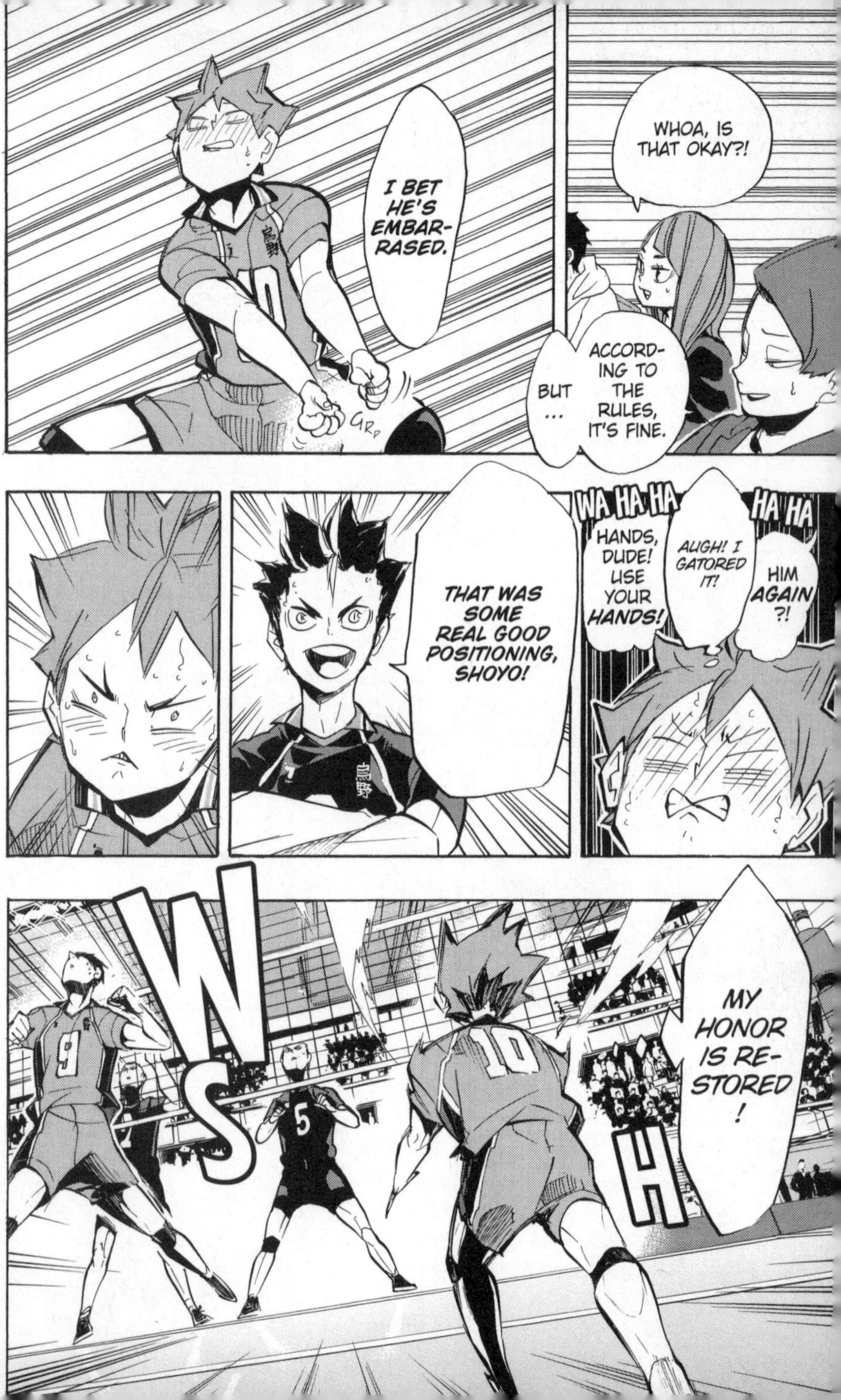
WHOA, IS THAT OKAY?!
ACCORDING TO THE RULES, IT'S FINE.
BUT ...
I BET HE'S EMBAR-RASED.
GRP
HA HA
HIM AGAIN?!
AUGH! I GATORED IT!
WA HA HA
HANDS, DUDE! USE YOUR HANDS!
THAT WAS SOME REAL GOOD POSITIONING, SHOYO!
MY HONOR IS RE-STORED!
W
S
H

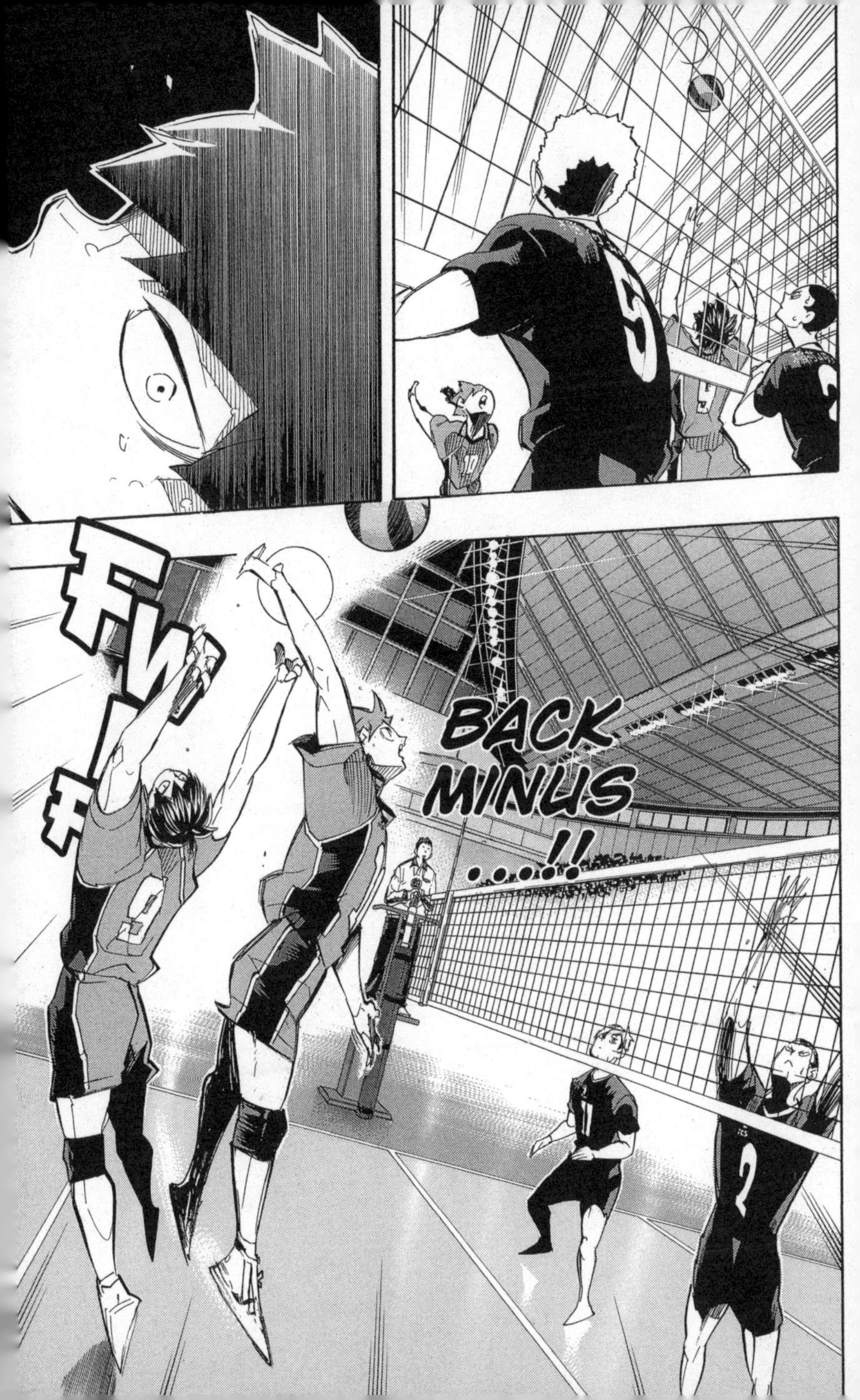
BACK MINUS ....!!

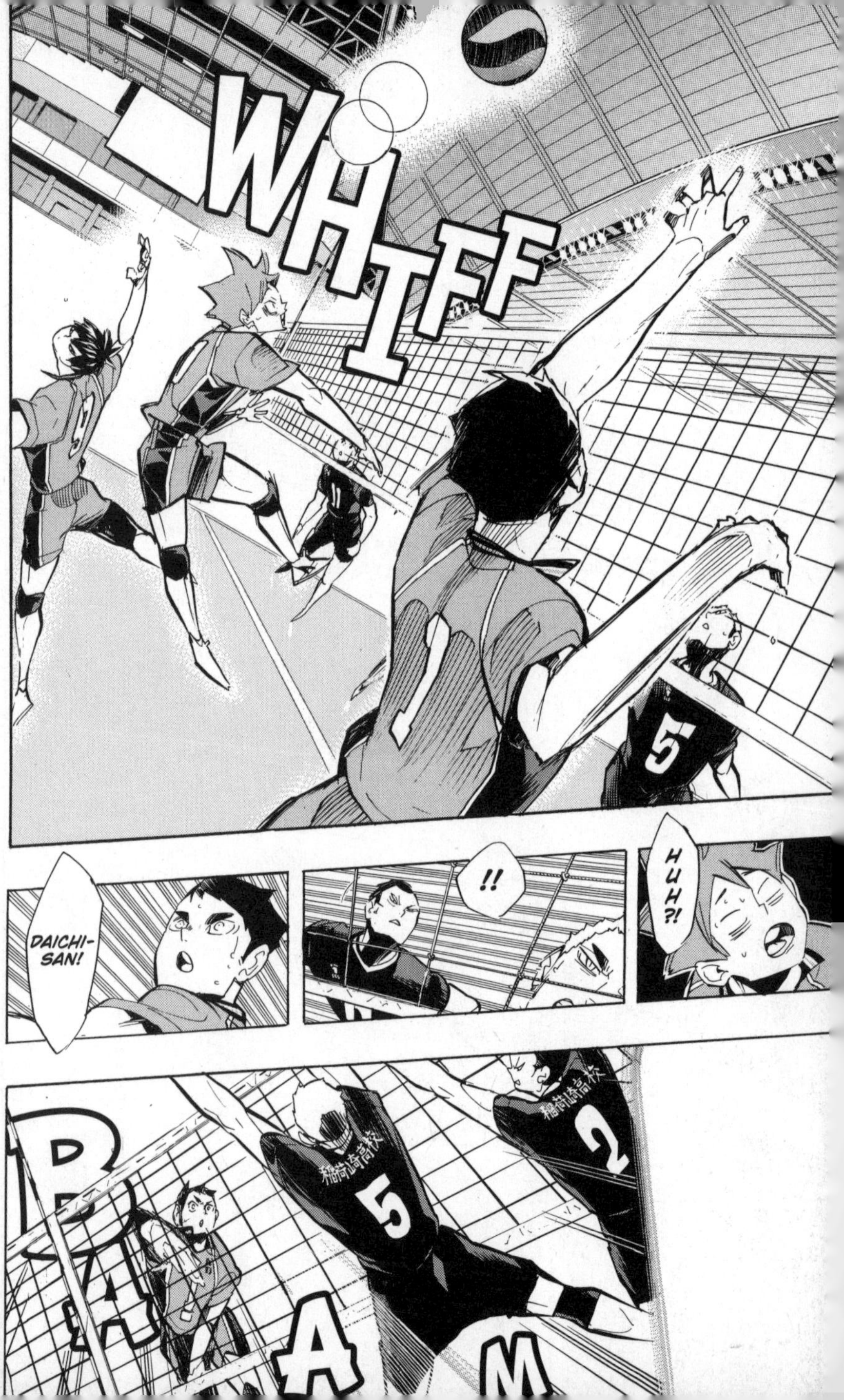
WHIFF
HUH?!
!!
DAICHI-SAN!
BAAM

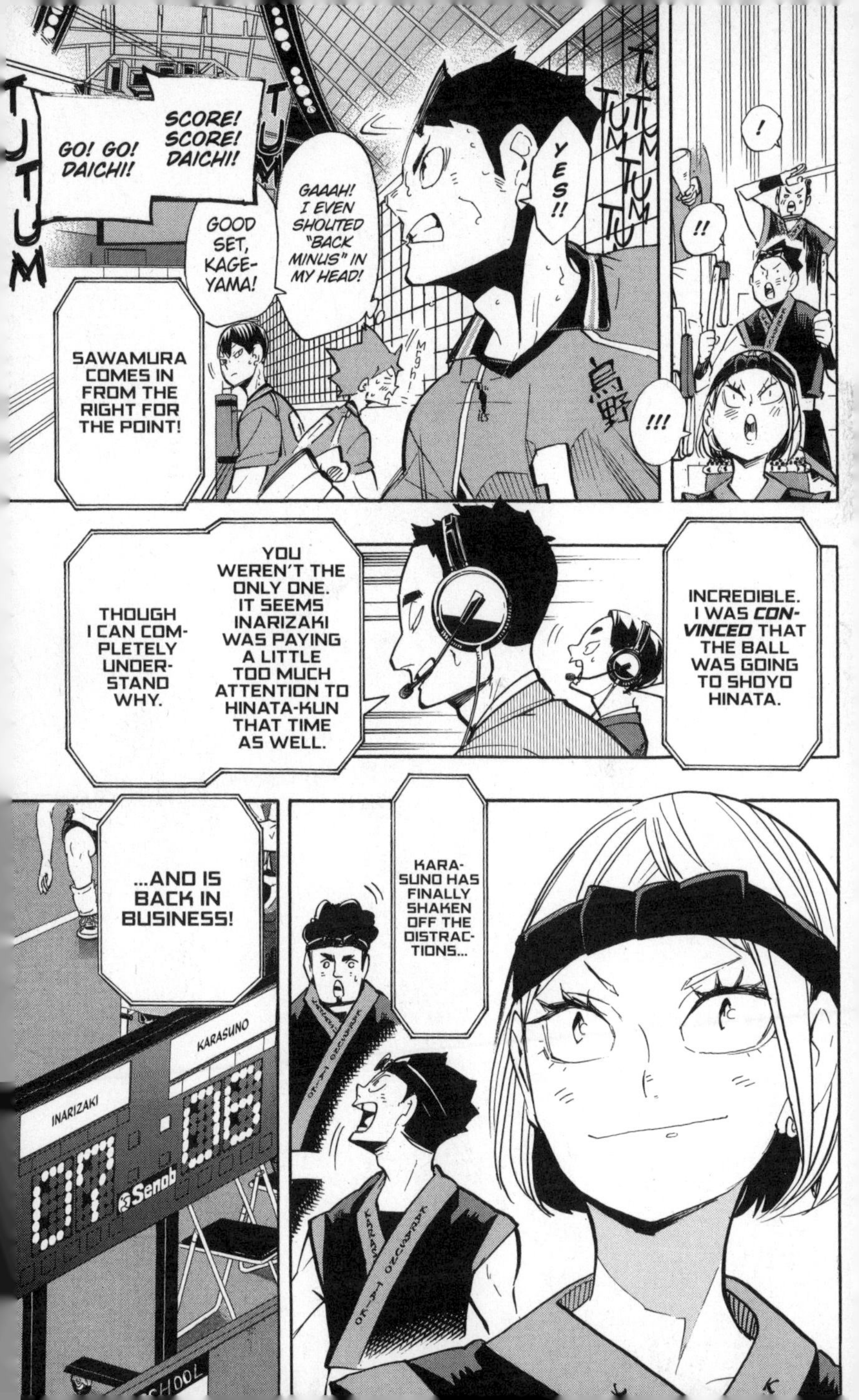
!
!!
!!!
YES!!
TUTUM TUTUM TUTUM
SCORE! SCORE! DAICHI!
GO! GO! DAICHI!
TUTUM
TUTUTUM
GAAAH! I EVEN SHOUTED "BACK MINUS" IN MY HEAD!
GOOD SET, KAGEYAMA!
Mgh!
SAWAMURA COMES IN FROM THE RIGHT FOR THE POINT!
INCREDIBLE. I WAS *CONVINCED* THAT THE BALL WAS GOING TO SHOYO HINATA.
YOU WEREN'T THE ONLY ONE. IT SEEMS INARIZAKI WAS PAYING A LITTLE TOO MUCH ATTENTION TO HINATA-KUN THAT TIME AS WELL.
THOUGH I CAN COMPLETELY UNDERSTAND WHY.
KARASUNO HAS FINALLY SHAKEN OFF THE DISTRACTIONS...
...AND IS BACK IN BUSINESS!
KARASUNO
INARIZAKI
07 08
Senob

THANKS!!

I'D LIKE TO THANK FUKUSHIMA PREFECTURE'S SOMA PUBLIC HIGH SCHOOL TAIKO CLUB FOR LETTING US OBSERVE THEIR PRACTICES IN ORDER TO DRAW THE CHEERLEADING SCENE IN THE PREVIOUS CHAPTER.

BACK BEFORE *HAIKYU!!* WAS EVEN THE FIRST SPARK OF AN IDEA IN MY MIND, I WENT TO WATCH THAT YEAR'S SPRING TOURNEY AND JUST HAPPENED TO SEE SOMA HIGH SCHOOL PLAY. THEIR CHEERLEADING SECTION WAS SO AMAZING THAT I TOLD MYSELF ON THE SPOT THAT SOMEDAY, IF I GOT THE CHANCE, I *HAD* TO MAKE THE PROTAGONISTS' CHEERLEADING SQUAD A TAIKO GROUP!

SO THANK YOU VERY MUCH TO BOTH THE CLUB MEMBERS AND THEIR ADVISERS. YOU WERE ALL REALLY AWESOME!!

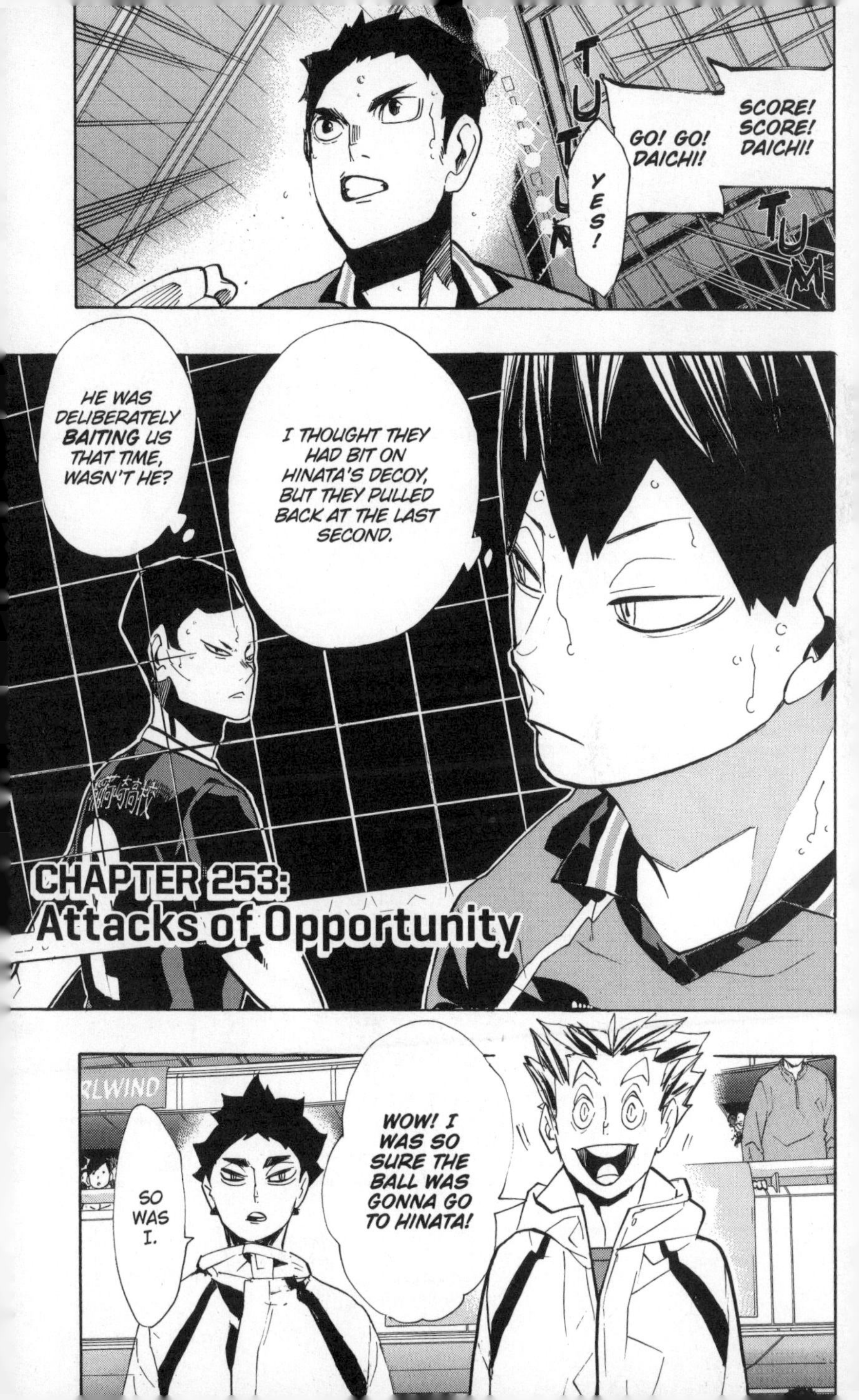
SCORE! SCORE! DAICHI!
TUM
GO! GO! DAICHI!
YES!
TUTUTUM
I THOUGHT THEY HAD BIT ON HINATA'S DECOY, BUT THEY PULLED BACK AT THE LAST SECOND.
HE WAS DELIBERATELY BAITING US THAT TIME, WASN'T HE?
CHAPTER 253:
Attacks of Opportunity
WOW! I WAS SO SURE THE BALL WAS GONNA GO TO HINATA!
SO WAS I.

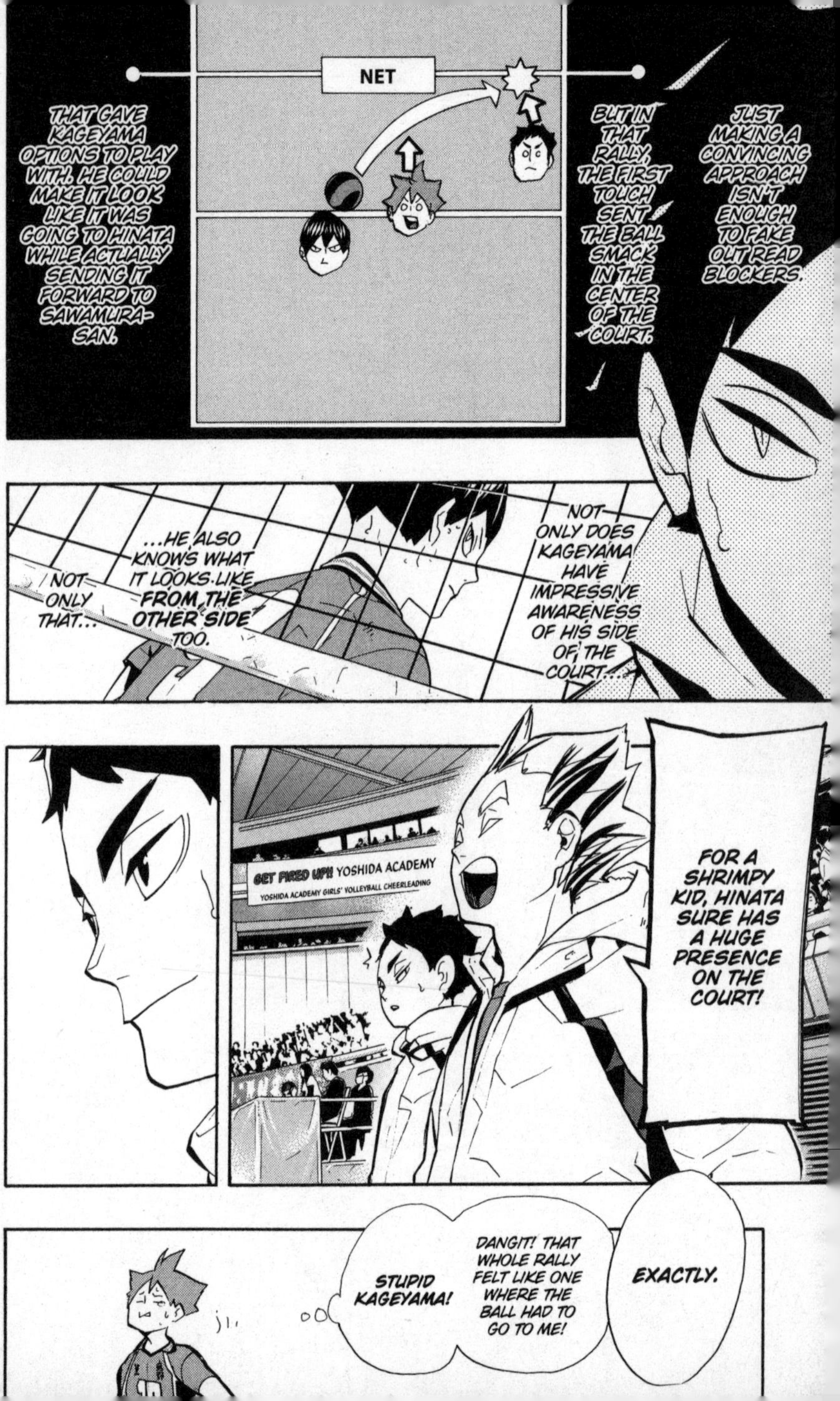

JUST MAKING A CONVINCING APPROACH ISN'T ENOUGH TO FAKE OUT READ BLOCKERS.
BUT IN THAT RALLY, THE FIRST TOUCH SENT THE BALL SMACK IN THE CENTER OF THE COURT.
NET
THAT GAVE KAGEYAMA OPTIONS TO PLAY WITH. HE COULD MAKE IT LOOK LIKE IT WAS GOING TO HINATA WHILE ACTUALLY SENDING IT FORWARD TO SAWAMURA-SAN.
NOT ONLY DOES KAGEYAMA HAVE IMPRESSIVE AWARENESS OF HIS SIDE OF THE COURT...
...HE ALSO KNOWS WHAT IT LOOKS LIKE FROM THE OTHER SIDE TOO.
NOT ONLY THAT...
FOR A SHRIMPY KID, HINATA SURE HAS A HUGE PRESENCE ON THE COURT!
GET FIRED UP!! YOSHIDA ACADEMY
YOSHIDA ACADEMY GIRLS' VOLLEYBALL CHEERLEADING
EXACTLY.
DANGIT! THAT WHOLE RALLY FELT LIKE ONE WHERE THE BALL HAD TO GO TO ME!
STUPID KAGEYAMA!

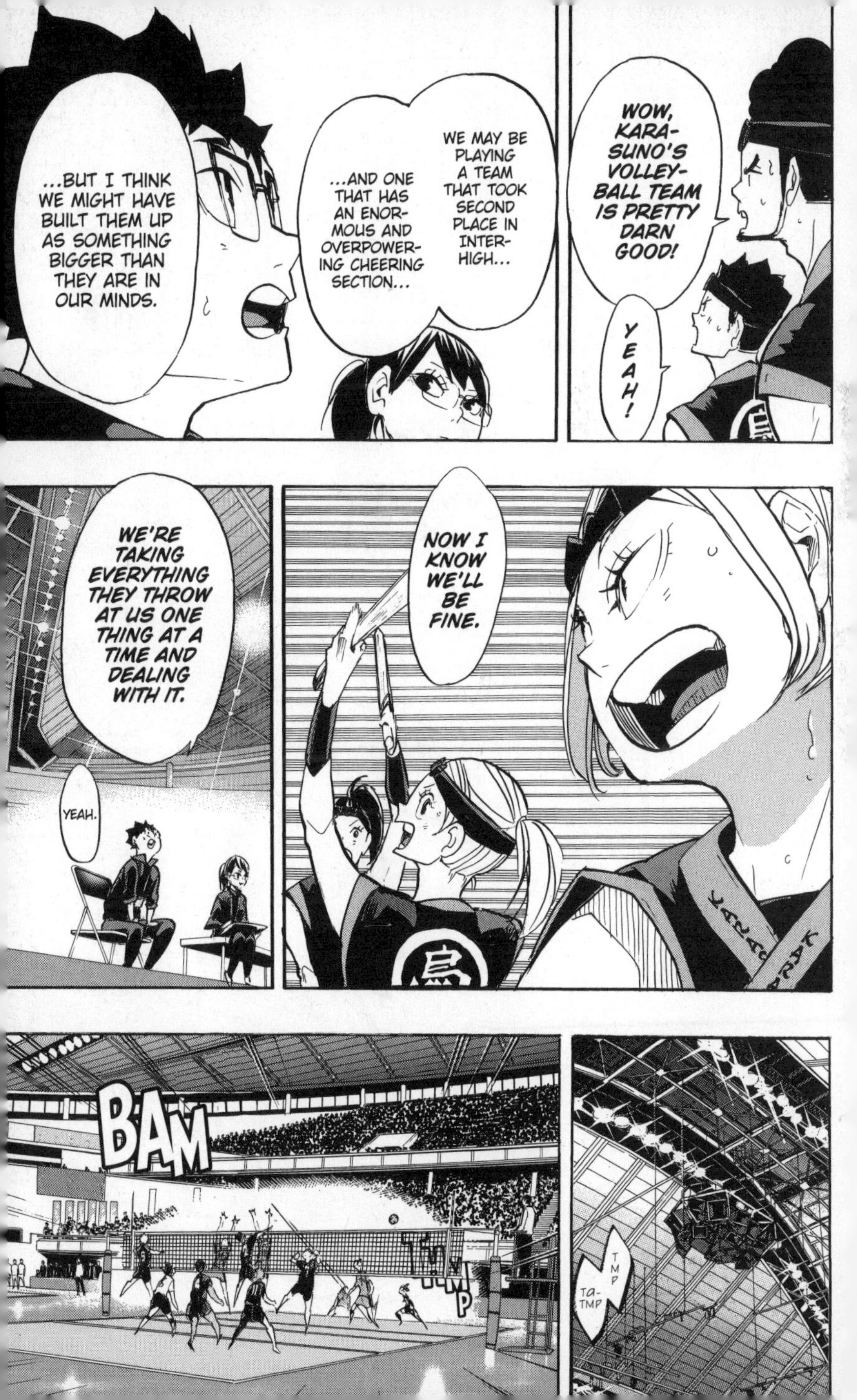
WOW, KARASUNO'S VOLLEYBALL TEAM IS PRETTY DARN GOOD!
YEAH!
WE MAY BE PLAYING A TEAM THAT TOOK SECOND PLACE IN INTER-HIGH...
...AND ONE THAT HAS AN ENORMOUS AND OVERPOWERING CHEERING SECTION...
...BUT I THINK WE MIGHT HAVE BUILT THEM UP AS SOMETHING BIGGER THAN THEY ARE IN OUR MINDS.
NOW I KNOW WE'LL BE FINE.
WE'RE TAKING EVERYTHING THEY THROW AT US ONE THING AT A TIME AND DEALING WITH IT.
YEAH.
TMP
TMP
TA-TMP
BAM
TMP

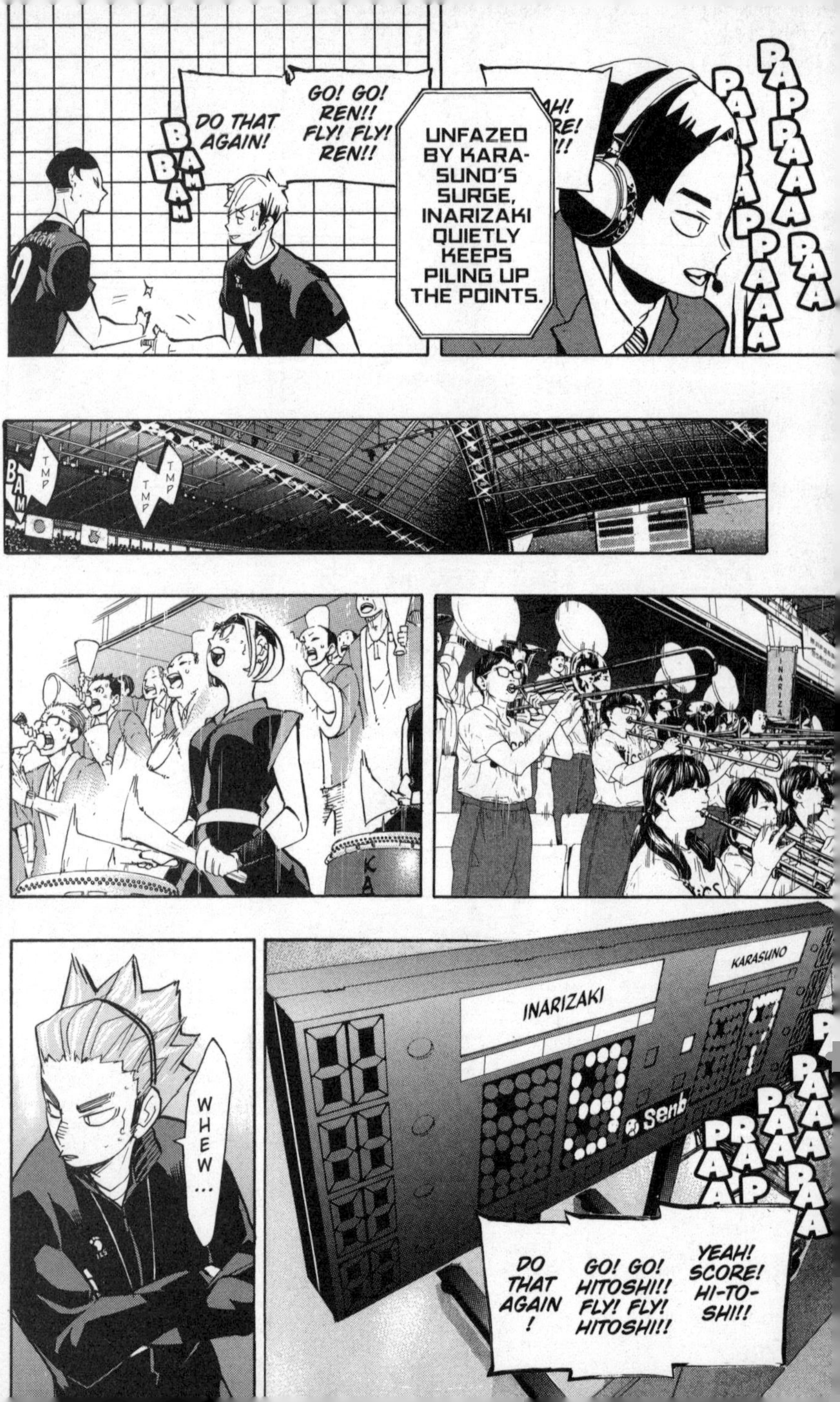

PAPAPAAAA
PAPAPAAAA PAA
UNFAZED BY KARASUNO'S SURGE, INARIZAKI QUIETLY KEEPS PILING UP THE POINTS.
GO! GO! REN!! FLY! FLY! REN!!
DO THAT AGAIN!
BAM BAM BAM
TMP TMP
TMP TMP
BAM
INARIZA
KA
KARASUNO
INARIZAKI
Senb
PAPAPAAAA
PRAAA
PAPAA
YEAH! SCORE! HI-TO-SHI!!!
GO! GO! HITOSHI!!! FLY! FLY! HITOSHI!!!
DO THAT AGAIN!
WHEW...

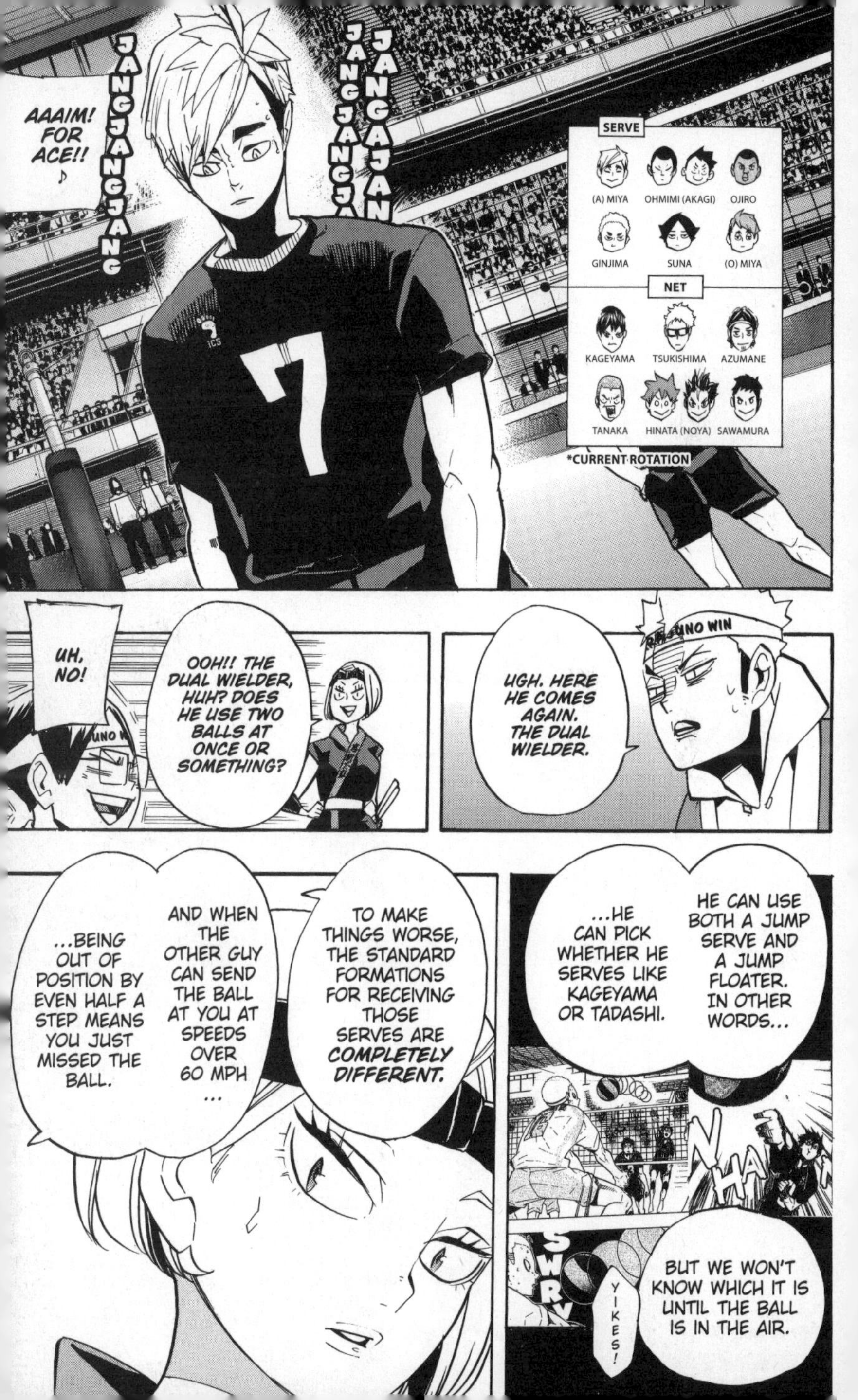
JANGAJAN
JANGJANGJA
SERVE
(A) MIYA
OHMIMI (AKAGI)
OJIRO
GINJIMA
SUNA
(O) MIYA
NET
KAGEYAMA
TSUKISHIMA
AZUMANE
TANAKA
HINATA (NOYA)
SAWAMURA
*CURRENT ROTATION
JANGJANGJANG
AAAIM! FOR ACE!! ♪
UNO WIN
UGH. HERE HE COMES AGAIN. THE DUAL WIELDER.
OOH!! THE DUAL WIELDER, HUH? DOES HE USE TWO BALLS AT ONCE OR SOMETHING?
UH, NO!
HE CAN USE BOTH A JUMP SERVE AND A JUMP FLOATER. IN OTHER WORDS...
...HE CAN PICK WHETHER HE SERVES LIKE KAGEYAMA OR TADASHI.
SWRV
YIKES!
BUT WE WON'T KNOW WHICH IT IS UNTIL THE BALL IS IN THE AIR.
TO MAKE THINGS WORSE, THE STANDARD FORMATIONS FOR RECEIVING THOSE SERVES ARE COMPLETELY DIFFERENT.
AND WHEN THE OTHER GUY CAN SEND THE BALL AT YOU AT SPEEDS OVER 60 MPH...
...BEING OUT OF POSITION BY EVEN HALF A STEP MEANS YOU JUST MISSED THE BALL.

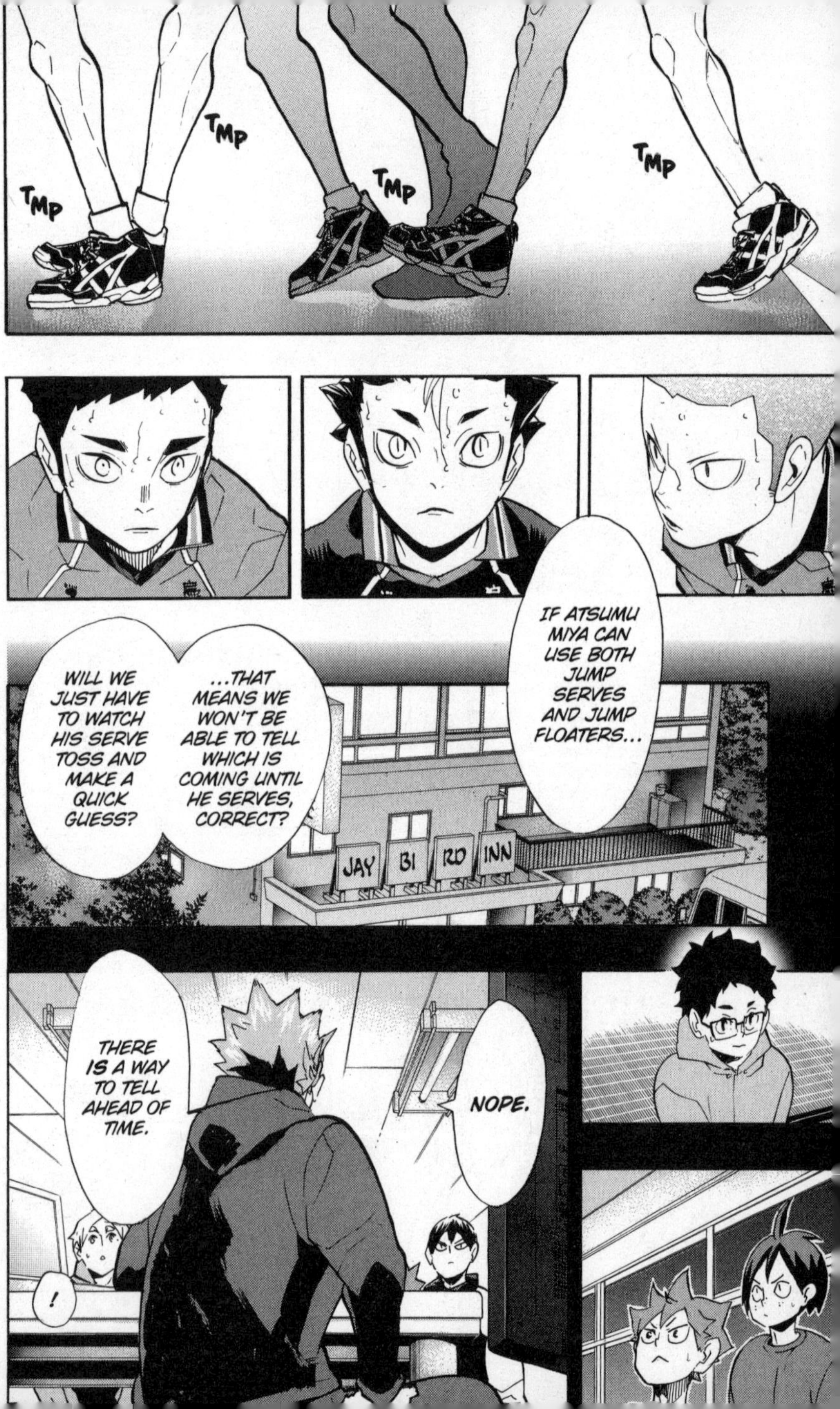
TMP
TMP
TMP
TMP
IF ATSUMU MIYA CAN USE BOTH JUMP SERVES AND JUMP FLOATERS...
...THAT MEANS WE WON'T BE ABLE TO TELL WHICH IS COMING UNTIL HE SERVES, CORRECT?
WILL WE JUST HAVE TO WATCH HIS SERVE TOSS AND MAKE A QUICK GUESS?
JAY BI RO INN
NOPE.
THERE IS A WAY TO TELL AHEAD OF TIME.
!

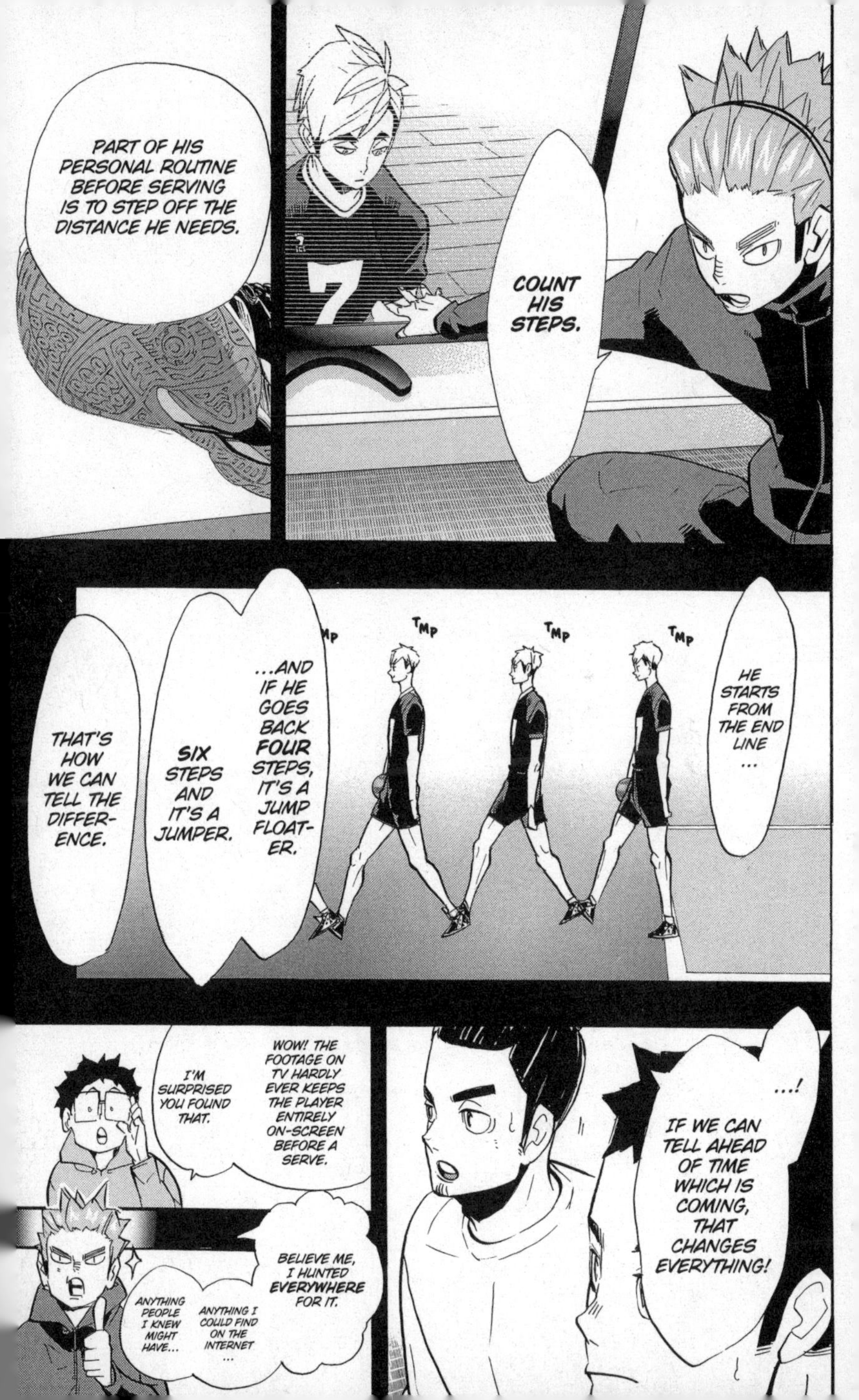
COUNT HIS STEPS.
PART OF HIS PERSONAL ROUTINE BEFORE SERVING IS TO STEP OFF THE DISTANCE HE NEEDS.
HE STARTS FROM THE END LINE ...
TMP
TMP
TMP
TMP
...AND IF HE GOES BACK FOUR STEPS, IT'S A JUMP FLOAT-ER.
SIX STEPS AND IT'S A JUMPER.
THAT'S HOW WE CAN TELL THE DIFFER-ENCE.
...!
IF WE CAN TELL AHEAD OF TIME WHICH IS COMING, THAT CHANGES EVERYTHING!
WOW! THE FOOTAGE ON TV HARDLY EVER KEEPS THE PLAYER ENTIRELY ON-SCREEN BEFORE A SERVE.
I'M SURPRISED YOU FOUND THAT.
BELIEVE ME, I HUNTED EVERYWHERE FOR IT.
ANYTHING I COULD FIND ON THE INTERNET ...
ANYTHING PEOPLE I KNEW MIGHT HAVE...

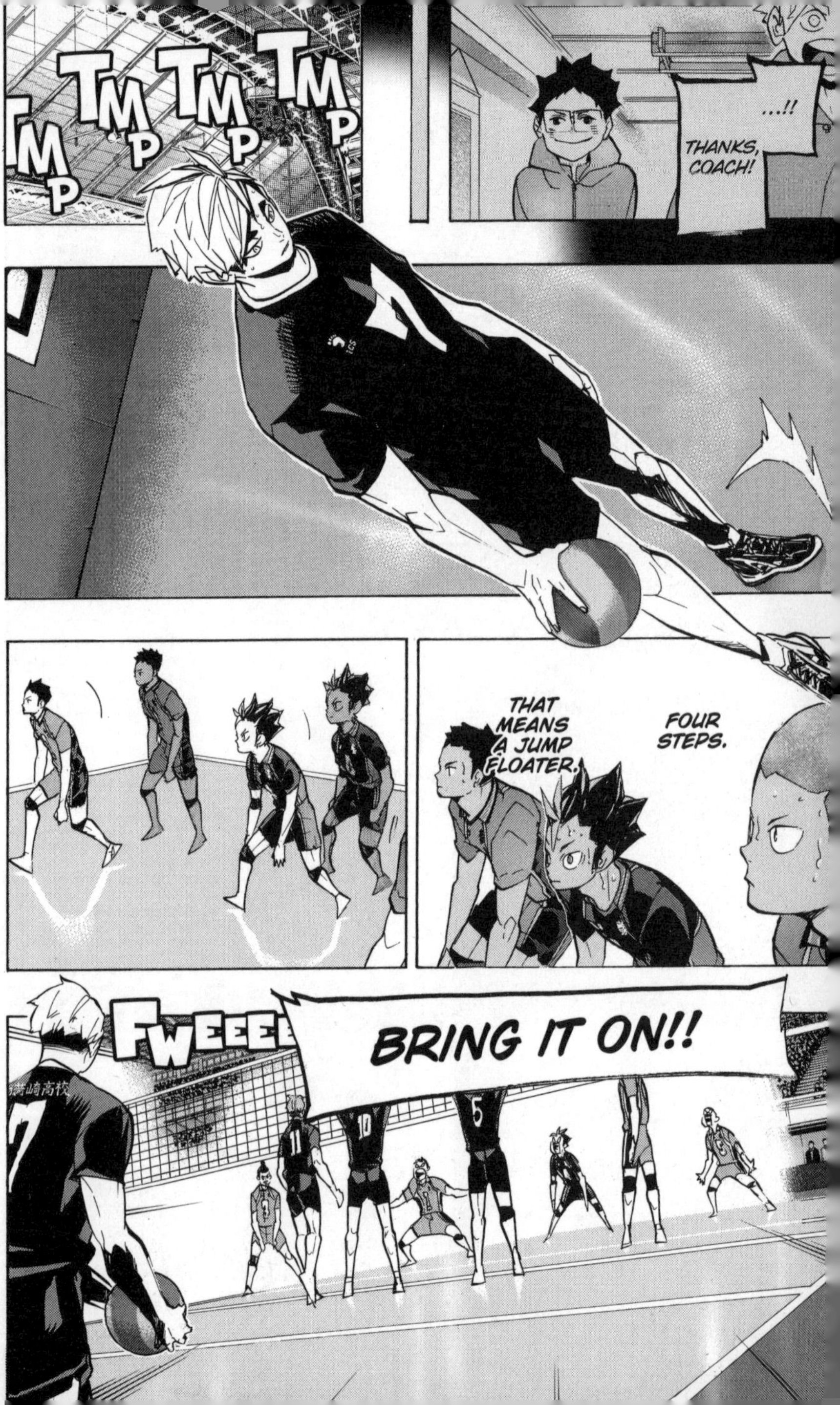
...!!
THANKS, COACH!
TMP TMP TMP TMP
FOUR STEPS.
THAT MEANS A JUMP FLOATER.
BRING IT ON!!
FWEEEE

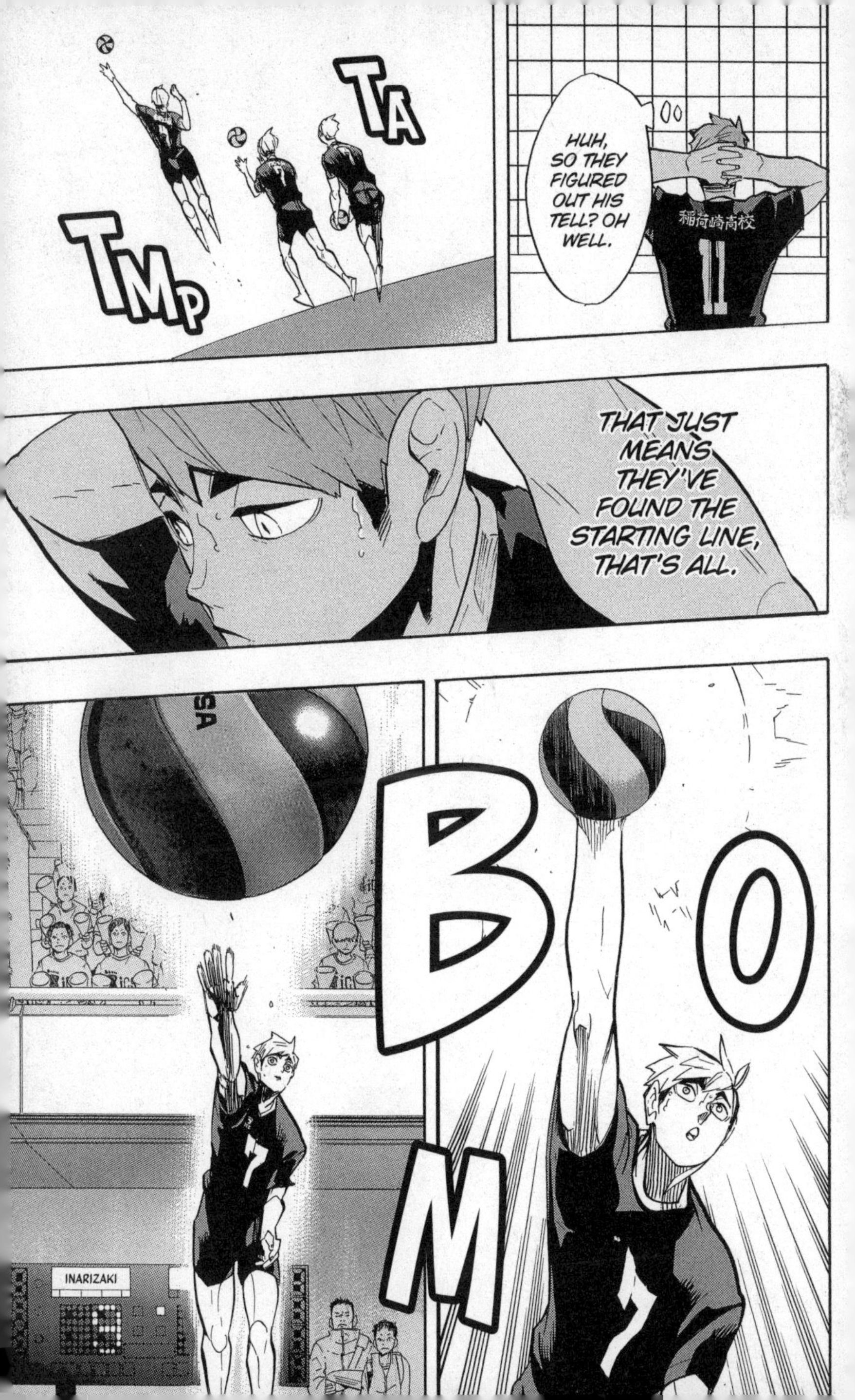
HUH, SO THEY FIGURED OUT HIS TELL? OH WELL.
稲荷崎高校
11
TA
TMP
THAT JUST MEANS THEY'VE FOUND THE STARTING LINE, THAT'S ALL.
BOOM
SA
INARIZAKI

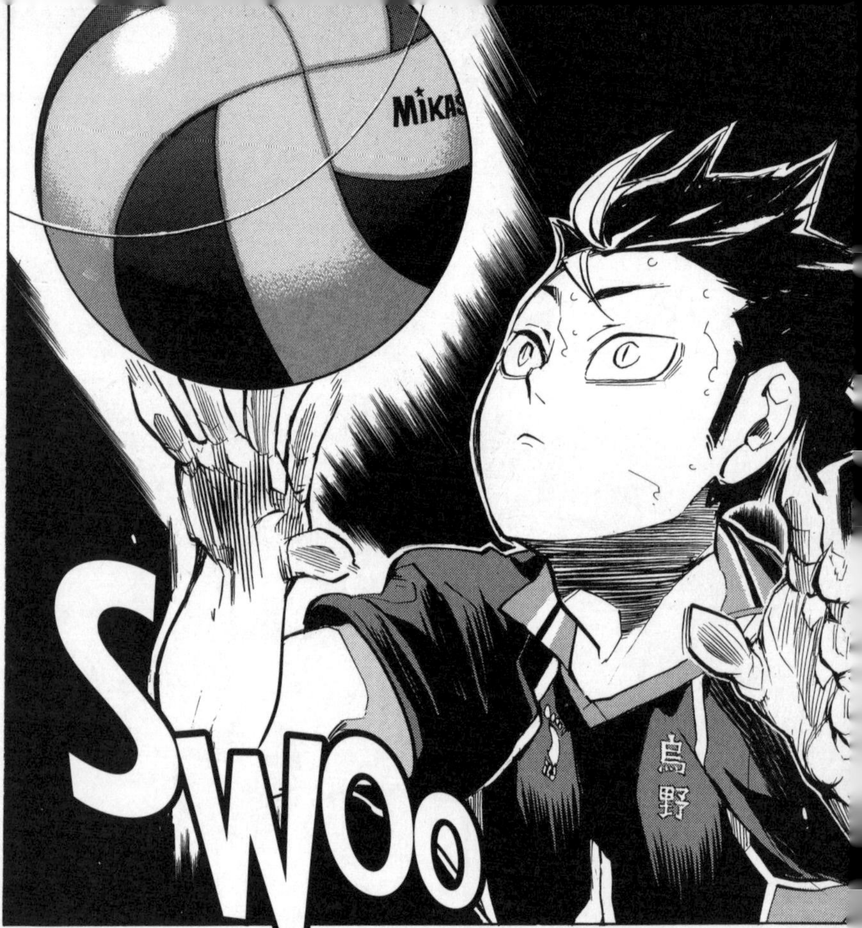
MIKAS
烏野
SWOO

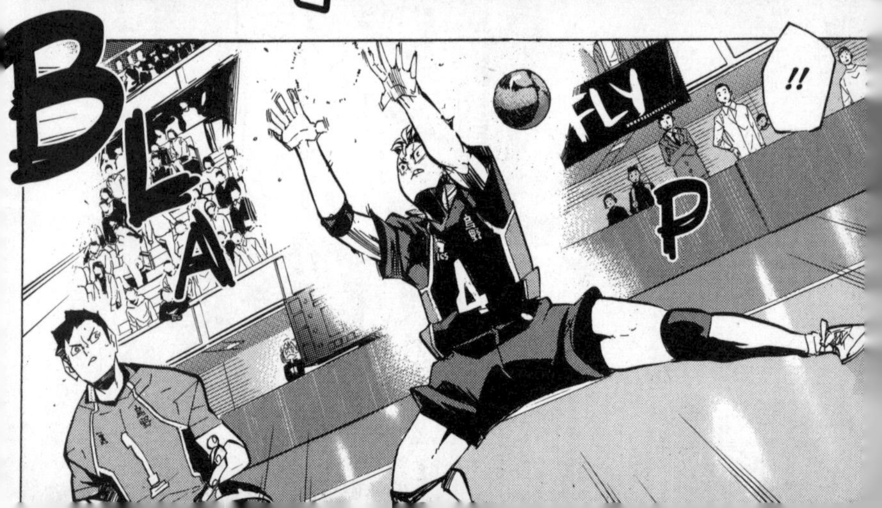
!!
FLY
BLAP

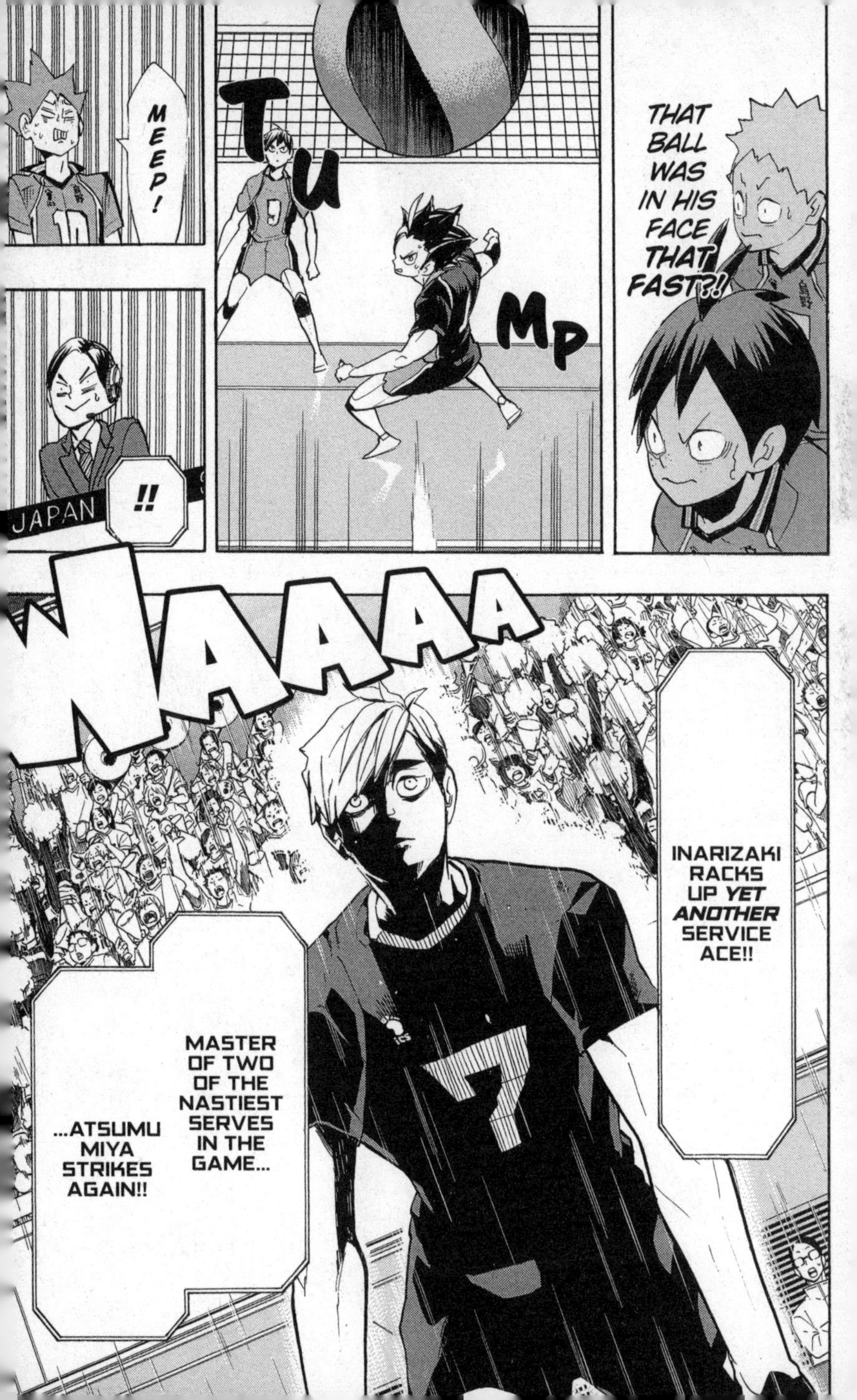

THAT BALL WAS IN HIS FACE THAT FAST?!
TU
MP
MEEP!
JAPAN
!!
WAAAA
INARIZAKI RACKS UP *YET ANOTHER* SERVICE ACE!!
MASTER OF TWO OF THE NASTIEST SERVES IN THE GAME...
...ATSUMU MIYA STRIKES AGAIN!!

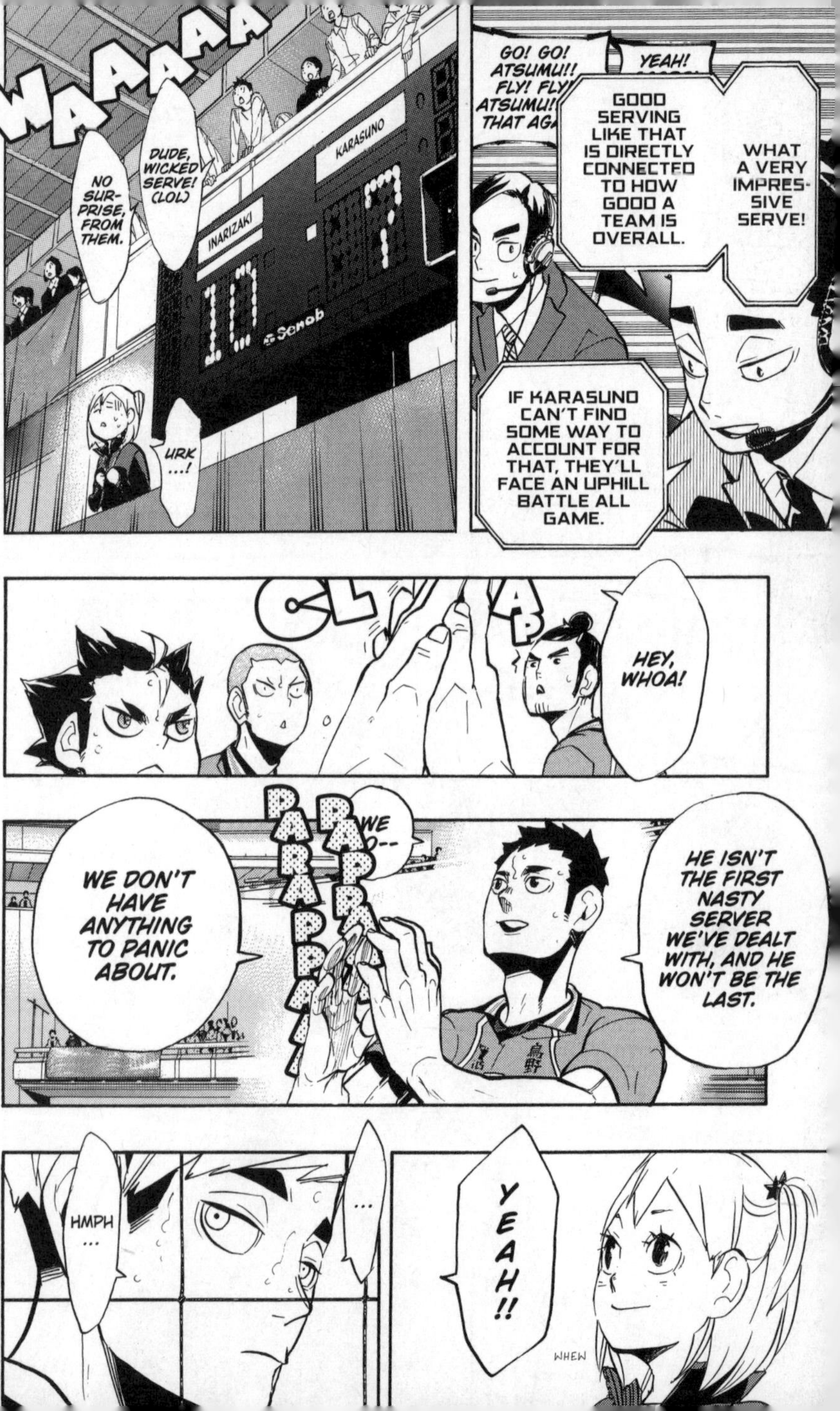
YEAH!
WHAT A VERY IMPRESSIVE SERVE!
GOOD SERVING LIKE THAT IS DIRECTLY CONNECTED TO HOW GOOD A TEAM IS OVERALL.
GO! GO! ATSUMU!! FLY! FLY! ATSUMU!! THAT AG
IF KARASUNO CAN'T FIND SOME WAY TO ACCOUNT FOR THAT, THEY'LL FACE AN UPHILL BATTLE ALL GAME.
WAAAAA
KARASUNO
INARIZAKI
DUDE, WICKED SERVE! (LOL)
NO SURPRISE, FROM THEM.
URK ...!
CLAP
HEY, WHOA!
HE ISN'T THE FIRST NASTY SERVER WE'VE DEALT WITH, AND HE WON'T BE THE LAST.
PARAPA
PARAPA
WE DO--
WE DON'T HAVE ANYTHING TO PANIC ABOUT.
YEAH!!
WHEW
...
HMPH ...

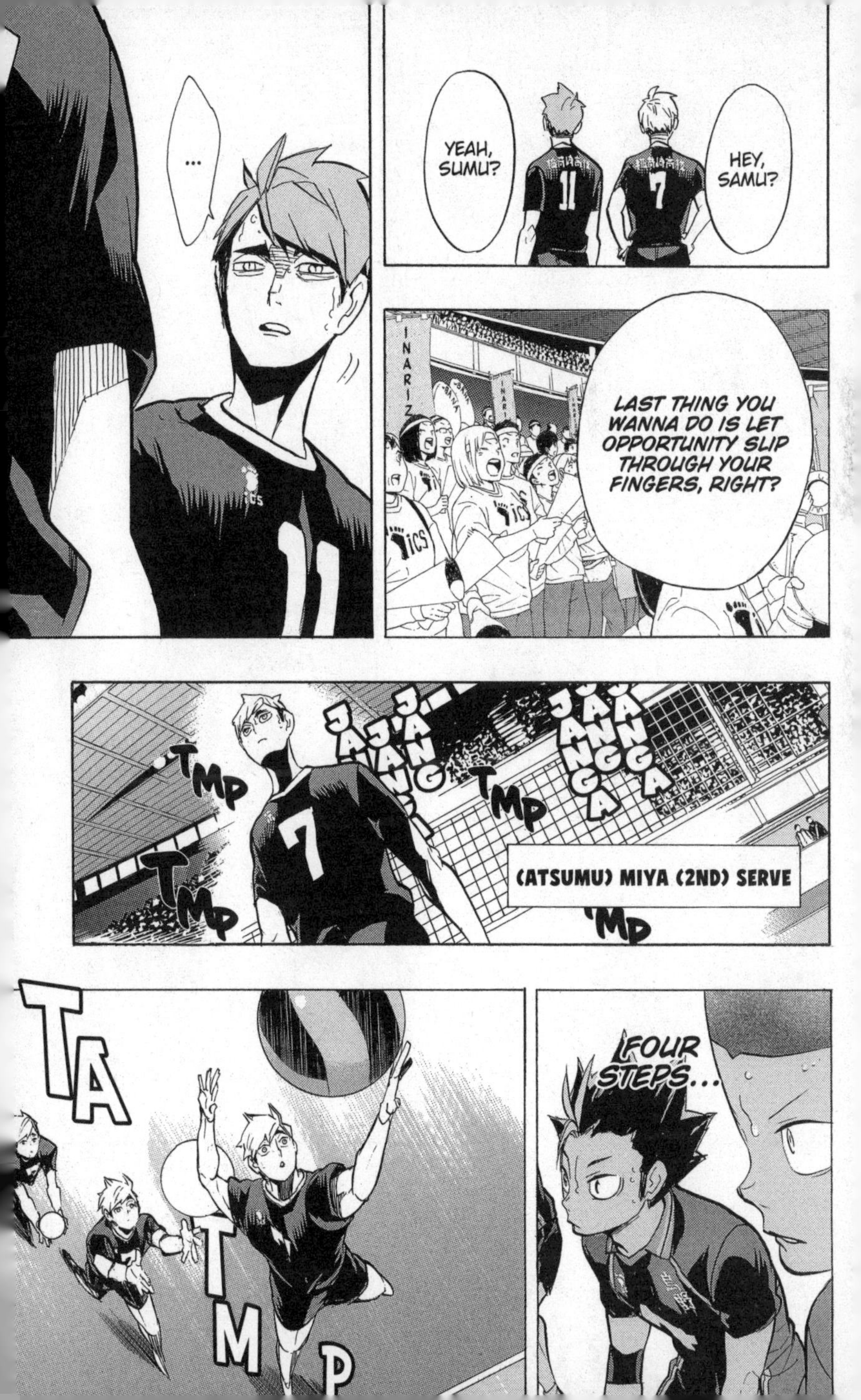
HEY, SAMU?
YEAH, SUMU?
LAST THING YOU WANNA DO IS LET OPPORTUNITY SLIP THROUGH YOUR FINGERS, RIGHT?
...
(ATSUMU) MIYA (2ND) SERVE
'MP
JAANGGA
JANGGA
TMP
JAANG
J...
TMP
TMP
FOUR STEPS...
TA
TMP

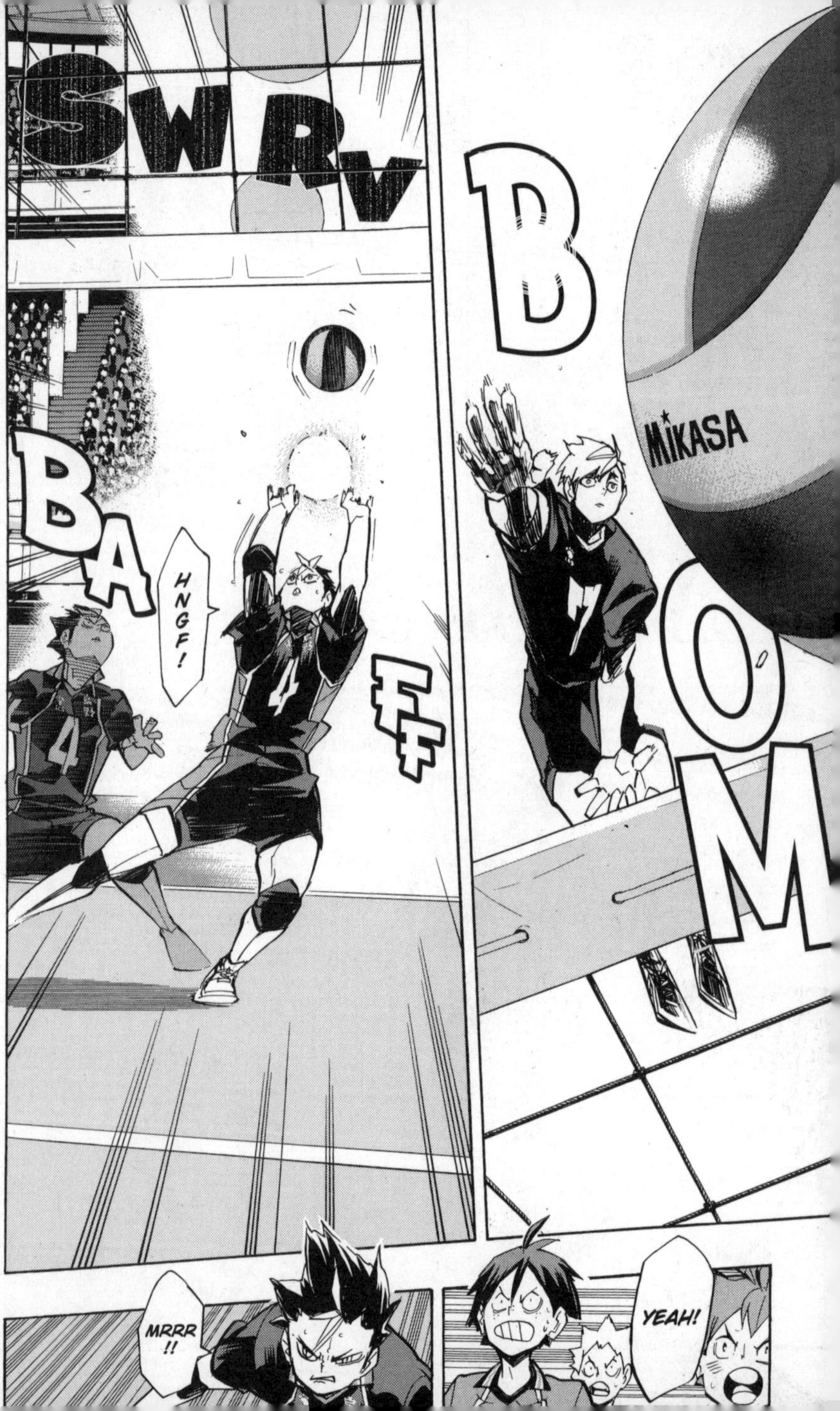
B
O
M
MIKASA
SWRV
BA
HNGF!
FF
YEAH!
MRRR!!

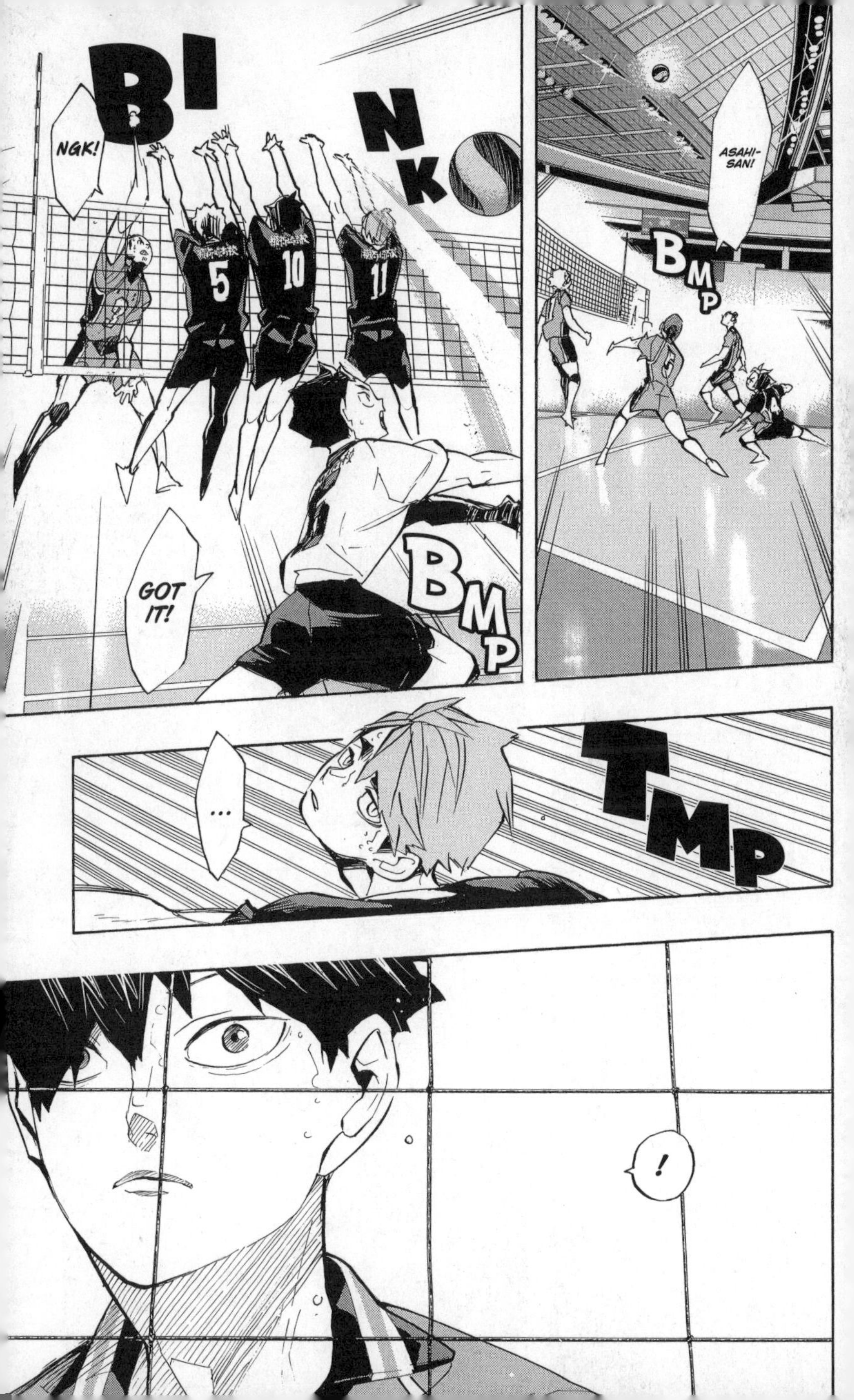

ASAHI-SAN!
BMP
BINK
NGK!
BMP
GOT IT!
TMP
...
!

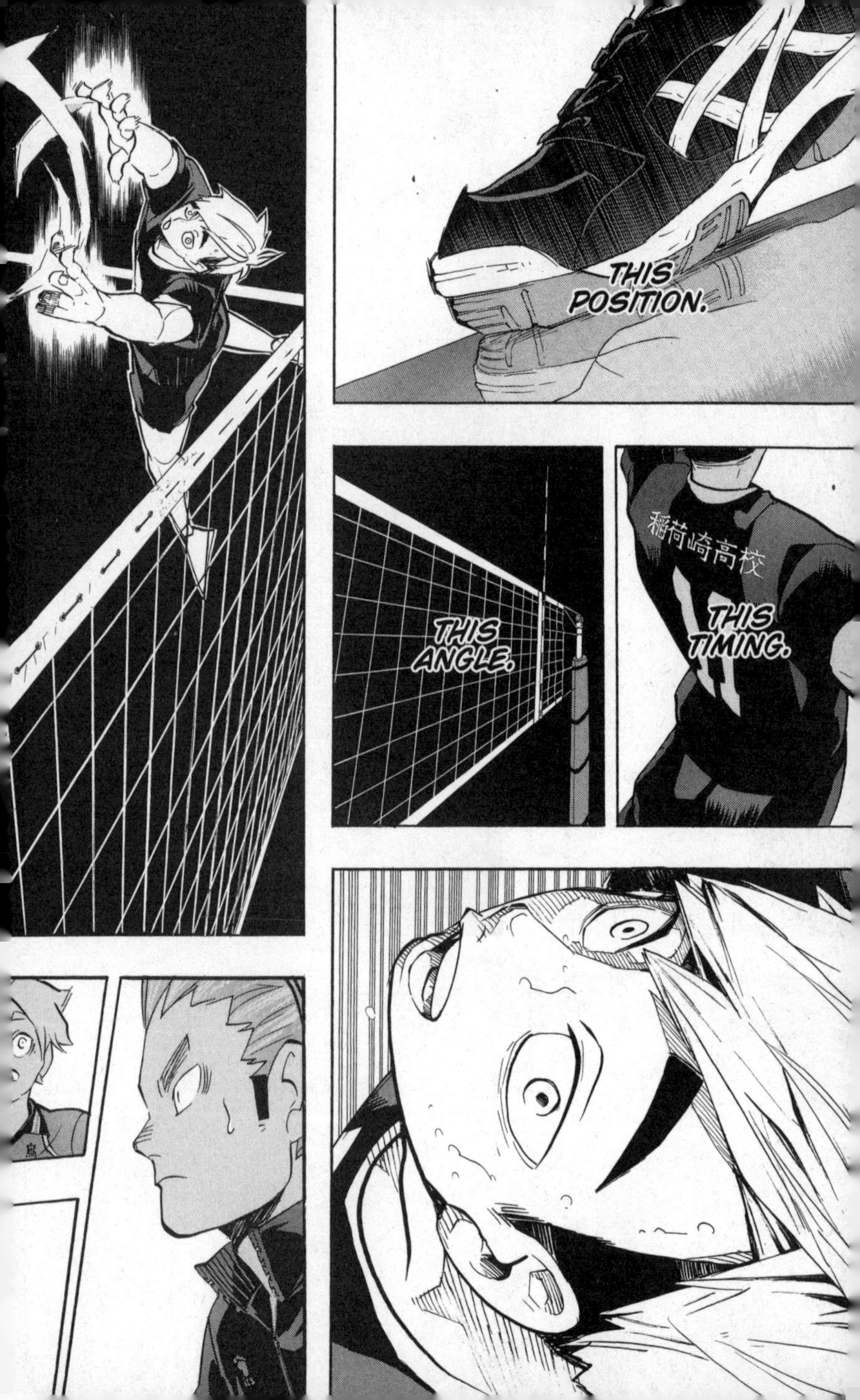
THIS POSITION.
稲荷崎高校
THIS TIMING.
THIS ANGLE.

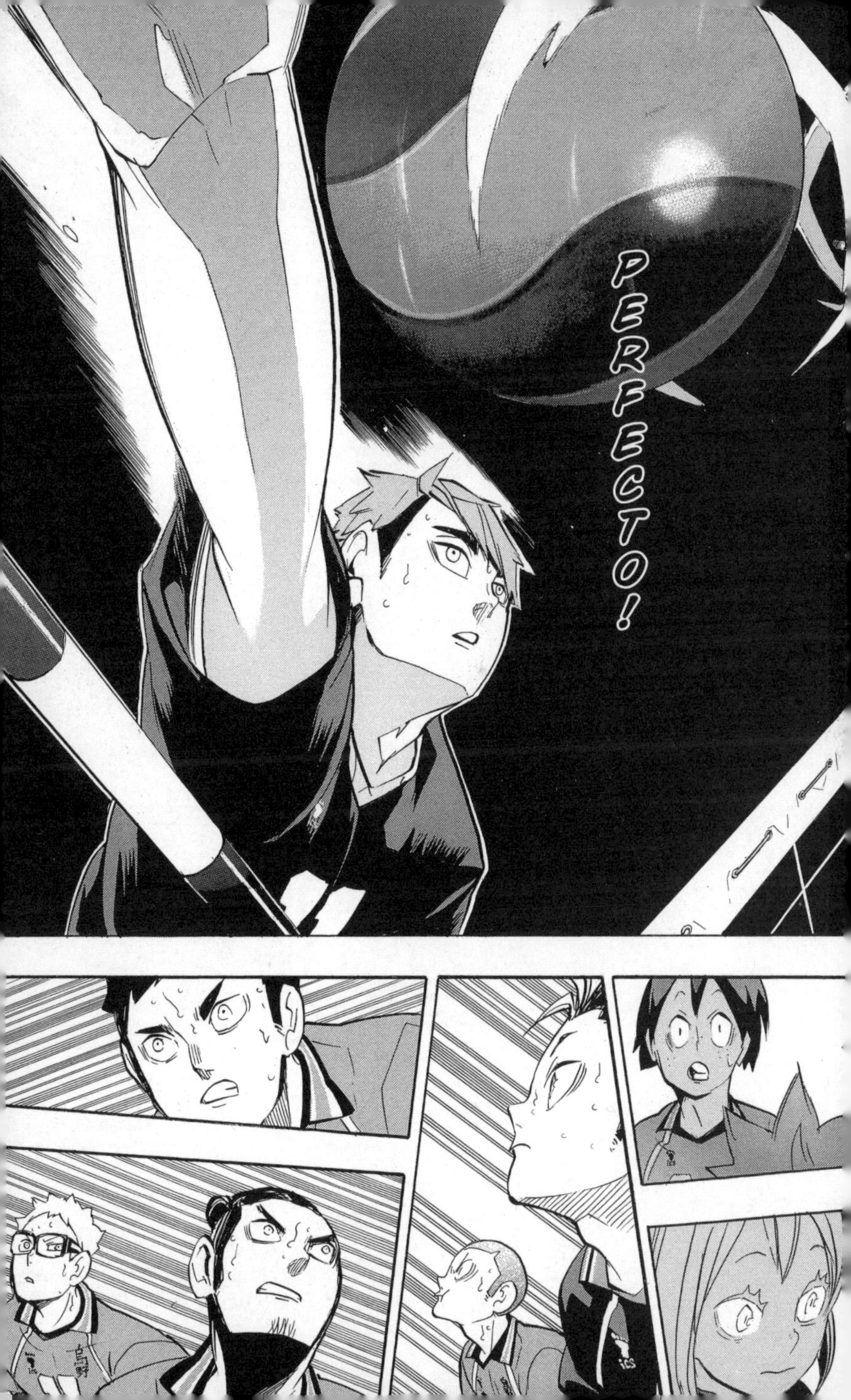
PERFECTO!

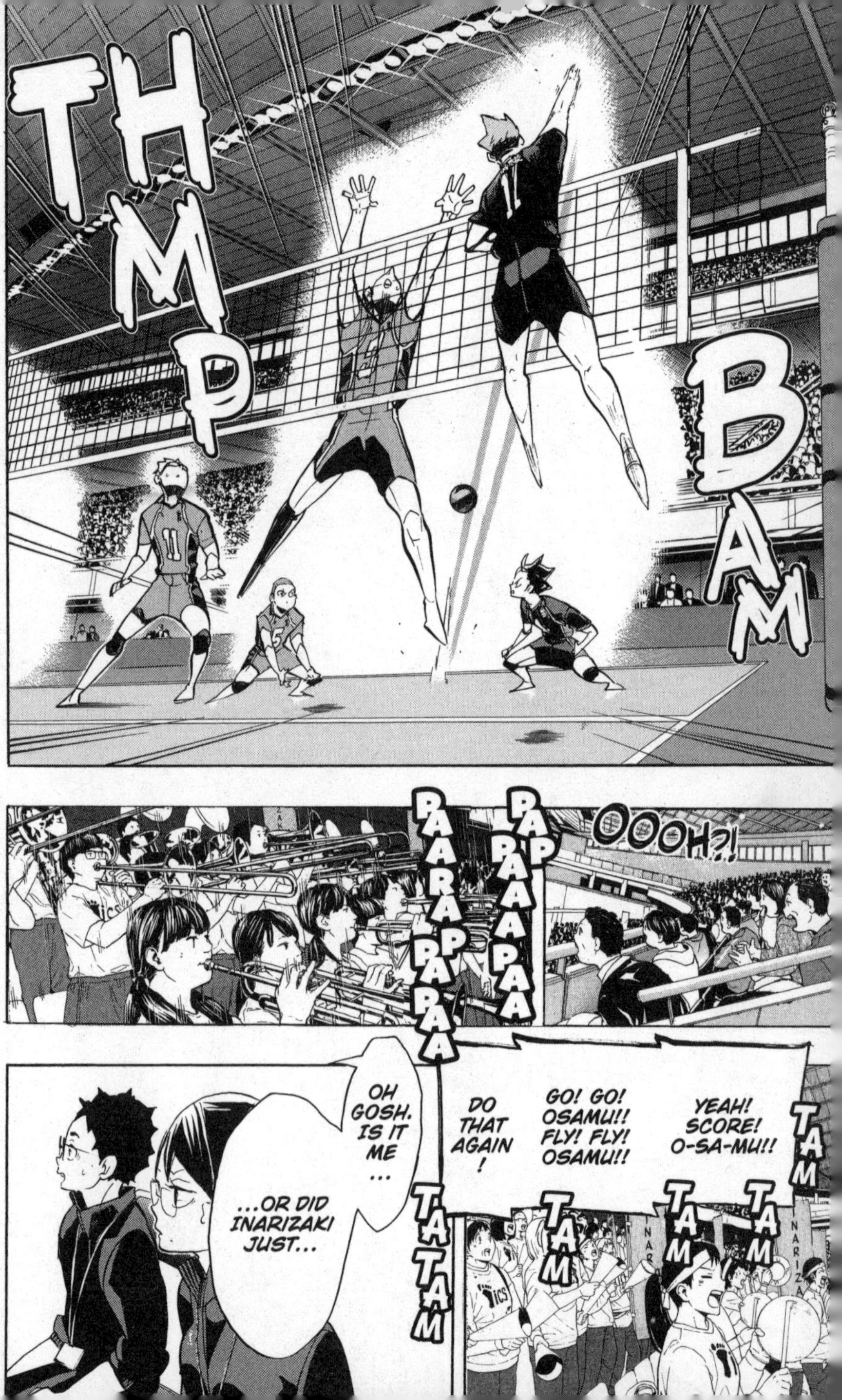
THMP
BAM
OOOH?!
PAP PAAAAA
PAARAP PAPAAA
YEAH! SCORE! O-SA-MU!!
GO! GO! OSAMU!! FLY! FLY! OSAMU!!
DO THAT AGAIN!
TAM
TAM
TAM
TAM
TATAM
OH GOSH. IS IT ME...
...OR DID INARIZAKI JUST...

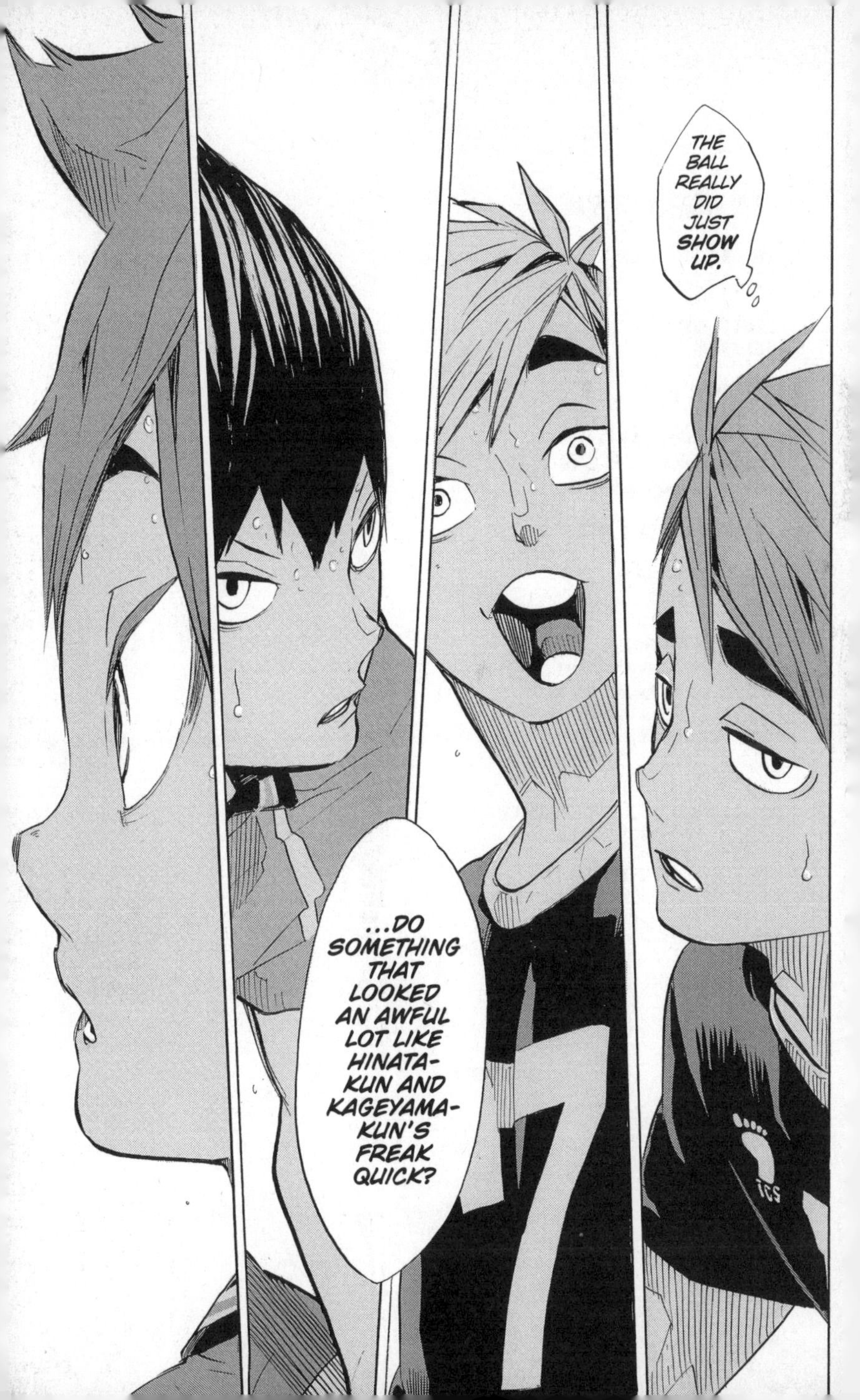
THE BALL REALLY DID JUST SHOW UP.
...DO SOMETHING THAT LOOKED AN AWFUL LOT LIKE HINATA-KUN AND KAGEYAMA-KUN'S FREAK QUICK?

ATSUMU MIYA

INARIZAKI HIGH SCHOOL
CLASS 2-2

POSITION:
SETTER

HEIGHT: 6'0"

WEIGHT: 162 LBS.
(AS OF JANUARY, 2ND YEAR OF HIGH SCHOOL)

BIRTHDAY: OCTOBER 5

FAVORITE FOOD:
FATTY TUNA

CURRENT WORRY:
IT'S GETTING TO THAT TIME OF YEAR WHEN HIS FINGERTIPS GET DRY AND CRACKED.

ABILITY PARAMETERS
(5-POINT SCALE)

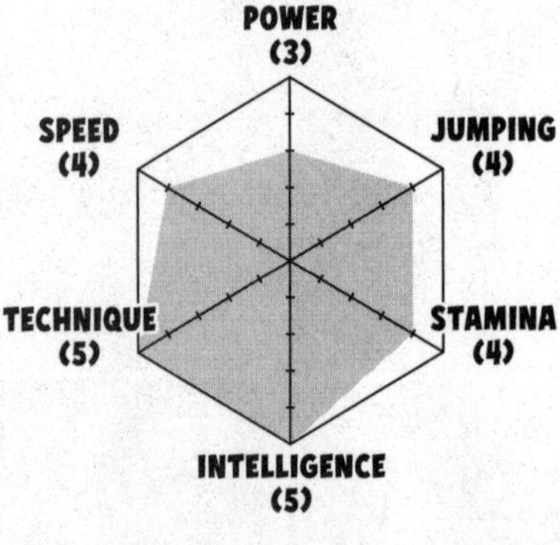
POWER (3)
JUMPING (4)
STAMINA (4)
INTELLIGENCE (5)
TECHNIQUE (5)
SPEED (4)

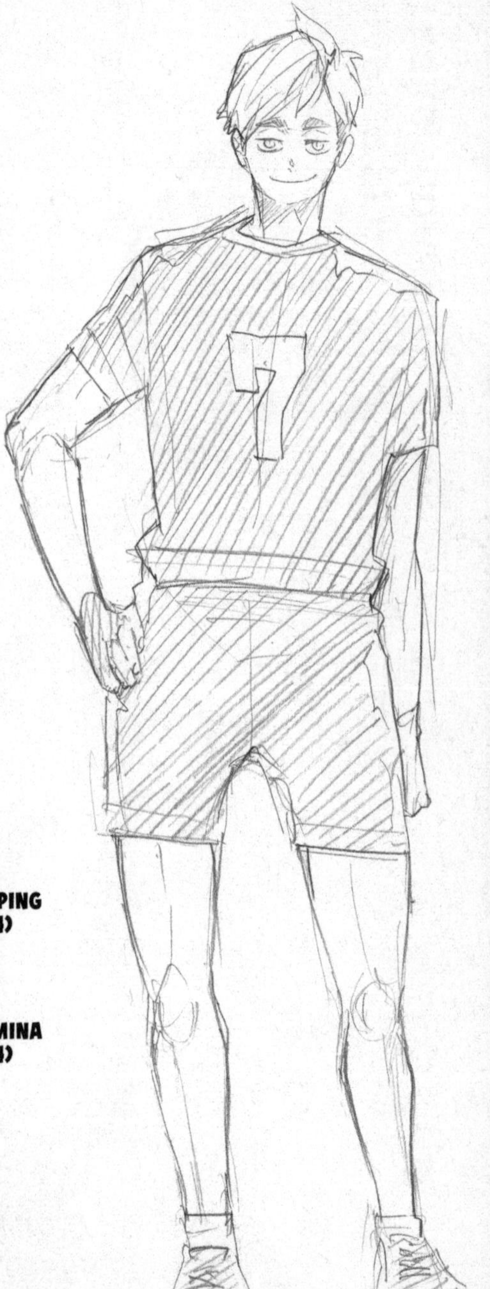
7

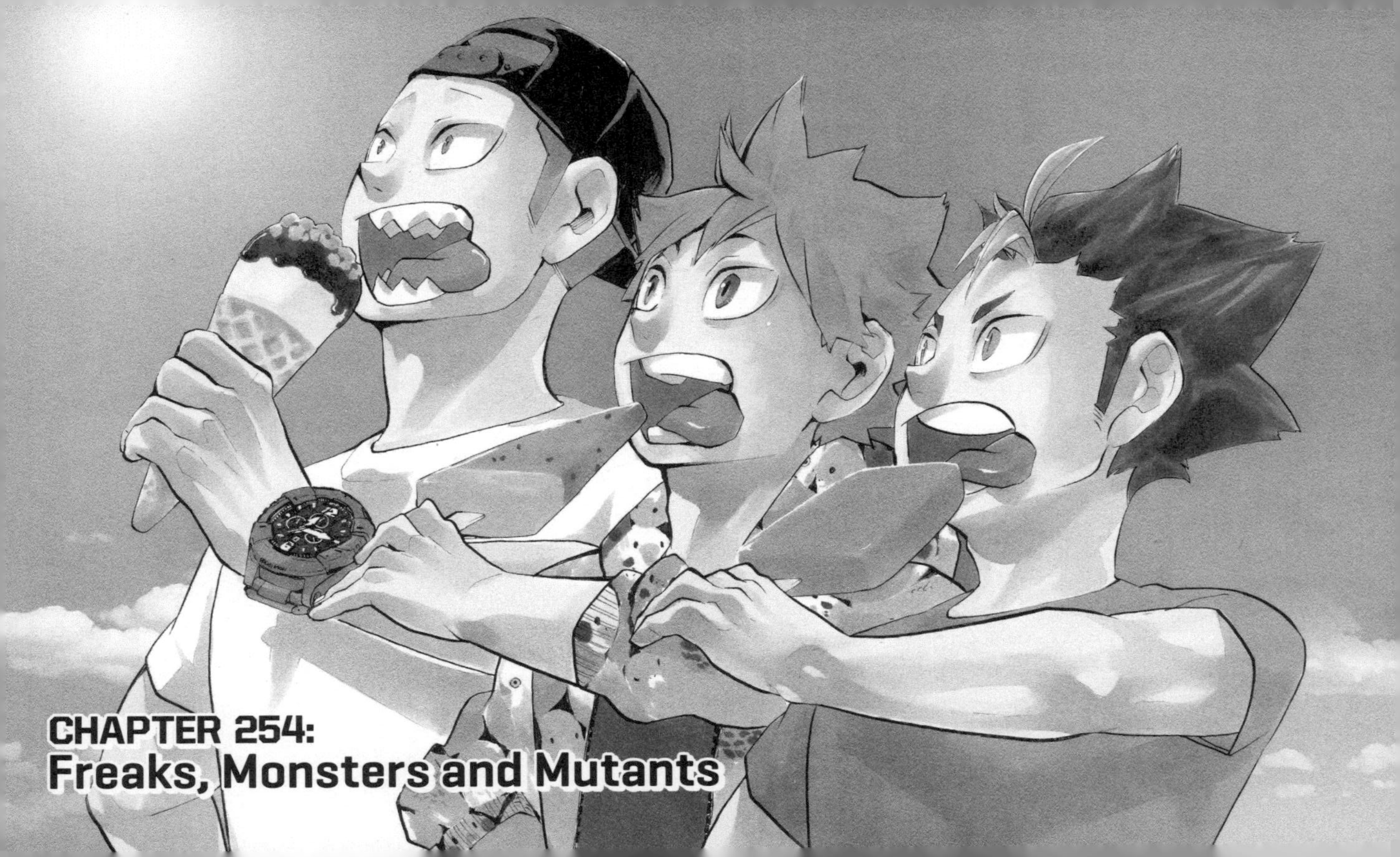
CHAPTER 254:
Freaks, Monsters and Mutants

HAIKYU!!

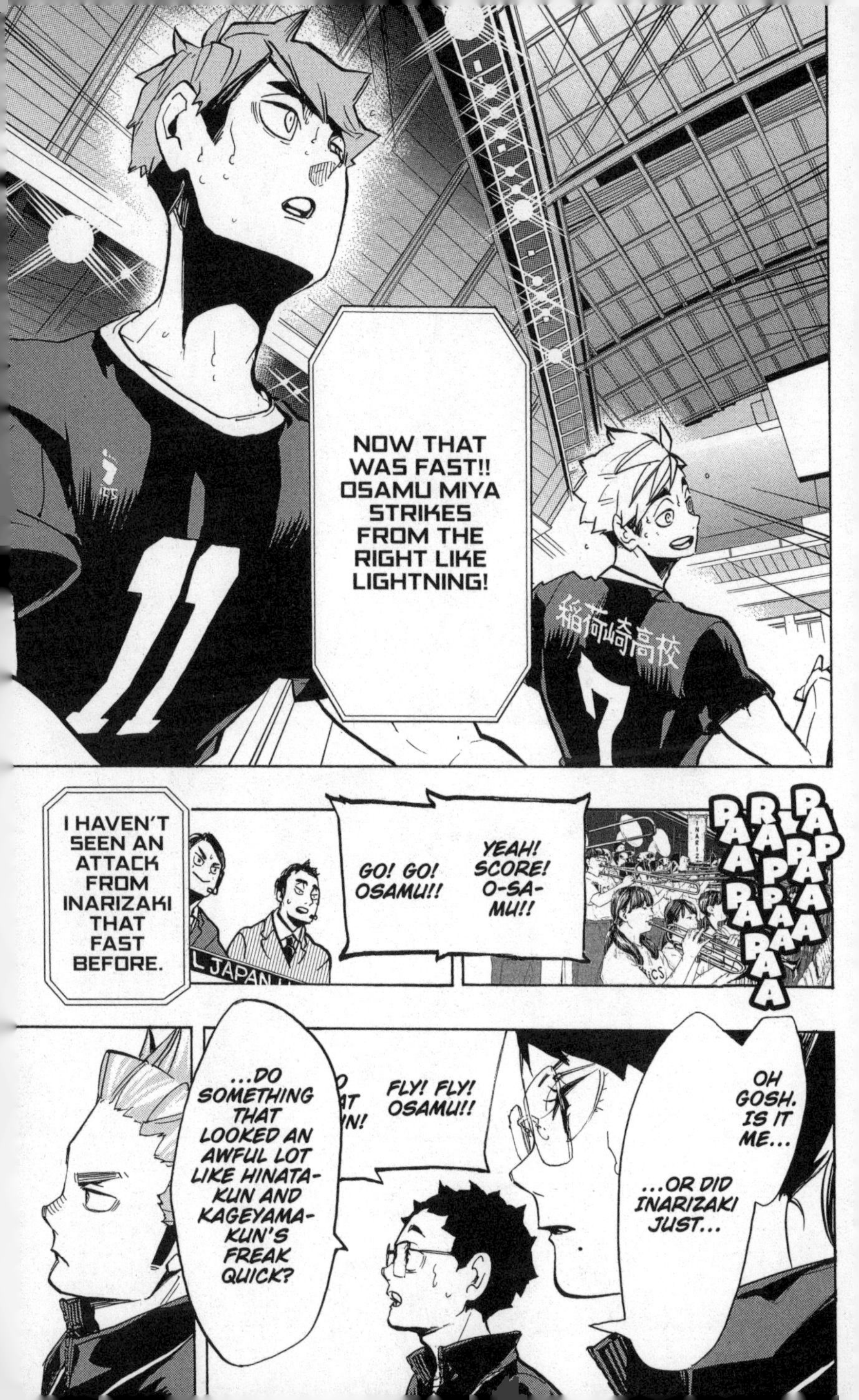
NOW THAT WAS FAST!! OSAMU MIYA STRIKES FROM THE RIGHT LIKE LIGHTNING!
稲荷崎高校
YEAH! SCORE! O-SA-MU!!
GO! GO! OSAMU!!
I HAVEN'T SEEN AN ATTACK FROM INARIZAKI THAT FAST BEFORE.
OH GOSH. IS IT ME...
...OR DID INARIZAKI JUST...
FLY! FLY! OSAMU!!
...DO SOMETHING THAT LOOKED AN AWFUL LOT LIKE HINATA-KUN AND KAGEYAMA-KUN'S FREAK QUICK?

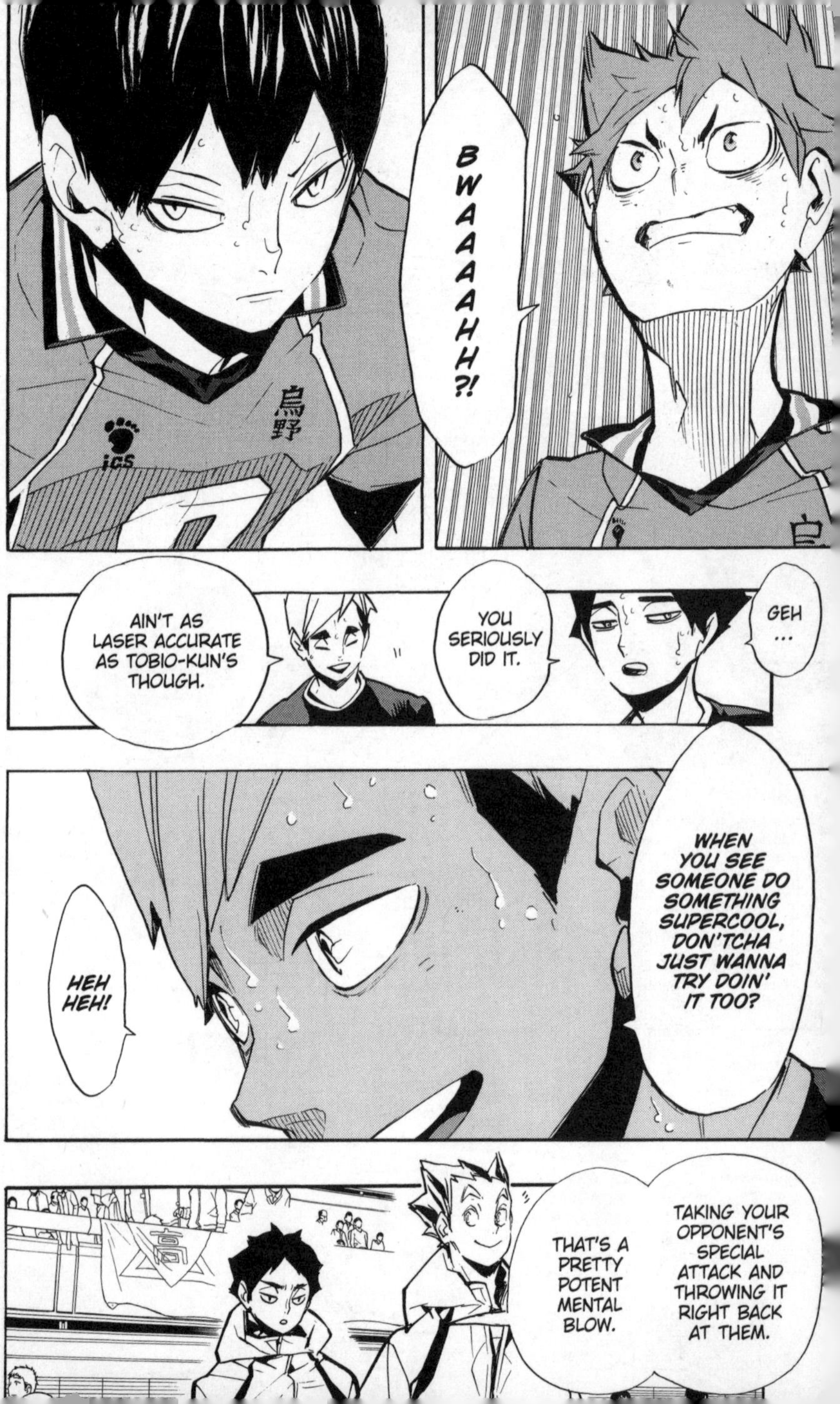
BWAAAAAHH?!
GEH ...
YOU SERIOUSLY DID IT.
AIN'T AS LASER ACCURATE AS TOBIO-KUN'S THOUGH.
WHEN YOU SEE SOMEONE DO SOMETHING SUPERCOOL, DON'TCHA JUST WANNA TRY DOIN' IT TOO?
HEH HEH!
TAKING YOUR OPPONENT'S SPECIAL ATTACK AND THROWING IT RIGHT BACK AT THEM.
THAT'S A PRETTY POTENT MENTAL BLOW.

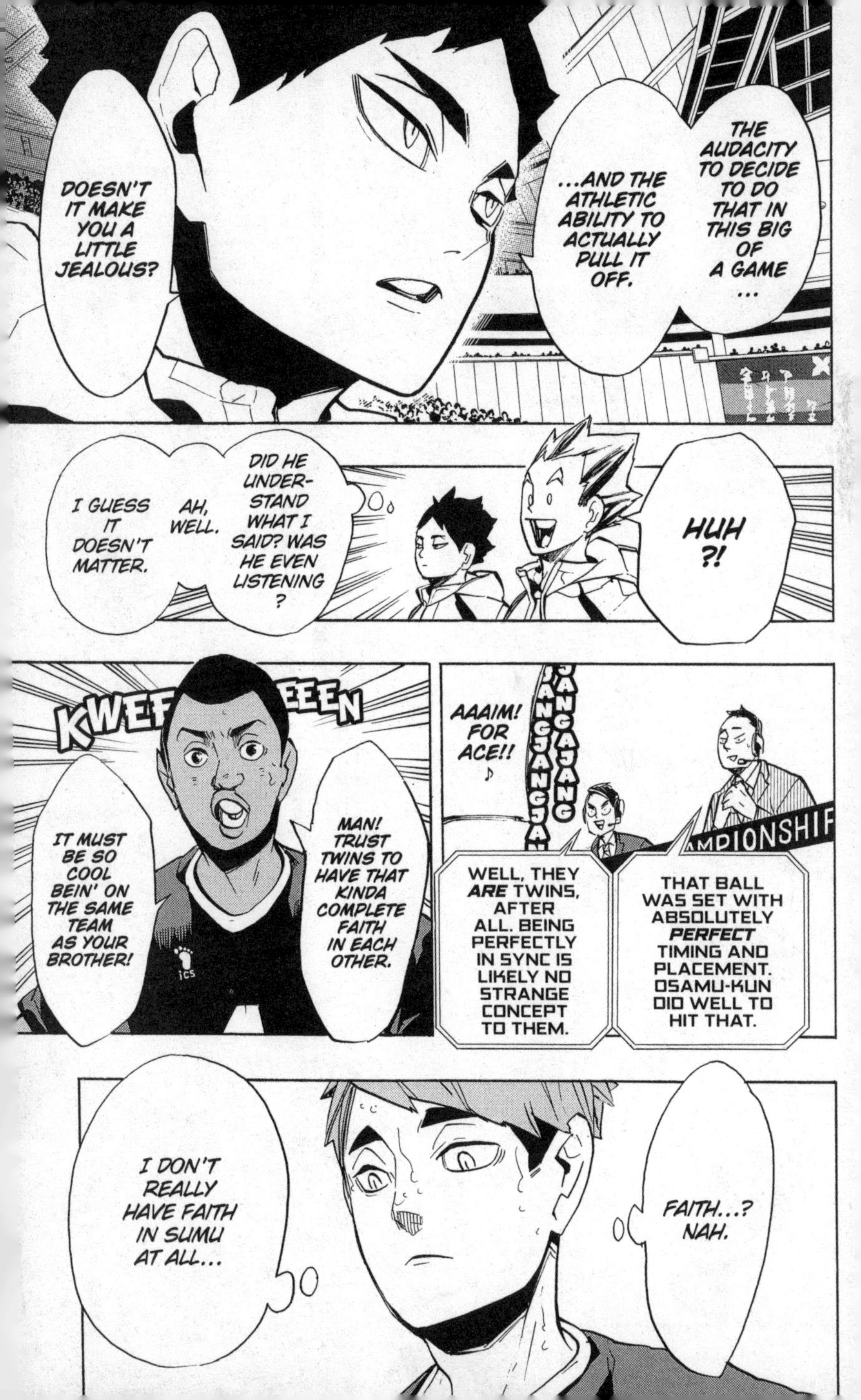
THE AUDACITY TO DECIDE TO DO THAT IN THIS BIG OF A GAME...
...AND THE ATHLETIC ABILITY TO ACTUALLY PULL IT OFF.
DOESN'T IT MAKE YOU A LITTLE JEALOUS?
HUH ?!
DID HE UNDER-STAND WHAT I SAID? WAS HE EVEN LISTENING ?
AH, WELL.
I GUESS IT DOESN'T MATTER.
JANGAJANG
JANGJANGJAN
AAAIM! FOR ACE!! ♪
THAT BALL WAS SET WITH ABSOLUTELY PERFECT TIMING AND PLACEMENT. OSAMU-KUN DID WELL TO HIT THAT.
WELL, THEY ARE TWINS, AFTER ALL. BEING PERFECTLY IN SYNC IS LIKELY NO STRANGE CONCEPT TO THEM.
KWEE
EEEN
MAN! TRUST TWINS TO HAVE THAT KINDA COMPLETE FAITH IN EACH OTHER.
IT MUST BE SO COOL BEIN' ON THE SAME TEAM AS YOUR BROTHER!
FAITH...? NAH.
I DON'T REALLY HAVE FAITH IN SUMU AT ALL...

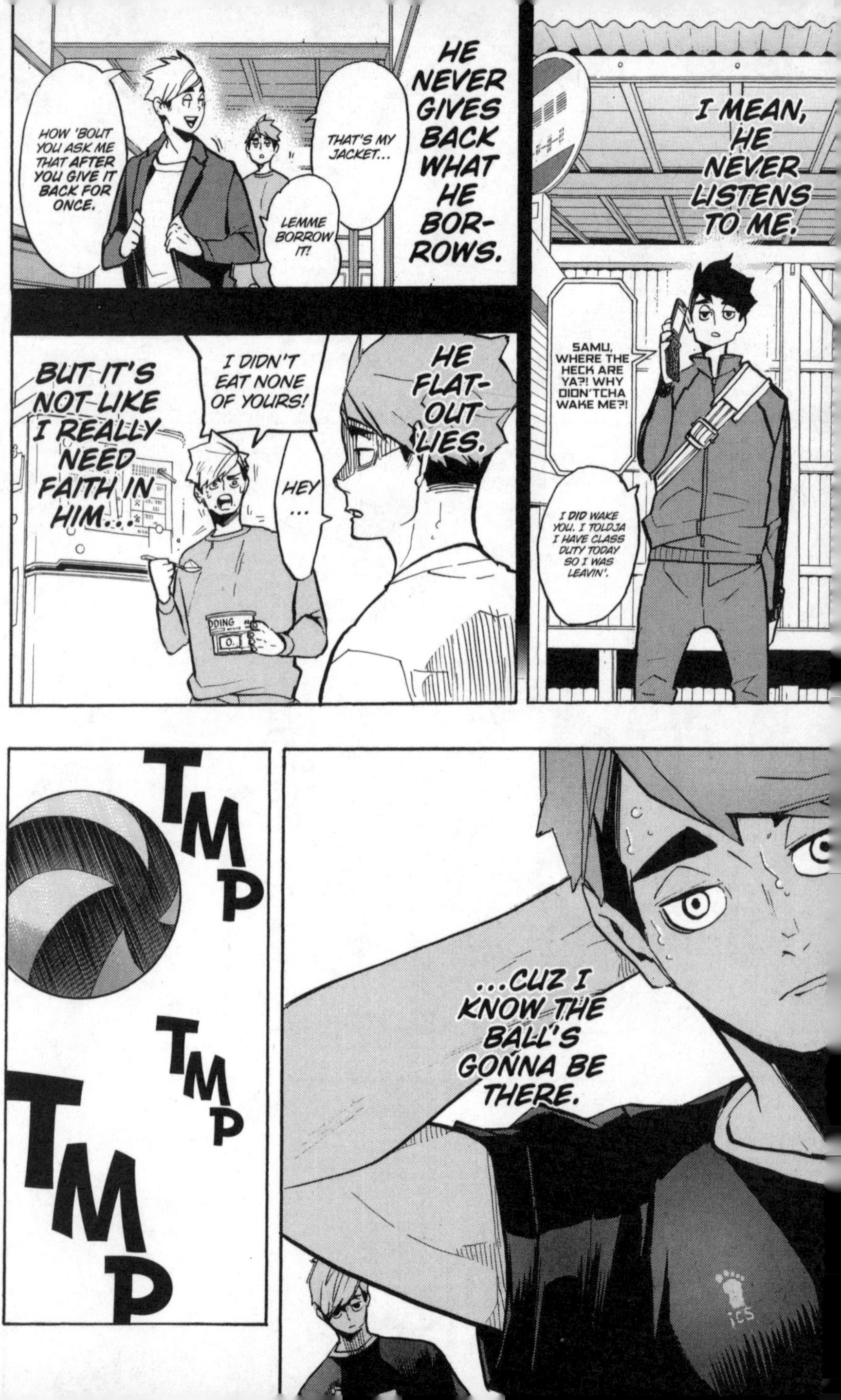

I MEAN, HE NEVER LISTENS TO ME.
SAMU, WHERE THE HECK ARE YA?! WHY DIDN'TCHA WAKE ME?!
I DID WAKE YOU. I TOLDJA I HAVE CLASS DUTY TODAY SO I WAS LEAVIN'.
HE NEVER GIVES BACK WHAT HE BORROWS.
THAT'S MY JACKET...
LEMME BORROW IT!
HOW 'BOUT YOU ASK ME THAT AFTER YOU GIVE IT BACK FOR ONCE.
HE FLAT-OUT LIES.
HEY ...
I DIDN'T EAT NONE OF YOURS!
BUT IT'S NOT LIKE I REALLY NEED FAITH IN HIM...
...CUZ I KNOW THE BALL'S GONNA BE THERE.
TMP
TMP
TMP

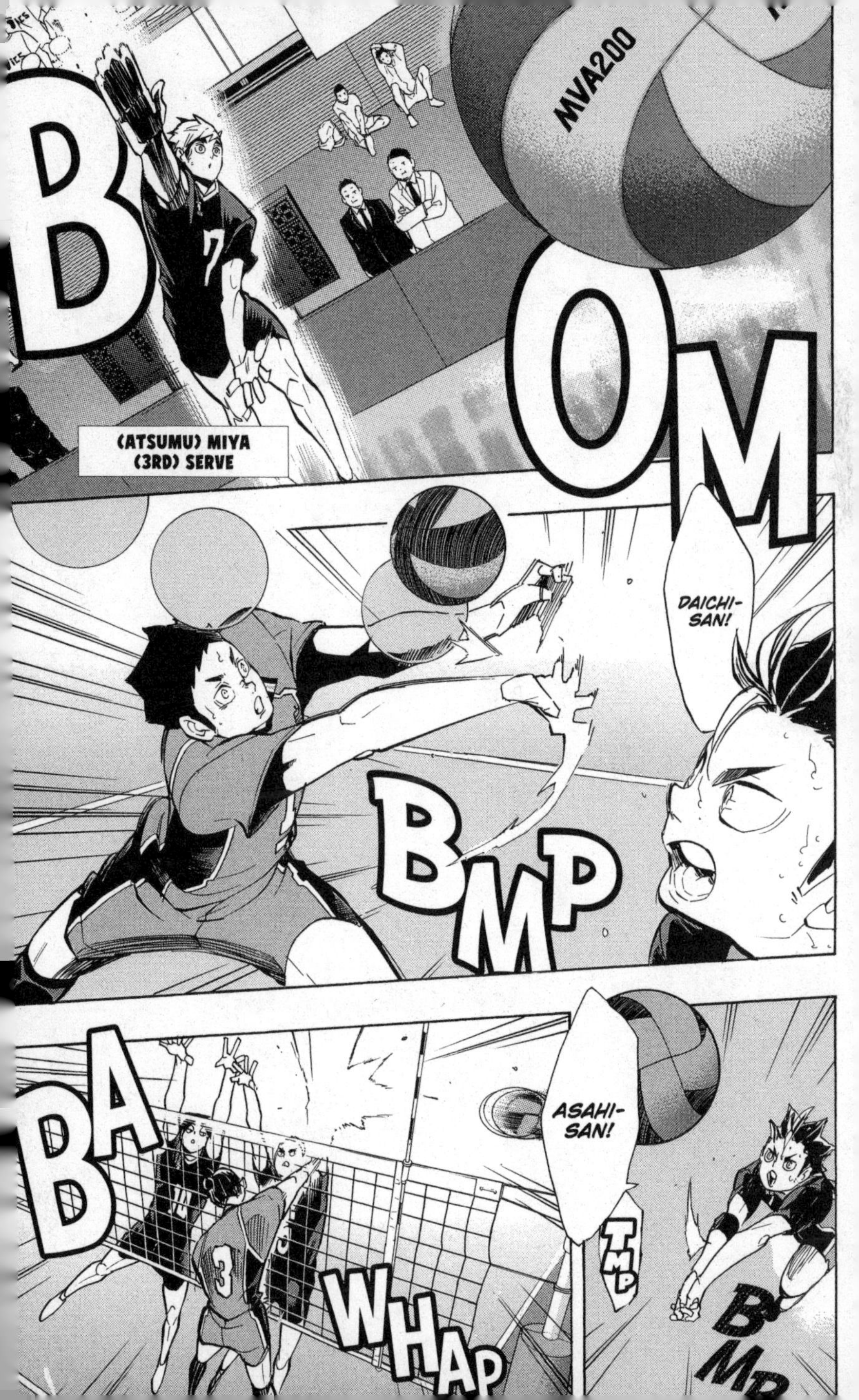
MVA200
BOOM
(ATSUMU) MIYA
(3RD) SERVE
DAICHI-SAN!
BMP
ASAHI-SAN!
TMP
WHAP
BA

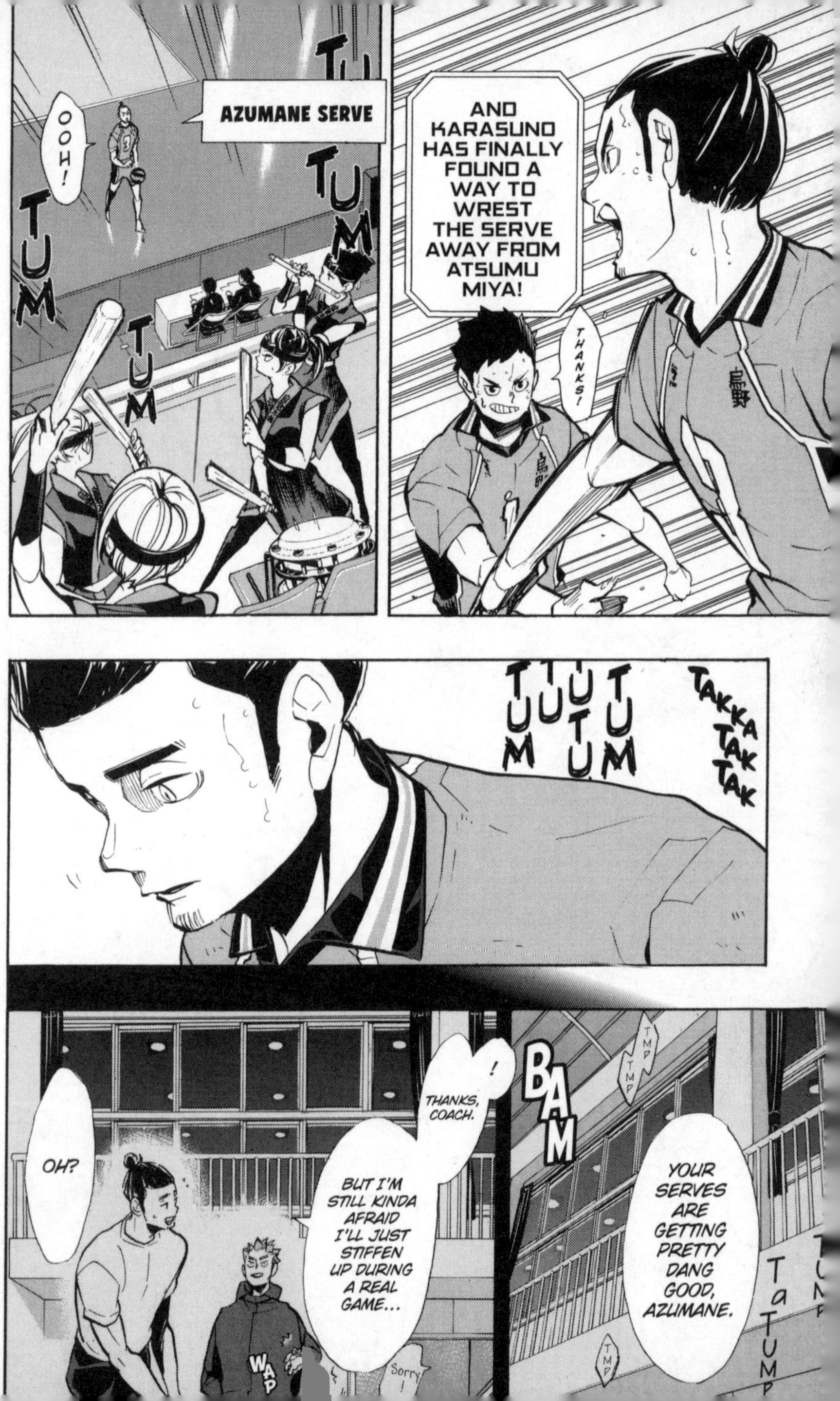
AND KARASUNO HAS FINALLY FOUND A WAY TO WREST THE SERVE AWAY FROM ATSUMU MIYA!
THANKS!
AZUMANE SERVE
OOH!
TUM
TUM
TUM
TUM
TAKKA TAK TAK
TUM TUM TUM TUM
TMP TMP
BAM
YOUR SERVES ARE GETTING PRETTY DANG GOOD, AZUMANE.
TaTUMP
TMP
!
THANKS, COACH.
BUT I'M STILL KINDA AFRAID I'LL JUST STIFFEN UP DURING A REAL GAME...
OH?
WAP
Sorry!

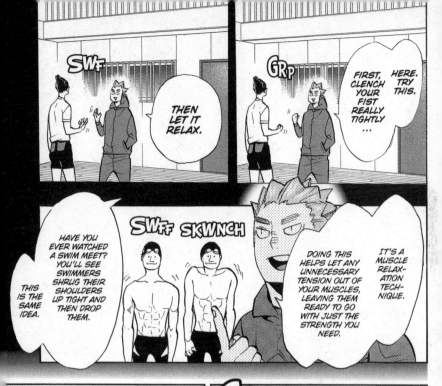

HERE. TRY THIS.
FIRST, CLENCH YOUR FIST REALLY TIGHTLY...
GRP
SWF
THEN LET IT RELAX.
IT'S A MUSCLE RELAXATION TECHNIQUE.
DOING THIS HELPS LET ANY UNNECESSARY TENSION OUT OF YOUR MUSCLES, LEAVING THEM READY TO GO WITH JUST THE STRENGTH YOU NEED.
SKWNCH
SWFF
HAVE YOU EVER WATCHED A SWIM MEET? YOU'LL SEE SWIMMERS SHRUG THEIR SHOULDERS UP TIGHT AND THEN DROP THEM.
THIS IS THE SAME IDEA.
GRRRRRRRRP

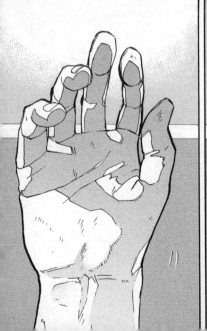

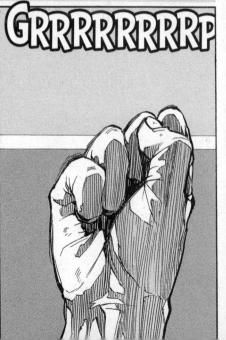

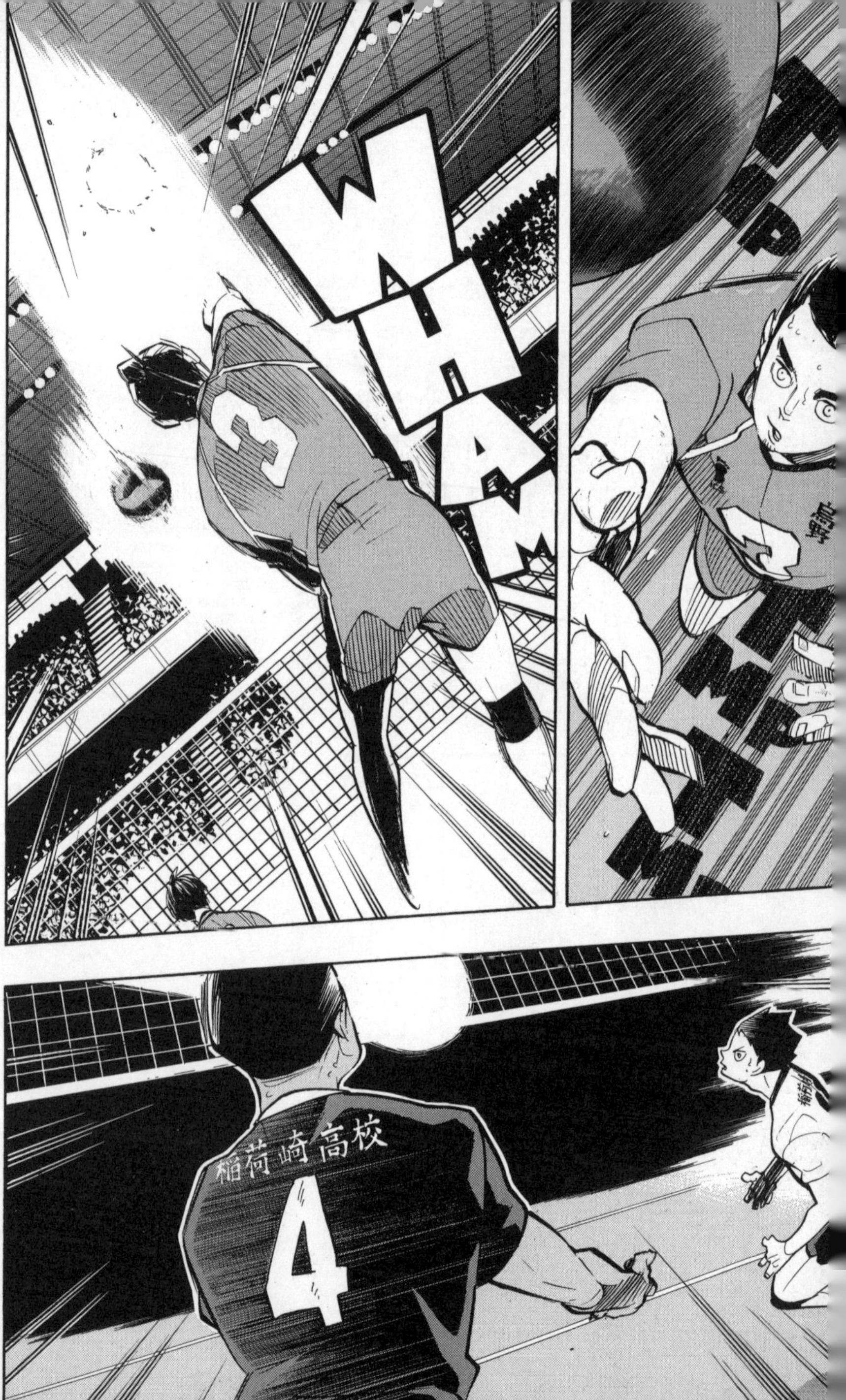
WHAM
稲荷崎高校

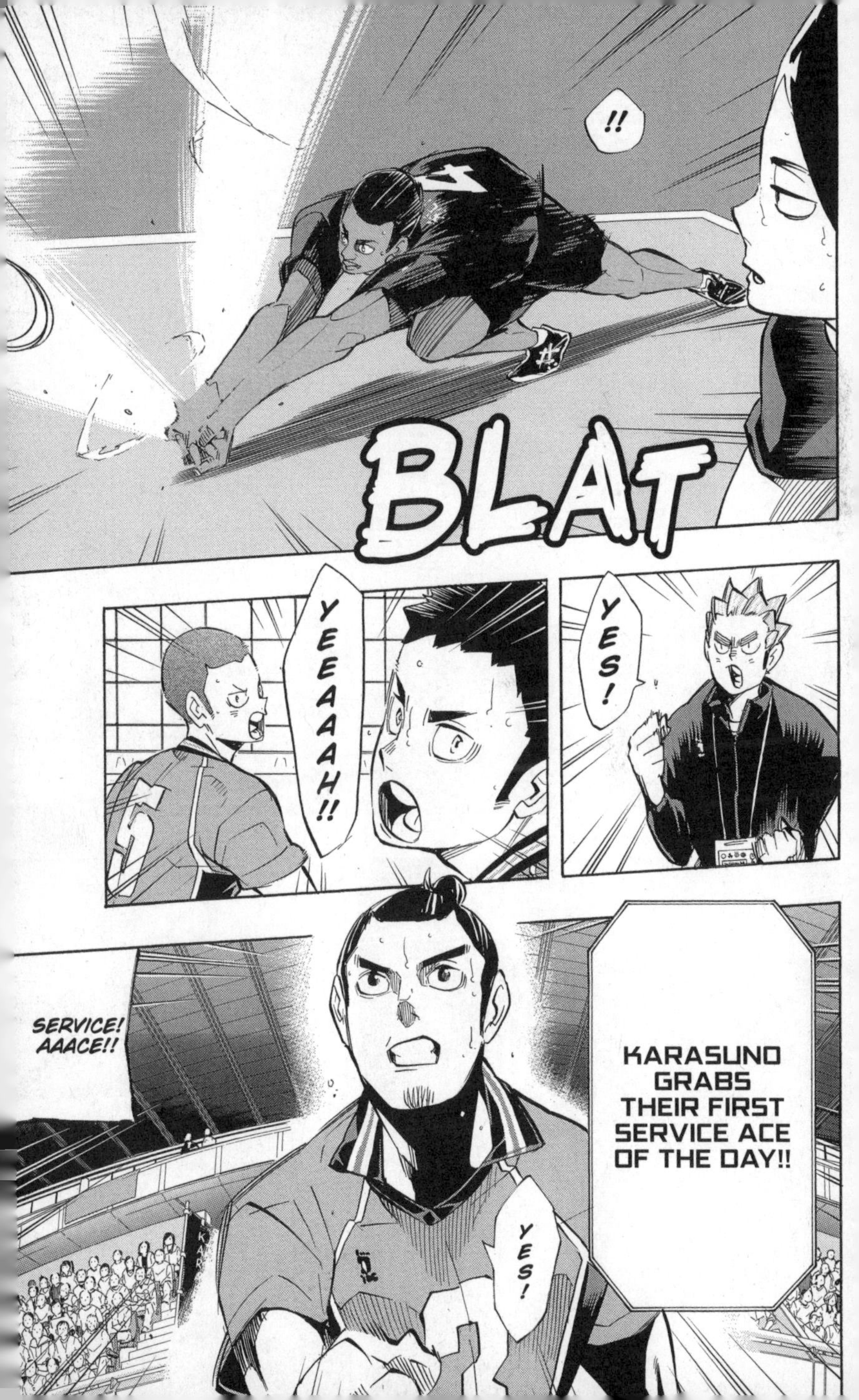

!!
BLAT
YES!
YEEAAAAH!!
KARASUNO GRABS THEIR FIRST SERVICE ACE OF THE DAY!!
YES!
SERVICE! AAACE!!

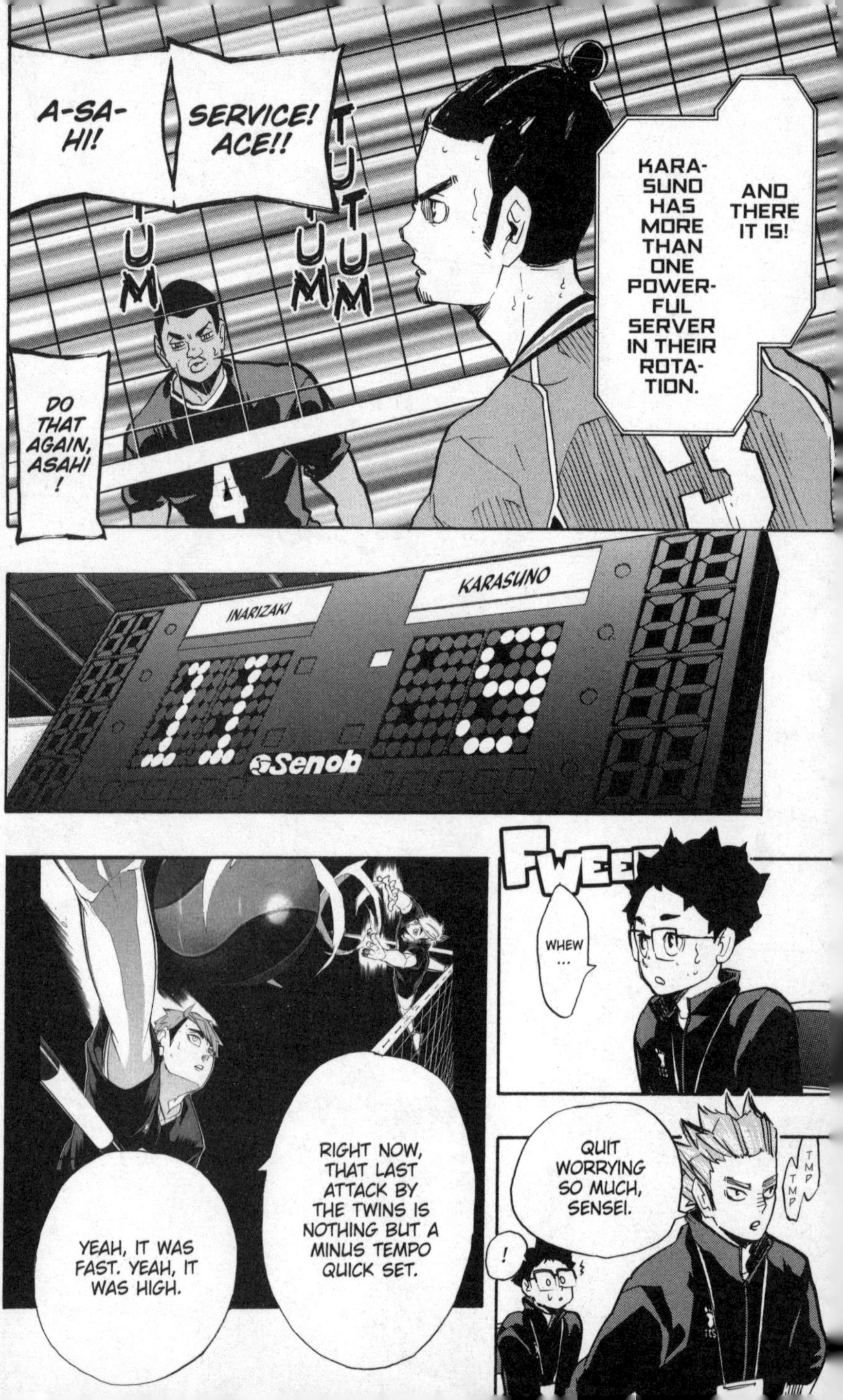
AND THERE IT IS!
KARASUNO HAS MORE THAN ONE POWERFUL SERVER IN THEIR ROTATION.
SERVICE! ACE!!
A-SA-HI!
TUTUMM
DO THAT AGAIN, ASAHI!
KARASUNO
INARIZAKI
Senob
FWEE
WHEW...
QUIT WORRYING SO MUCH, SENSEI.
TMP TMP
!
RIGHT NOW, THAT LAST ATTACK BY THE TWINS IS NOTHING BUT A MINUS TEMPO QUICK SET.
YEAH, IT WAS FAST. YEAH, IT WAS HIGH.

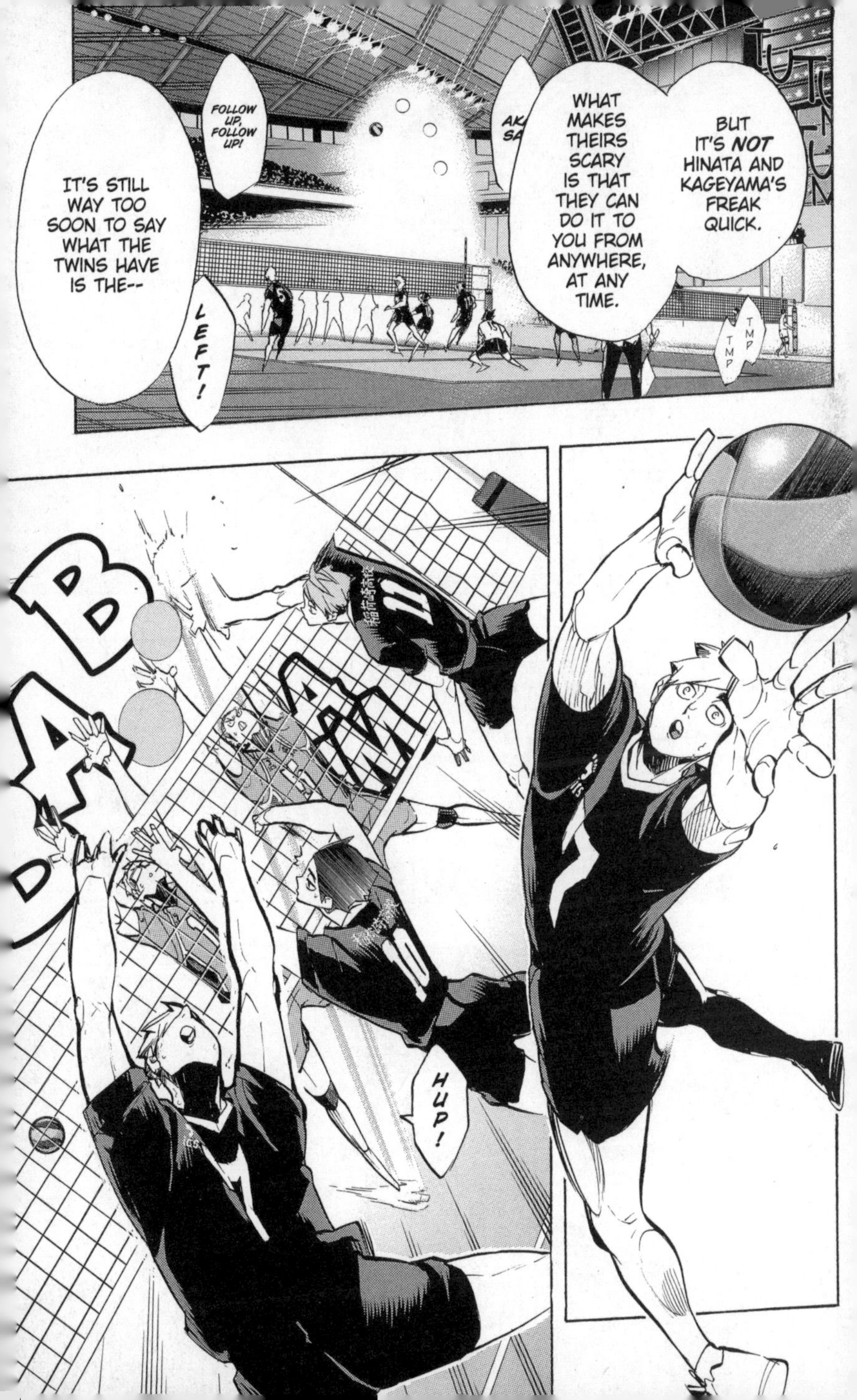

BUT IT'S NOT HINATA AND KAGEYAMA'S FREAK QUICK.
WHAT MAKES THEIRS SCARY IS THAT THEY CAN DO IT TO YOU FROM ANYWHERE, AT ANY TIME.
TMP TMP
FOLLOW UP, FOLLOW UP!
IT'S STILL WAY TOO SOON TO SAY WHAT THE TWINS HAVE IS THE--
LEFT!
BAM
HUP!

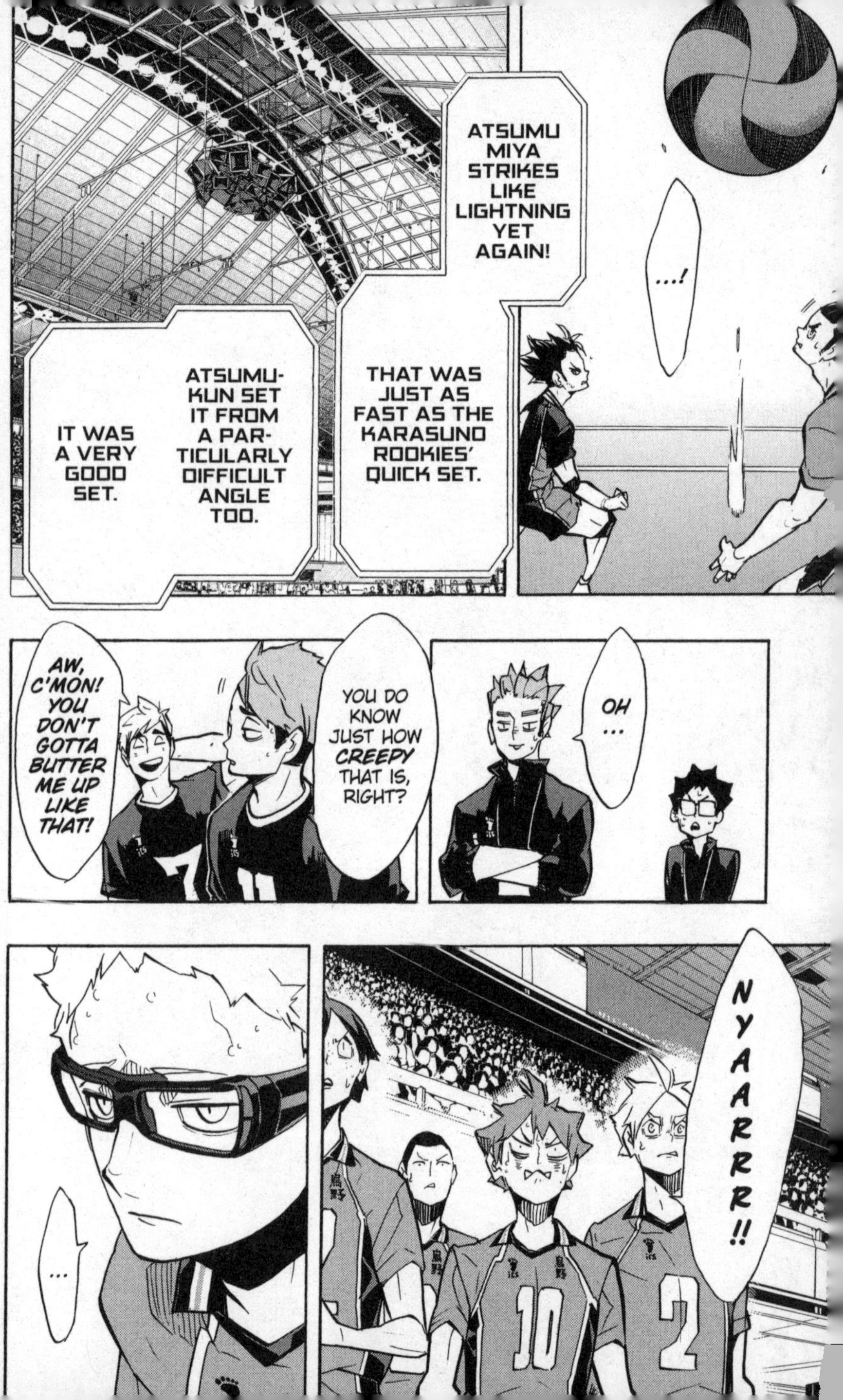
...!
ATSUMU MIYA STRIKES LIKE LIGHTNING YET AGAIN!
THAT WAS JUST AS FAST AS THE KARASUNO ROOKIES' QUICK SET.
ATSUMU-KUN SET IT FROM A PARTICULARLY DIFFICULT ANGLE TOO.
IT WAS A VERY GOOD SET.
OH ...
YOU DO KNOW JUST HOW *CREEPY* THAT IS, RIGHT?
AW, C'MON! YOU DON'T GOTTA BUTTER ME UP LIKE THAT!
NYAARRR!!
...

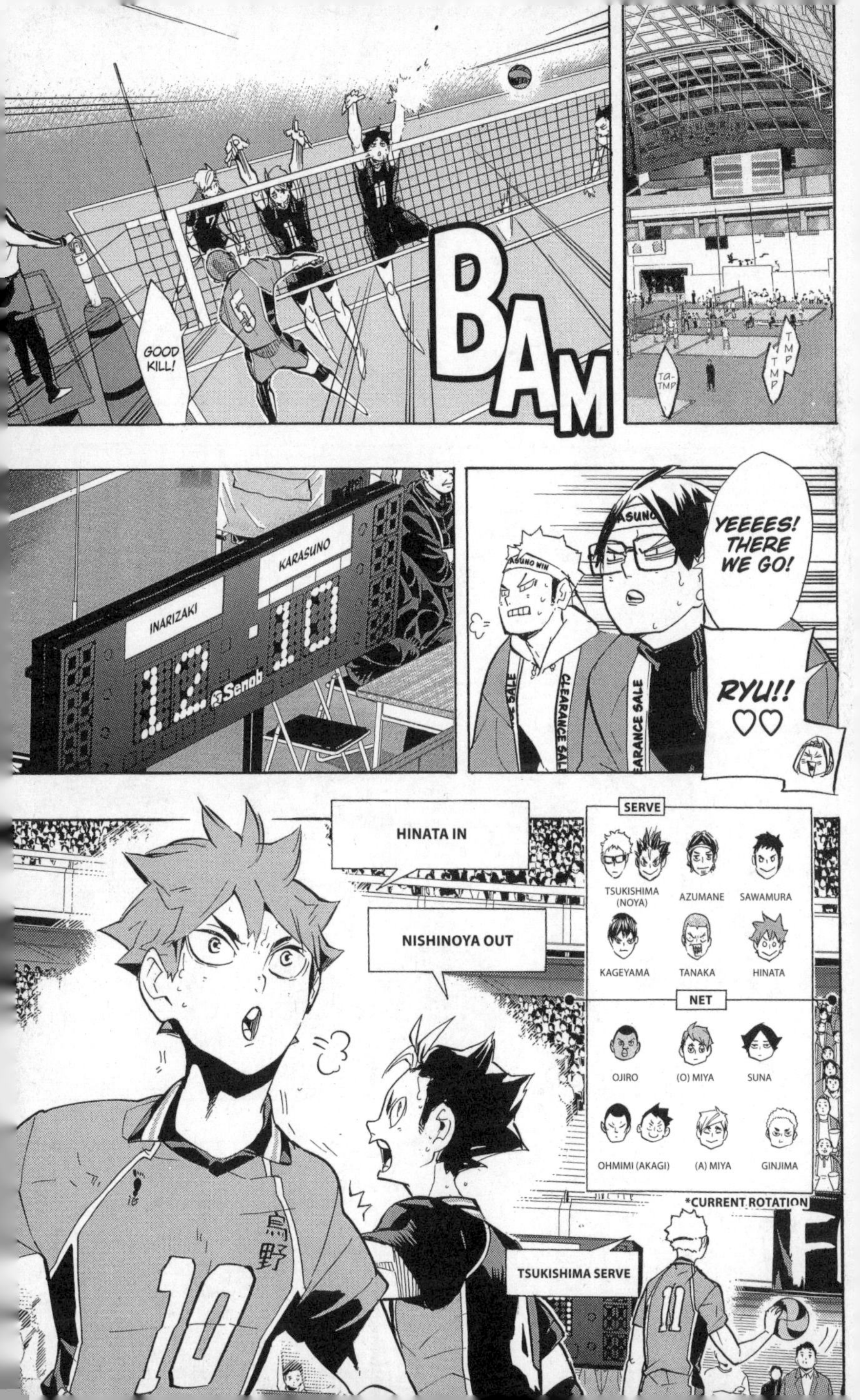

TMP TMP TMP
TA-TMP
BAM
GOOD KILL!
YEEEES! THERE WE GO!
RYU!! ♡♡
CLEARANCE SALE
KARASUNO
INARIZAKI
12
10
Senob
SERVE
TSUKISHIMA (NOYA)
AZUMANE
SAWAMURA
KAGEYAMA
TANAKA
HINATA
NET
OJIRO
(O) MIYA
SUNA
OHMIMI (AKAGI)
(A) MIYA
GINJIMA
*CURRENT ROTATION
HINATA IN
NISHINOYA OUT
TSUKISHIMA SERVE

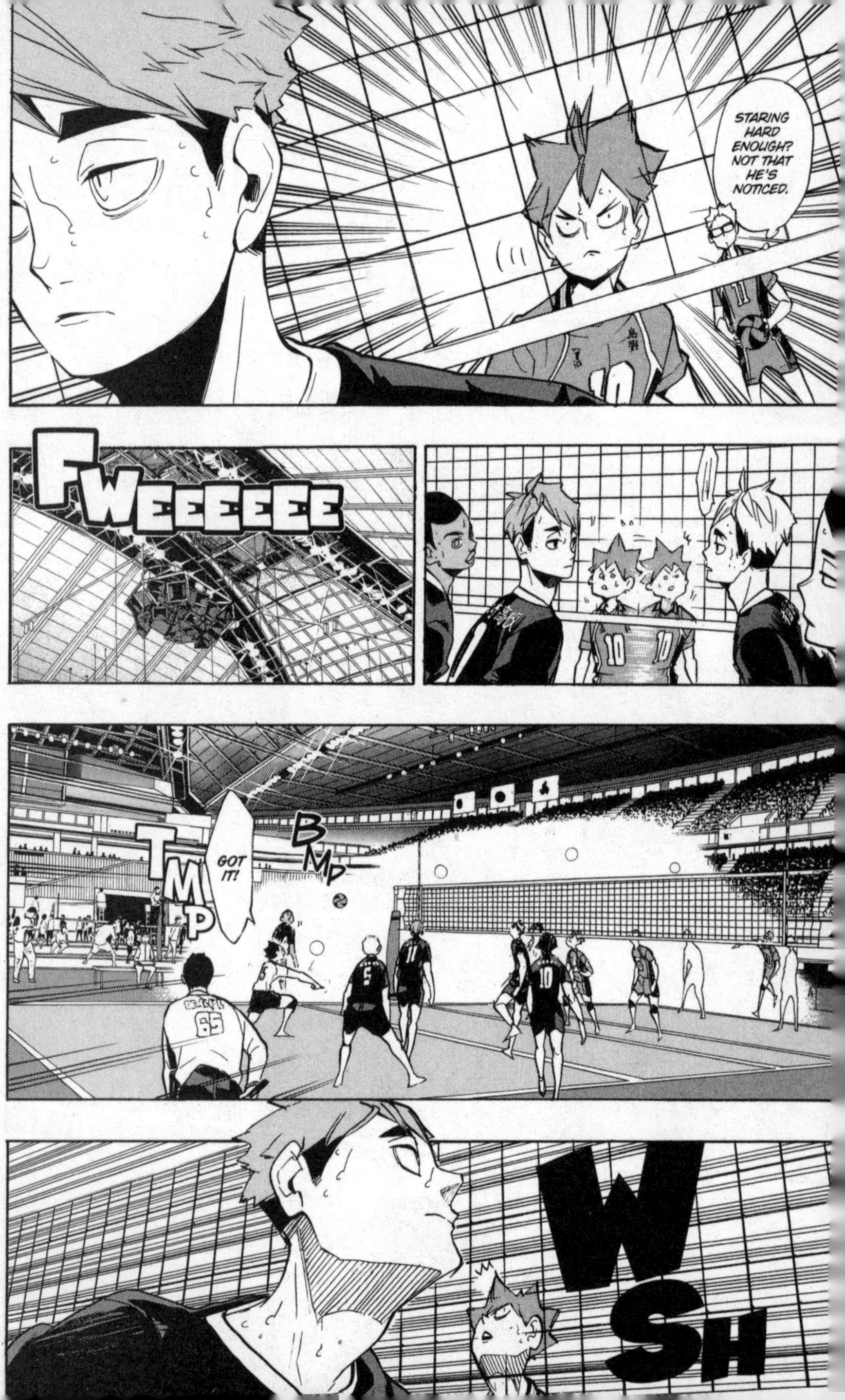
STARING HARD ENOUGH? NOT THAT HE'S NOTICED.
FWEEEEEE
GOT IT!
BMP
TMP
WSH

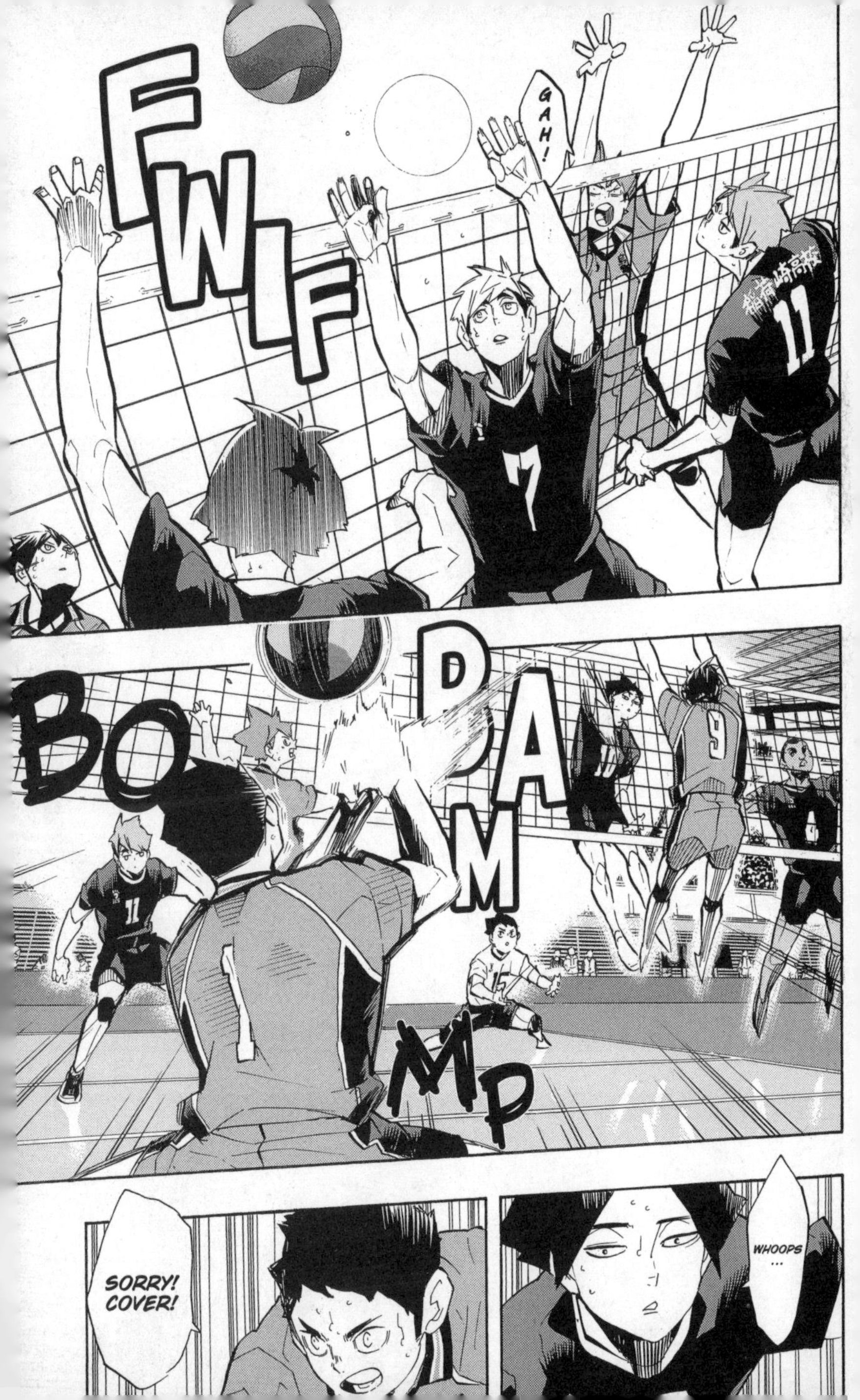
FWIF
GAH!
DAM
BO
MMP
WHOOPS ...
SORRY! COVER!

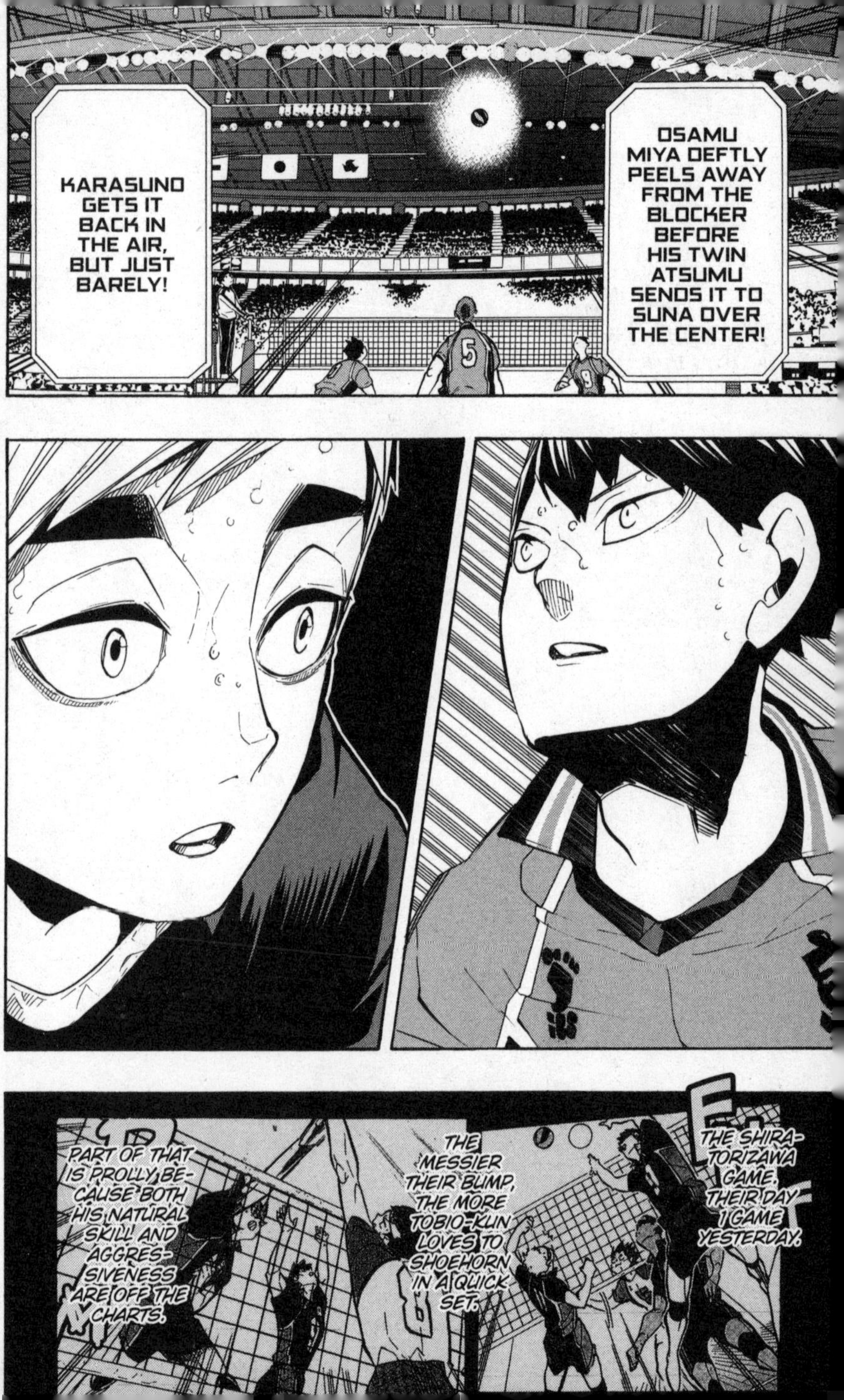
OSAMU MIYA DEFTLY PEELS AWAY FROM THE BLOCKER BEFORE HIS TWIN ATSUMU SENDS IT TO SUNA OVER THE CENTER!
KARASUNO GETS IT BACK IN THE AIR, BUT JUST BARELY!
THE SHIRATORIZAWA GAME. THEIR DAY 1 GAME YESTERDAY.
THE MESSIER THEIR BUMP, THE MORE TOBIO-KUN LOVES TO SHOEHORN IN A QUICK SET.
PART OF THAT IS PROLLY BECAUSE BOTH HIS NATURAL SKILL AND AGGRESSIVENESS ARE OFF THE CHARTS.

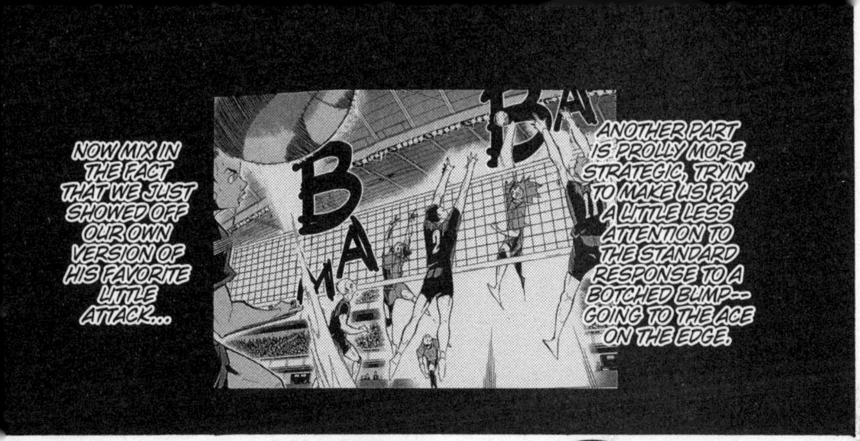
ANOTHER PART IS PROLLY MORE STRATEGIC, TRYIN' TO MAKE US PAY A LITTLE LESS ATTENTION TO THE STANDARD RESPONSE TO A BOTCHED BUMP-- GOING TO THE ACE ON THE EDGE.
BA
BAM
NOW MIX IN THE FACT THAT WE JUST SHOWED OFF OUR OWN VERSION OF HIS FAVORITE LITTLE ATTACK...
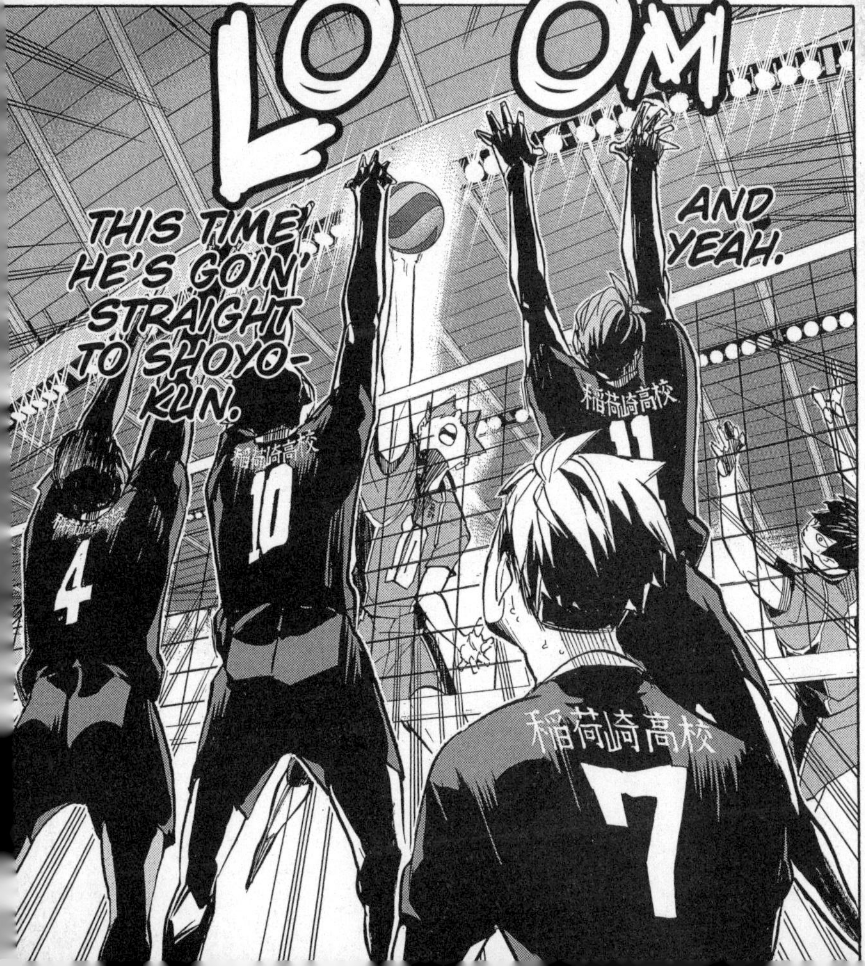
LO OM
AND YEAH.
THIS TIME... HE'S GOIN' STRAIGHT TO SHOYO-KUN.

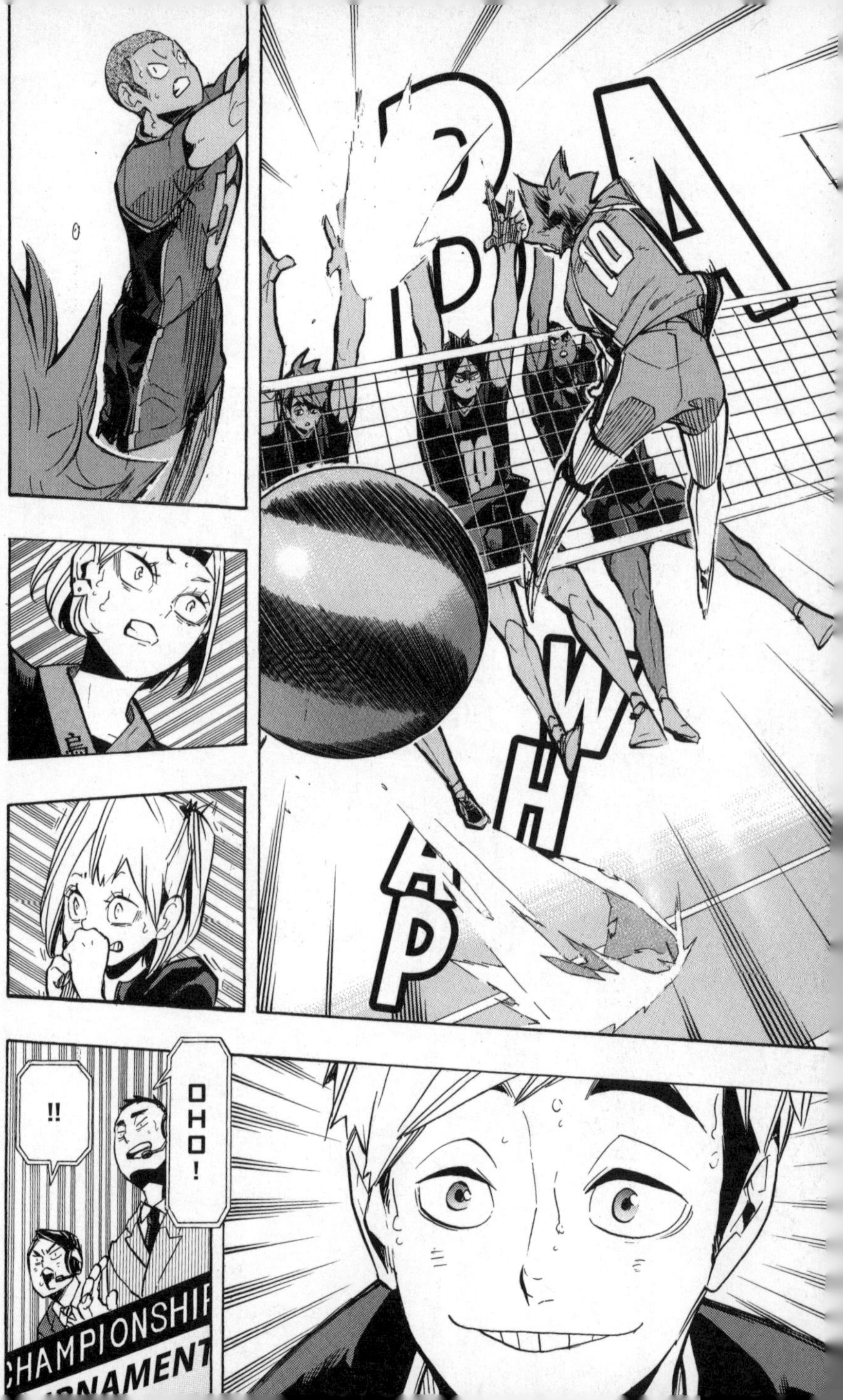
BA
WHAP
OHO!
!!

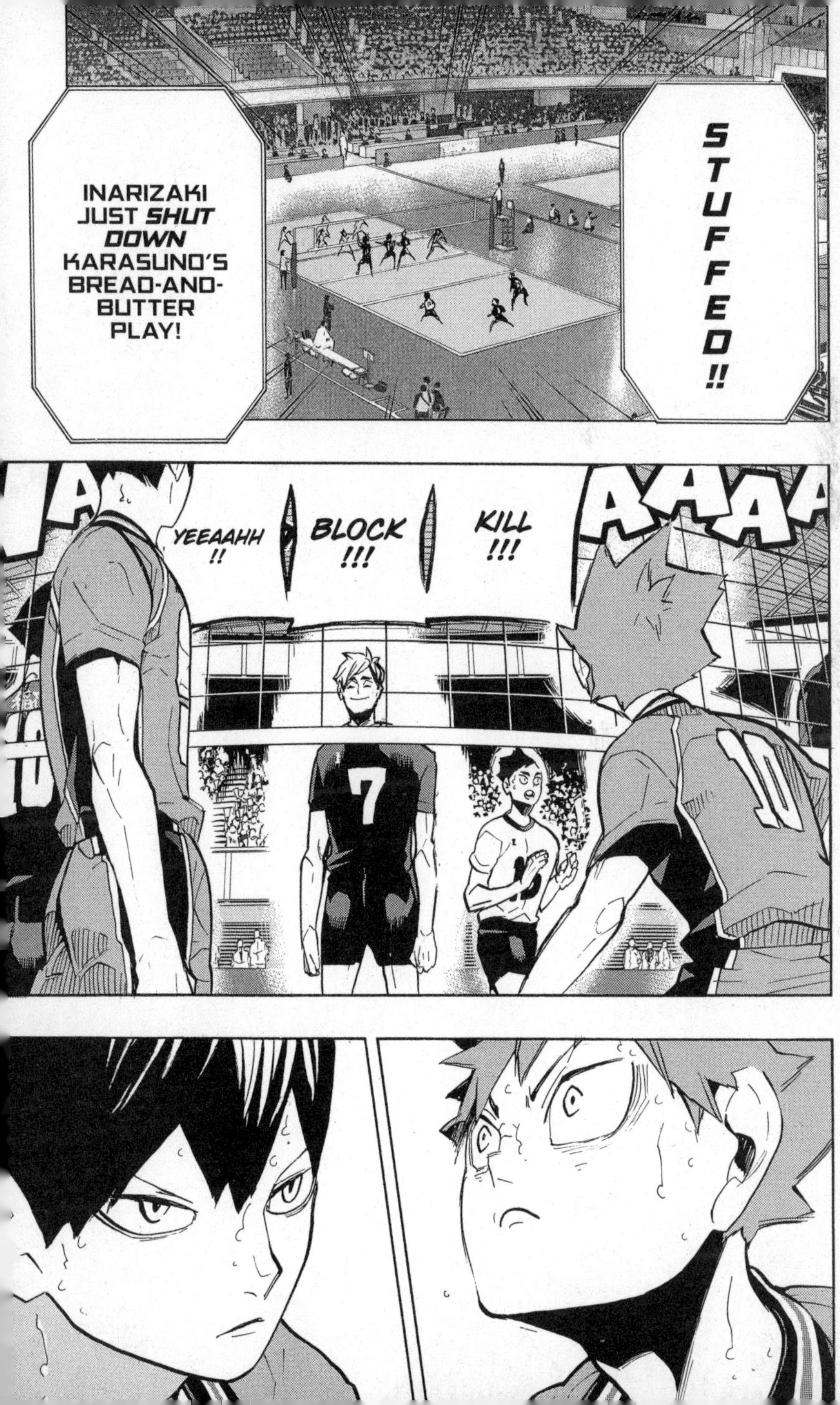
STUFFED!!
INARIZAKI JUST SHUT DOWN KARASUNO'S BREAD-AND-BUTTER PLAY!
AAAA
KILL !!!
BLOCK !!!
YEEAAHH !!

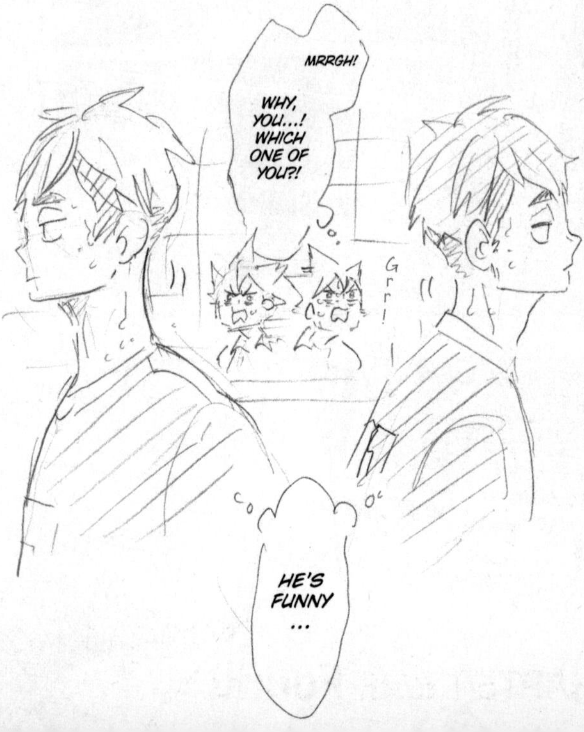
MRRGH!
WHY, YOU...! WHICH ONE OF YOU?!
Grr!
HE'S FUNNY ...

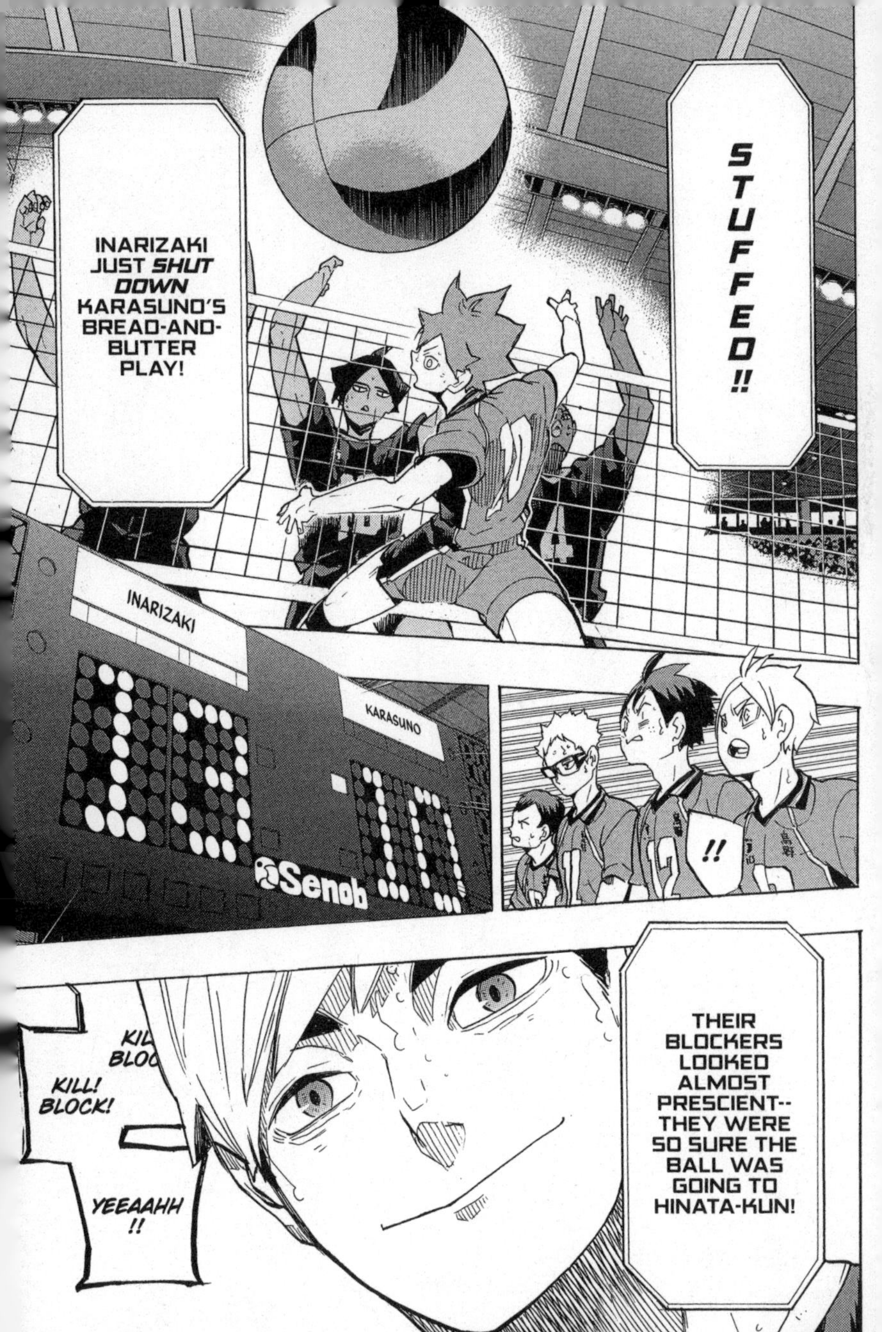
STUFFED!!
INARIZAKI JUST SHUT DOWN KARASUNO'S BREAD-AND-BUTTER PLAY!
!!
INARIZAKI
KARASUNO
Senob
THEIR BLOCKERS LOOKED ALMOST PRESCIENT-- THEY WERE SO SURE THE BALL WAS GOING TO HINATA-KUN!
KILL! BLOCK!
YEEAAHH!!

CHAPTER 255: Found

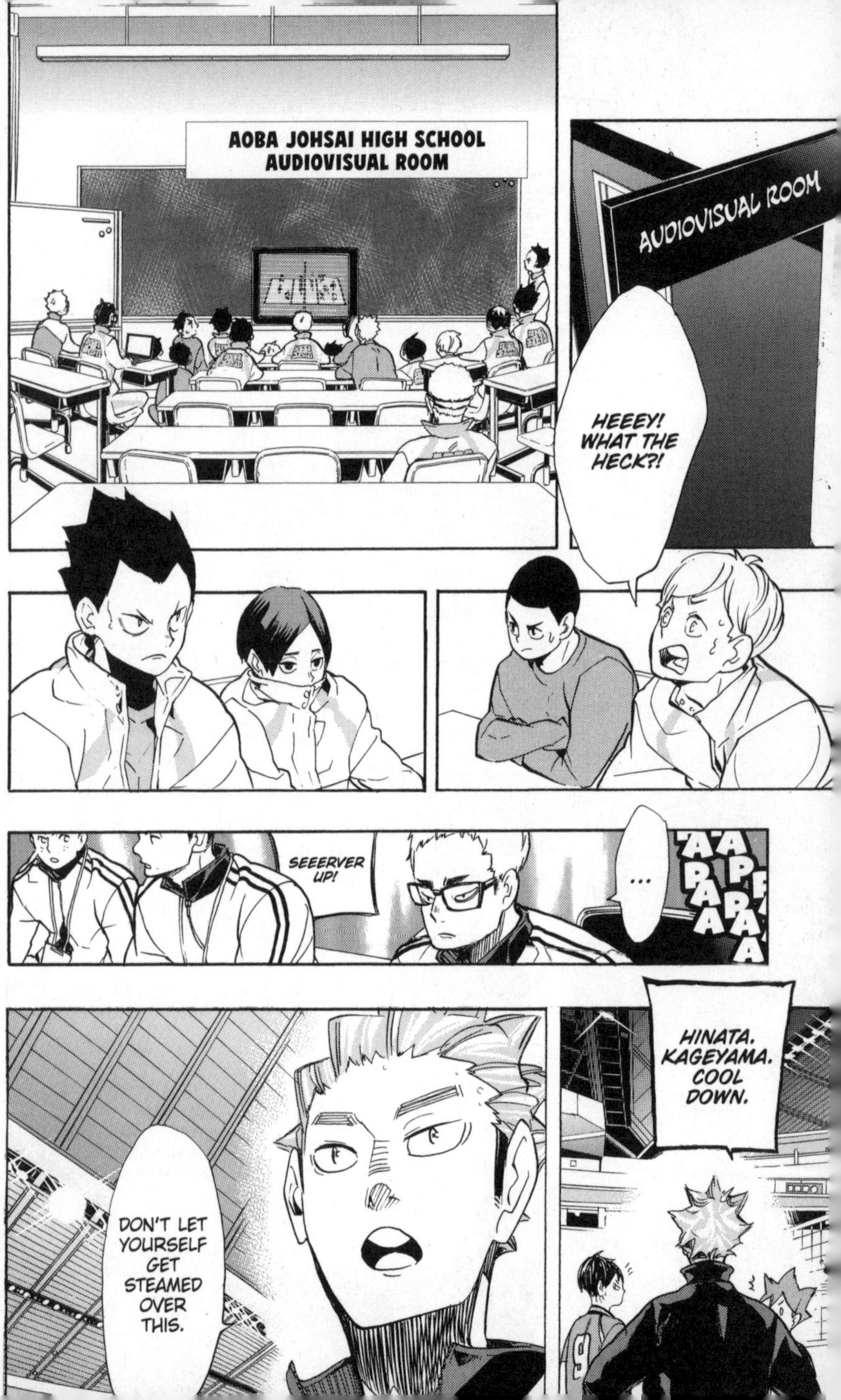
AUDIOVISUAL ROOM
HEEEY! WHAT THE HECK?!
AOBA JOHSAI HIGH SCHOOL AUDIOVISUAL ROOM
PAPAPA
...
SEEERVER UP!
HINATA. KAGEYAMA. COOL DOWN.
DON'T LET YOURSELF GET STEAMED OVER THIS.

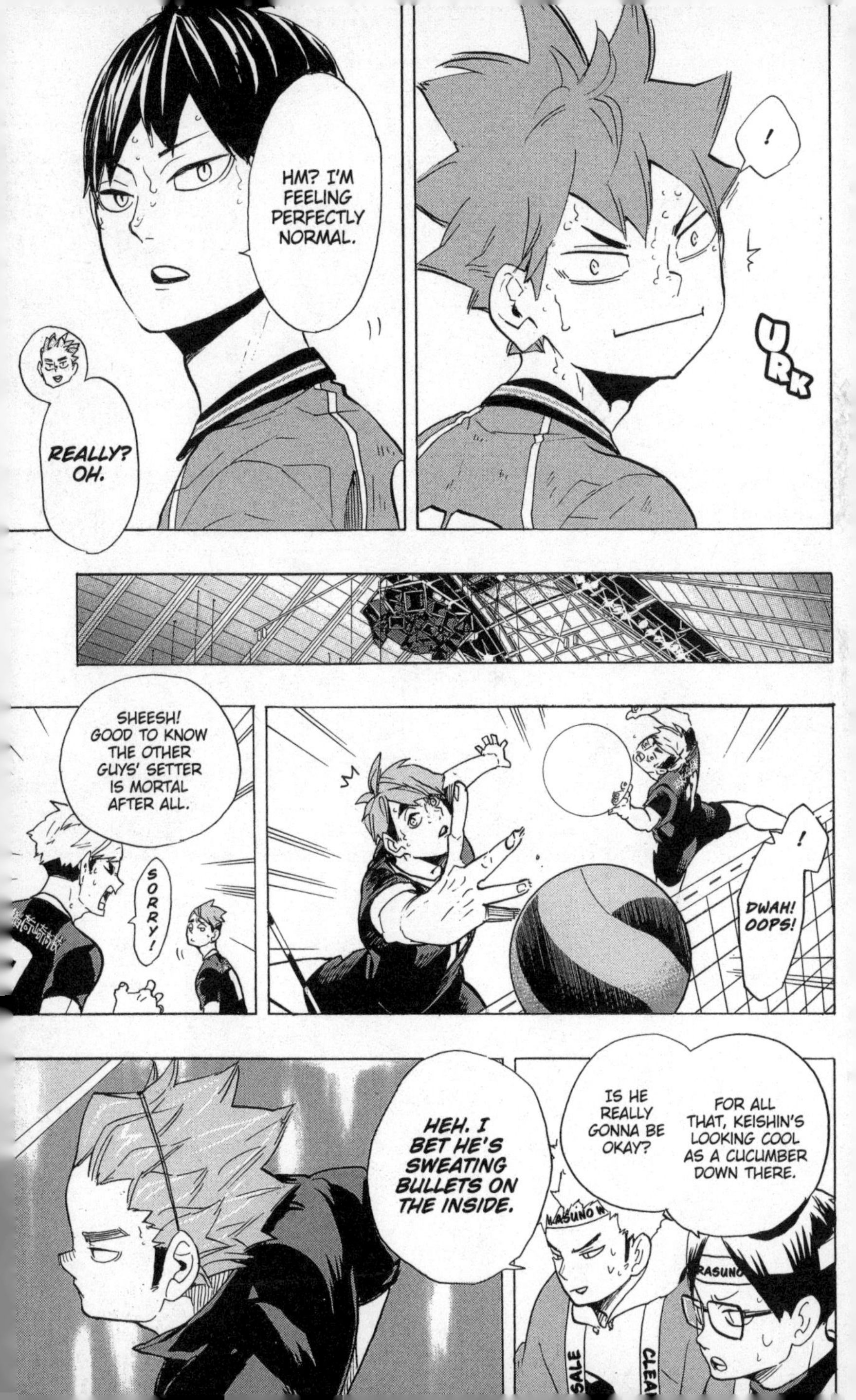

!
URK
HM? I'M FEELING PERFECTLY NORMAL.
REALLY? OH.
!
DWAH! OOPS!
SHEESH! GOOD TO KNOW THE OTHER GUYS' SETTER IS MORTAL AFTER ALL.
SORRY!
FOR ALL THAT, KEISHIN'S LOOKING COOL AS A CUCUMBER DOWN THERE.
IS HE REALLY GONNA BE OKAY?
HEH. I BET HE'S SWEATING BULLETS ON THE INSIDE.

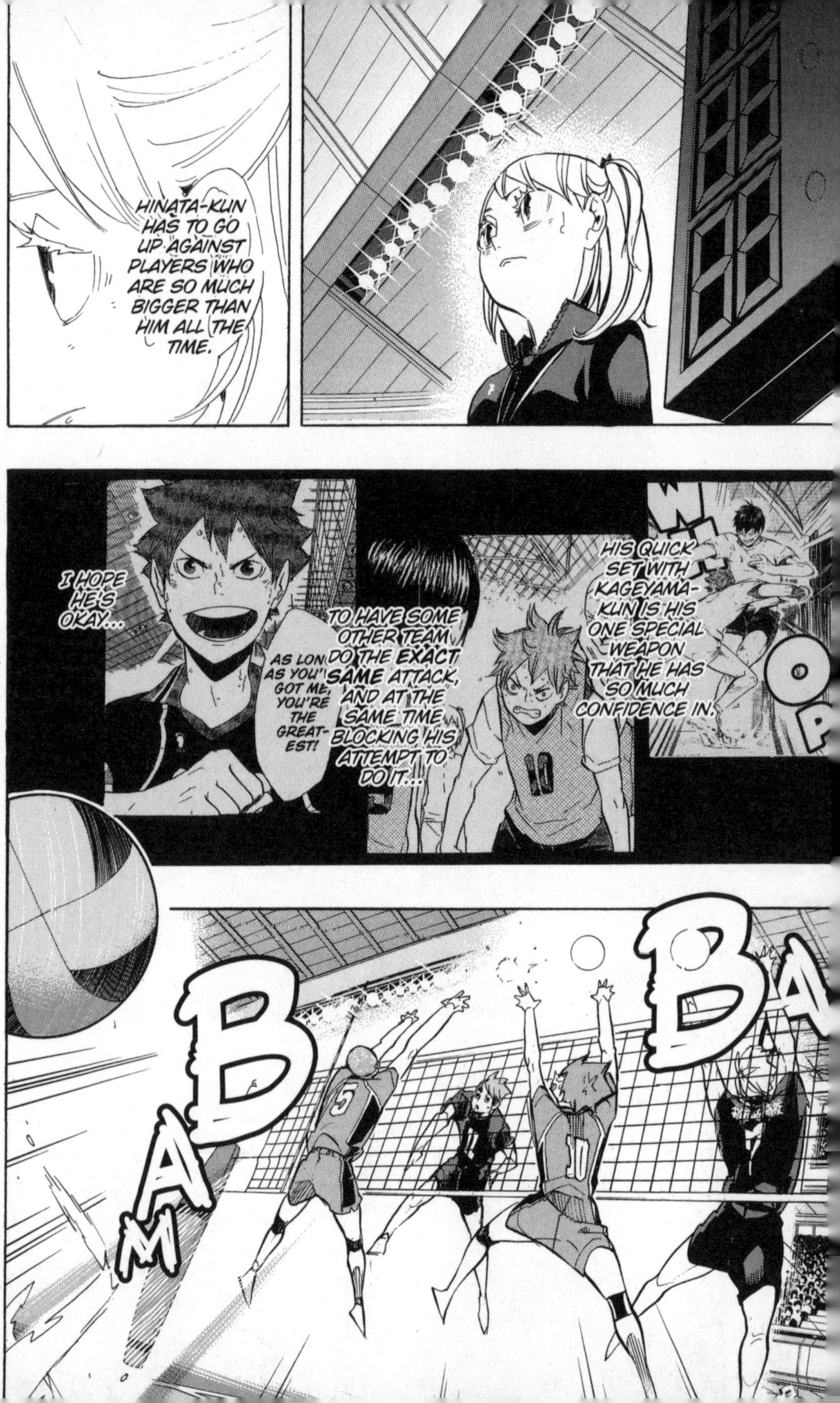
HINATA-KUN HAS TO GO UP AGAINST PLAYERS WHO ARE SO MUCH BIGGER THAN HIM ALL THE TIME.
HIS QUICK SET WITH KAGEYAMA-KUN IS HIS ONE SPECIAL WEAPON THAT HE HAS SO MUCH CONFIDENCE IN.
TO HAVE SOME OTHER TEAM DO THE **EXACT SAME** ATTACK, AND AT THE SAME TIME BLOCKING HIS ATTEMPT TO DO IT...
AS LON AS YOU'' GOT ME, YOU'RE THE GREAT-EST!
I HOPE HE'S OKAY...
BA
BAM

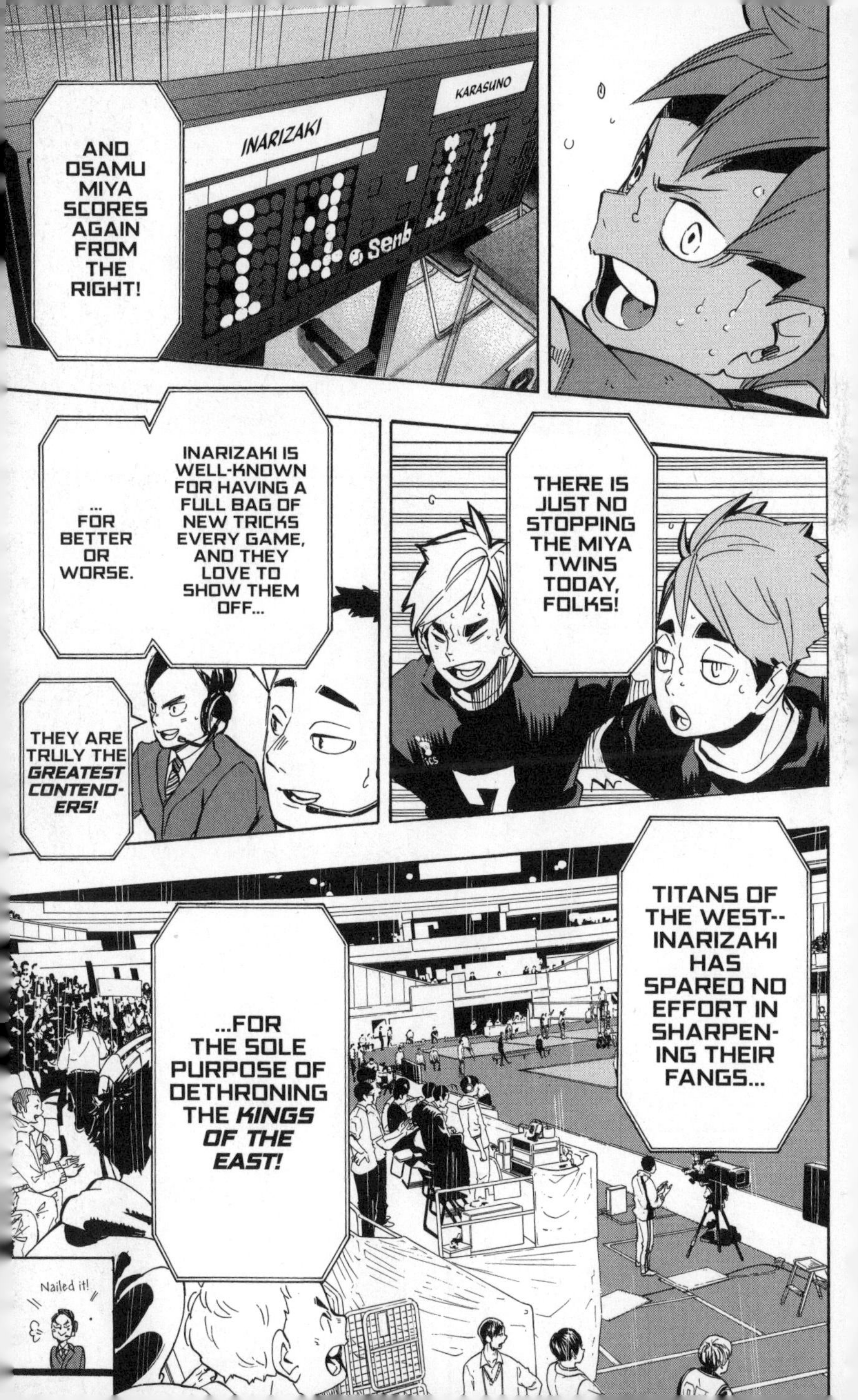
KARASUNO
INARIZAKI
AND OSAMU MIYA SCORES AGAIN FROM THE RIGHT!
THERE IS JUST NO STOPPING THE MIYA TWINS TODAY, FOLKS!
INARIZAKI IS WELL-KNOWN FOR HAVING A FULL BAG OF NEW TRICKS EVERY GAME, AND THEY LOVE TO SHOW THEM OFF...
...FOR BETTER OR WORSE.
THEY ARE TRULY THE *GREATEST CONTENDERS!*
TITANS OF THE WEST--INARIZAKI HAS SPARED NO EFFORT IN SHARPENING THEIR FANGS...
...FOR THE SOLE PURPOSE OF DETHRONING THE *KINGS OF THE EAST!*
Nailed it!

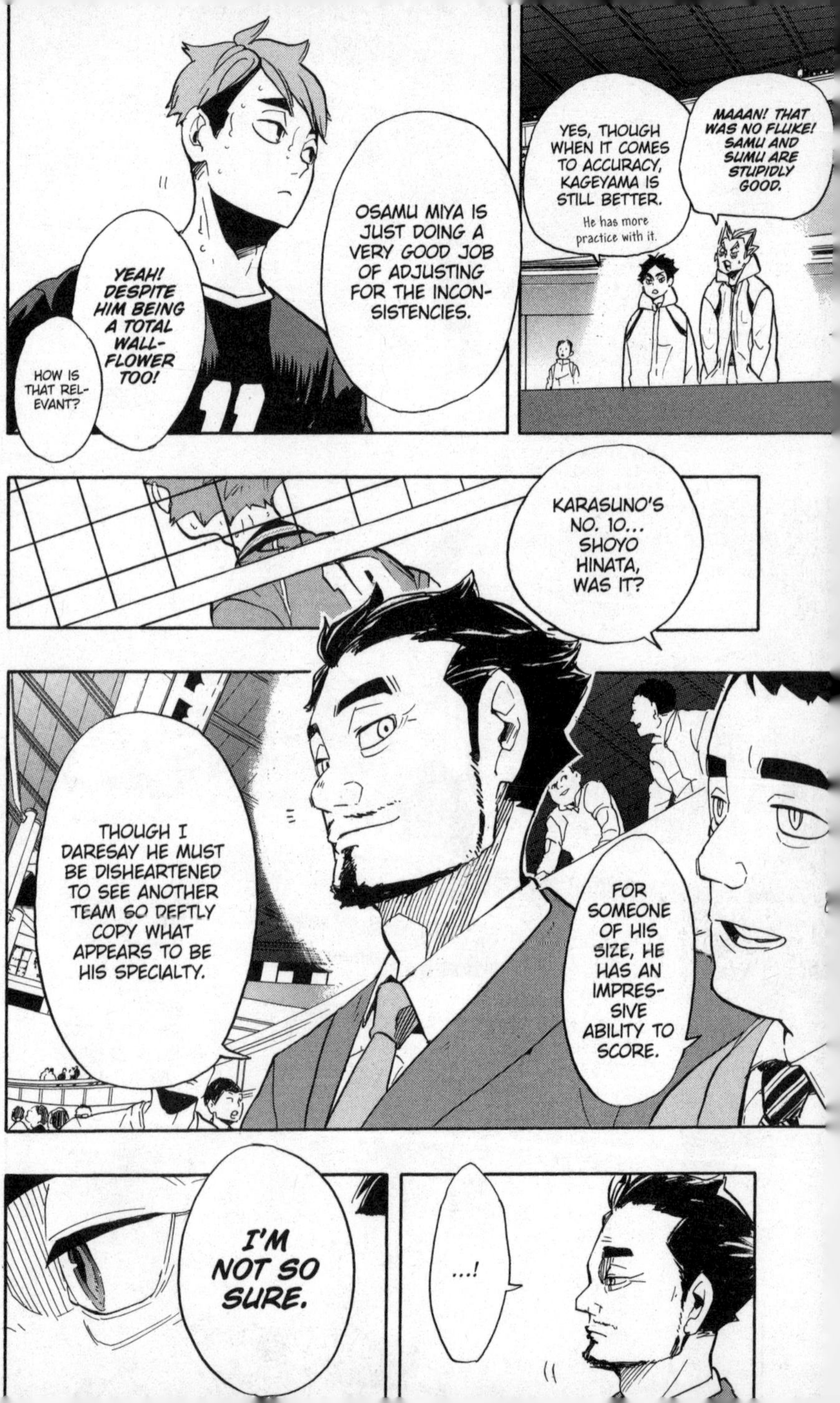
MAAAN! THAT WAS NO FLUKE! SAMU AND SUMU ARE STUPIDLY GOOD.
YES, THOUGH WHEN IT COMES TO ACCURACY, KAGEYAMA IS STILL BETTER.
He has more practice with it.
OSAMU MIYA IS JUST DOING A VERY GOOD JOB OF ADJUSTING FOR THE INCONSISTENCIES.
YEAH! DESPITE HIM BEING A TOTAL WALLFLOWER TOO!
HOW IS THAT RELEVANT?
KARASUNO'S NO. 10... SHOYO HINATA, WAS IT?
FOR SOMEONE OF HIS SIZE, HE HAS AN IMPRESSIVE ABILITY TO SCORE.
THOUGH I DARESAY HE MUST BE DISHEARTENED TO SEE ANOTHER TEAM SO DEFTLY COPY WHAT APPEARS TO BE HIS SPECIALTY.
...!
I'M NOT SO SURE.

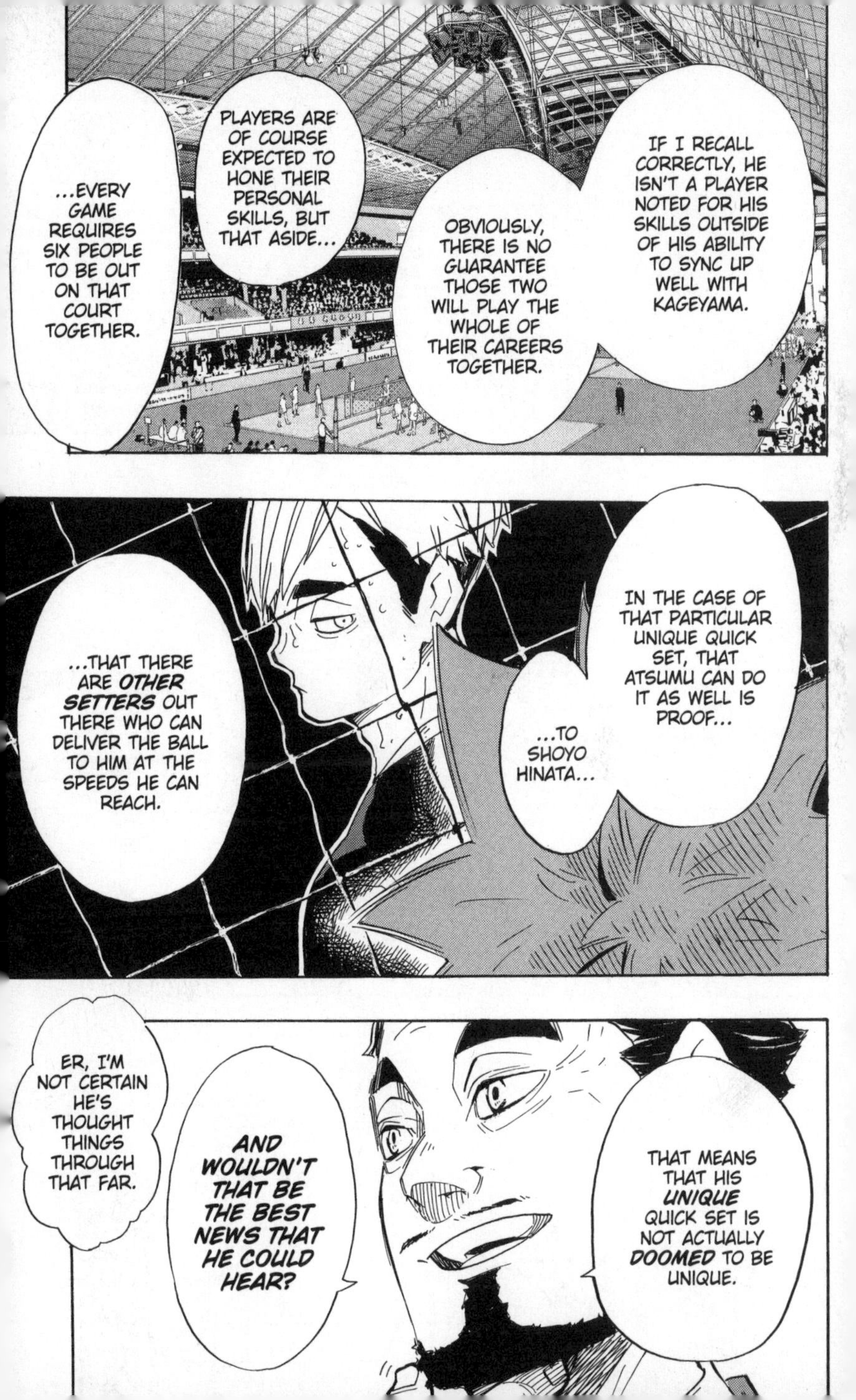
IF I RECALL CORRECTLY, HE ISN'T A PLAYER NOTED FOR HIS SKILLS OUTSIDE OF HIS ABILITY TO SYNC UP WELL WITH KAGEYAMA.
OBVIOUSLY, THERE IS NO GUARANTEE THOSE TWO WILL PLAY THE WHOLE OF THEIR CAREERS TOGETHER.
PLAYERS ARE OF COURSE EXPECTED TO HONE THEIR PERSONAL SKILLS, BUT THAT ASIDE...
...EVERY GAME REQUIRES SIX PEOPLE TO BE OUT ON THAT COURT TOGETHER.
IN THE CASE OF THAT PARTICULAR UNIQUE QUICK SET, THAT ATSUMU CAN DO IT AS WELL IS PROOF...
...TO SHOYO HINATA...
...THAT THERE ARE ***OTHER SETTERS*** OUT THERE WHO CAN DELIVER THE BALL TO HIM AT THE SPEEDS HE CAN REACH.
THAT MEANS THAT HIS ***UNIQUE*** QUICK SET IS NOT ACTUALLY ***DOOMED*** TO BE UNIQUE.
AND WOULDN'T THAT BE THE BEST NEWS THAT HE COULD HEAR?
ER, I'M NOT CERTAIN HE'S THOUGHT THINGS THROUGH THAT FAR.

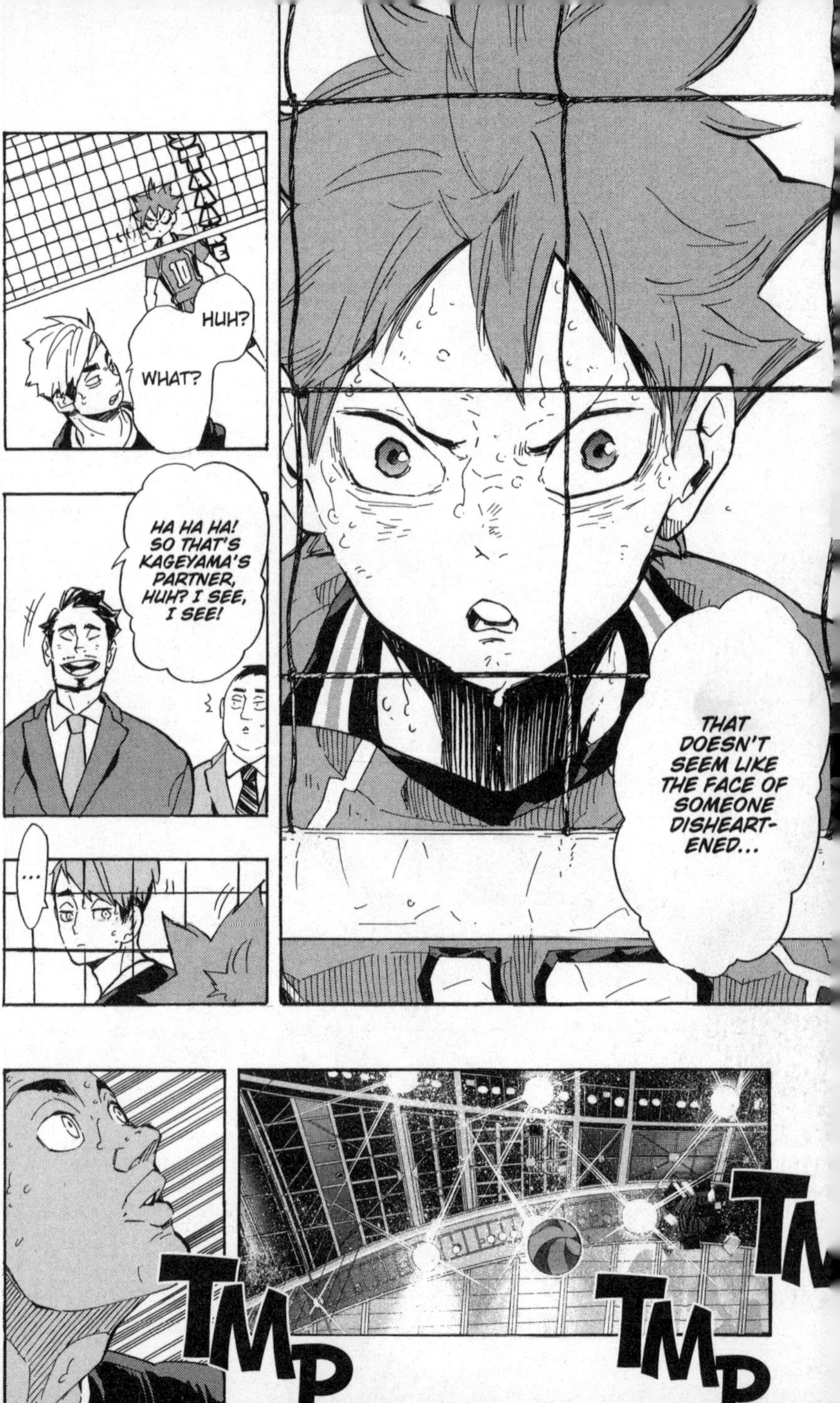
THAT DOESN'T SEEM LIKE THE FACE OF SOMEONE DISHEART-ENED...
HUH?
WHAT?
HA HA HA! SO THAT'S KAGEYAMA'S PARTNER, HUH? I SEE, I SEE!
...
TMP
TMP
TM
TMP

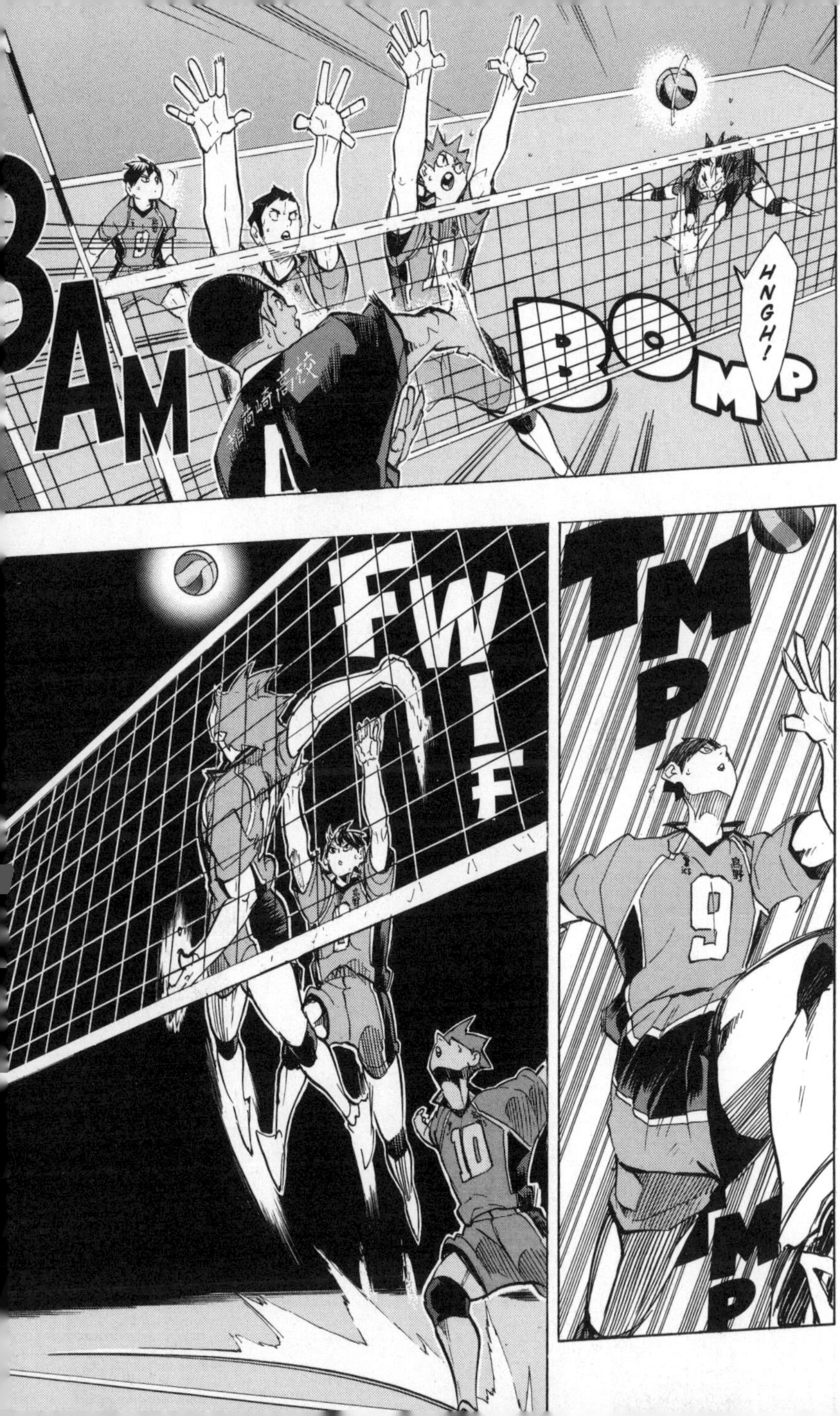
HNGH!
DOOMP
BAM
TMP
FWIF

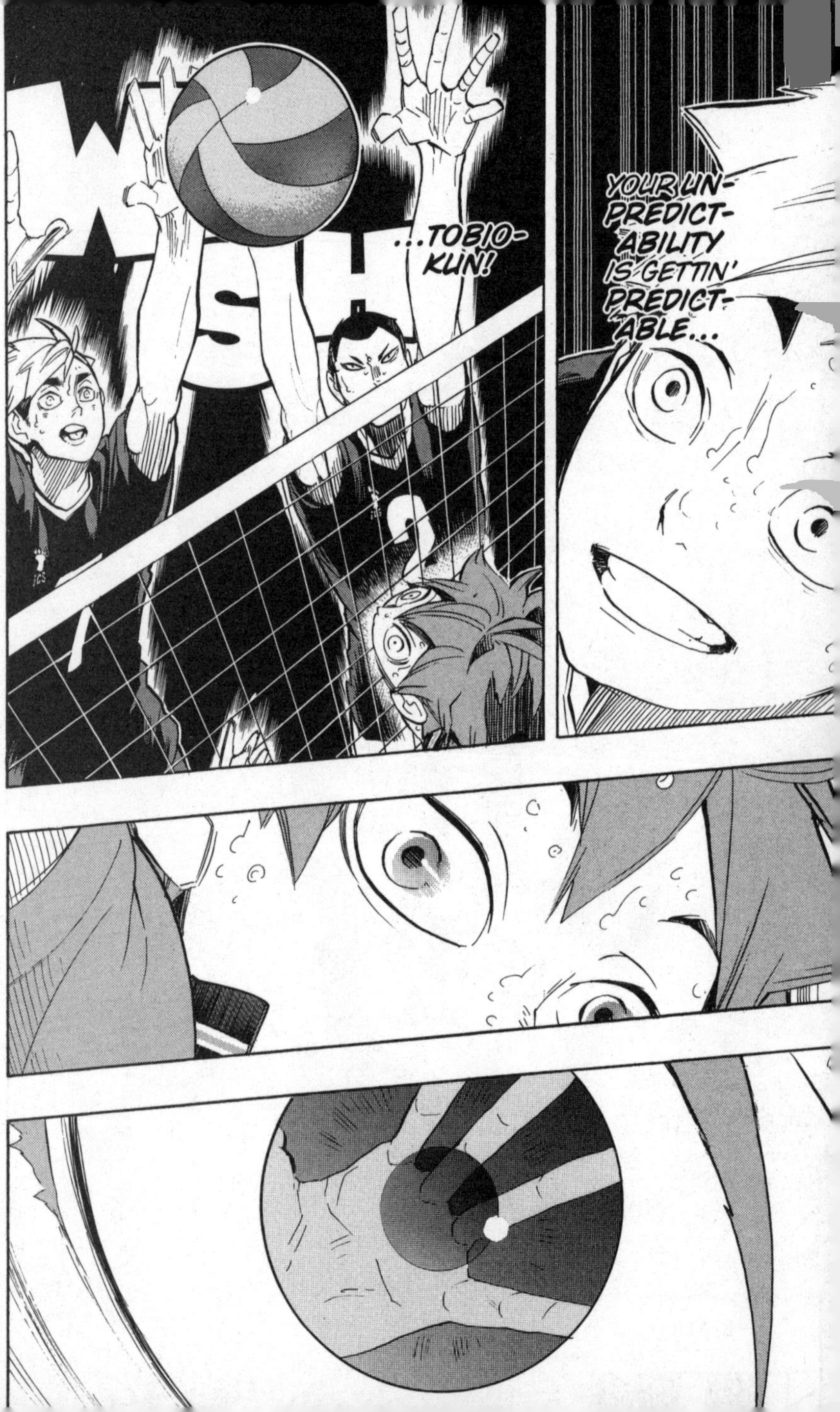
YOUR UN-PREDICT-ABILITY IS GETTIN' PREDICT-ABLE...
...TOBIO-KUN!

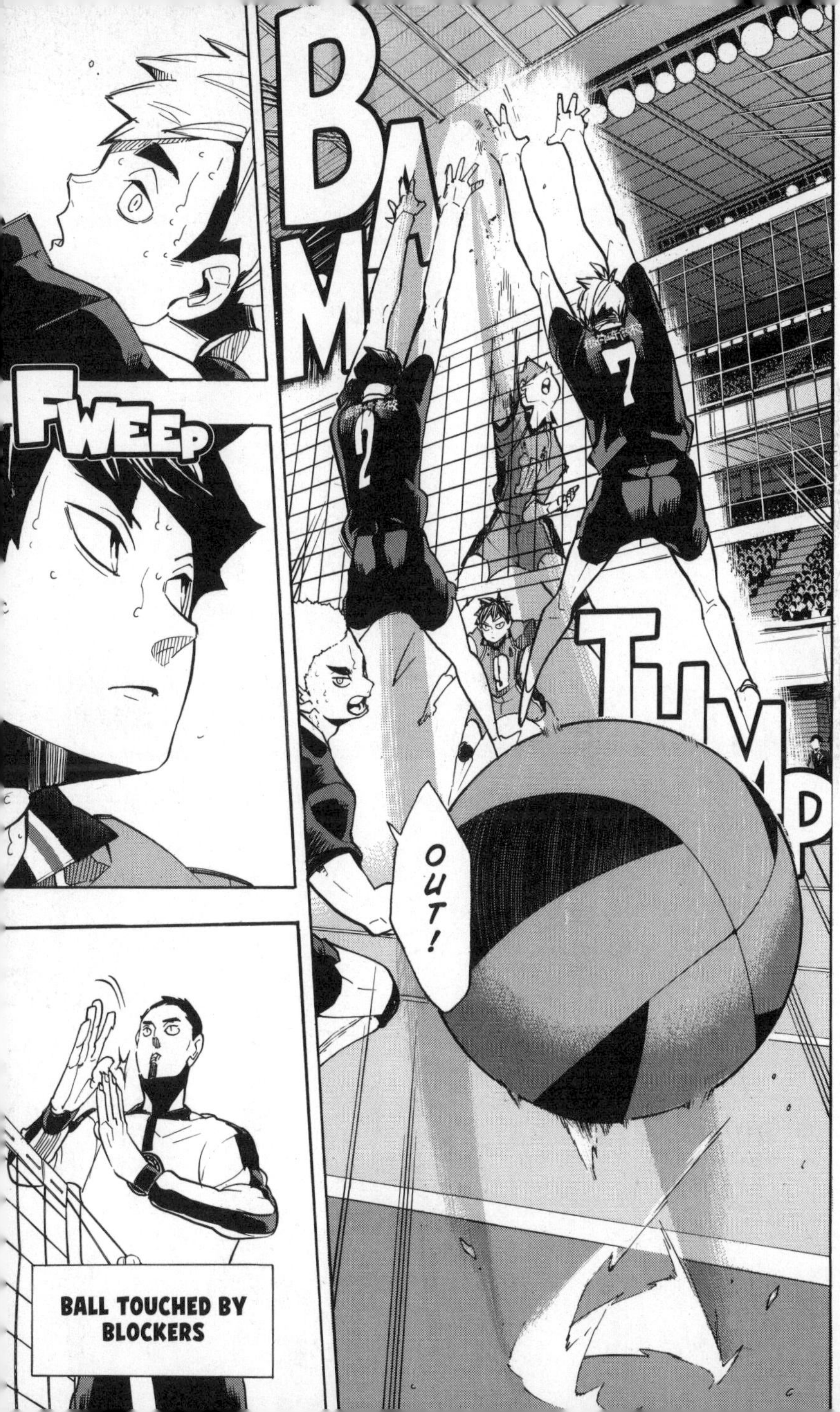
BAM
THUMP
OUT!
FWEEP
BALL TOUCHED BY BLOCKERS

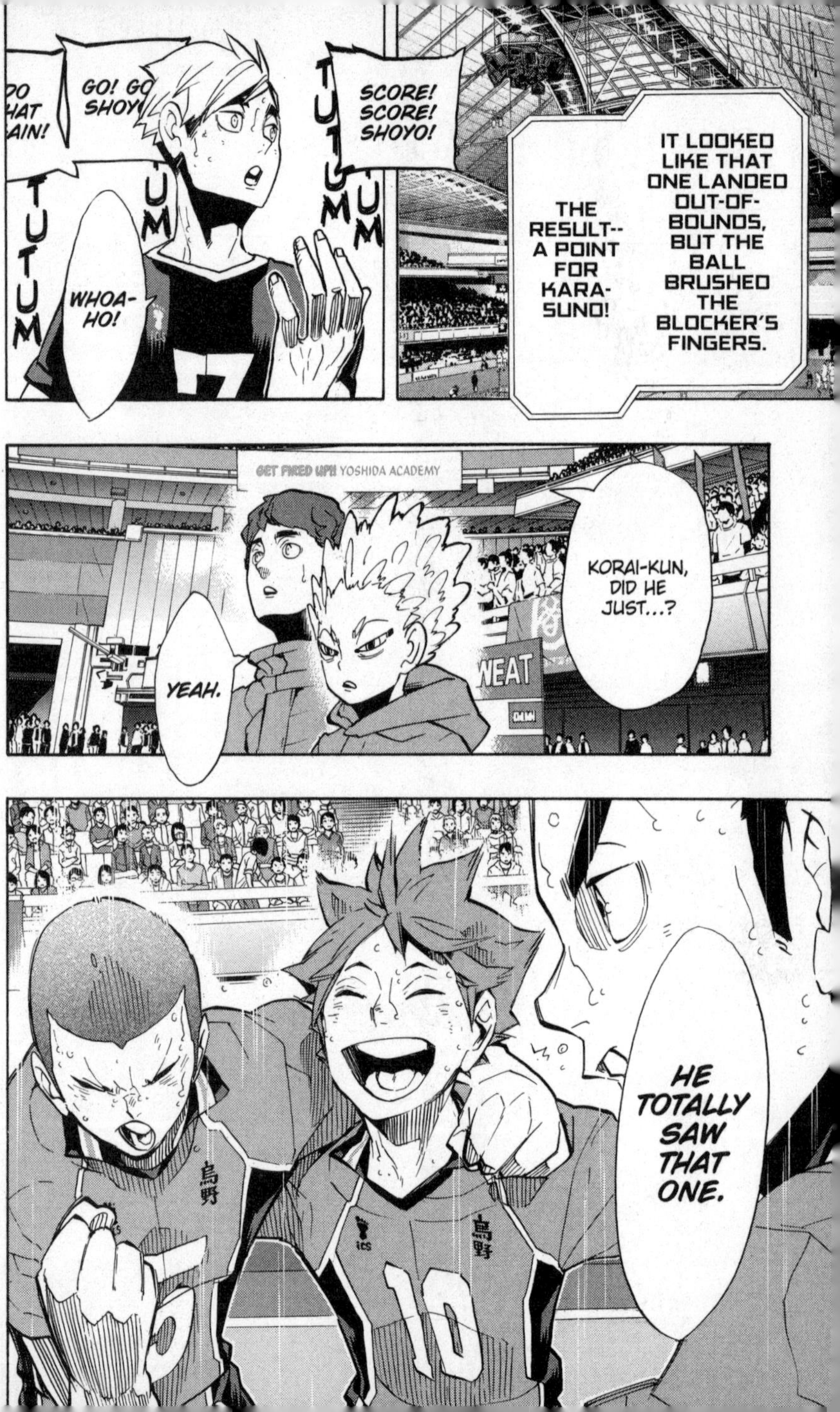
THE RESULT-- A POINT FOR KARASUNO!
IT LOOKED LIKE THAT ONE LANDED OUT-OF-BOUNDS, BUT THE BALL BRUSHED THE BLOCKER'S FINGERS.
TUTUM TUTUM
SCORE! SCORE! SHOYO!
GO! GO SHOYO
DO HAT AIN!
TUTUM TUTUM
WHOA-HO!
GET FIRED UP!! YOSHIDA ACADEMY
KORAI-KUN, DID HE JUST...?
YEAH.
HE TOTALLY SAW THAT ONE.

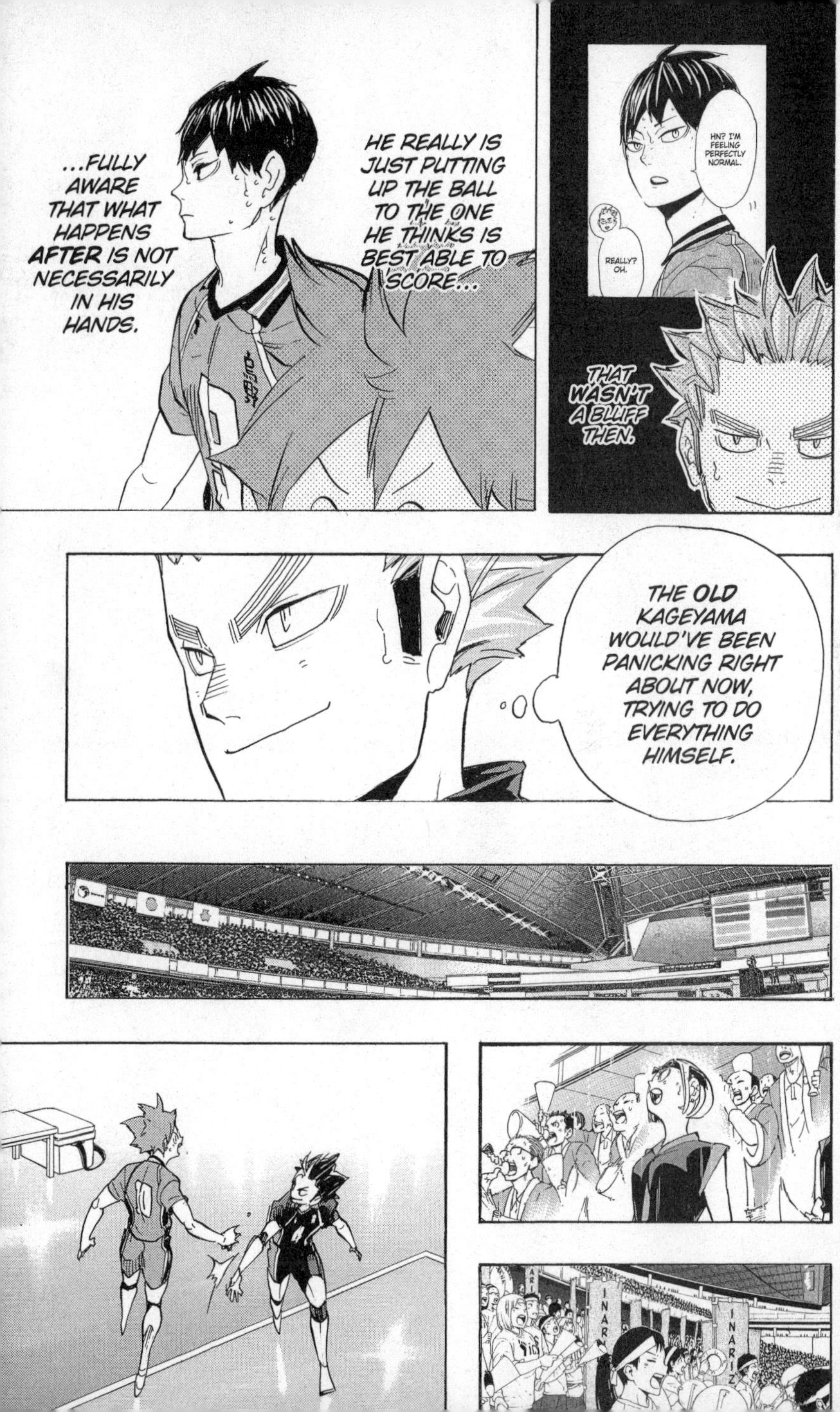
HN? I'M FEELING PERFECTLY NORMAL.
REALLY? OH.
THAT WASN'T A BLUFF THEN.
HE REALLY IS JUST PUTTING UP THE BALL TO THE ONE HE THINKS IS BEST ABLE TO SCORE...
...FULLY AWARE THAT WHAT HAPPENS AFTER IS NOT NECESSARILY IN HIS HANDS.
THE OLD KAGEYAMA WOULD'VE BEEN PANICKING RIGHT ABOUT NOW, TRYING TO DO EVERYTHING HIMSELF.
INARI

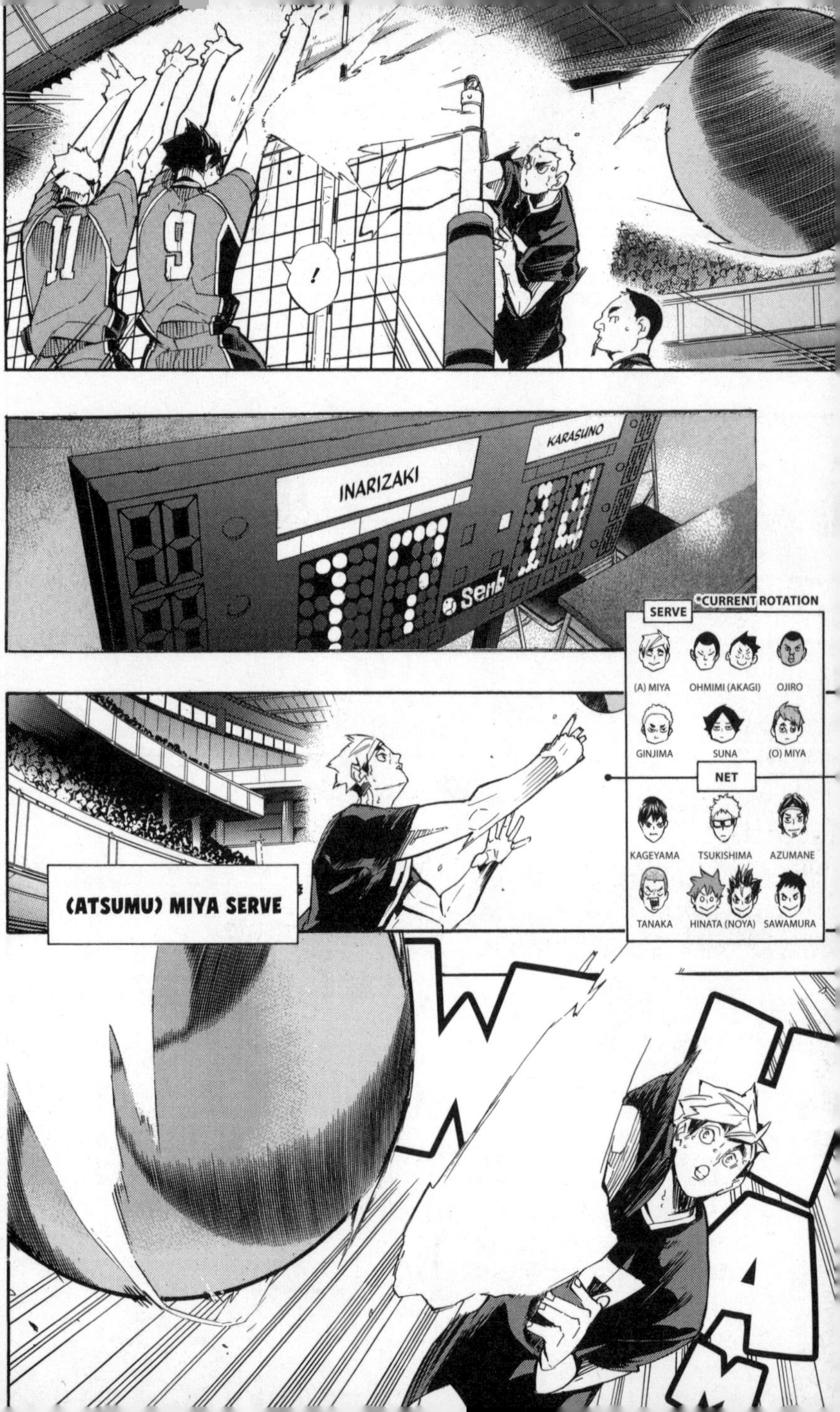
!
INARIZAKI
KARASUNO
*CURRENT ROTATION
SERVE
(A) MIYA
OHMIMI (AKAGI)
OJIRO
GINJIMA
SUNA
(O) MIYA
NET
KAGEYAMA
TSUKISHIMA
AZUMANE
TANAKA
HINATA (NOYA)
SAWAMURA
(ATSUMU) MIYA SERVE

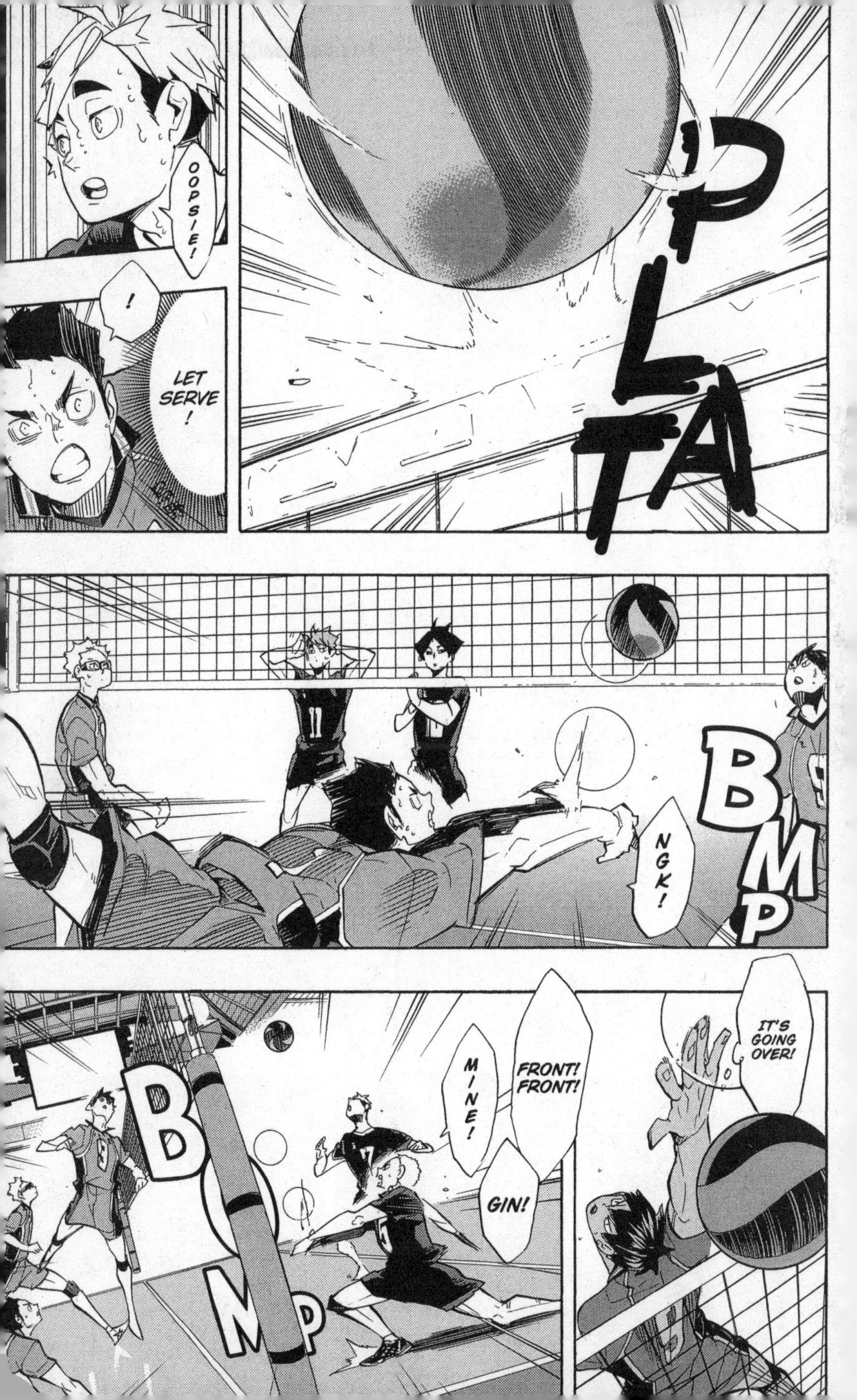
PLAP
OOPSIE!
!
LET SERVE!
BMP
NGK!
IT'S GOING OVER!
FRONT! FRONT!
MINE!
GIN!
BMP

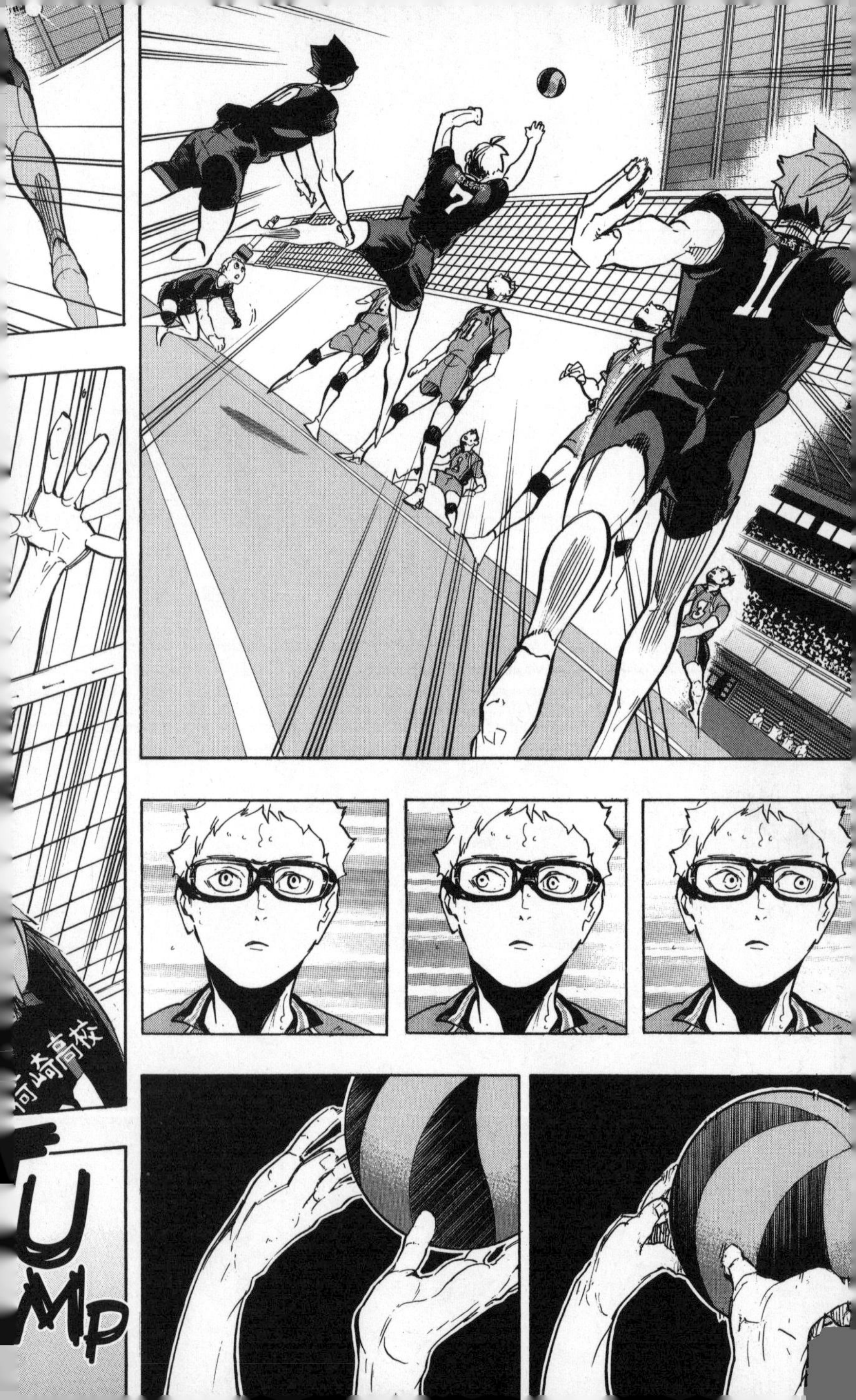
河崎高校
UMP

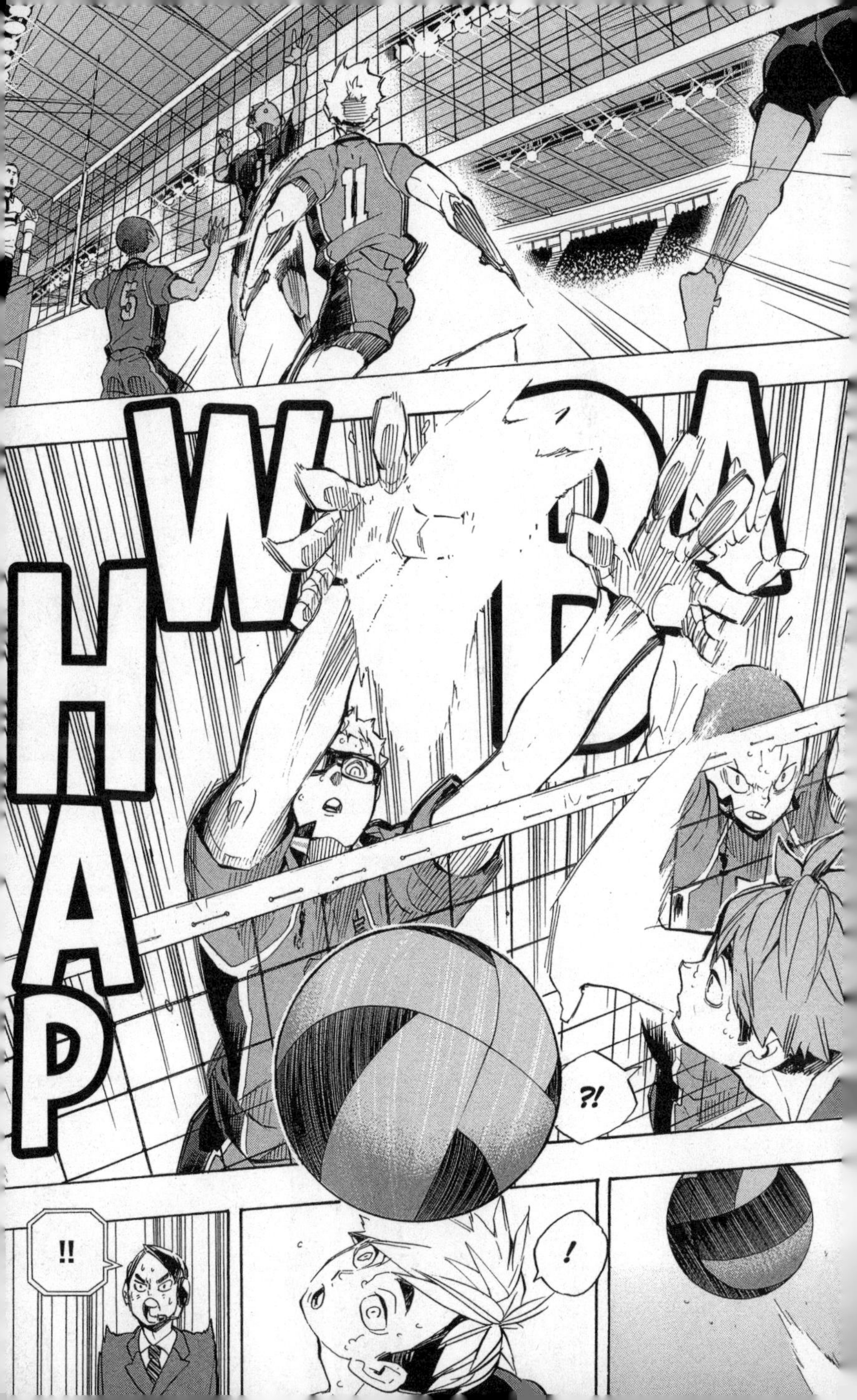
WHAP
?!
!
!!

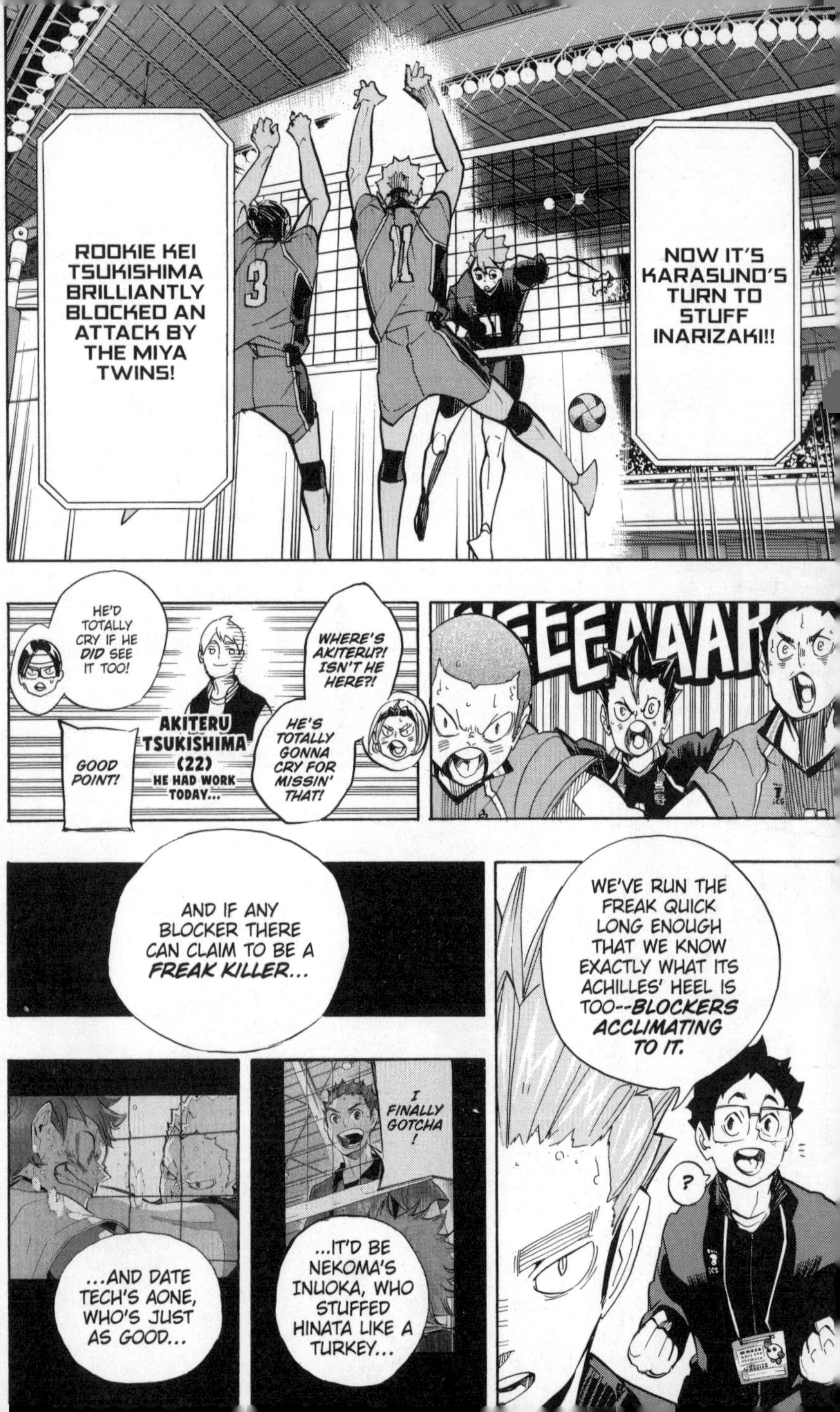
NOW IT'S KARASUNO'S TURN TO STUFF INARIZAKI!!
ROOKIE KEI TSUKISHIMA BRILLIANTLY BLOCKED AN ATTACK BY THE MIYA TWINS!
EEAAA
WHERE'S AKITERU?! ISN'T HE HERE?!
HE'S TOTALLY GONNA CRY FOR MISSIN' THAT!
HE'D TOTALLY CRY IF HE DID SEE IT TOO!
AKITERU TSUKISHIMA (22)
HE HAD WORK TODAY...
GOOD POINT!
WE'VE RUN THE FREAK QUICK LONG ENOUGH THAT WE KNOW EXACTLY WHAT ITS ACHILLES' HEEL IS TOO--BLOCKERS ACCLIMATING TO IT.
?
AND IF ANY BLOCKER THERE CAN CLAIM TO BE A FREAK KILLER...
I FINALLY GOTCHA!
...IT'D BE NEKOMA'S INUOKA, WHO STUFFED HINATA LIKE A TURKEY...
...AND DATE TECH'S AONE, WHO'S JUST AS GOOD...

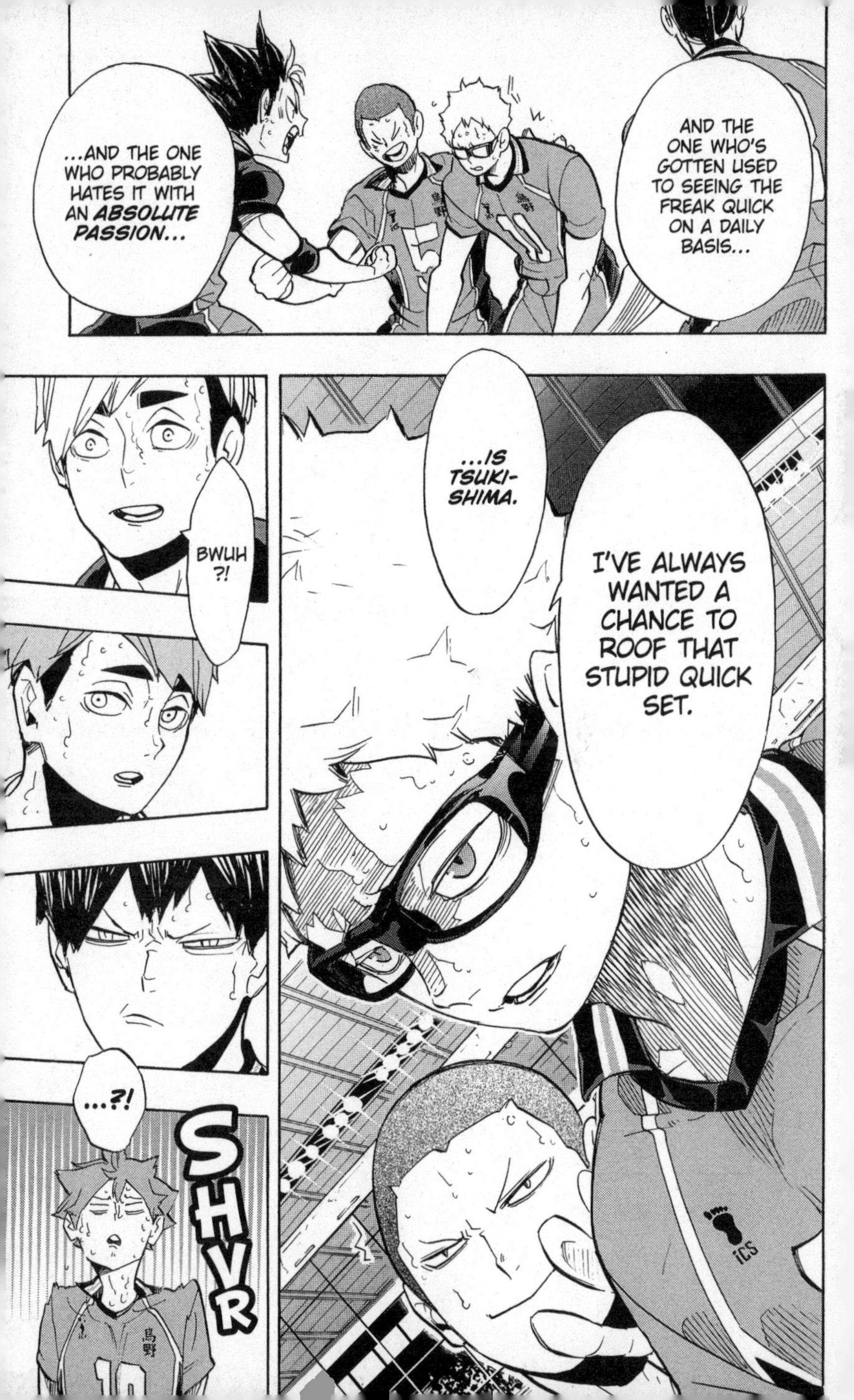
AND THE ONE WHO'S GOTTEN USED TO SEEING THE FREAK QUICK ON A DAILY BASIS...
...AND THE ONE WHO PROBABLY HATES IT WITH AN ABSOLUTE PASSION...
...IS TSUKISHIMA.
I'VE ALWAYS WANTED A CHANCE TO ROOF THAT STUPID QUICK SET.
BWUH ?!
...?!
SHVR

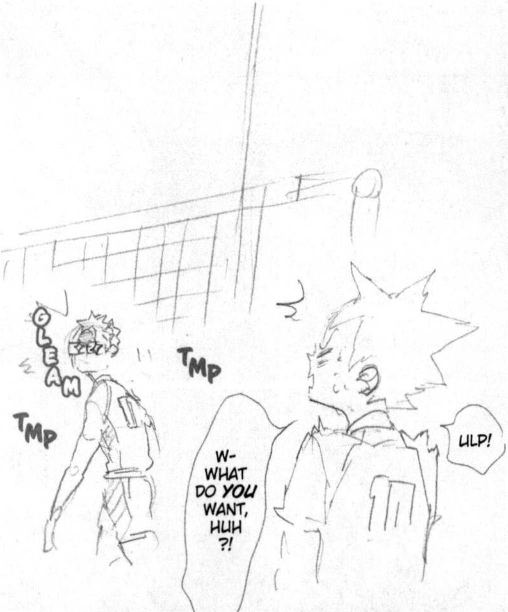
ULP!
TMP
GLEAM
W-WHAT DO YOU WANT, HUH?!
TMP

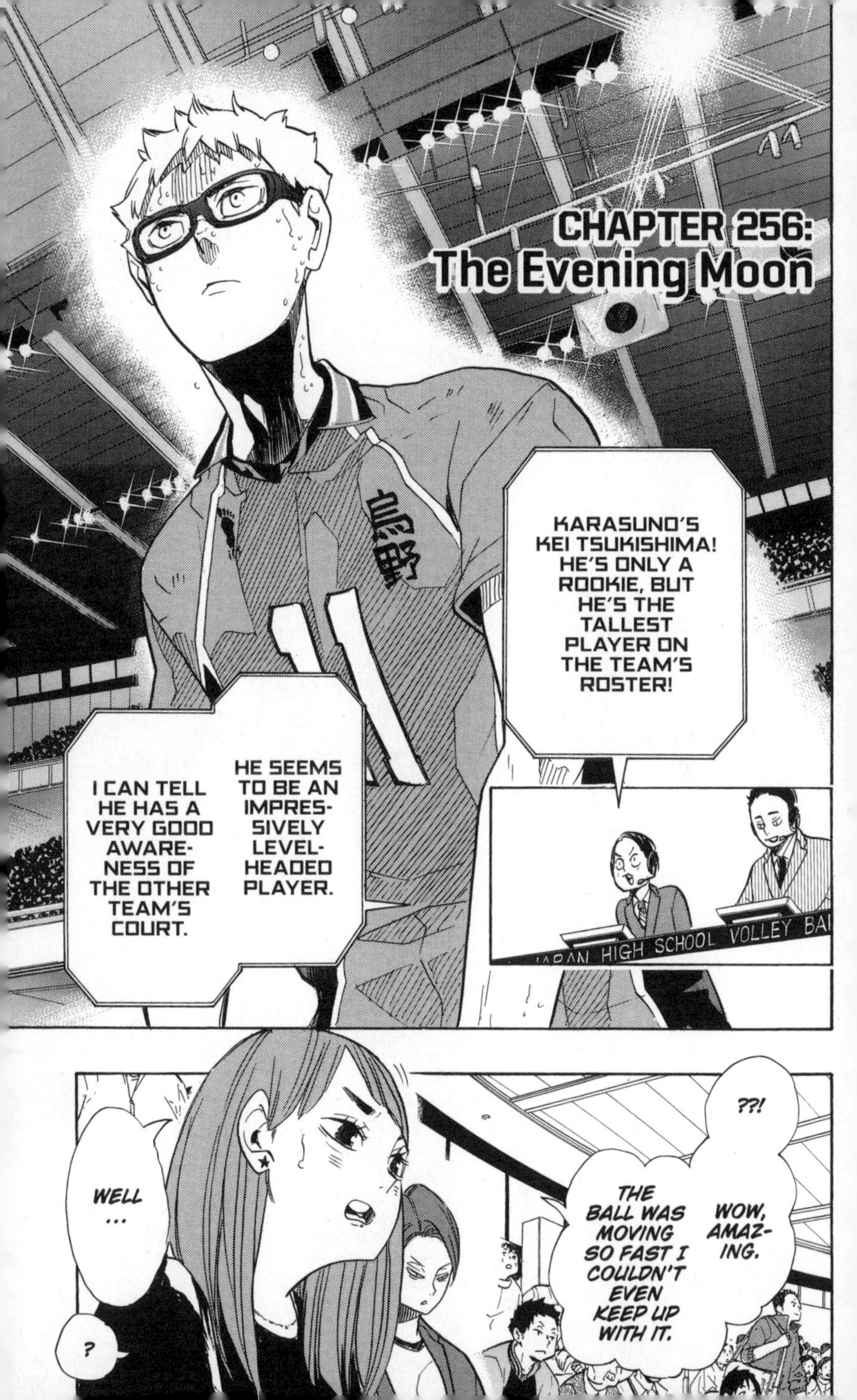
CHAPTER 256:
The Evening Moon
KARASUNO'S KEI TSUKISHIMA! HE'S ONLY A ROOKIE, BUT HE'S THE TALLEST PLAYER ON THE TEAM'S ROSTER!
HE SEEMS TO BE AN IMPRES-SIVELY LEVEL-HEADED PLAYER.
I CAN TELL HE HAS A VERY GOOD AWARE-NESS OF THE OTHER TEAM'S COURT.
??!
WOW, AMAZ-ING.
THE BALL WAS MOVING SO FAST I COULDN'T EVEN KEEP UP WITH IT.
WELL ...
?

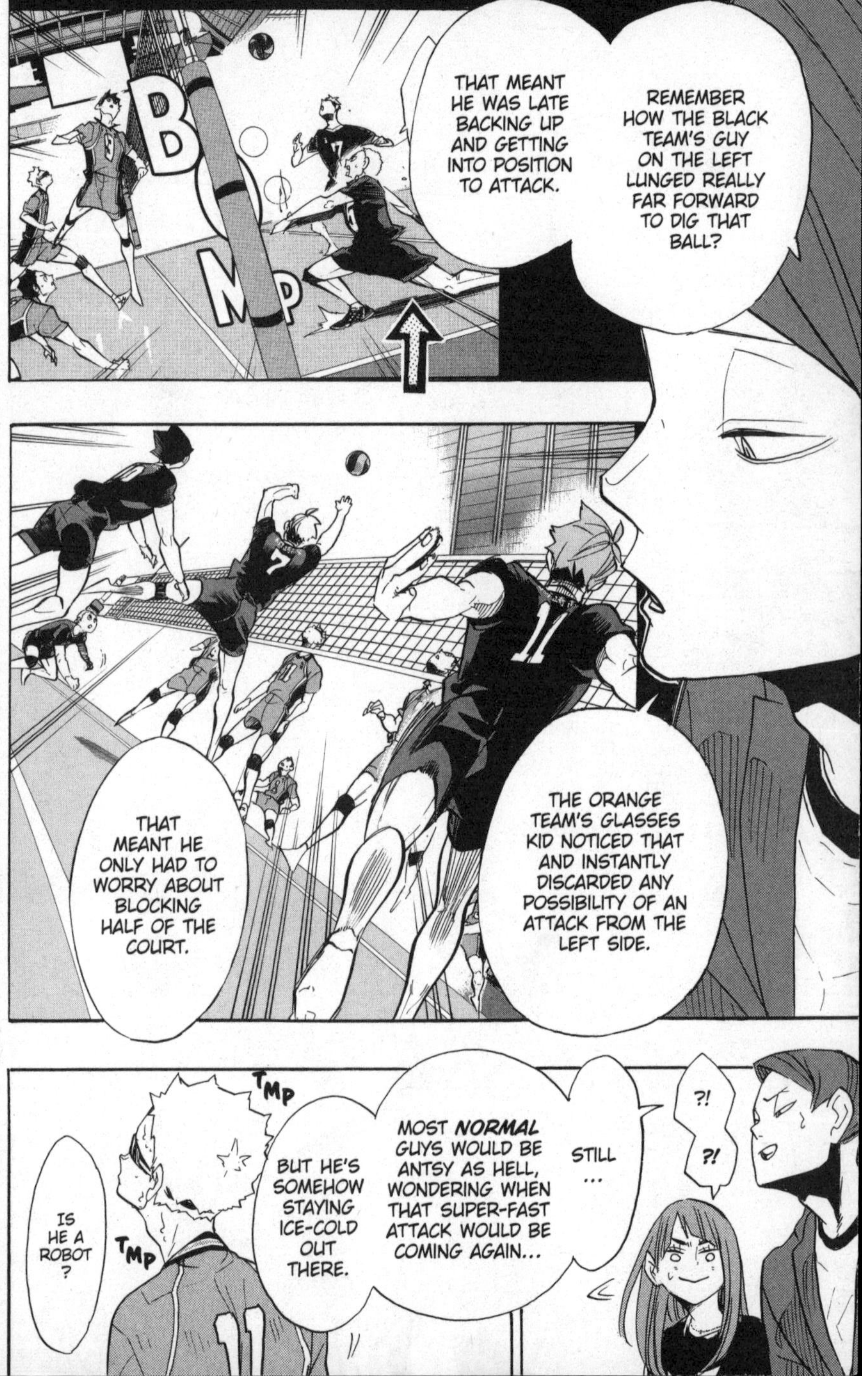
REMEMBER HOW THE BLACK TEAM'S GUY ON THE LEFT LUNGED REALLY FAR FORWARD TO DIG THAT BALL?
BOMP
THAT MEANT HE WAS LATE BACKING UP AND GETTING INTO POSITION TO ATTACK.
THE ORANGE TEAM'S GLASSES KID NOTICED THAT AND INSTANTLY DISCARDED ANY POSSIBILITY OF AN ATTACK FROM THE LEFT SIDE.
THAT MEANT HE ONLY HAD TO WORRY ABOUT BLOCKING HALF OF THE COURT.
?!
?!
STILL...
MOST ***NORMAL*** GUYS WOULD BE ANTSY AS HELL, WONDERING WHEN THAT SUPER-FAST ATTACK WOULD BE COMING AGAIN...
TMP
BUT HE'S SOMEHOW STAYING ICE-COLD OUT THERE.
TMP
IS HE A ROBOT?

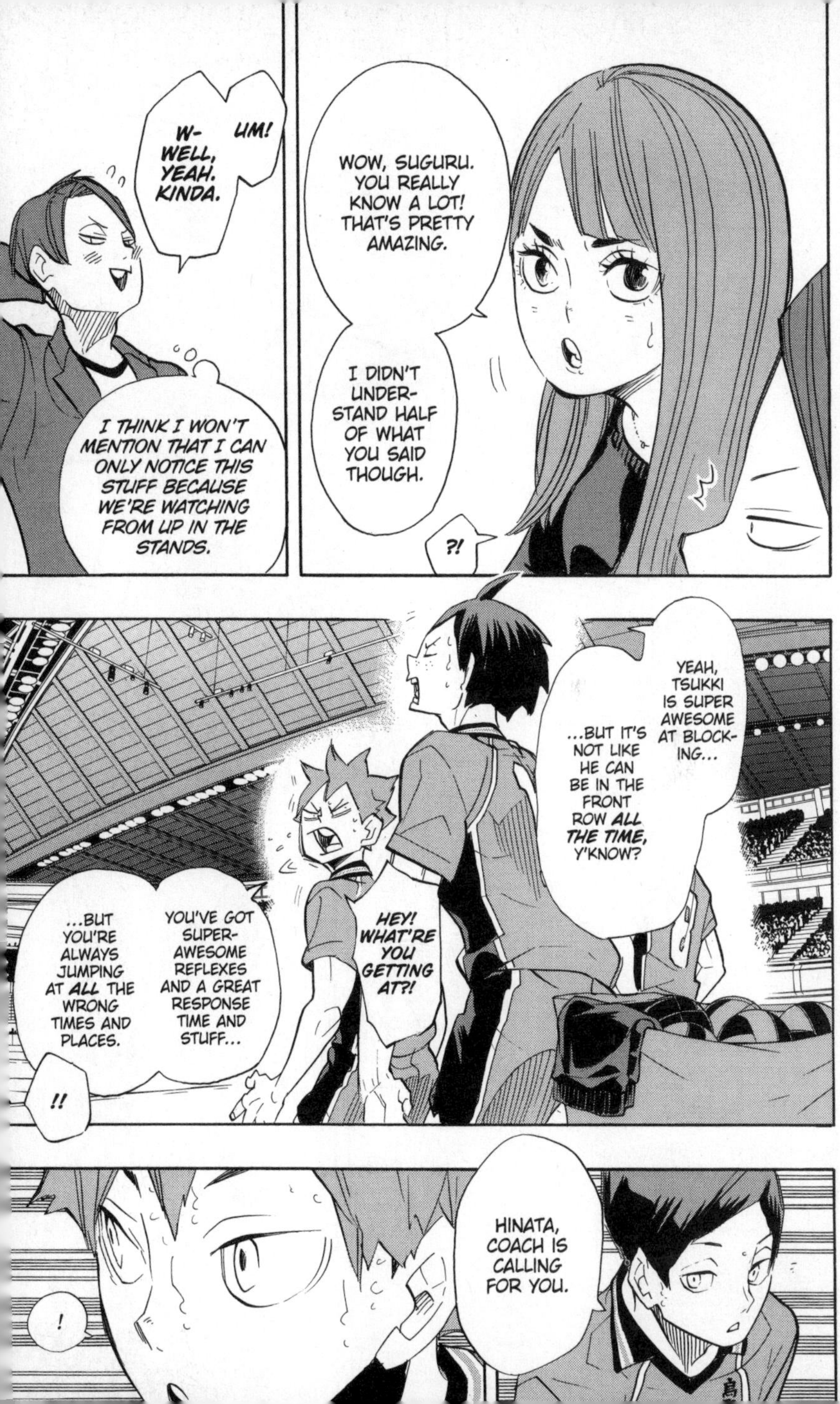
WOW, SUGURU. YOU REALLY KNOW A LOT! THAT'S PRETTY AMAZING.
I DIDN'T UNDER-STAND HALF OF WHAT YOU SAID THOUGH.
?!
UM!
W-WELL, YEAH. KINDA.
I THINK I WON'T MENTION THAT I CAN ONLY NOTICE THIS STUFF BECAUSE WE'RE WATCHING FROM UP IN THE STANDS.
YEAH, TSUKKI IS SUPER AWESOME AT BLOCK-ING...
...BUT IT'S NOT LIKE HE CAN BE IN THE FRONT ROW ALL THE TIME, Y'KNOW?
HEY! WHAT'RE YOU GETTING AT?!
YOU'VE GOT SUPER-AWESOME REFLEXES AND A GREAT RESPONSE TIME AND STUFF...
...BUT YOU'RE ALWAYS JUMPING AT ALL THE WRONG TIMES AND PLACES.
!!
HINATA, COACH IS CALLING FOR YOU.
!

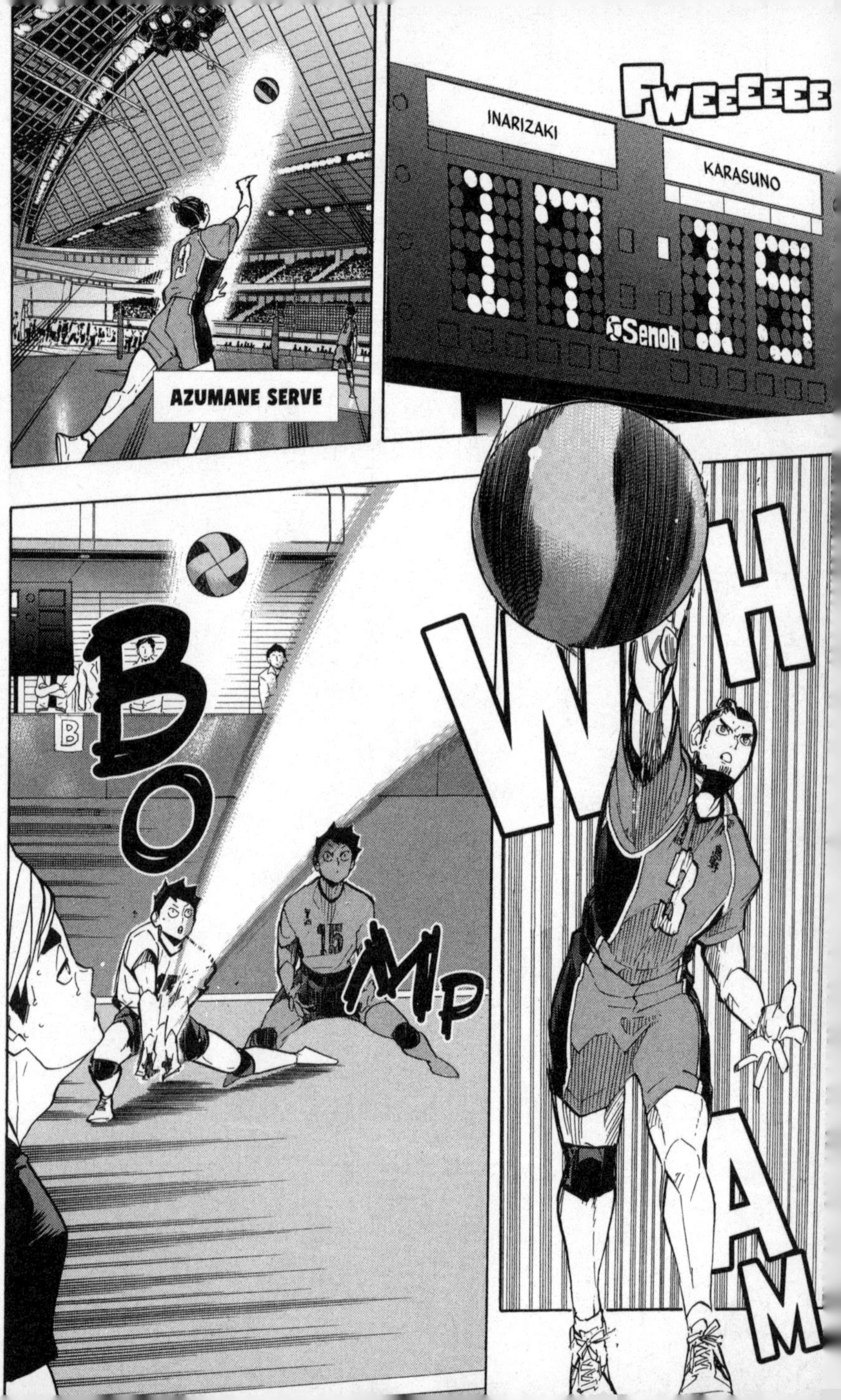
FWEEEEEE
INARIZAKI
KARASUNO
17 : 15
Senoh
AZUMANE SERVE
WHAM
BOMP
B

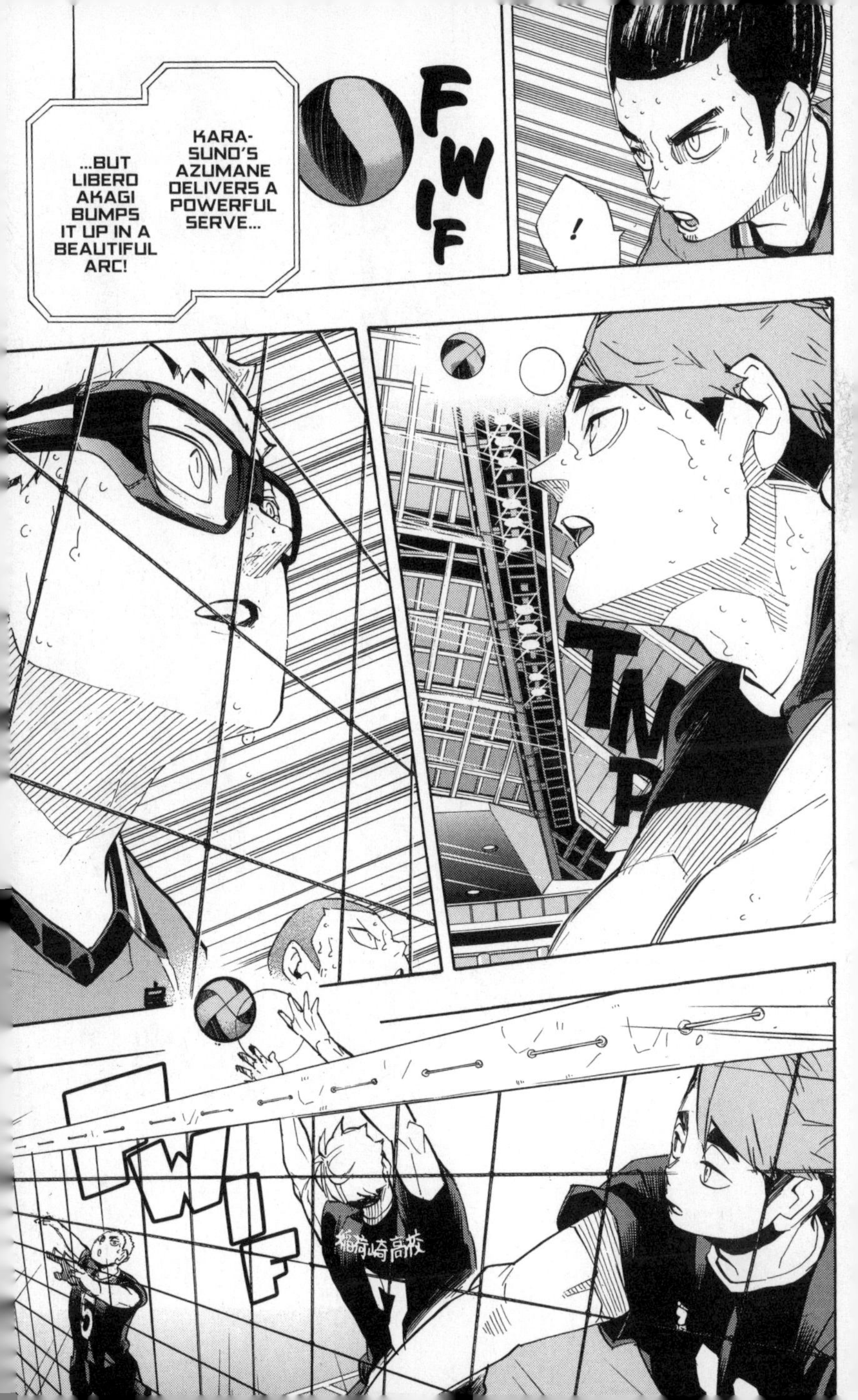
!
FWIF
KARA-SUNO'S AZUMANE DELIVERS A POWERFUL SERVE...
...BUT LIBERO AKAGI BUMPS IT UP IN A BEAUTIFUL ARC!
TMP
FWIF
稲荷崎高校

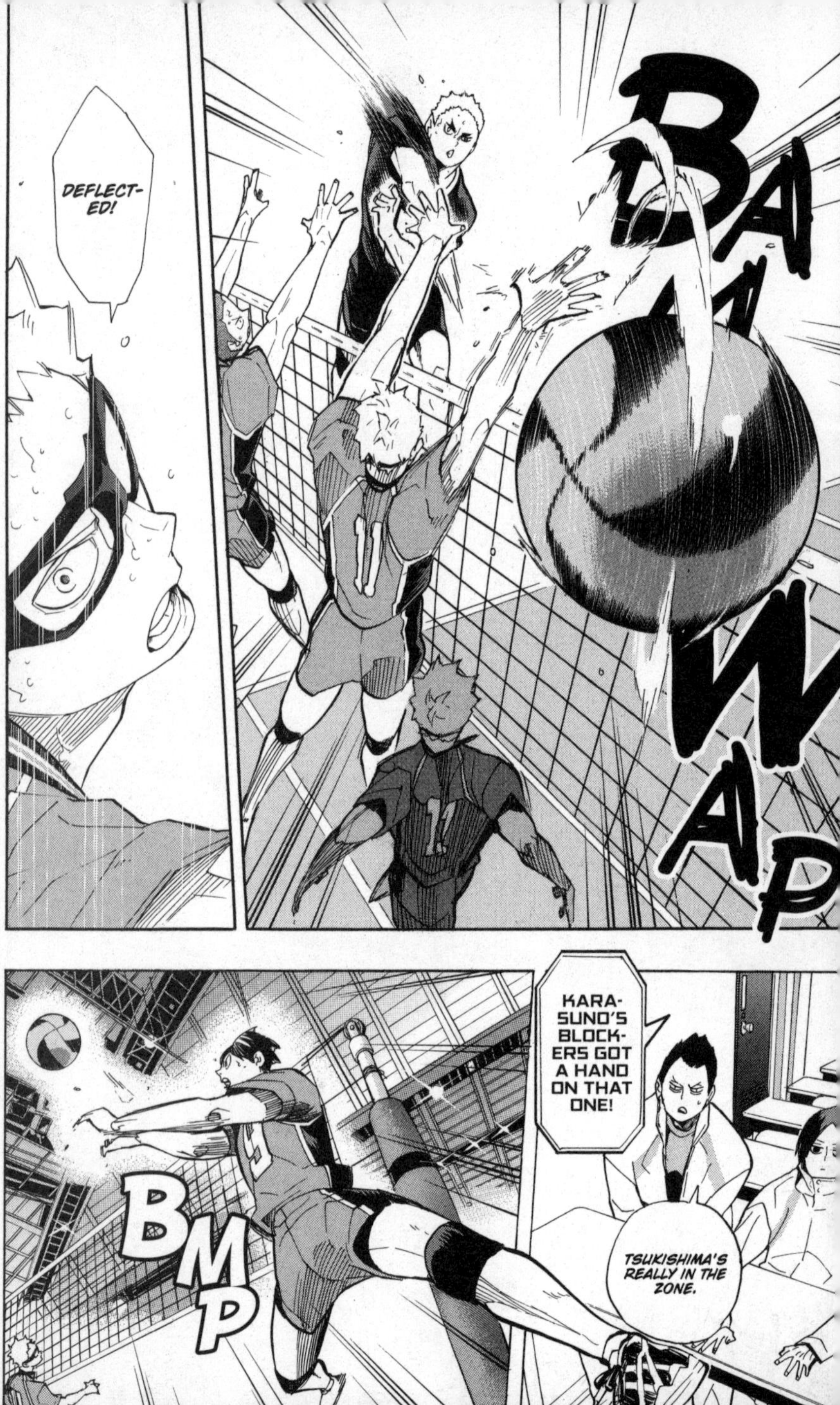
BAWAP
DEFLECT-ED!
KARA-SUNO'S BLOCK-ERS GOT A HAND ON THAT ONE!
TSUKISHIMA'S REALLY IN THE ZONE.
BMP

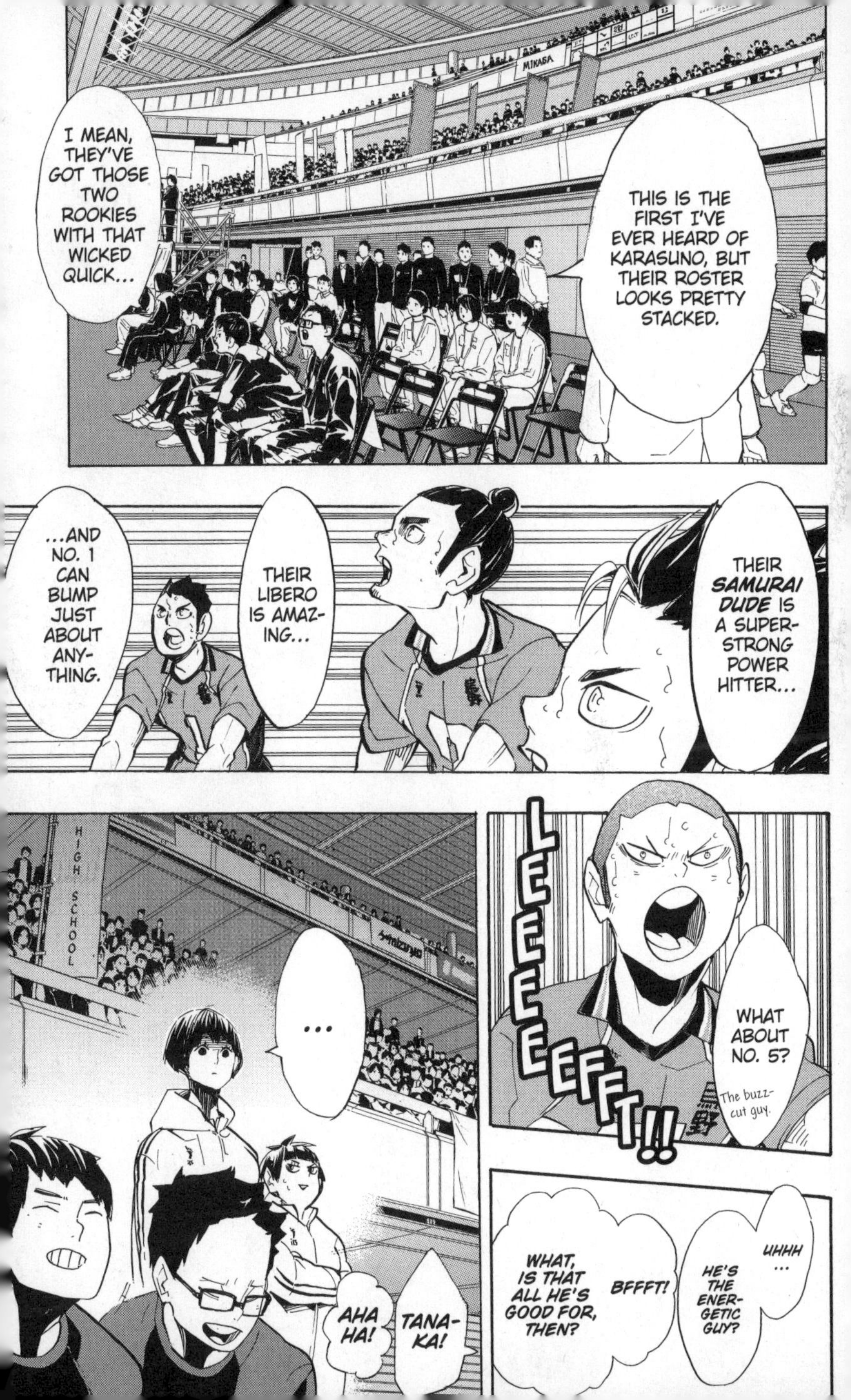
MIKASA
THIS IS THE FIRST I'VE EVER HEARD OF KARASUNO, BUT THEIR ROSTER LOOKS PRETTY STACKED.
I MEAN, THEY'VE GOT THOSE TWO ROOKIES WITH THAT WICKED QUICK...
THEIR ***SAMURAI DUDE*** IS A SUPER-STRONG POWER HITTER...
THEIR LIBERO IS AMAZING...
...AND NO. 1 CAN BUMP JUST ABOUT ANYTHING.
LEEEEEFFT!!
WHAT ABOUT NO. 5?
The buzz-cut guy.
UHHH...
HE'S THE ENERGETIC GUY?
BFFFT!
WHAT, IS THAT ALL HE'S GOOD FOR, THEN?
HIGH SCHOOL
...
TANAKA!
AHA HA!

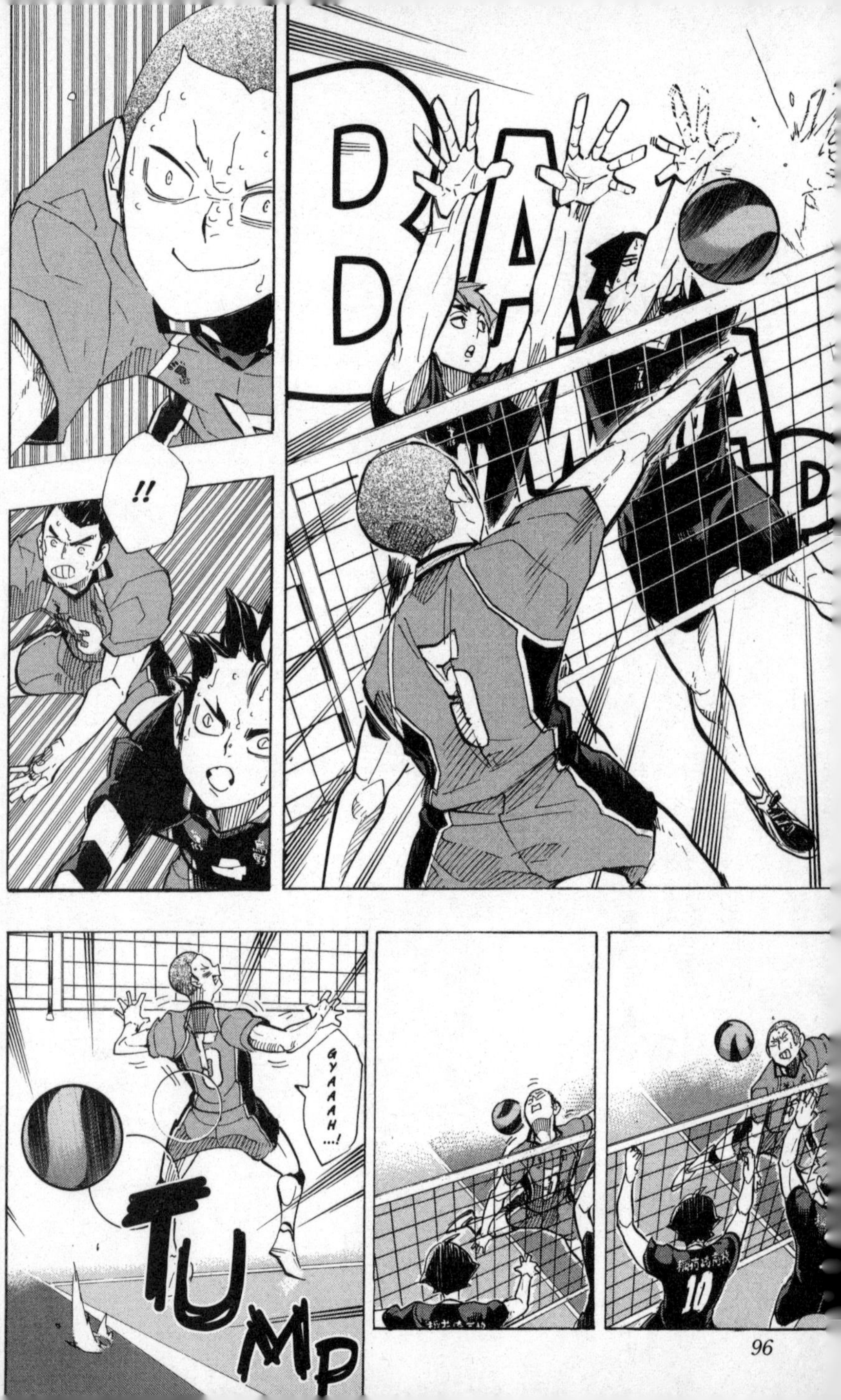
DDAAD
!!
GYAAAAH...!
TUMP

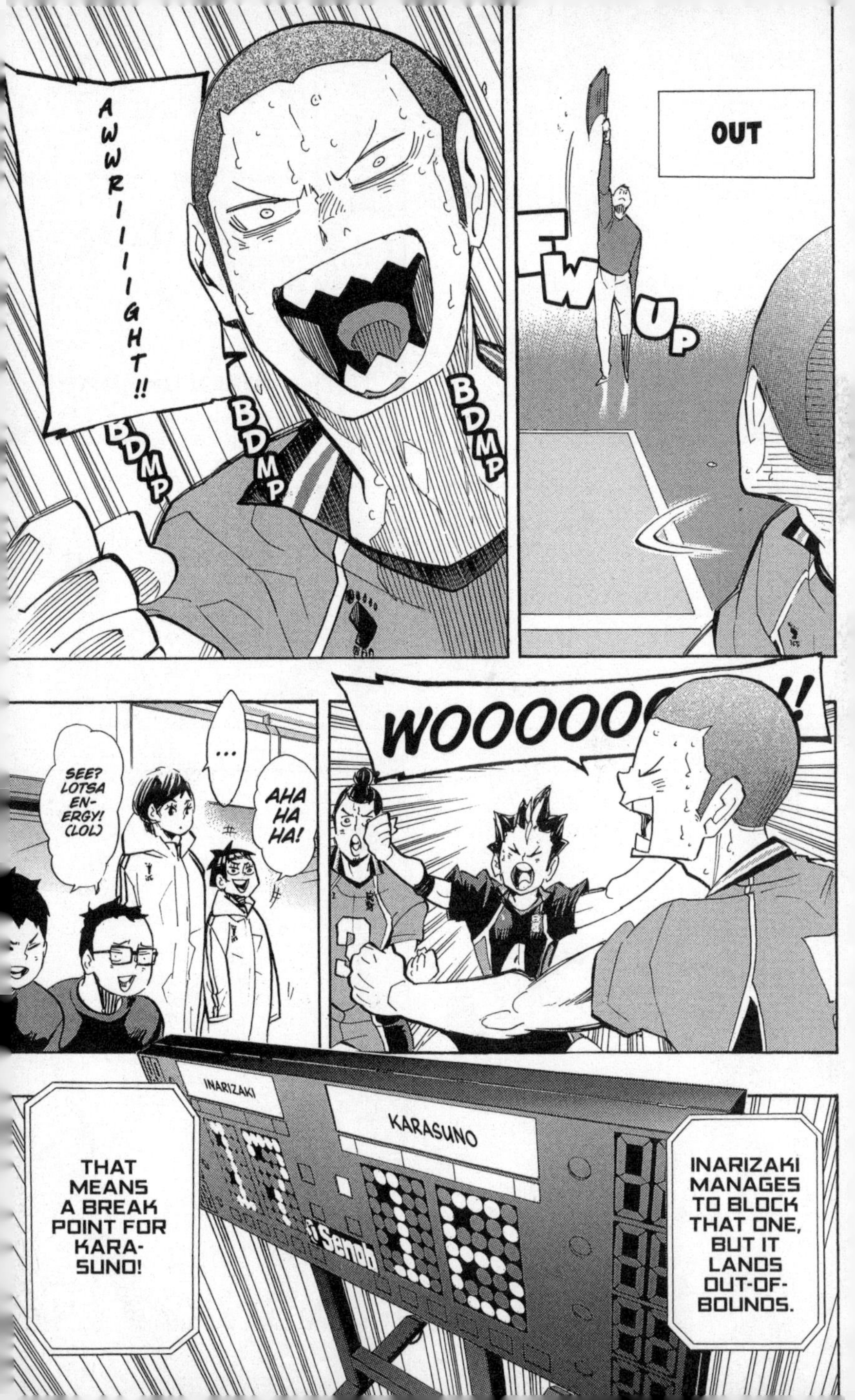
OUT
FWUP
AWWRIIIIIGHT!!
BDMP
BDMP
BDMP
WOOOOOO!!
...
AHA HA HA!
SEE? LOTSA ENERGY! (LOL)
INARIZAKI MANAGES TO BLOCK THAT ONE, BUT IT LANDS OUT-OF-BOUNDS.
INARIZAKI
KARASUNO
Senoh
THAT MEANS A BREAK POINT FOR KARASUNO!

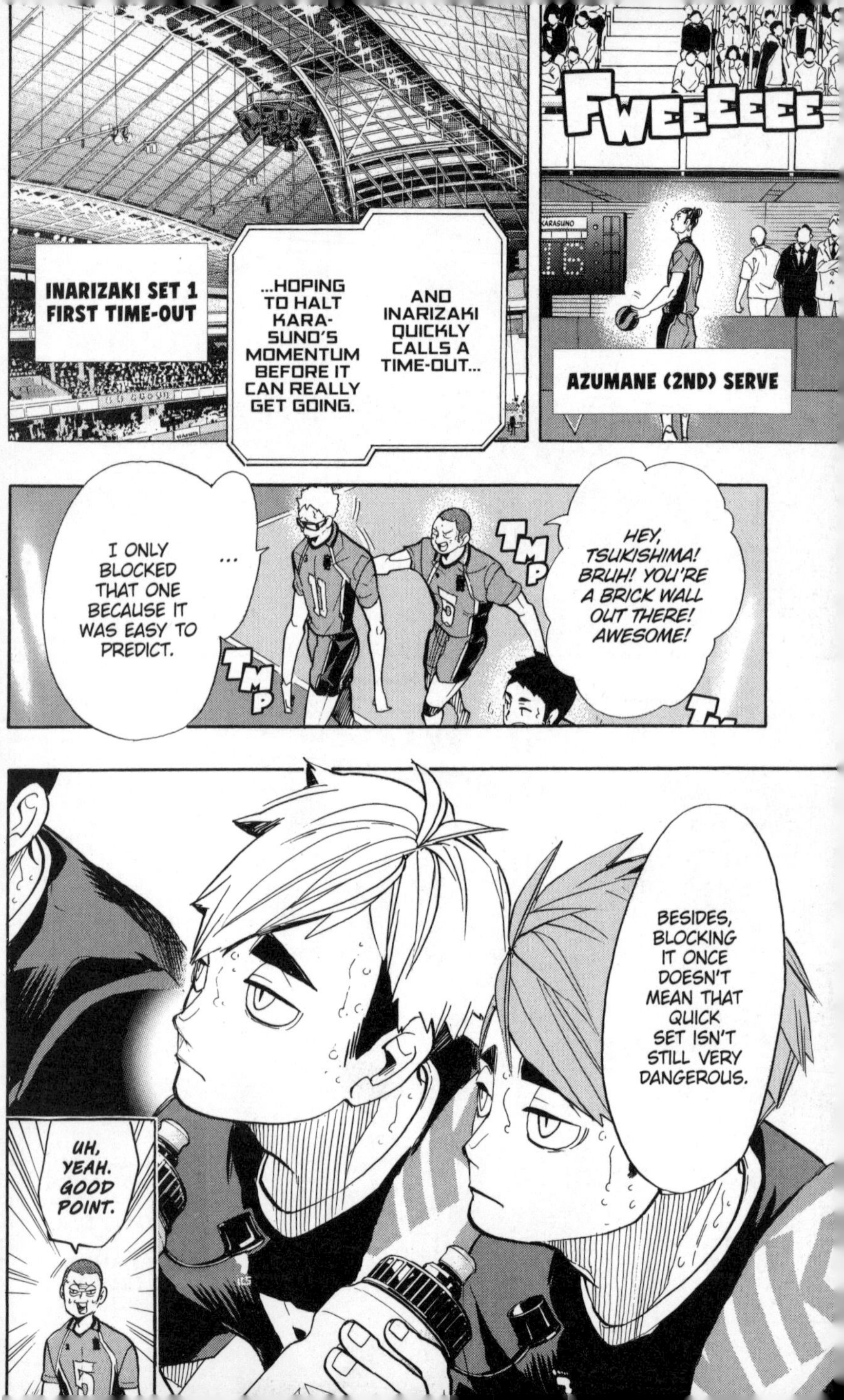
FWEEEEEE
AZUMANE (2ND) SERVE
AND INARIZAKI QUICKLY CALLS A TIME-OUT...
...HOPING TO HALT KARASUNO'S MOMENTUM BEFORE IT CAN REALLY GET GOING.
INARIZAKI SET 1 FIRST TIME-OUT
HEY, TSUKISHIMA! BRUH! YOU'RE A BRICK WALL OUT THERE! AWESOME!
TMP
TMP
...
I ONLY BLOCKED THAT ONE BECAUSE IT WAS EASY TO PREDICT.
BESIDES, BLOCKING IT ONCE DOESN'T MEAN THAT QUICK SET ISN'T STILL VERY DANGEROUS.
UH, YEAH. GOOD POINT.

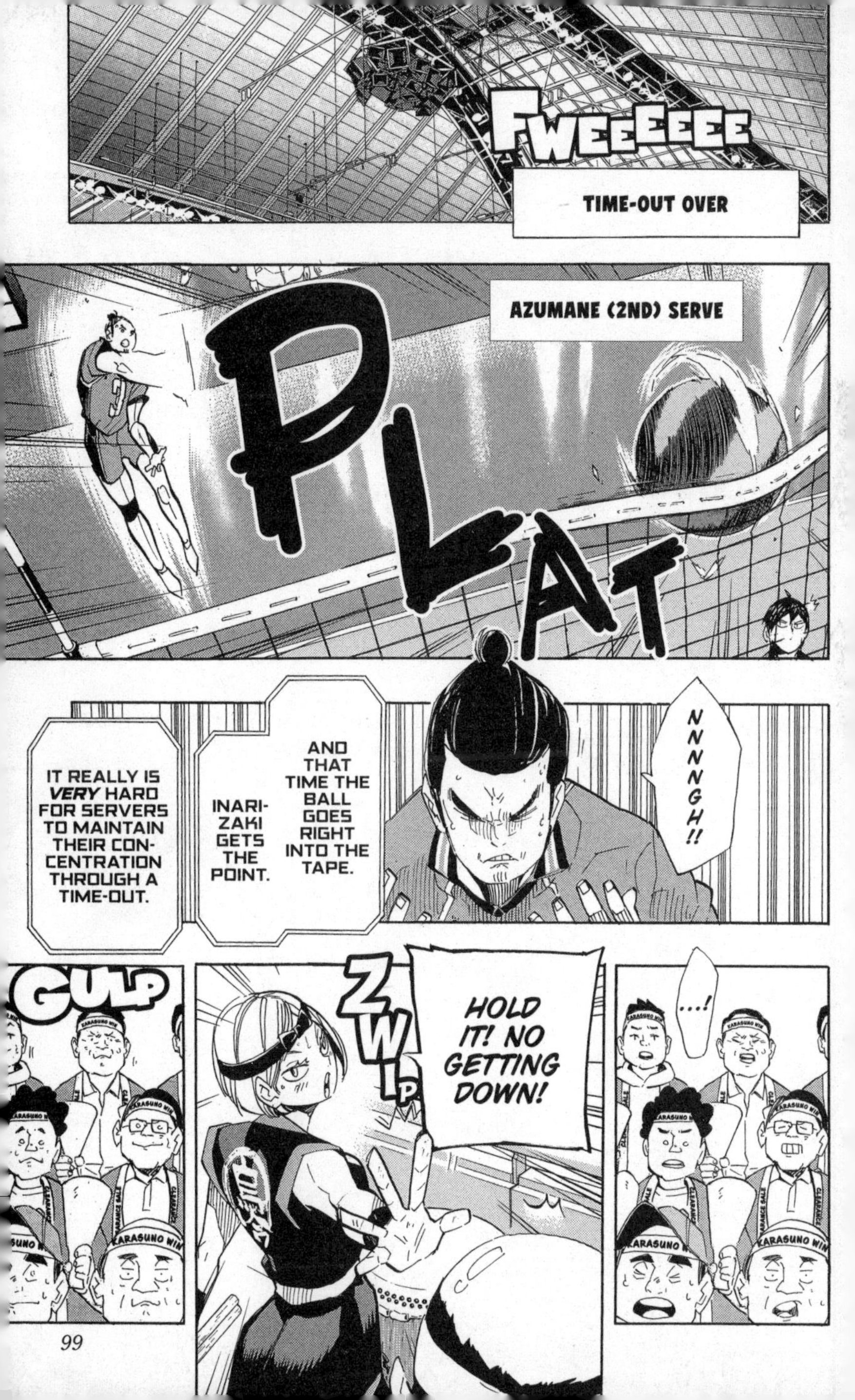
FWEEEEEE
TIME-OUT OVER
AZUMANE (2ND) SERVE
PLAT
NNNNGH!!
AND THAT TIME THE BALL GOES RIGHT INTO THE TAPE.
INARI-ZAKI GETS THE POINT.
IT REALLY IS *VERY* HARD FOR SERVERS TO MAINTAIN THEIR CON-CENTRATION THROUGH A TIME-OUT.
...!
HOLD IT! NO GETTING DOWN!
ZWIP
GULP

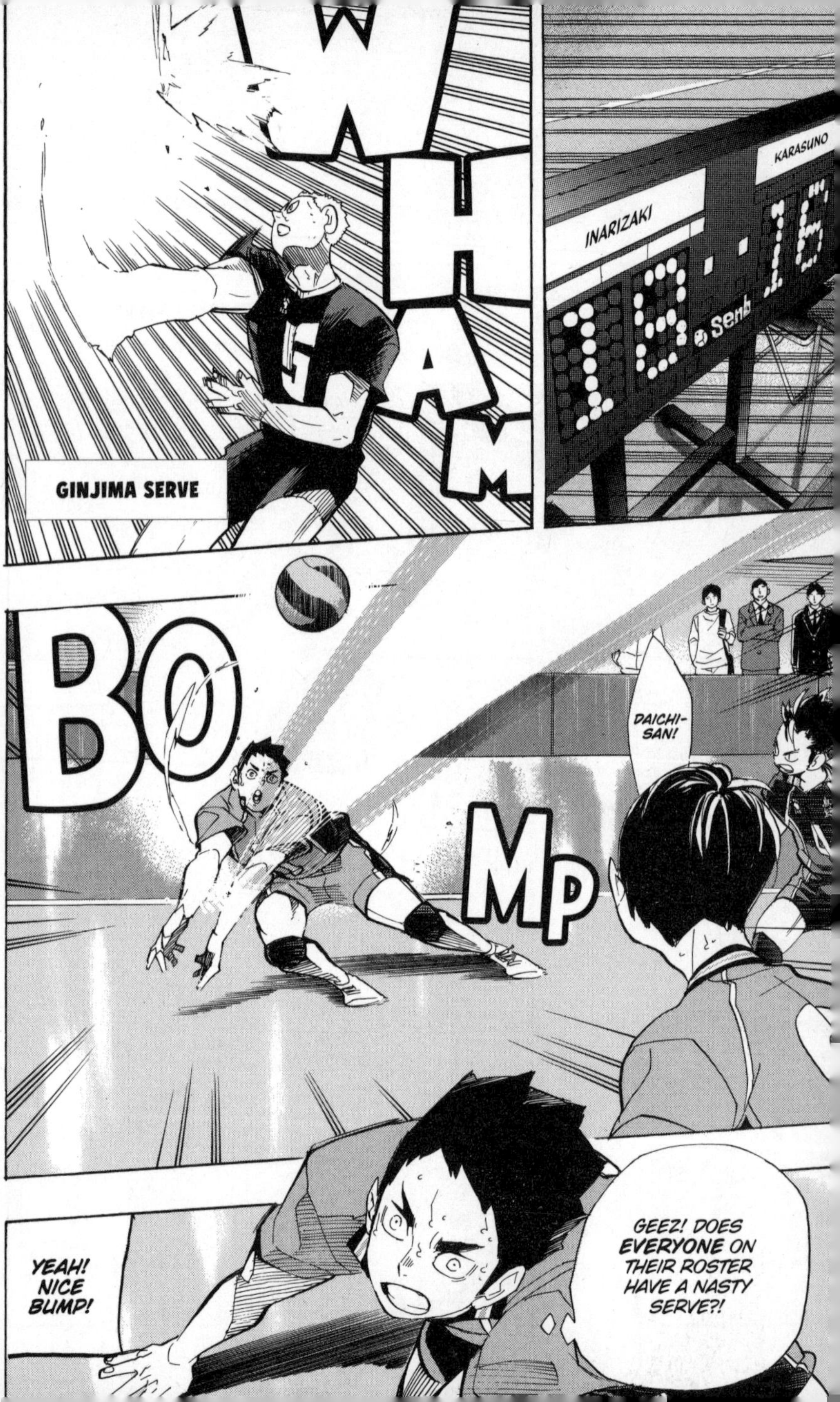

INARIZAKI
KARASUNO
WHAM
GINJIMA SERVE
BOOMP
DAICHI-SAN!
GEEZ! DOES EVERYONE ON THEIR ROSTER HAVE A NASTY SERVE?!
YEAH! NICE BUMP!

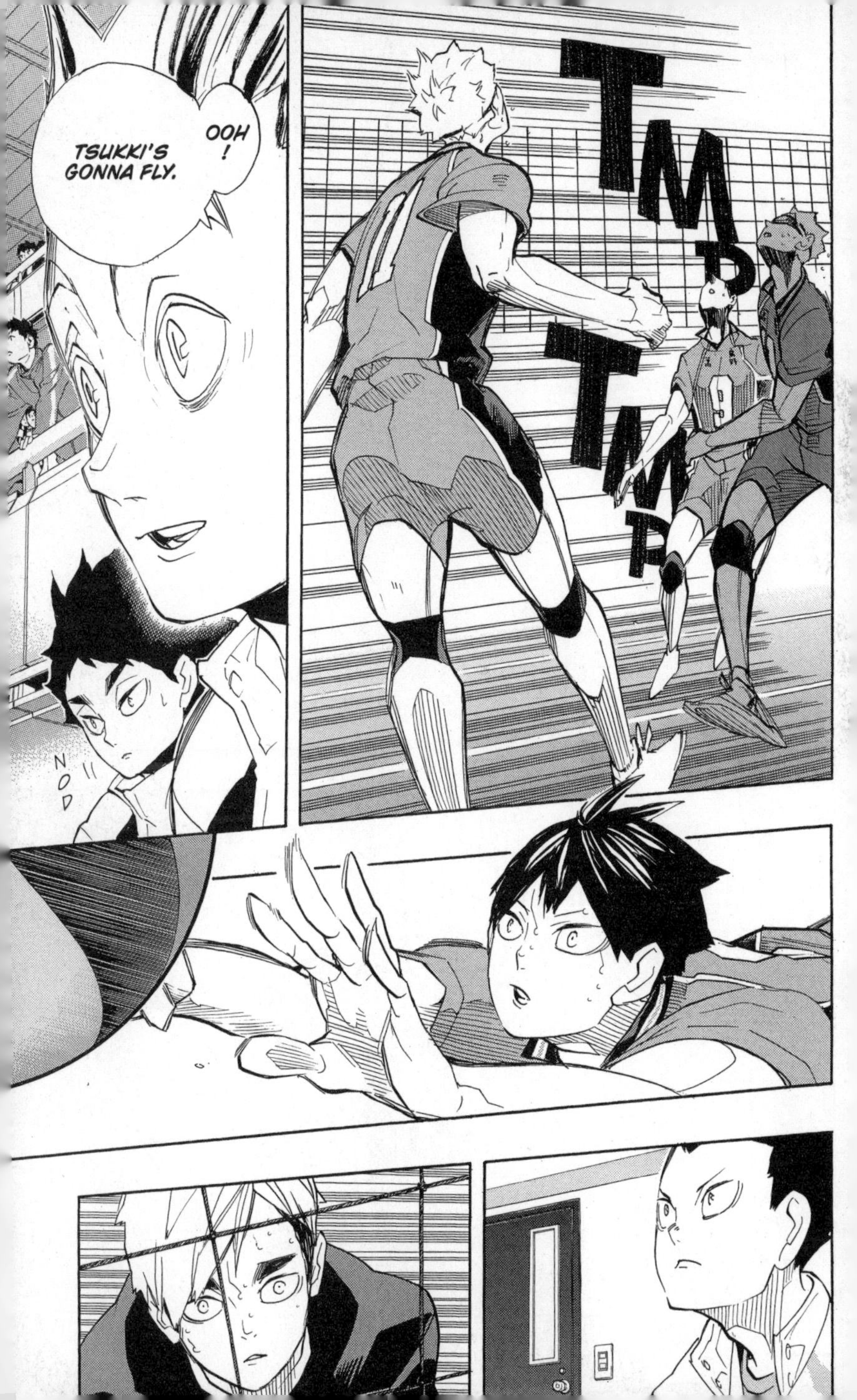
TMP
TMP
TMP
TMP
OOH!
TSUKKI'S GONNA FLY.
NOD

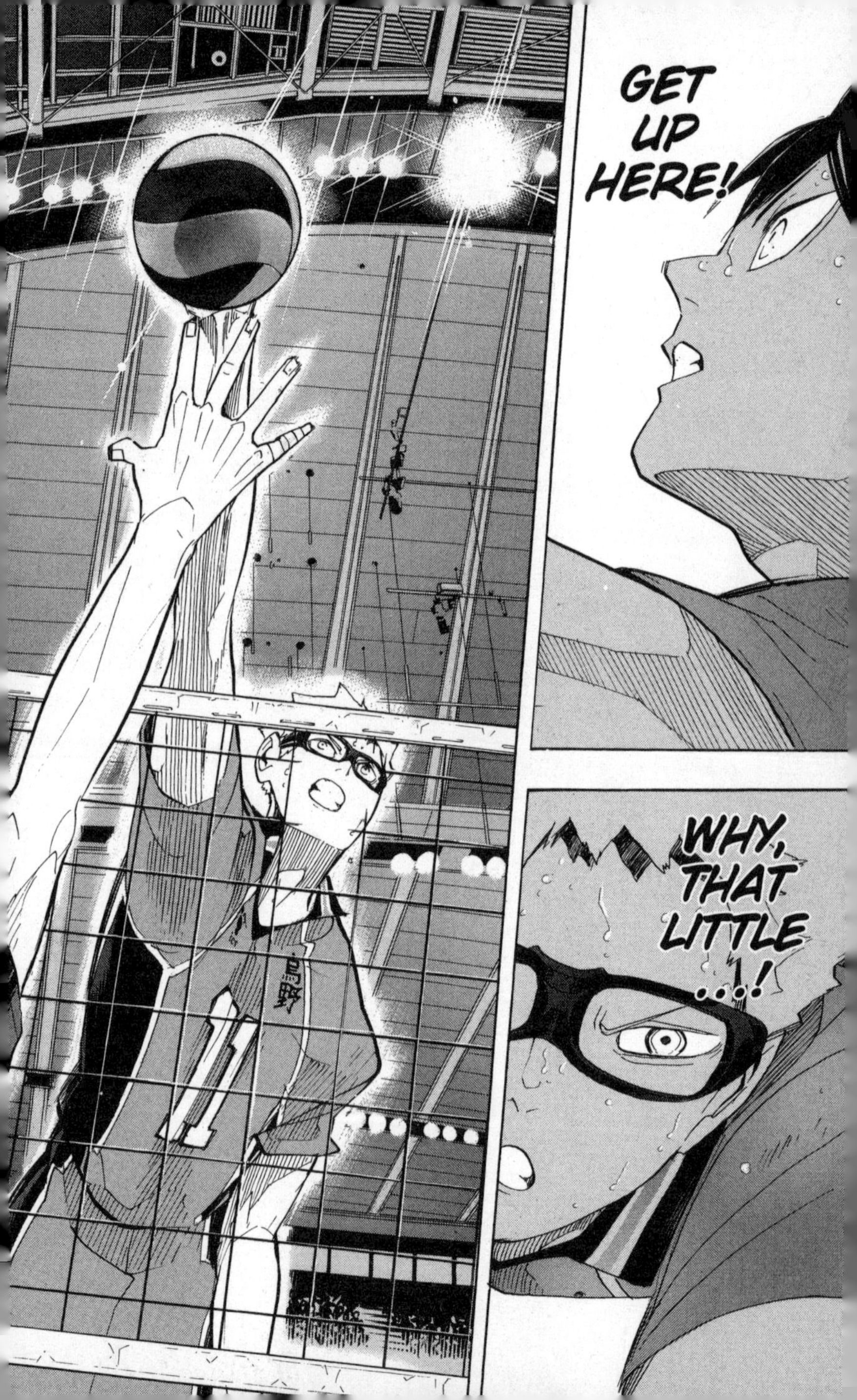
GET UP HERE!
WHY, THAT LITTLE ...!

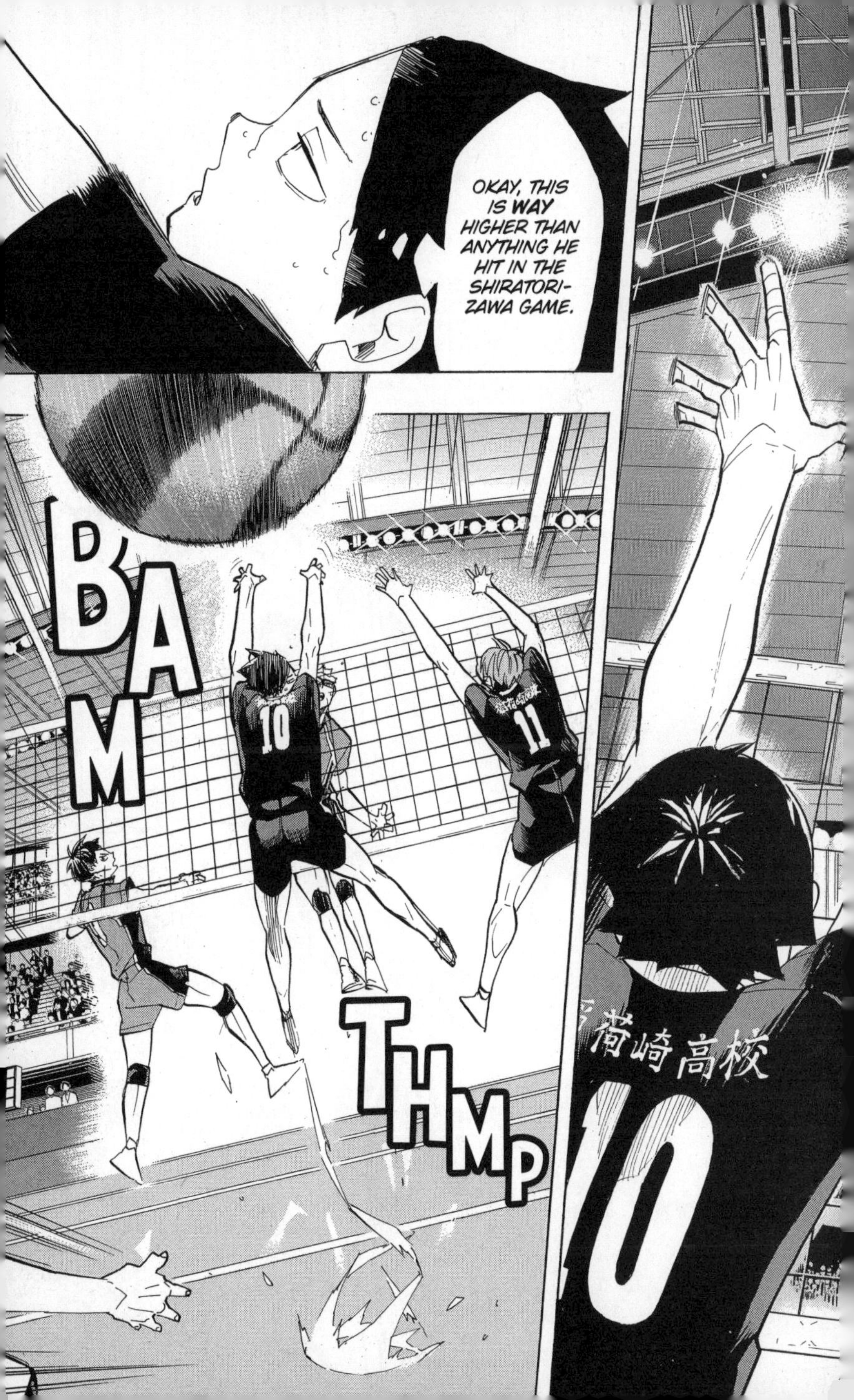
荷崎高校
10
OKAY, THIS IS WAY HIGHER THAN ANYTHING HE HIT IN THE SHIRATORI-ZAWA GAME.
BAM
10
11
THMP

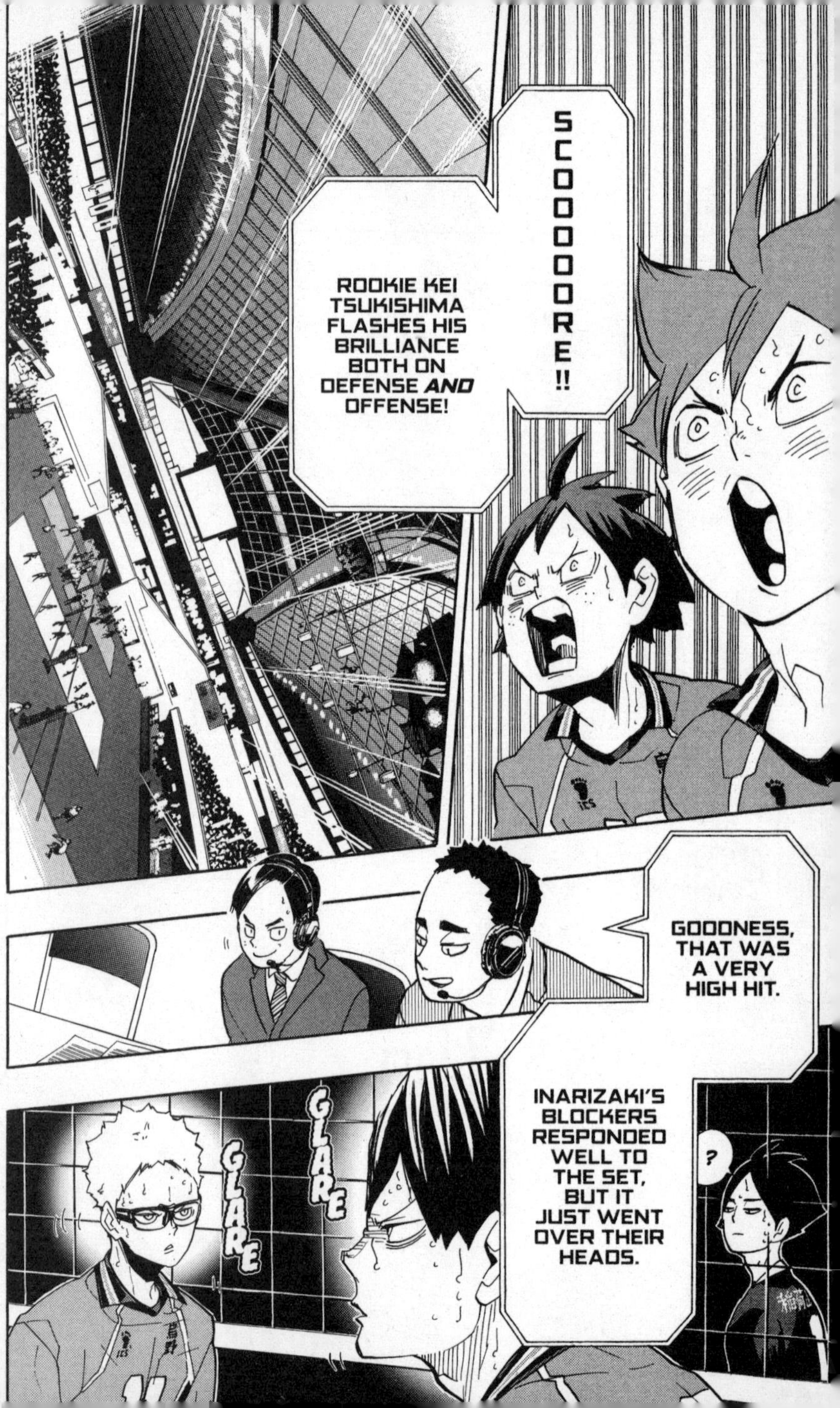
SCOOOOOORE!!
ROOKIE KEI TSUKISHIMA FLASHES HIS BRILLIANCE BOTH ON DEFENSE *AND* OFFENSE!
GOODNESS, THAT WAS A VERY HIGH HIT.
INARIZAKI'S BLOCKERS RESPONDED WELL TO THE SET, BUT IT JUST WENT OVER THEIR HEADS.
?
GLARE
GLARE

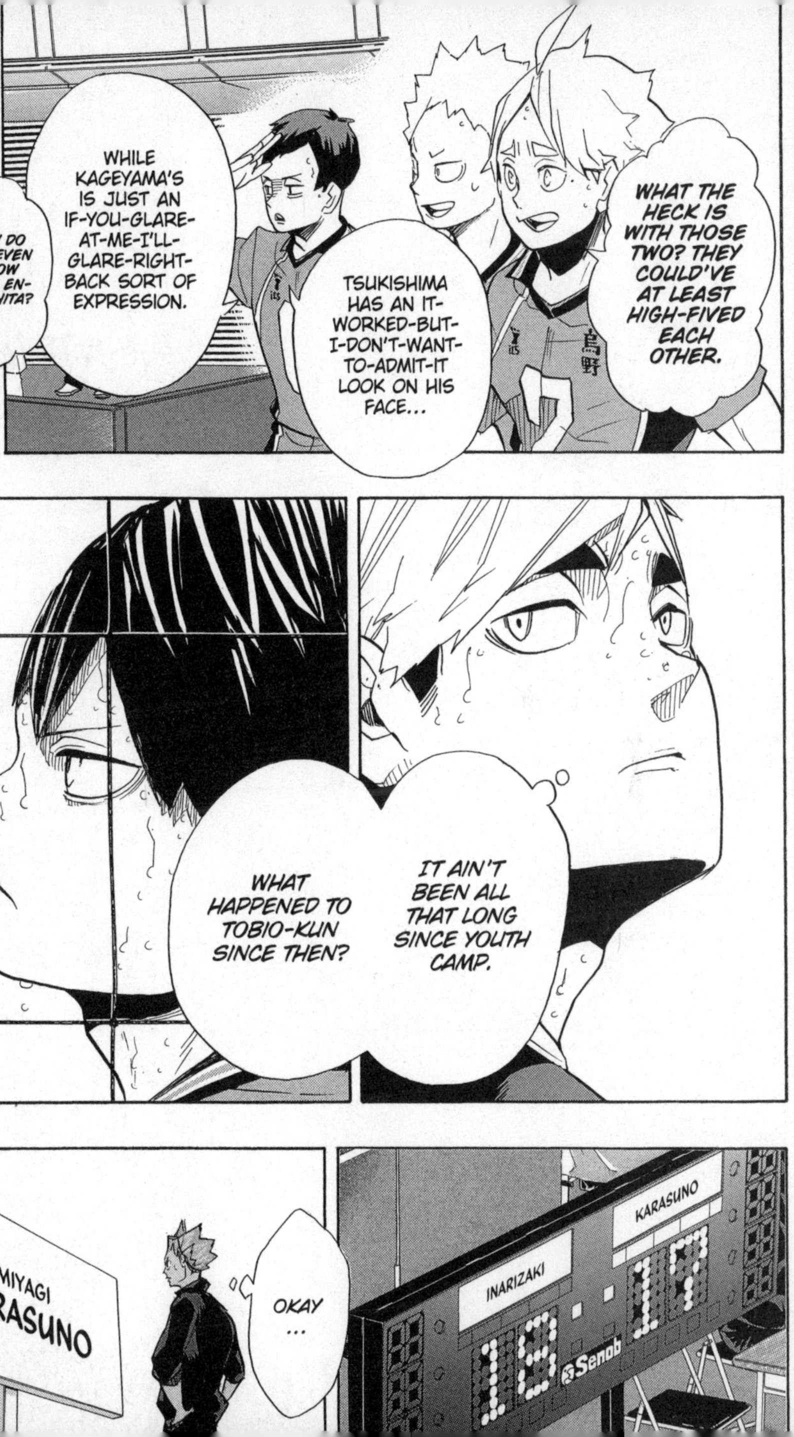
WHAT THE HECK IS WITH THOSE TWO? THEY COULD'VE AT LEAST HIGH-FIVED EACH OTHER.
TSUKISHIMA HAS AN IT-WORKED-BUT-I-DON'T-WANT-TO-ADMIT-IT LOOK ON HIS FACE...
WHILE KAGEYAMA'S IS JUST AN IF-YOU-GLARE-AT-ME-I'LL-GLARE-RIGHT-BACK SORT OF EXPRESSION.
HOW DO YOU EVEN KNOW THAT, ENNOSHITA?
IT AIN'T BEEN ALL THAT LONG SINCE YOUTH CAMP.
WHAT HAPPENED TO TOBIO-KUN SINCE THEN?
KARASUNO
INARIZAKI
Senob
MIYAGI KARASUNO
OKAY ...

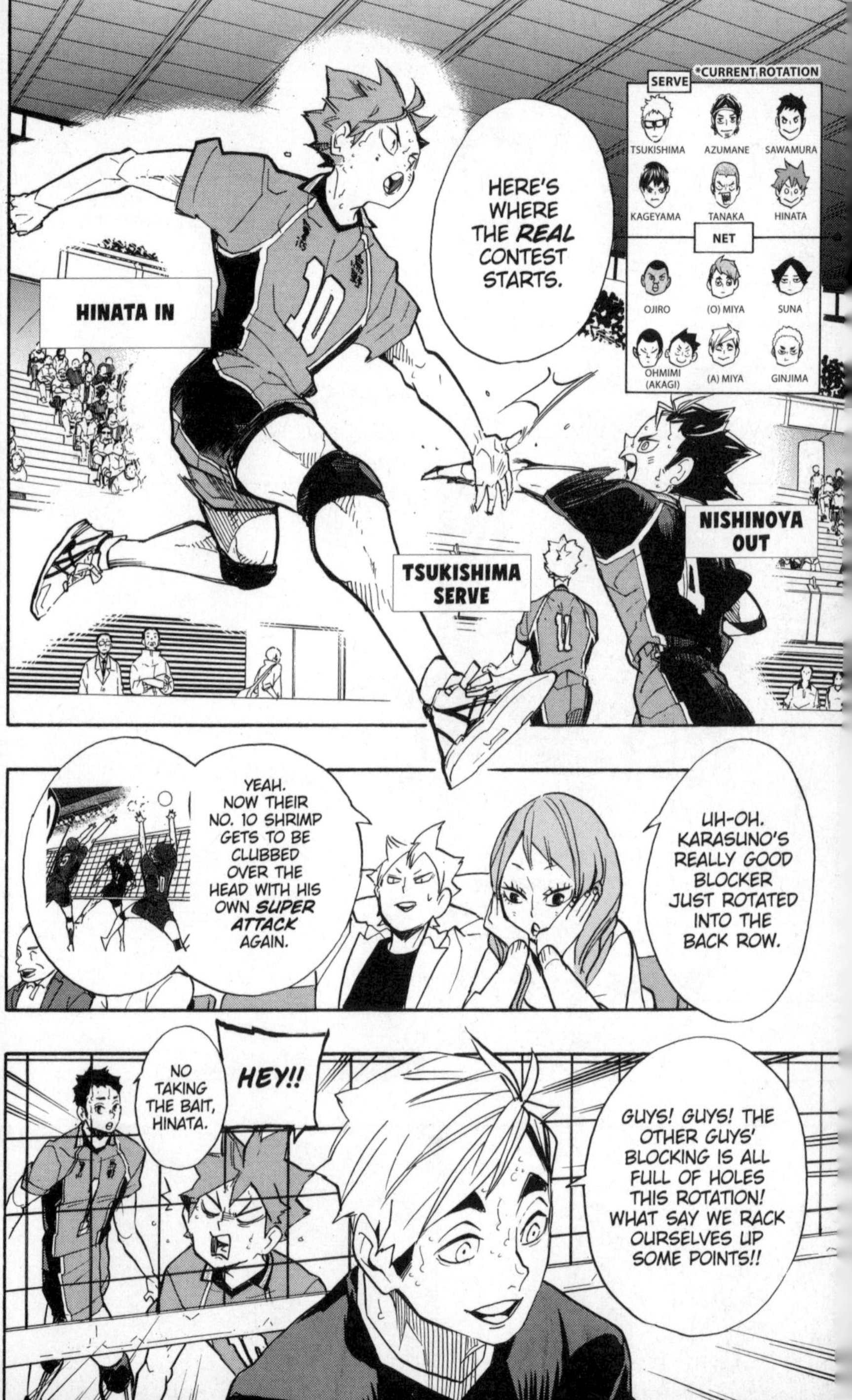
*CURRENT ROTATION
SERVE
TSUKISHIMA
AZUMANE
SAWAMURA
KAGEYAMA
TANAKA
HINATA
NET
OJIRO
(O) MIYA
SUNA
OHMIMI (AKAGI)
(A) MIYA
GINJIMA
HERE'S WHERE THE *REAL* CONTEST STARTS.
HINATA IN
NISHINOYA OUT
TSUKISHIMA SERVE
UH-OH. KARASUNO'S REALLY GOOD BLOCKER JUST ROTATED INTO THE BACK ROW.
YEAH. NOW THEIR NO. 10 SHRIMP GETS TO BE CLUBBED OVER THE HEAD WITH HIS OWN *SUPER ATTACK* AGAIN.
GUYS! GUYS! THE OTHER GUYS' BLOCKING IS ALL FULL OF HOLES THIS ROTATION! WHAT SAY WE RACK OURSELVES UP SOME POINTS!!
HEY!!
NO TAKING THE BAIT, HINATA.

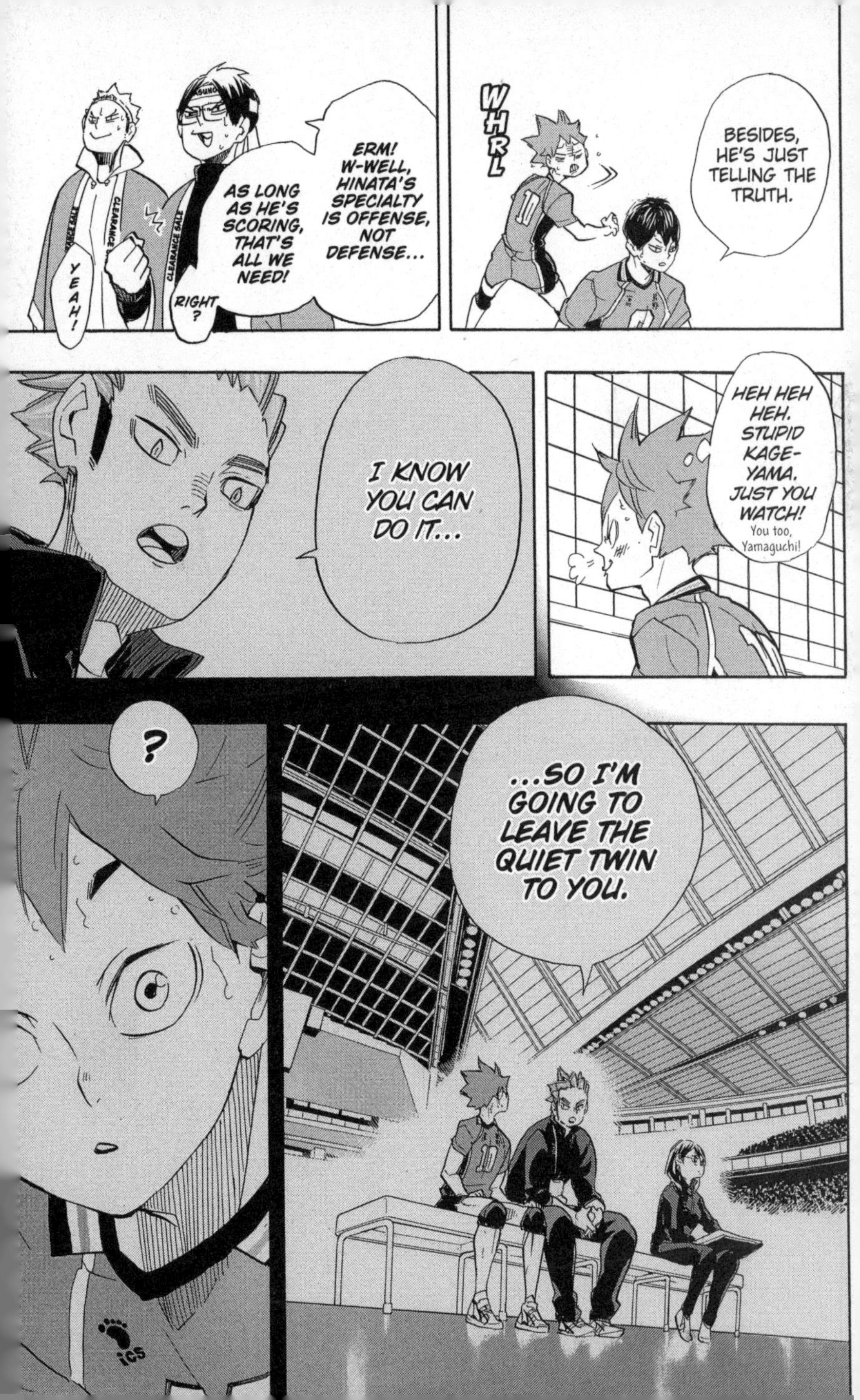
WHRL
BESIDES, HE'S JUST TELLING THE TRUTH.
ERM! W-WELL, HINATA'S SPECIALTY IS OFFENSE, NOT DEFENSE...
AS LONG AS HE'S SCORING, THAT'S ALL WE NEED!
RIGHT?
YEAH!
HEH HEH HEH. STUPID KAGE-YAMA. JUST YOU WATCH!
You too, Yamaguchi!
I KNOW YOU CAN DO IT...
...SO I'M GOING TO LEAVE THE QUIET TWIN TO YOU.
?

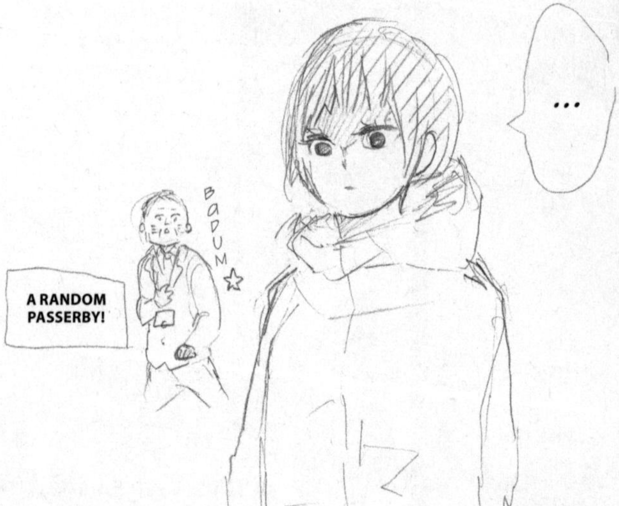
...
BADUM☆
A RANDOM PASSERBY!

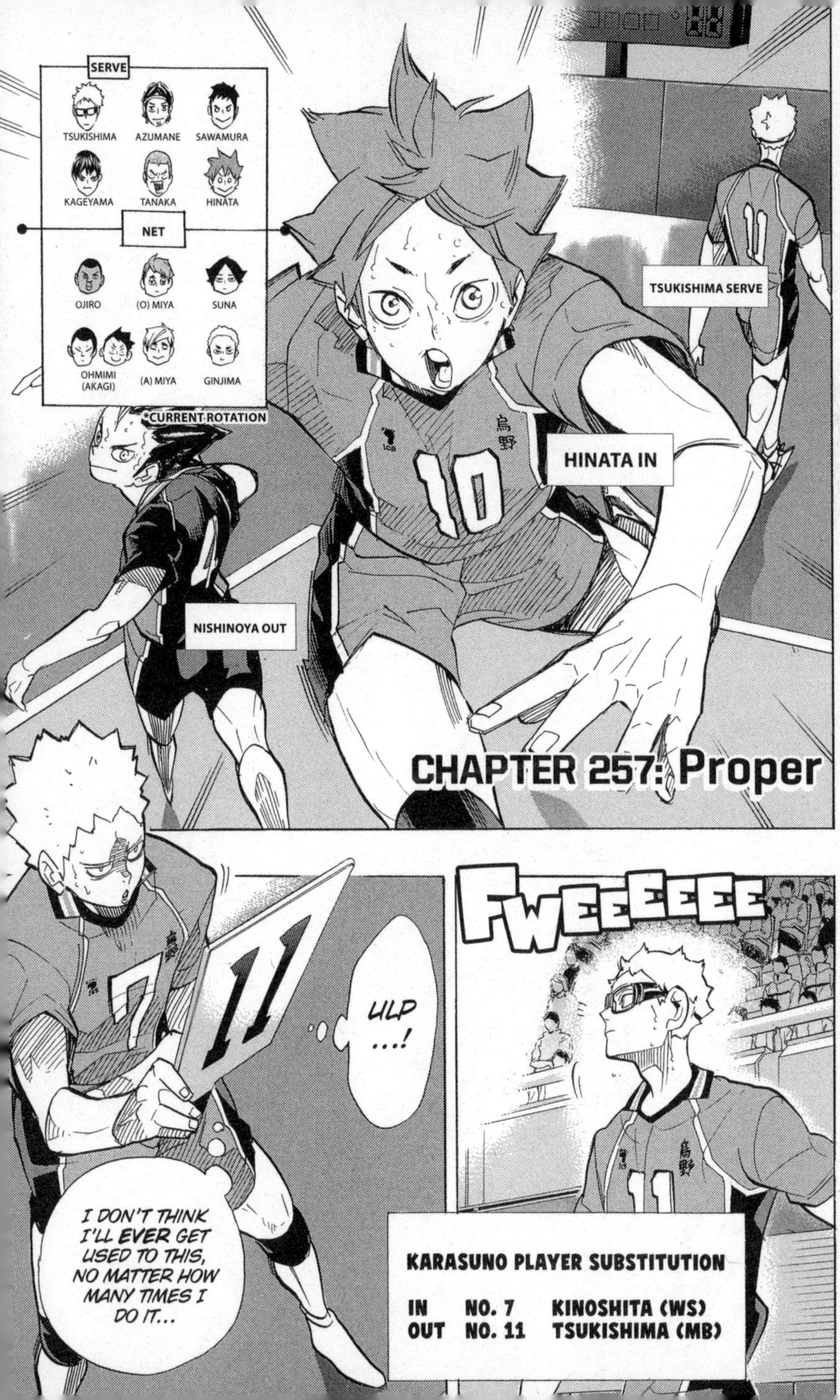
TSUKISHIMA SERVE
HINATA IN
SERVE
TSUKISHIMA
AZUMANE
SAWAMURA
KAGEYAMA
TANAKA
HINATA
NET
OJIRO
(O) MIYA
SUNA
OHMIMI (AKAGI)
(A) MIYA
GINJIMA
*CURRENT ROTATION
NISHINOYA OUT
CHAPTER 257: Proper
FWEEEEEE
KARASUNO PLAYER SUBSTITUTION
IN NO. 7 KINOSHITA (WS)
OUT NO. 11 TSUKISHIMA (MB)
ULP ...!
I DON'T THINK I'LL EVER GET USED TO THIS, NO MATTER HOW MANY TIMES I DO IT...

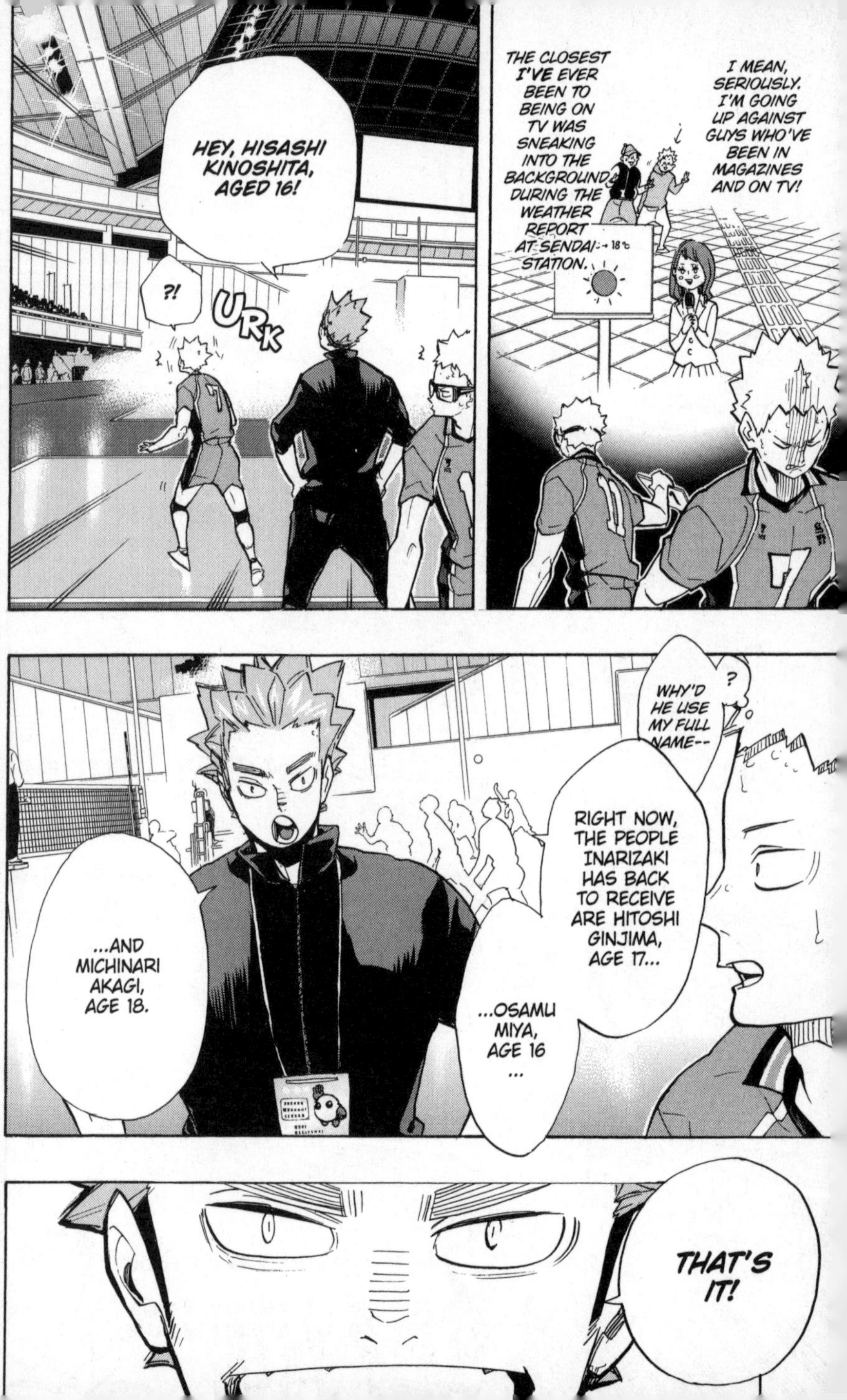
I MEAN, SERIOUSLY. I'M GOING UP AGAINST GUYS WHO'VE BEEN IN MAGAZINES AND ON TV!
THE CLOSEST I'VE EVER BEEN TO BEING ON TV WAS SNEAKING INTO THE BACKGROUND DURING THE WEATHER REPORT AT SENDAI STATION.
HEY, HISASHI KINOSHITA, AGED 16!
?!
URK
?
WHY'D HE USE MY FULL NAME--
RIGHT NOW, THE PEOPLE INARIZAKI HAS BACK TO RECEIVE ARE HITOSHI GINJIMA, AGE 17...
...OSAMU MIYA, AGE 16 ...
...AND MICHINARI AKAGI, AGE 18.
THAT'S IT!

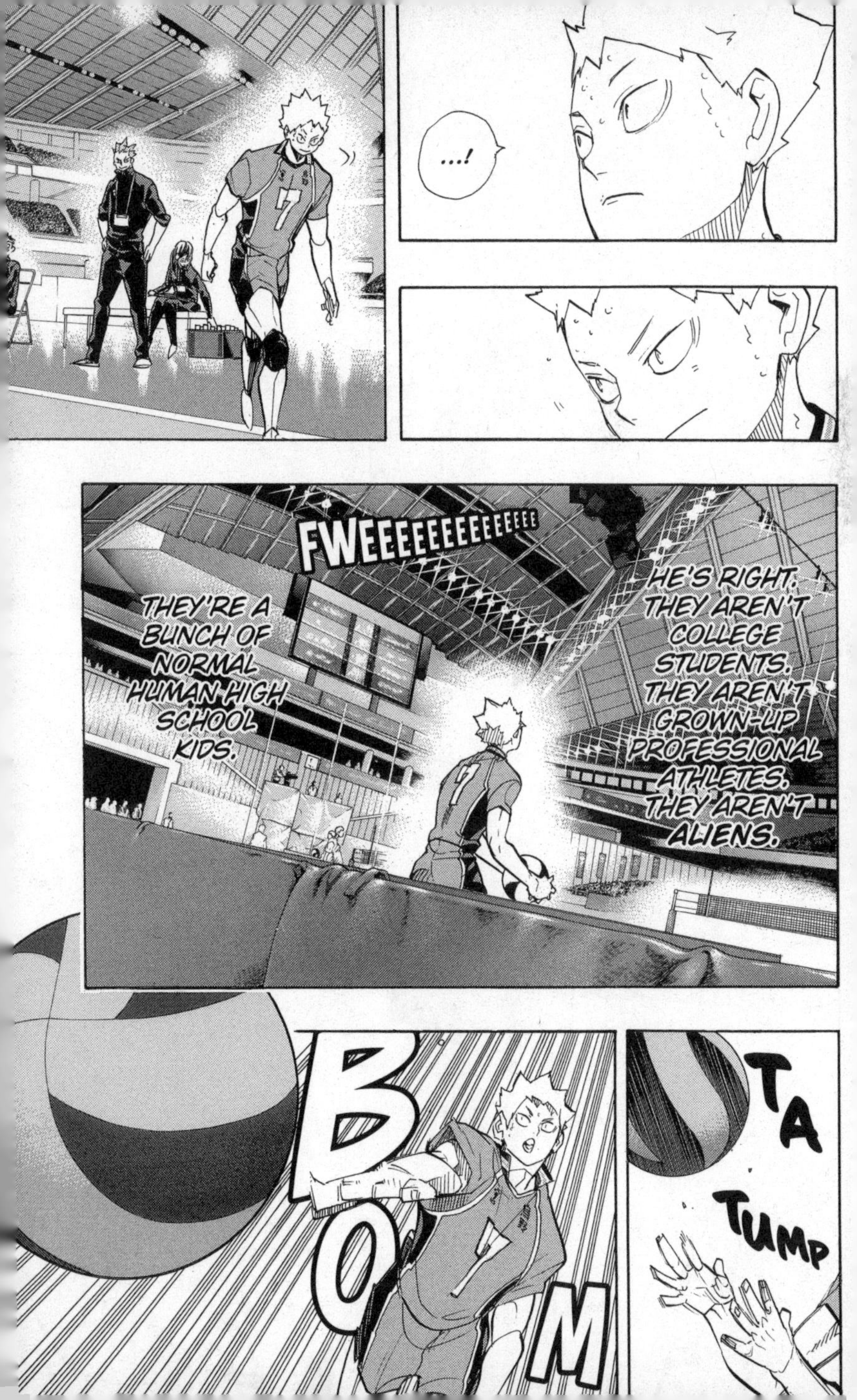
...!
FWEEEEEEEEEEEEE
HE'S RIGHT. THEY AREN'T COLLEGE STUDENTS. THEY AREN'T GROWN-UP PROFESSIONAL ATHLETES. THEY AREN'T ALIENS.
THEY'RE A BUNCH OF NORMAL HUMAN HIGH SCHOOL KIDS.
TA
TUMP
BOOM

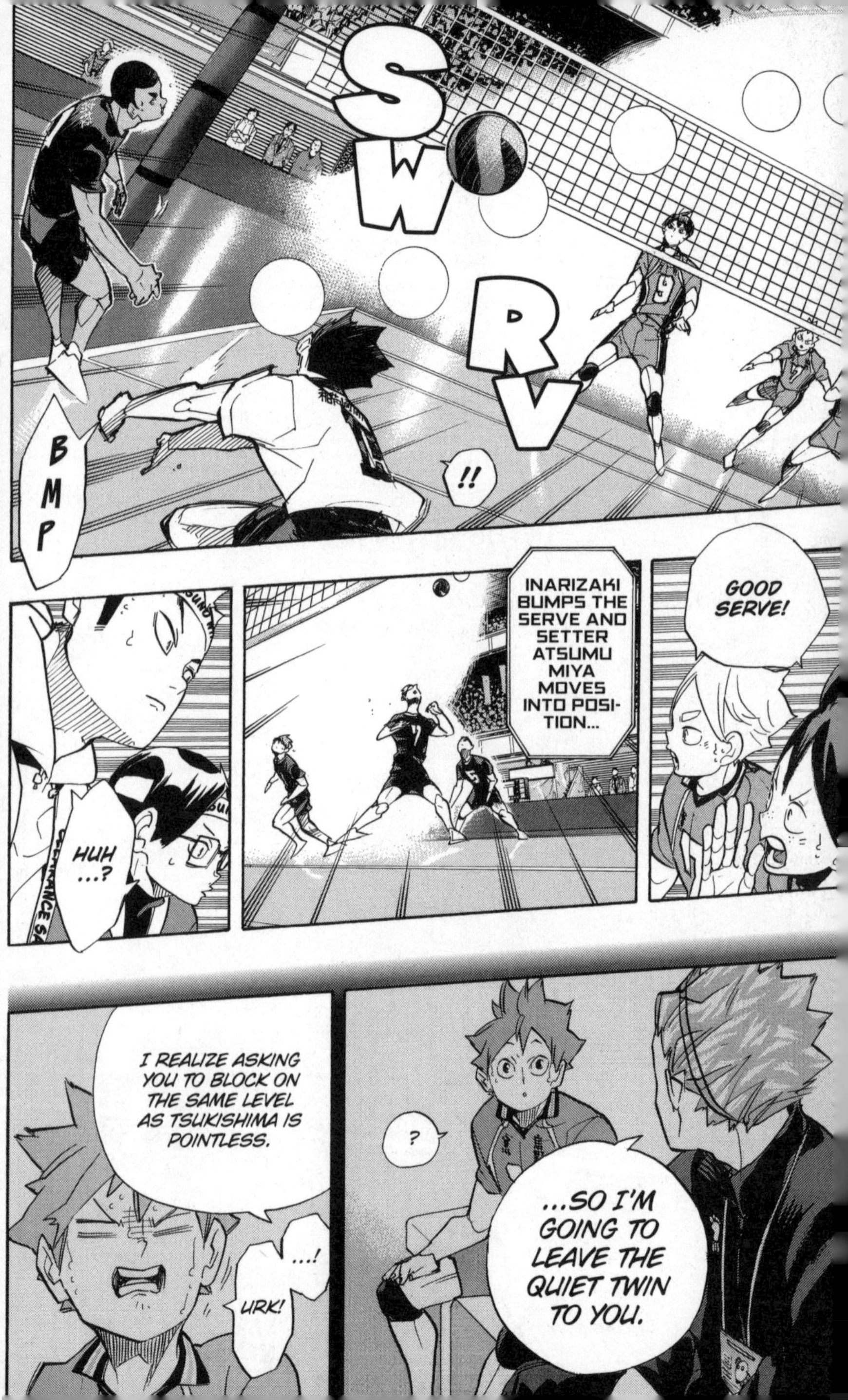
SWRV
!!
BMP
GOOD SERVE!
INARIZAKI BUMPS THE SERVE AND SETTER ATSUMU MIYA MOVES INTO POSITION...
HUH ...?
?
...SO I'M GOING TO LEAVE THE QUIET TWIN TO YOU.
I REALIZE ASKING YOU TO BLOCK ON THE SAME LEVEL AS TSUKISHIMA IS POINTLESS.
...!
URK!

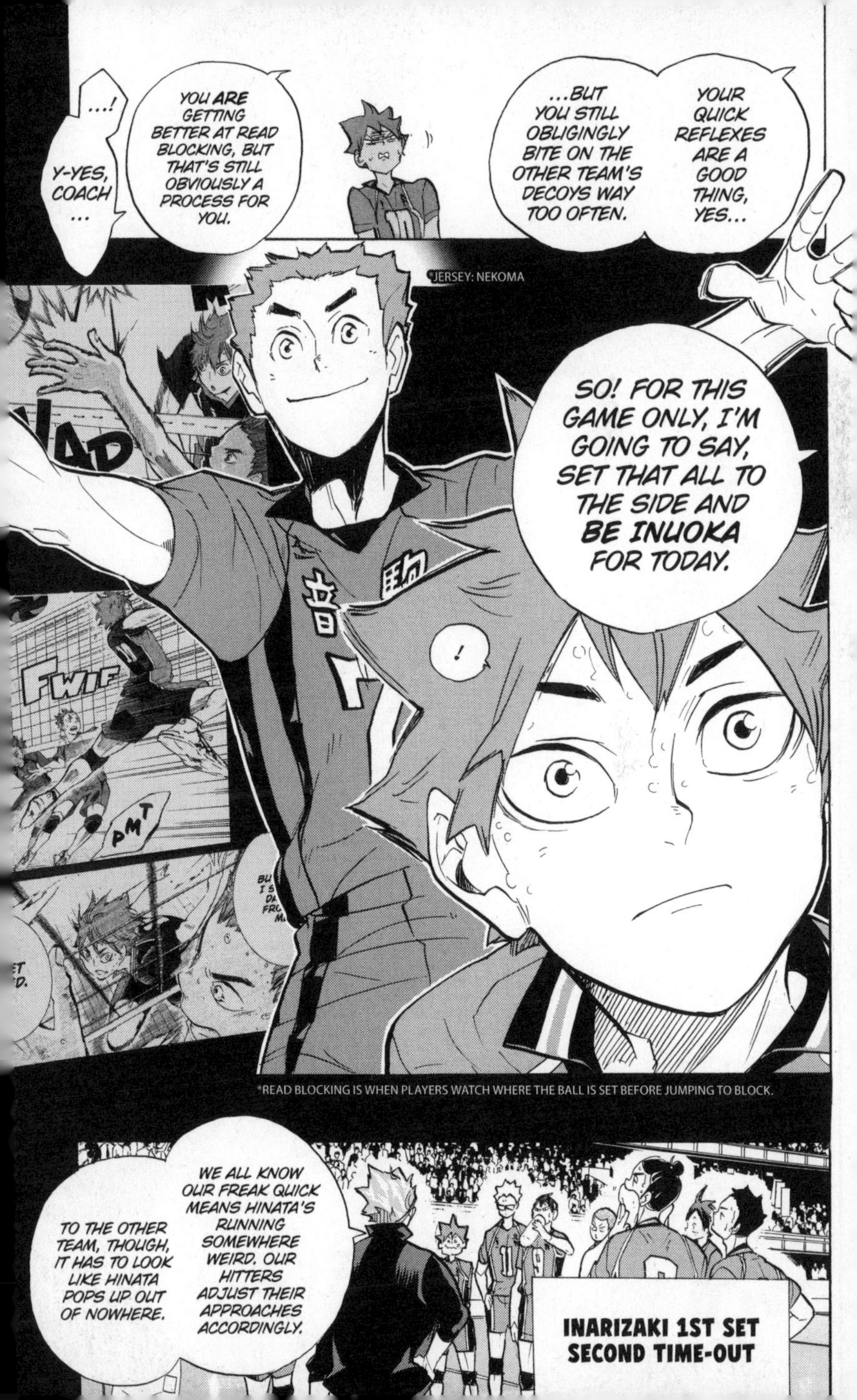
YOUR QUICK REFLEXES ARE A GOOD THING, YES...
...BUT YOU STILL OBLIGINGLY BITE ON THE OTHER TEAM'S DECOYS WAY TOO OFTEN.
YOU ARE GETTING BETTER AT READ BLOCKING, BUT THAT'S STILL OBVIOUSLY A PROCESS FOR YOU.
...!
Y-YES, COACH...
*JERSEY: NEKOMA
SO! FOR THIS GAME ONLY, I'M GOING TO SAY, SET THAT ALL TO THE SIDE AND BE INUOKA FOR TODAY.
!
WAD
FWIF
PMT
*READ BLOCKING IS WHEN PLAYERS WATCH WHERE THE BALL IS SET BEFORE JUMPING TO BLOCK.
WE ALL KNOW OUR FREAK QUICK MEANS HINATA'S RUNNING SOMEWHERE WEIRD. OUR HITTERS ADJUST THEIR APPROACHES ACCORDINGLY.
TO THE OTHER TEAM, THOUGH, IT HAS TO LOOK LIKE HINATA POPS UP OUT OF NOWHERE.
INARIZAKI 1ST SET SECOND TIME-OUT

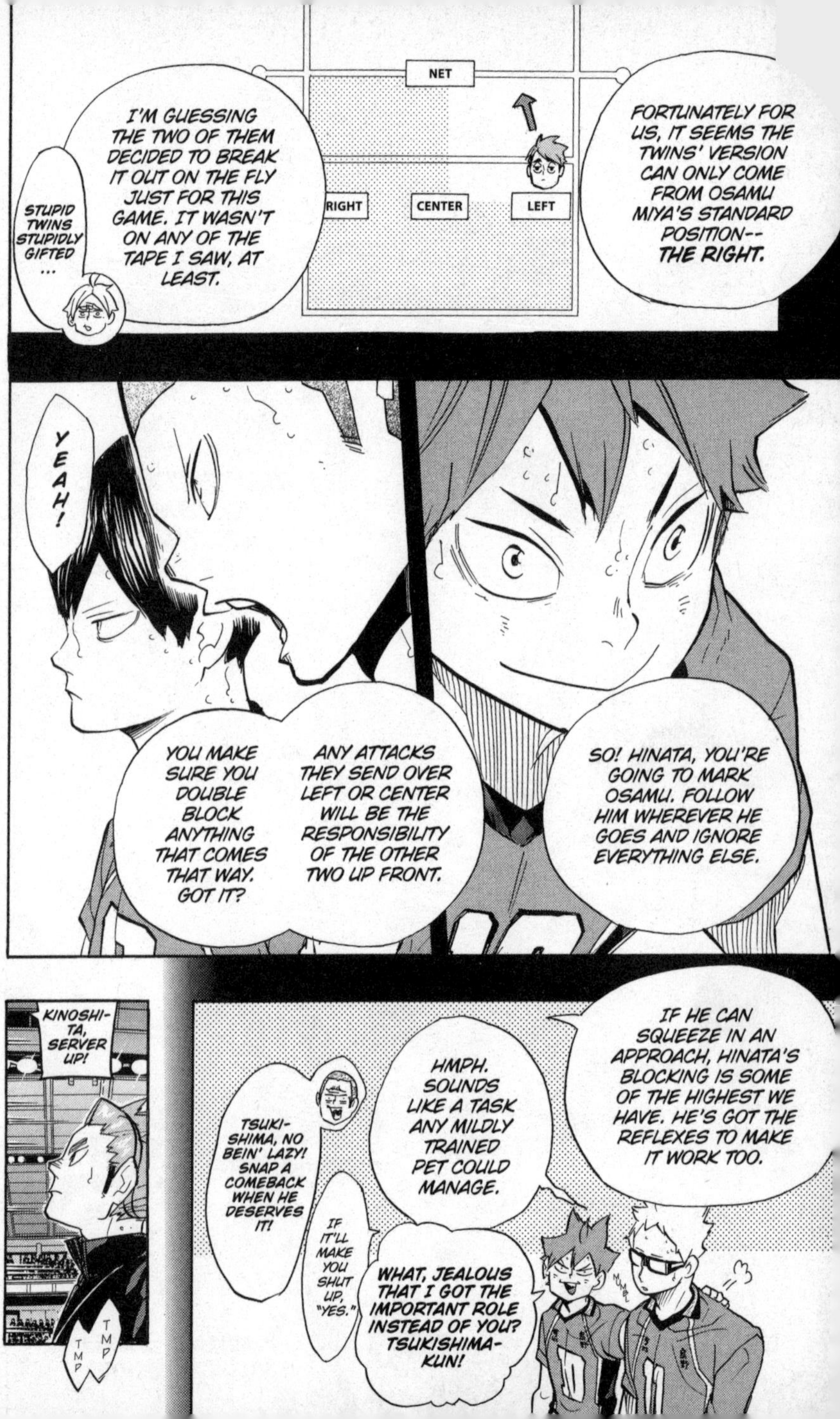
FORTUNATELY FOR US, IT SEEMS THE TWINS' VERSION CAN ONLY COME FROM OSAMU MIYA'S STANDARD POSITION-- THE RIGHT.
NET
LEFT
CENTER
RIGHT
I'M GUESSING THE TWO OF THEM DECIDED TO BREAK IT OUT ON THE FLY JUST FOR THIS GAME. IT WASN'T ON ANY OF THE TAPE I SAW, AT LEAST.
STUPID TWINS STUPIDLY GIFTED...
SO! HINATA, YOU'RE GOING TO MARK OSAMU. FOLLOW HIM WHEREVER HE GOES AND IGNORE EVERYTHING ELSE.
ANY ATTACKS THEY SEND OVER LEFT OR CENTER WILL BE THE RESPONSIBILITY OF THE OTHER TWO UP FRONT.
YOU MAKE SURE YOU DOUBLE BLOCK ANYTHING THAT COMES THAT WAY. GOT IT?
YEAH!
IF HE CAN SQUEEZE IN AN APPROACH, HINATA'S BLOCKING IS SOME OF THE HIGHEST WE HAVE. HE'S GOT THE REFLEXES TO MAKE IT WORK TOO.
HMPH. SOUNDS LIKE A TASK ANY MILDLY TRAINED PET COULD MANAGE.
TSUKISHIMA, NO BEIN' LAZY! SNAP A COMEBACK WHEN HE DESERVES IT!
WHAT, JEALOUS THAT I GOT THE IMPORTANT ROLE INSTEAD OF YOU? TSUKISHIMA-KUN!
MUMBL
IF IT'LL MAKE YOU SHUT UP, "YES."
KINOSHITA, SERVER UP!
TMP
TMP

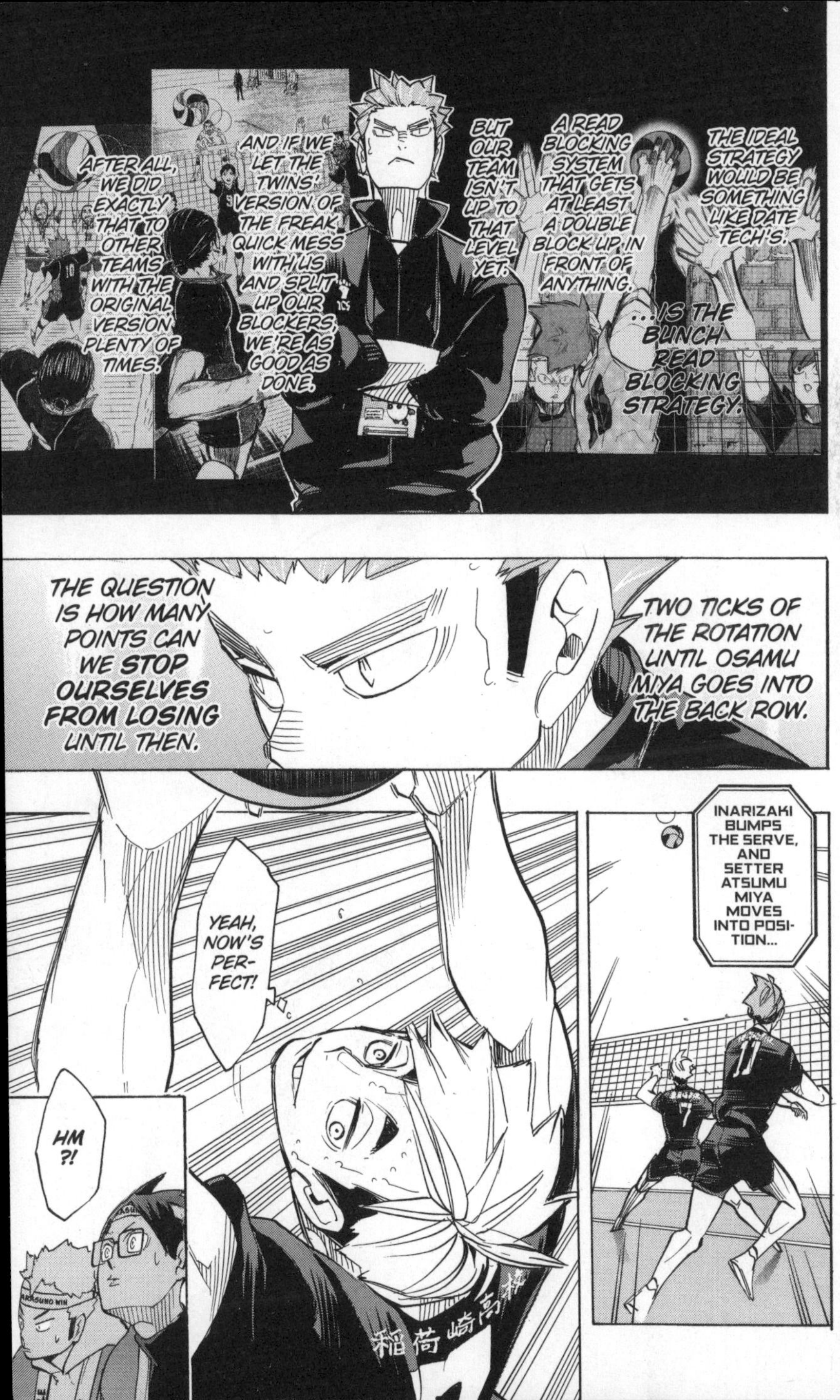

THE IDEAL STRATEGY WOULD BE SOMETHING LIKE DATE TECH'S.
...IS THE BUNCH READ BLOCKING STRATEGY.
A READ BLOCKING SYSTEM THAT GETS AT LEAST A DOUBLE BLOCK UP IN FRONT OF ANYTHING.
BUT OUR TEAM ISN'T UP TO THAT LEVEL YET.
AND IF WE LET THE TWINS' VERSION OF THE FREAK QUICK MESS WITH US AND SPLIT UP OUR BLOCKERS, WE'RE AS GOOD AS DONE.
AFTER ALL, WE DID EXACTLY THAT TO OTHER TEAMS WITH THE ORIGINAL VERSION PLENTY OF TIMES.
TWO TICKS OF THE ROTATION UNTIL OSAMU MIYA GOES INTO THE BACK ROW.
THE QUESTION IS HOW MANY POINTS CAN WE STOP OURSELVES FROM LOSING UNTIL THEN.
INARIZAKI BUMPS THE SERVE, AND SETTER ATSUMU MIYA MOVES INTO POSITION...
YEAH, NOW'S PERFECT!
HM ?!

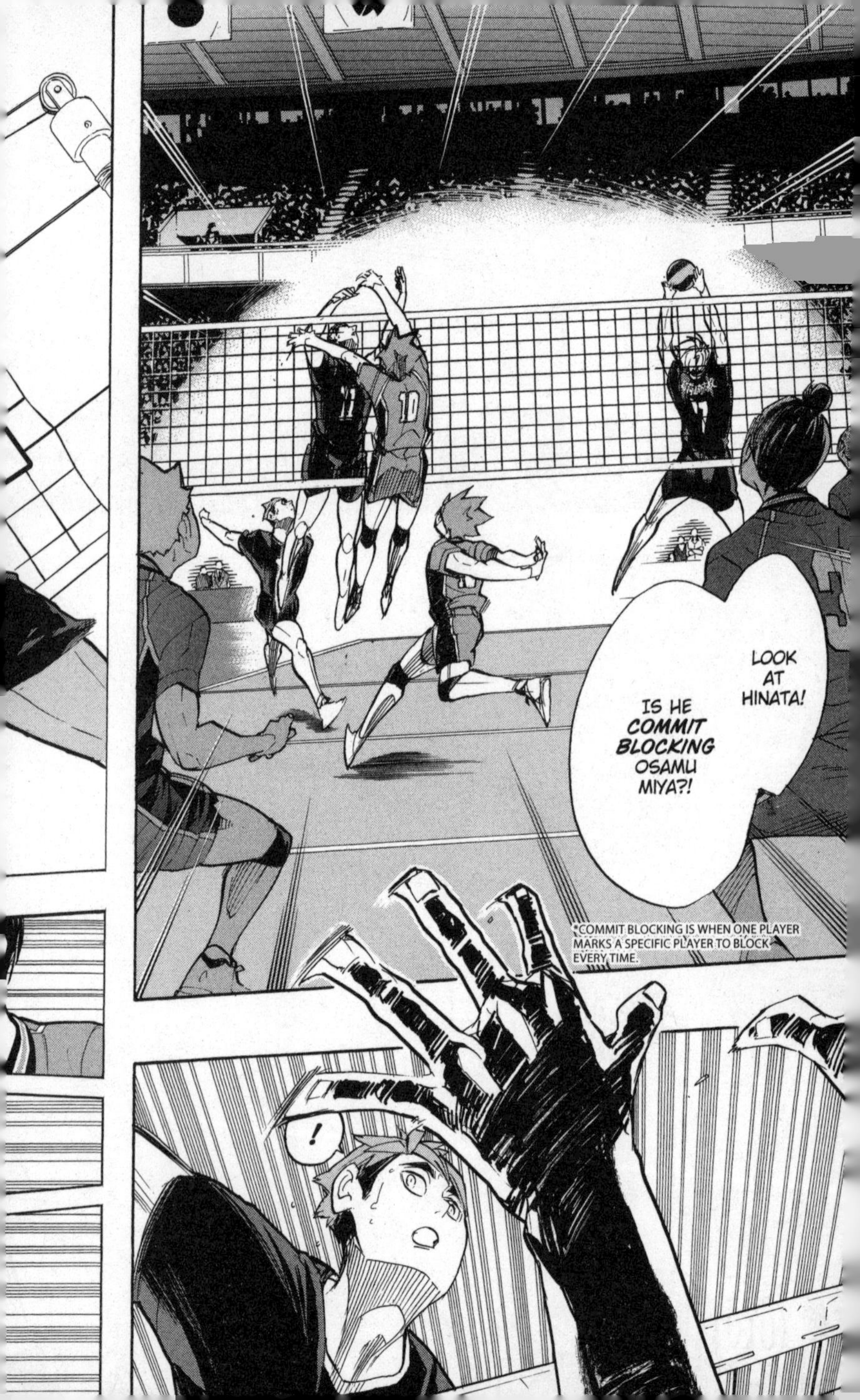
LOOK AT HINATA!
IS HE COMMIT BLOCKING OSAMU MIYA?!
*COMMIT BLOCKING IS WHEN ONE PLAYER MARKS A SPECIFIC PLAYER TO BLOCK EVERY TIME.
!

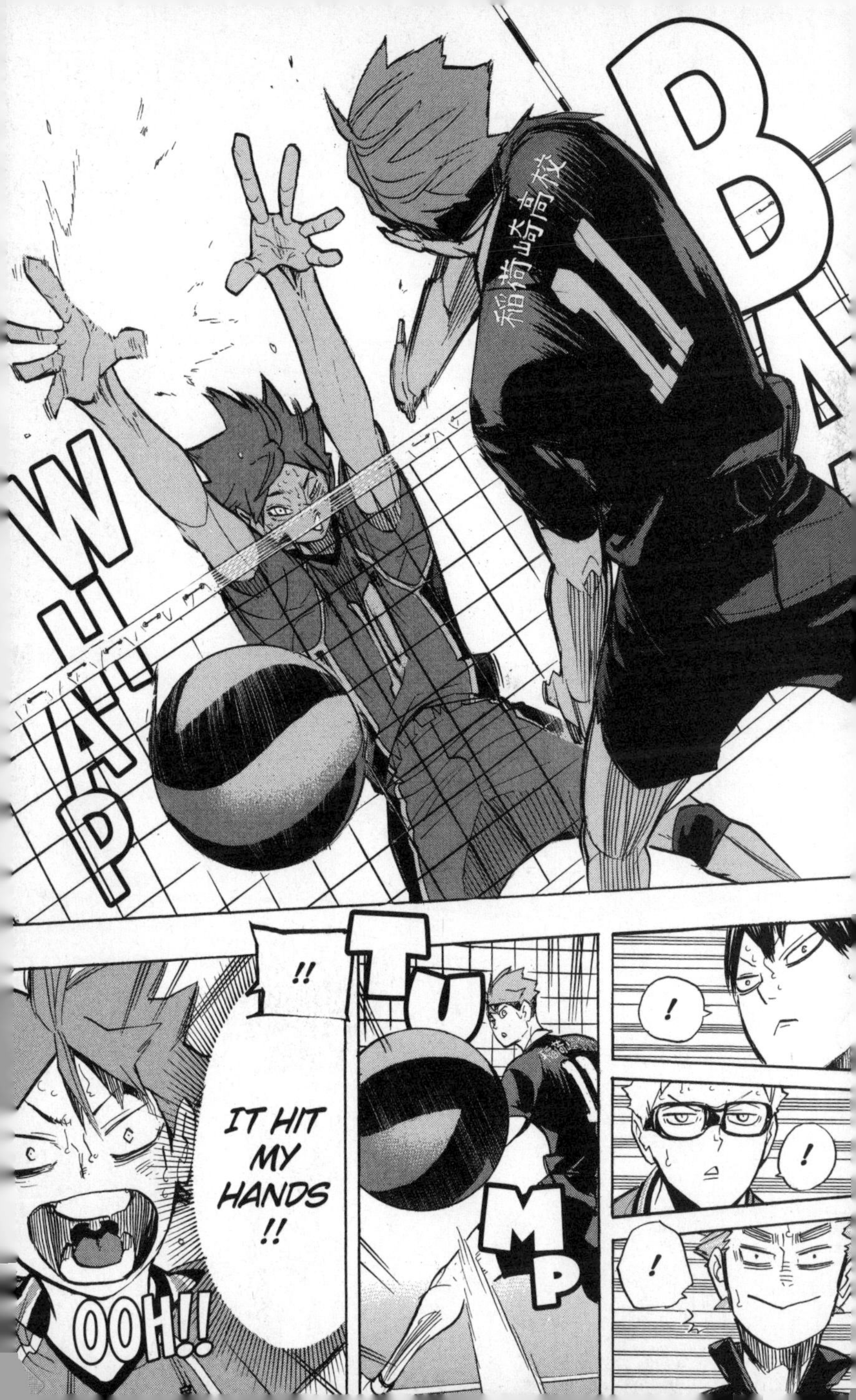

BA
WHAP
!
!
!
!!
TU
MP
IT HIT MY HANDS!!
OOH!!

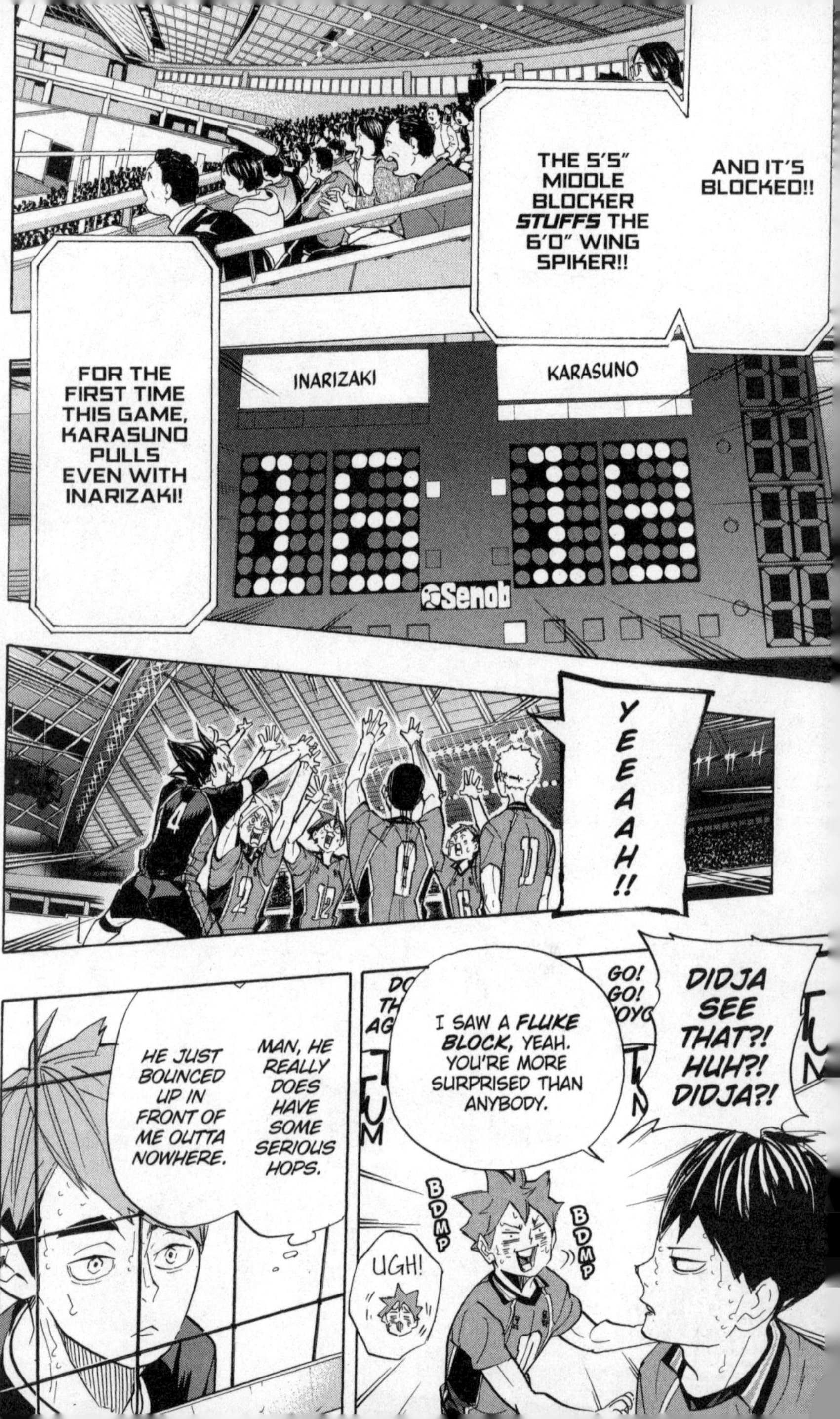
AND IT'S BLOCKED!!
THE 5'5" MIDDLE BLOCKER **STUFFS** THE 6'0" WING SPIKER!!
INARIZAKI
KARASUNO
Senob
FOR THE FIRST TIME THIS GAME, KARASUNO PULLS EVEN WITH INARIZAKI!
YEEAAAH!!
DIDJA SEE THAT?! HUH?! DIDJA?!
I SAW A **FLUKE BLOCK,** YEAH. YOU'RE MORE SURPRISED THAN ANYBODY.
BDMP
BDMP
UGH!
MAN, HE REALLY DOES HAVE SOME SERIOUS HOPS.
HE JUST BOUNCED UP IN FRONT OF ME OUTTA NOWHERE.

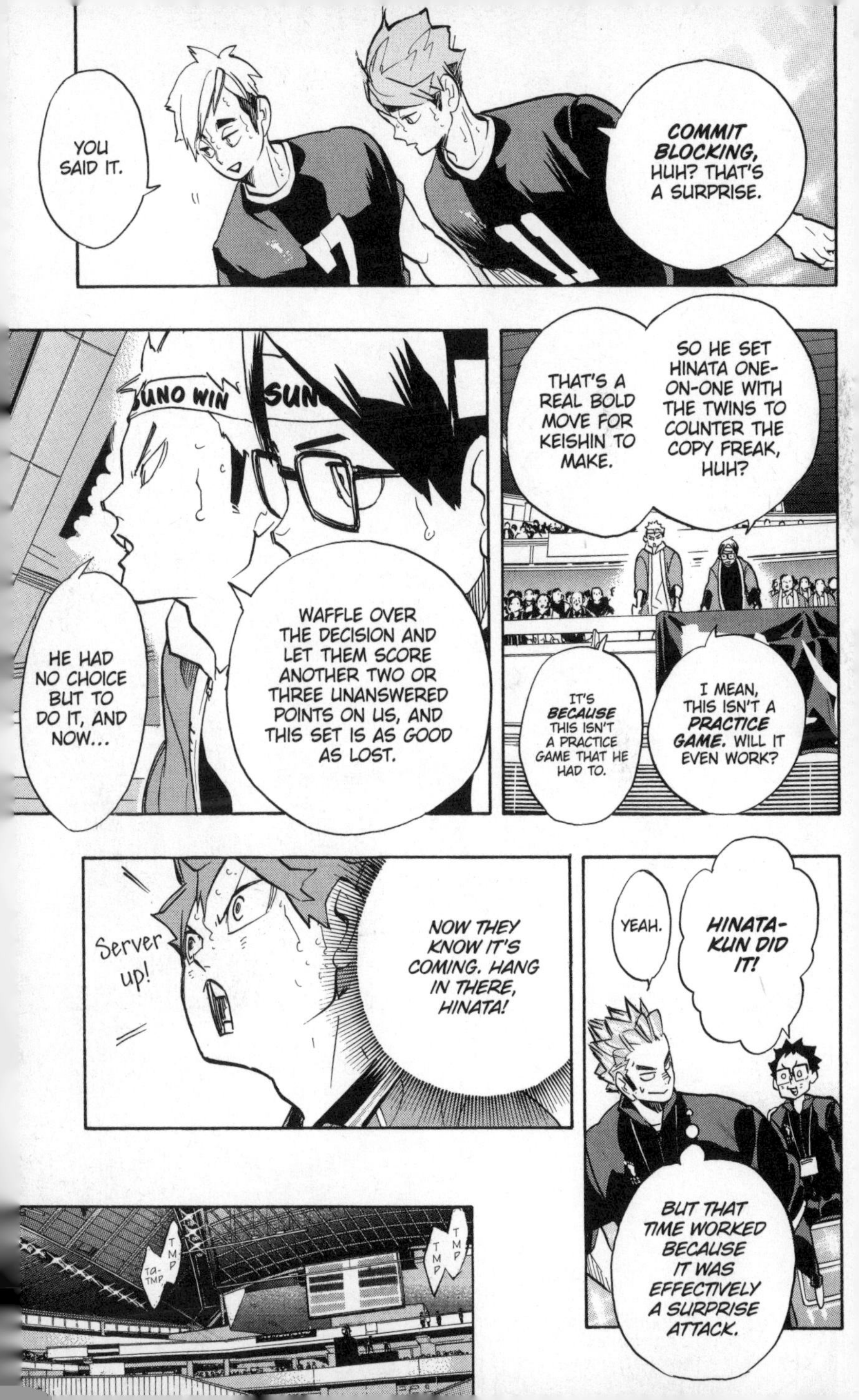
COMMIT BLOCKING, HUH? THAT'S A SURPRISE.
YOU SAID IT.
SO HE SET HINATA ONE-ON-ONE WITH THE TWINS TO COUNTER THE COPY FREAK, HUH?
THAT'S A REAL BOLD MOVE FOR KEISHIN TO MAKE.
I MEAN, THIS ISN'T A PRACTICE GAME. WILL IT EVEN WORK?
IT'S BECAUSE THIS ISN'T A PRACTICE GAME THAT HE HAD TO.
WAFFLE OVER THE DECISION AND LET THEM SCORE ANOTHER TWO OR THREE UNANSWERED POINTS ON US, AND THIS SET IS AS GOOD AS LOST.
HE HAD NO CHOICE BUT TO DO IT, AND NOW...
HINATA-KUN DID IT!
YEAH.
BUT THAT TIME WORKED BECAUSE IT WAS EFFECTIVELY A SURPRISE ATTACK.
NOW THEY KNOW IT'S COMING. HANG IN THERE, HINATA!
Server up!
TMP TMP
TA-TMP TMP

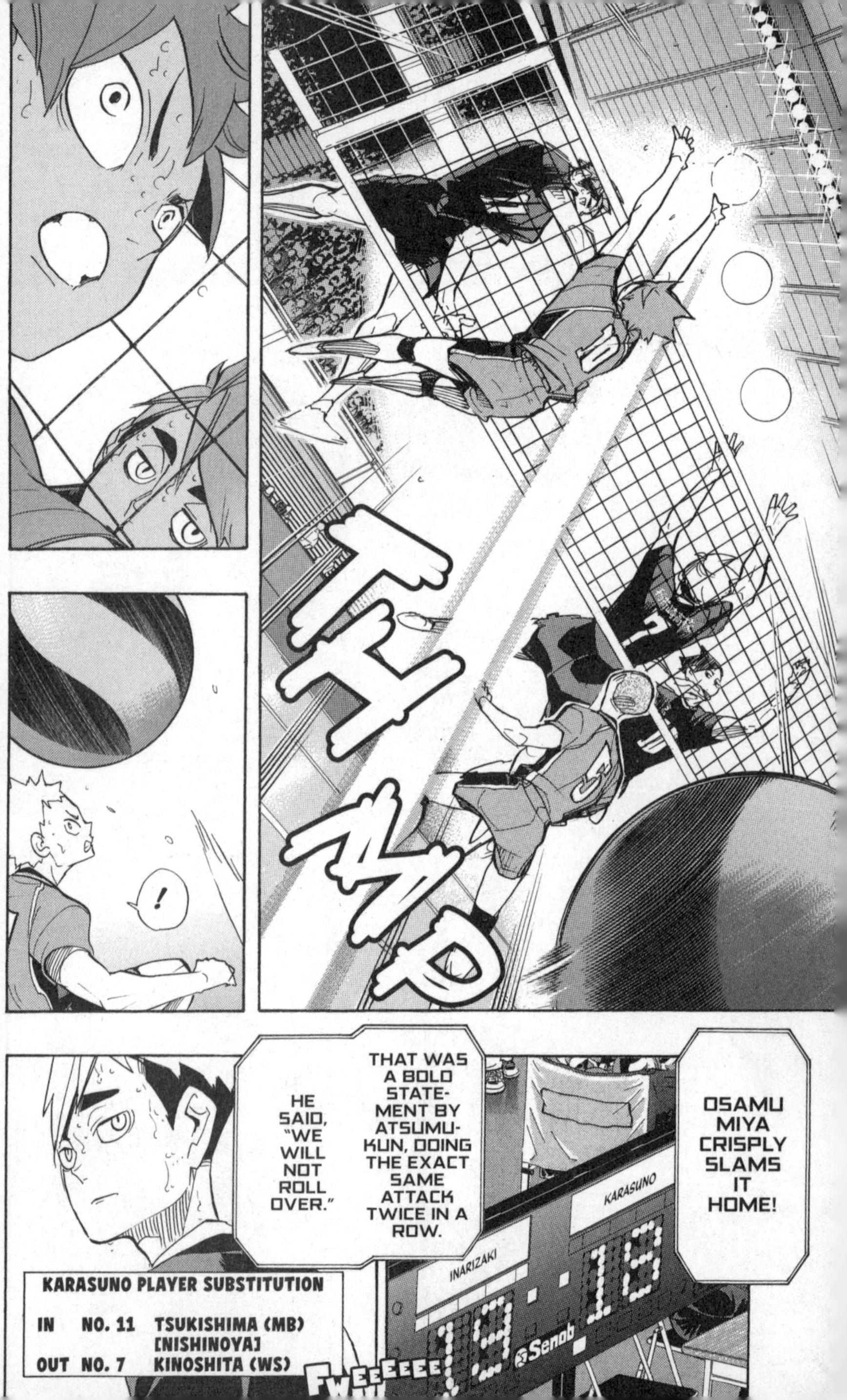
THMP
!
OSAMU MIYA CRISPLY SLAMS IT HOME!
KARASUNO
INARIZAKI
THAT WAS A BOLD STATEMENT BY ATSUMU-KUN, DOING THE EXACT SAME ATTACK TWICE IN A ROW.
HE SAID, "WE WILL NOT ROLL OVER."
KARASUNO PLAYER SUBSTITUTION
IN NO. 11 TSUKISHIMA (MB) [NISHINOYA]
OUT NO. 7 KINOSHITA (WS)
FWEEEEEEE

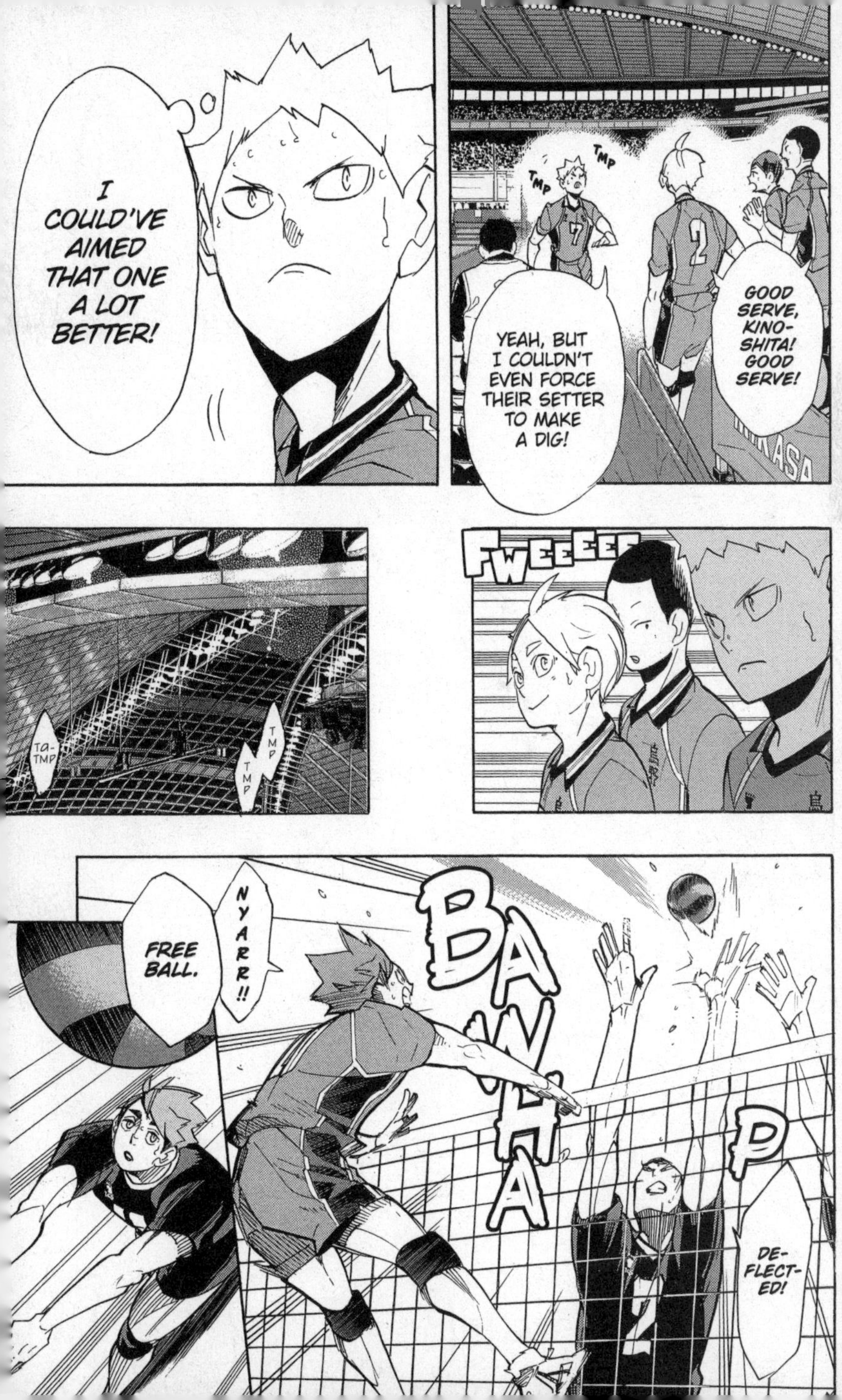
TMP
TMP
GOOD SERVE, KINOSHITA! GOOD SERVE!
YEAH, BUT I COULDN'T EVEN FORCE THEIR SETTER TO MAKE A DIG!
I COULD'VE AIMED THAT ONE A LOT BETTER!
FWEEEEE
TMP
TMP
Ta-TMP
BANHAP
NYARR!!
FREE BALL.
DE-FLECT-ED!

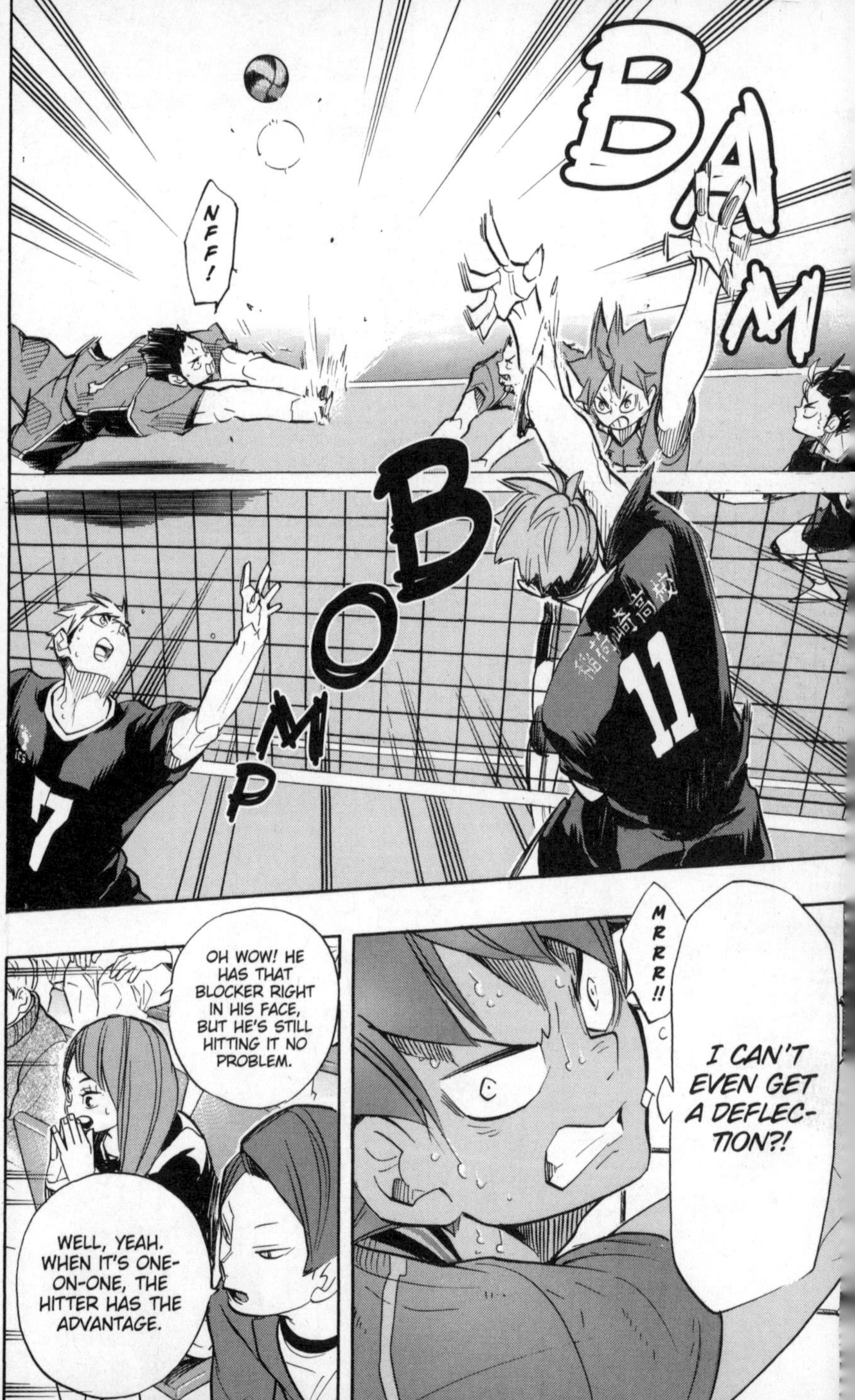
BAM
NFF!
BOMP
MRRR!!
I CAN'T EVEN GET A DEFLECTION?!
OH WOW! HE HAS THAT BLOCKER RIGHT IN HIS FACE, BUT HE'S STILL HITTING IT NO PROBLEM.
WELL, YEAH. WHEN IT'S ONE-ON-ONE, THE HITTER HAS THE ADVANTAGE.
11
7

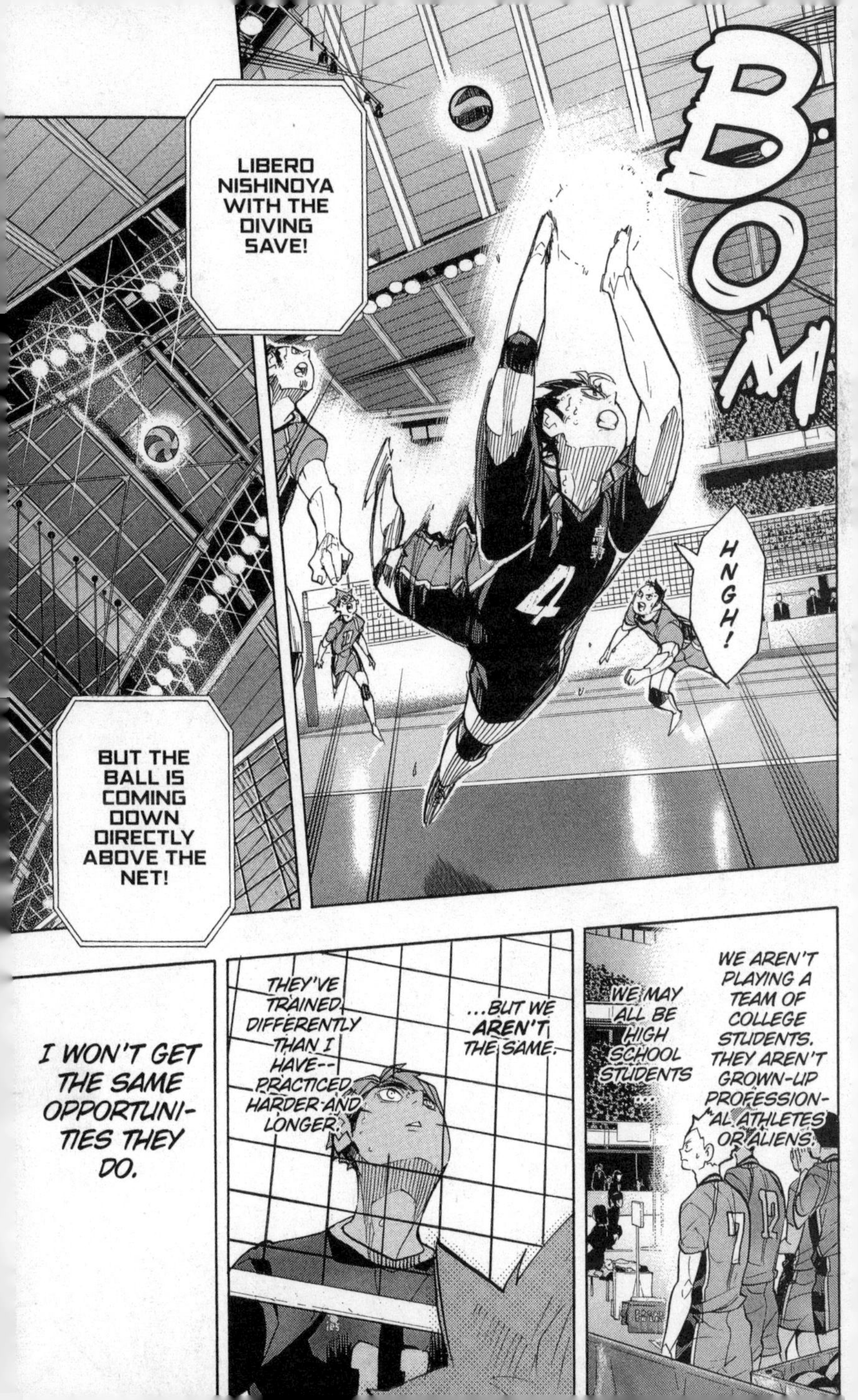
BOOM
LIBERO NISHINOYA WITH THE DIVING SAVE!
HNGH!
BUT THE BALL IS COMING DOWN DIRECTLY ABOVE THE NET!
WE AREN'T PLAYING A TEAM OF COLLEGE STUDENTS. THEY AREN'T GROWN-UP PROFESSIONAL ATHLETES OR ALIENS.
WE MAY ALL BE HIGH SCHOOL STUDENTS...
...BUT WE AREN'T THE SAME.
THEY'VE TRAINED DIFFERENTLY THAN I HAVE--PRACTICED HARDER AND LONGER.
I WON'T GET THE SAME OPPORTUNITIES THEY DO.

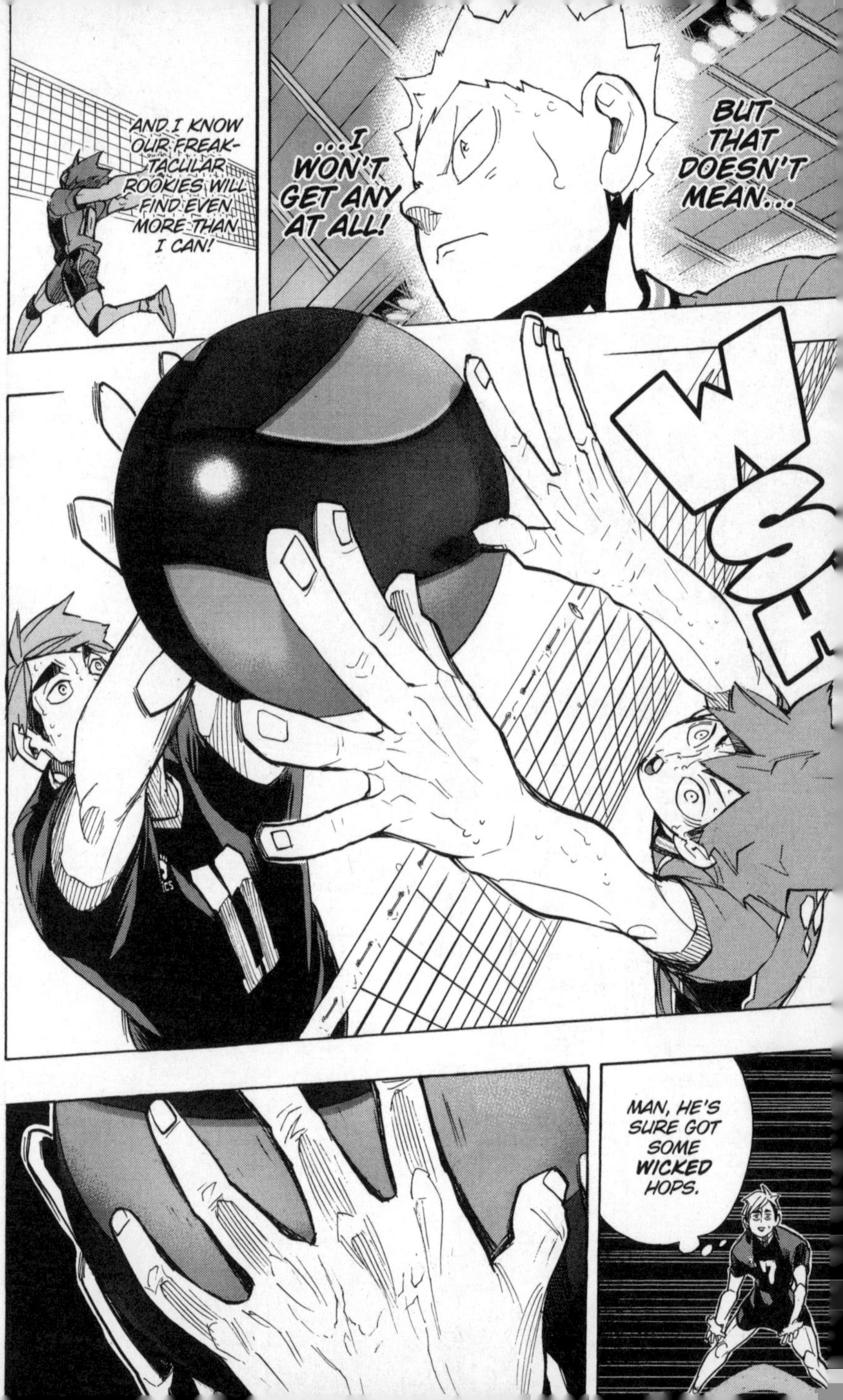
BUT THAT DOESN'T MEAN...
...I WON'T GET ANY AT ALL!
AND I KNOW OUR FREAK-TACULAR ROOKIES WILL FIND EVEN MORE THAN I CAN!
WSH
MAN, HE'S SURE GOT SOME WICKED HOPS.

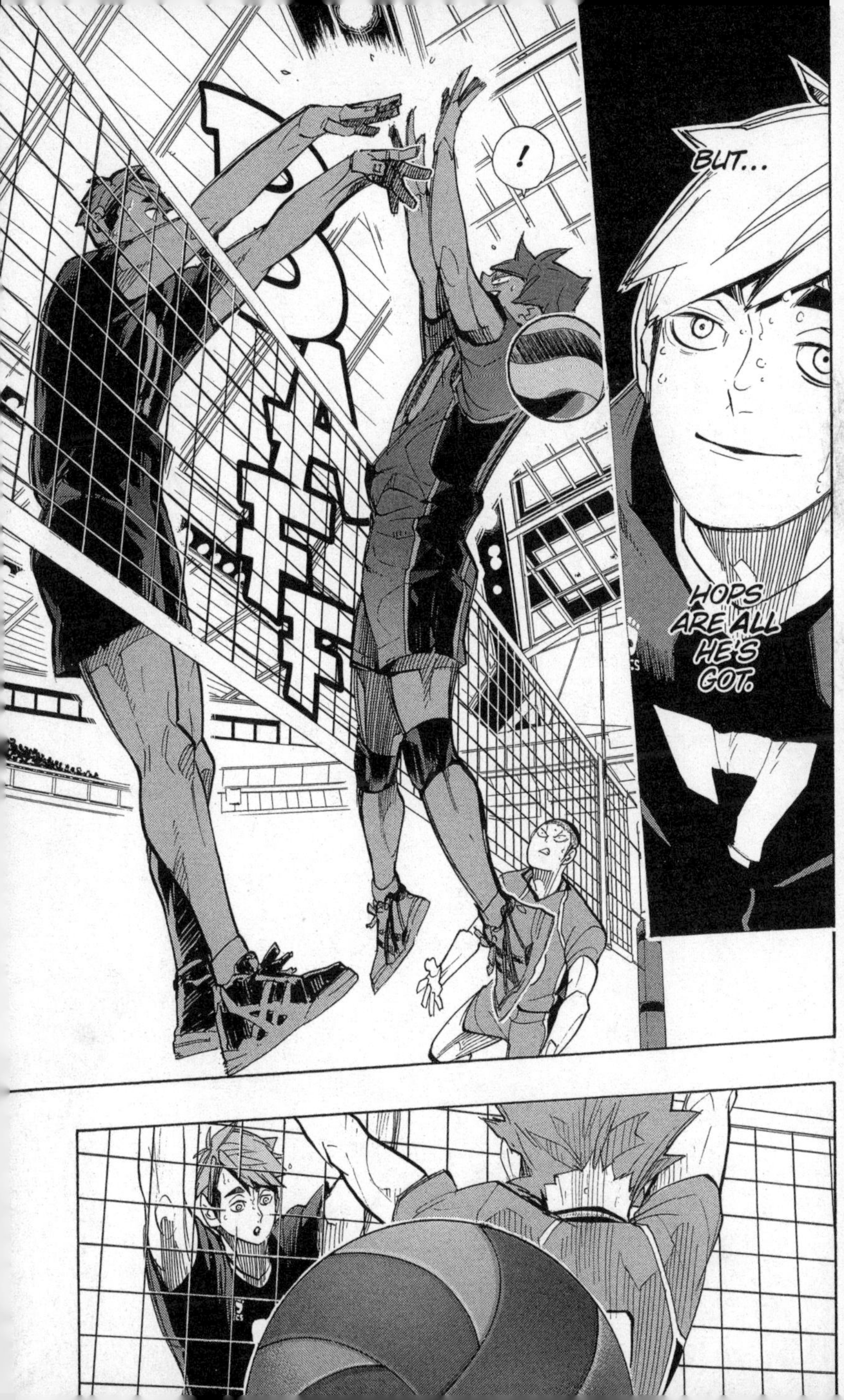
BUT...
HOPS ARE ALL HE'S GOT.
!

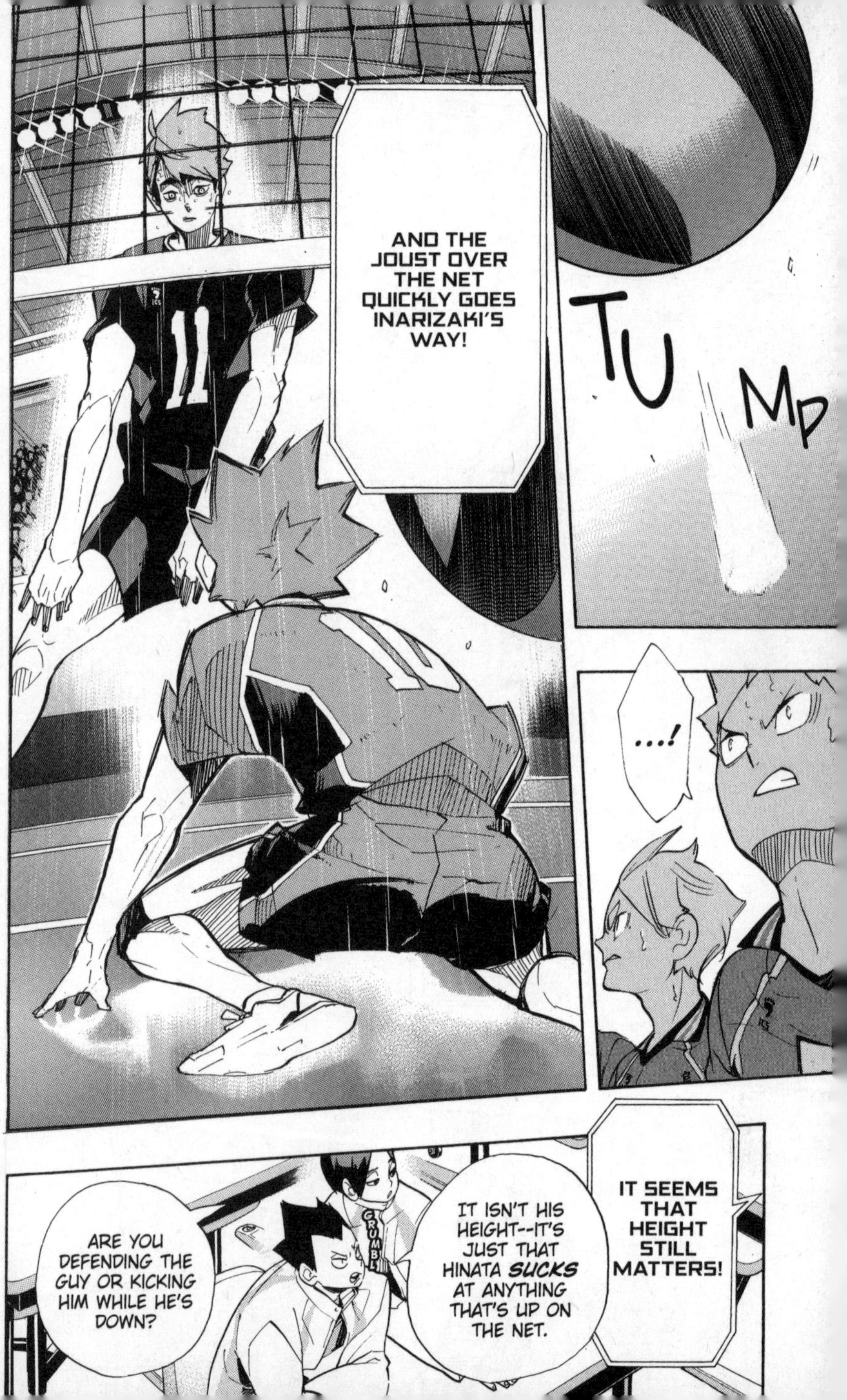
TUMP
...!
AND THE JOUST OVER THE NET QUICKLY GOES INARIZAKI'S WAY!
IT SEEMS THAT HEIGHT STILL MATTERS!
IT ISN'T HIS HEIGHT--IT'S JUST THAT HINATA ***SUCKS*** AT ANYTHING THAT'S UP ON THE NET.
GRUMBL
ARE YOU DEFENDING THE GUY OR KICKING HIM WHILE HE'S DOWN?

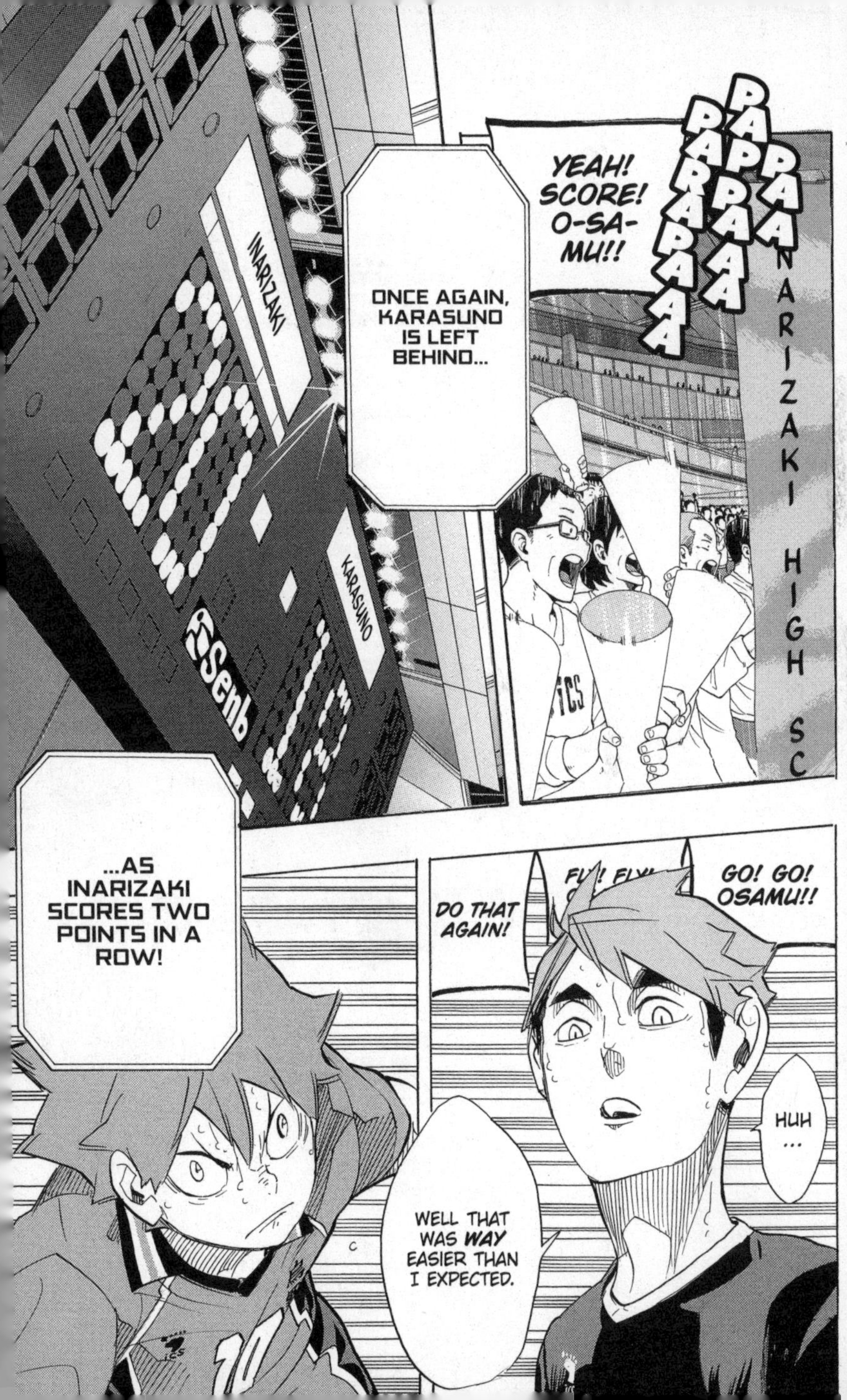
PAPAPAA PAPAPAAA PAPAPAAAA
YEAH! SCORE! O-SA-MU!!
INARIZAKI HIGH SC
ONCE AGAIN, KARASUNO IS LEFT BEHIND...
INARIZAKI
KARASUNO
Senb
GO! GO! OSAMU!!
DO THAT AGAIN!
HUH ...
WELL THAT WAS *WAY* EASIER THAN I EXPECTED.
...AS INARIZAKI SCORES TWO POINTS IN A ROW!

OSAMU MIYA

**INARIZAKI HIGH SCHOOL
CLASS 2-1**

**POSITION:
WING SPIKER**

HEIGHT: 6'0"

**WEIGHT: 164 LBS.
(AS OF JANUARY, 2ND YEAR
OF HIGH SCHOOL)**

BIRTHDAY: OCTOBER 5

**FAVORITE FOOD:
FOOD**

**CURRENT WORRY:
HE'S NOT SURE HE'LL BE
ABLE TO DECIDE WHAT HE
WANTS TO HAVE FOR HIS
LAST MEAL EVER.**

**ABILITY PARAMETERS
(5-POINT SCALE)**

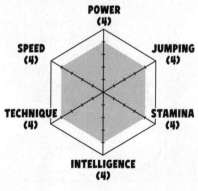

POWER
(4)

JUMPING
(4)

SPEED
(4)

STAMINA
(4)

TECHNIQUE
(4)

INTELLIGENCE
(4)

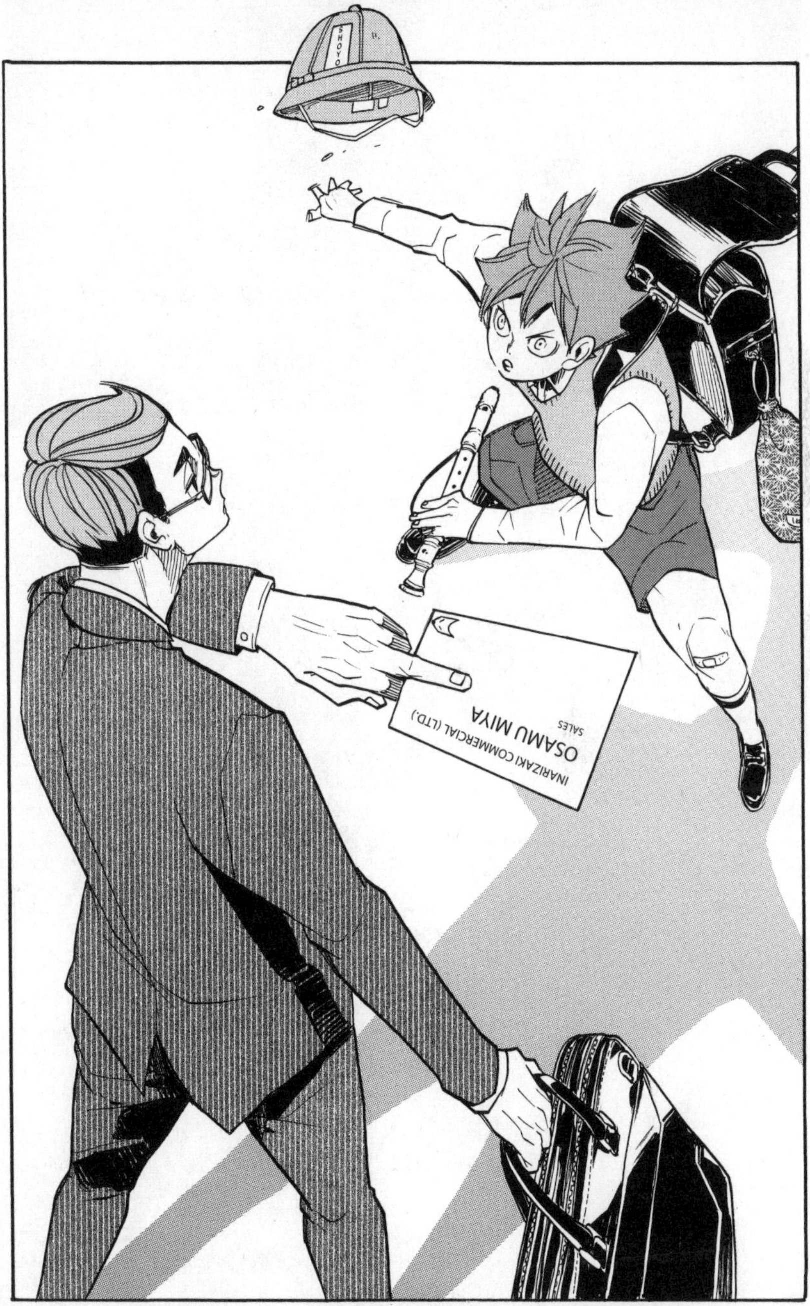
INARIZAKI COMMERCIAL (LTD.)
OSAMU MIYA
SALES

CHAPTER 258: Experience Levels

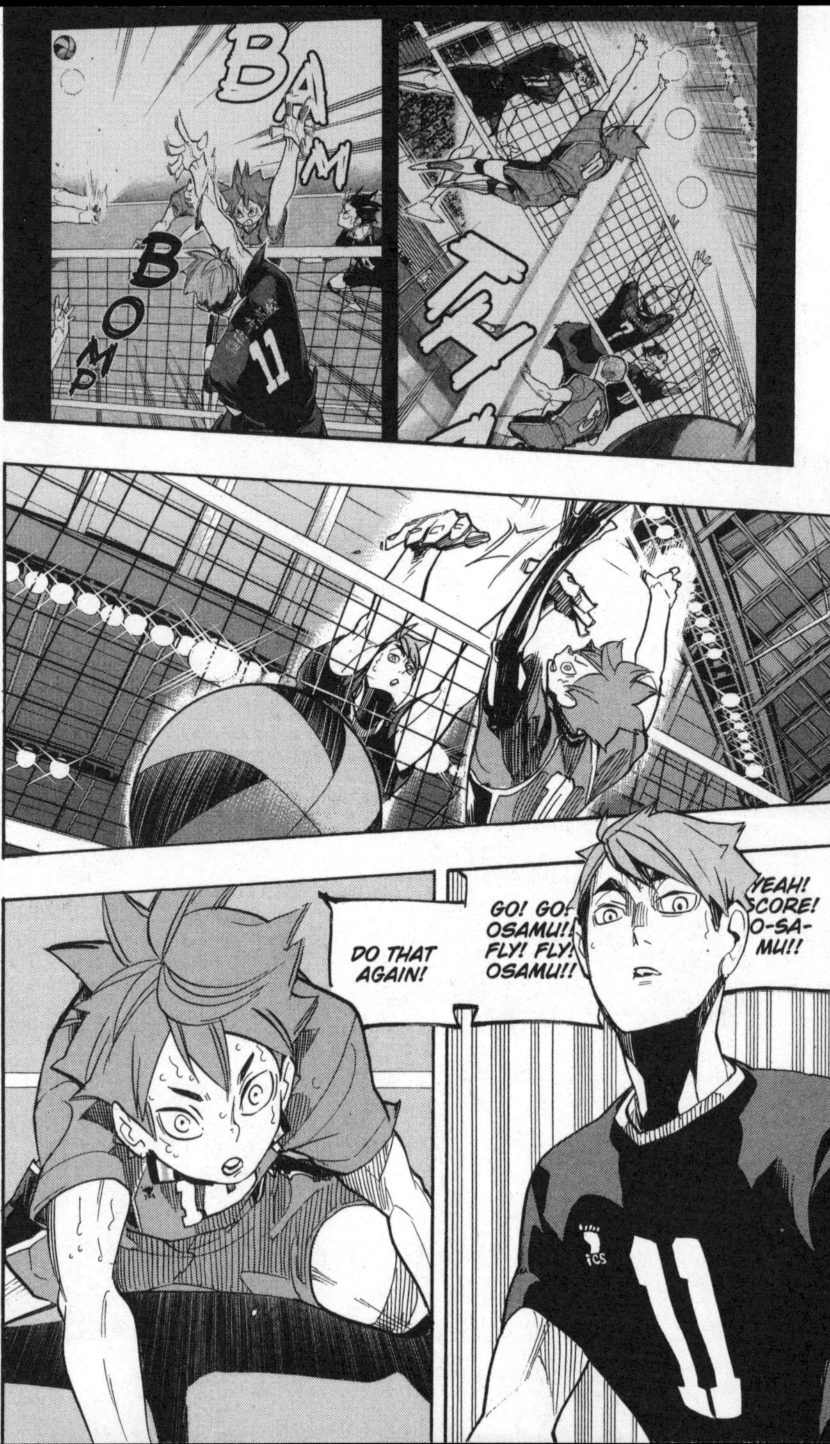
TH
BAM
BOMP
YEAH! SCORE! O-SA-MU!!
GO! GO! OSAMU!! FLY! FLY! OSAMU!!
DO THAT AGAIN!

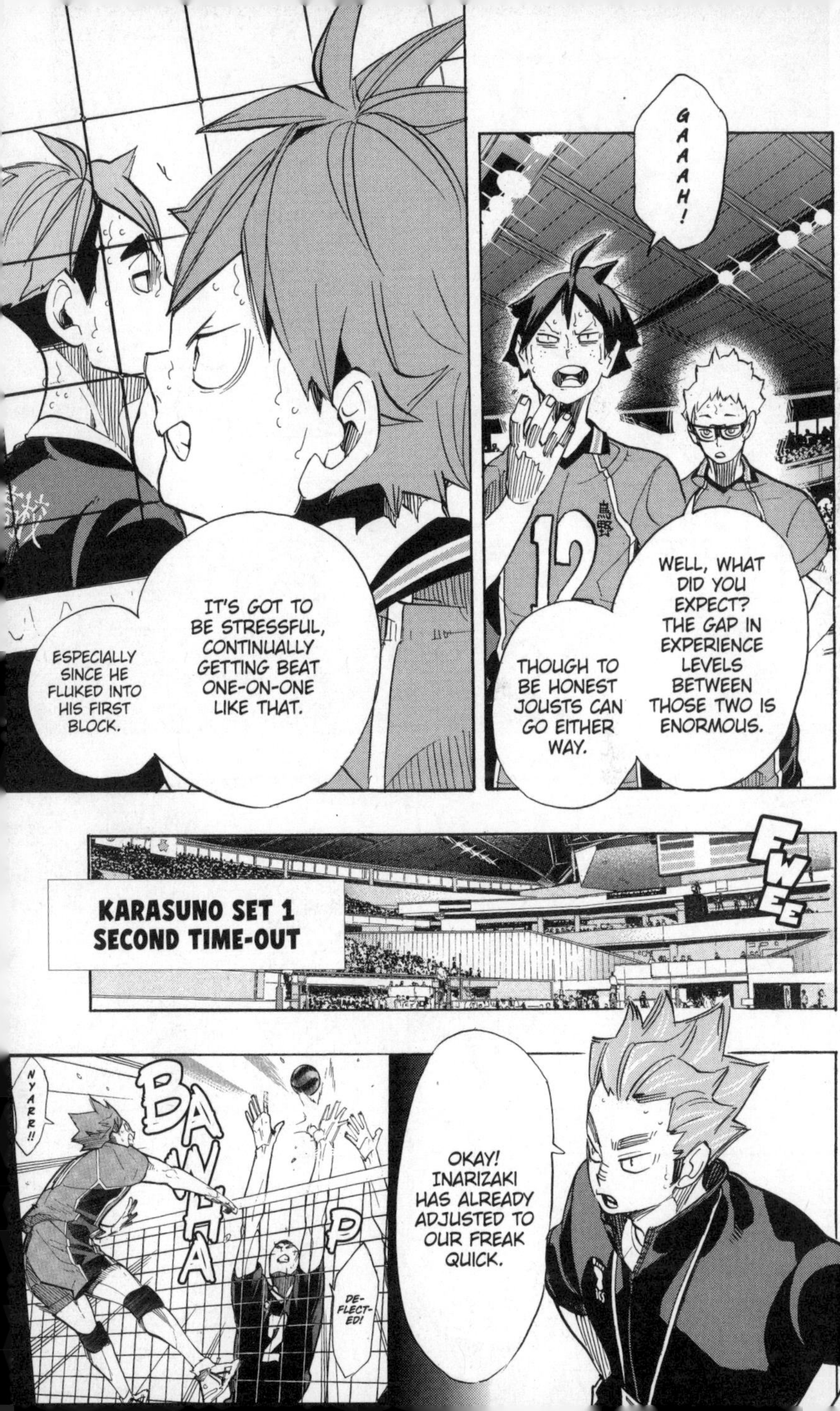
GAAAH!
WELL, WHAT DID YOU EXPECT? THE GAP IN EXPERIENCE LEVELS BETWEEN THOSE TWO IS ENORMOUS.
THOUGH TO BE HONEST JOUSTS CAN GO EITHER WAY.
IT'S GOT TO BE STRESSFUL, CONTINUALLY GETTING BEAT ONE-ON-ONE LIKE THAT.
ESPECIALLY SINCE HE FLUKED INTO HIS FIRST BLOCK.
FWEE
KARASUNO SET 1 SECOND TIME-OUT
OKAY! INARIZAKI HAS ALREADY ADJUSTED TO OUR FREAK QUICK.
NYARR!!
BAWHAP
DE-FLECT-ED!

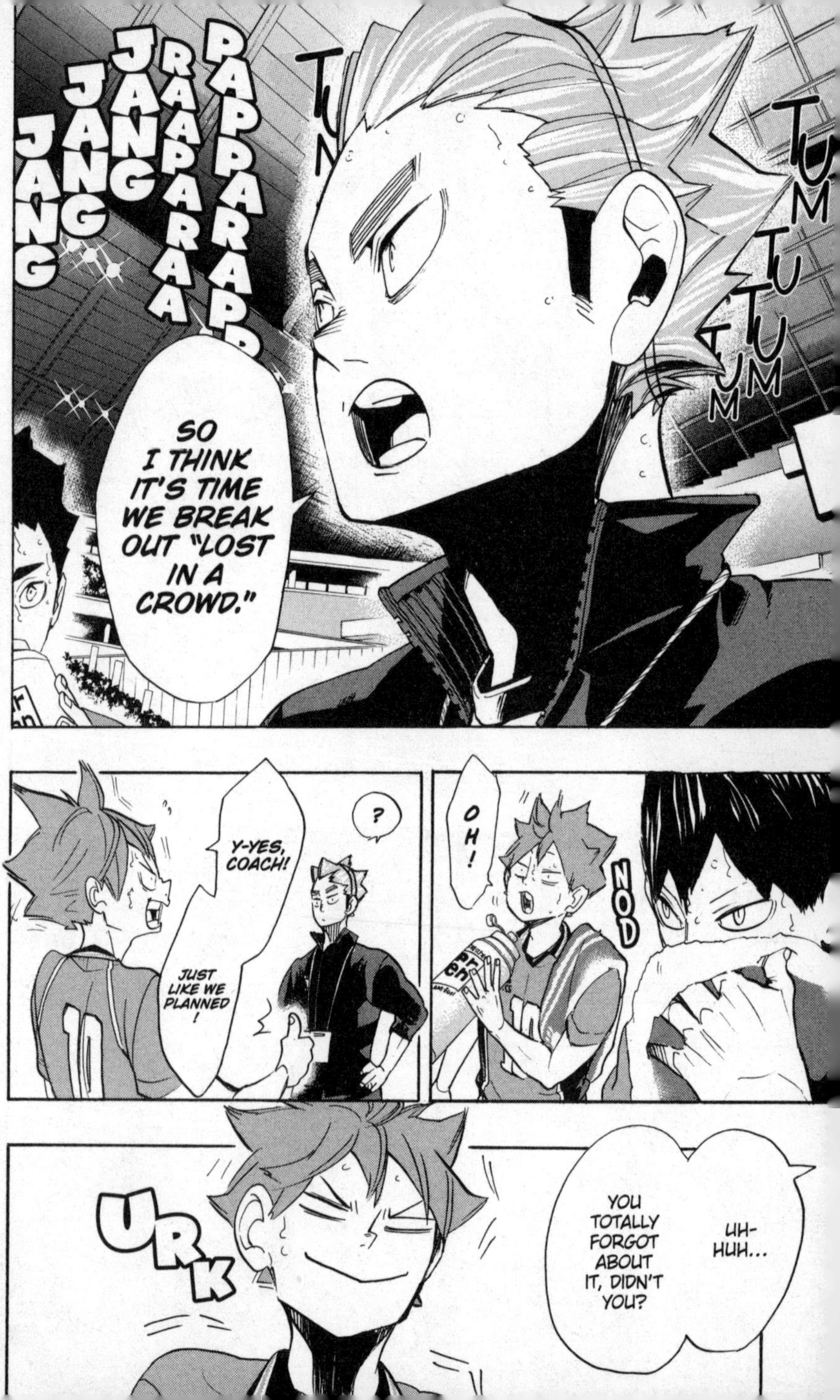
TUM TUM TUM TUM
TUN
PAPPARAPP
RAAPARAA
JANGANG
JANGANG
JANG
SO I THINK IT'S TIME WE BREAK OUT "LOST IN A CROWD."
NOD
OH!
?
Y-YES, COACH!
JUST LIKE WE PLANNED!
YOU TOTALLY FORGOT ABOUT IT, DIDN'T YOU?
UH-HUH...
URK

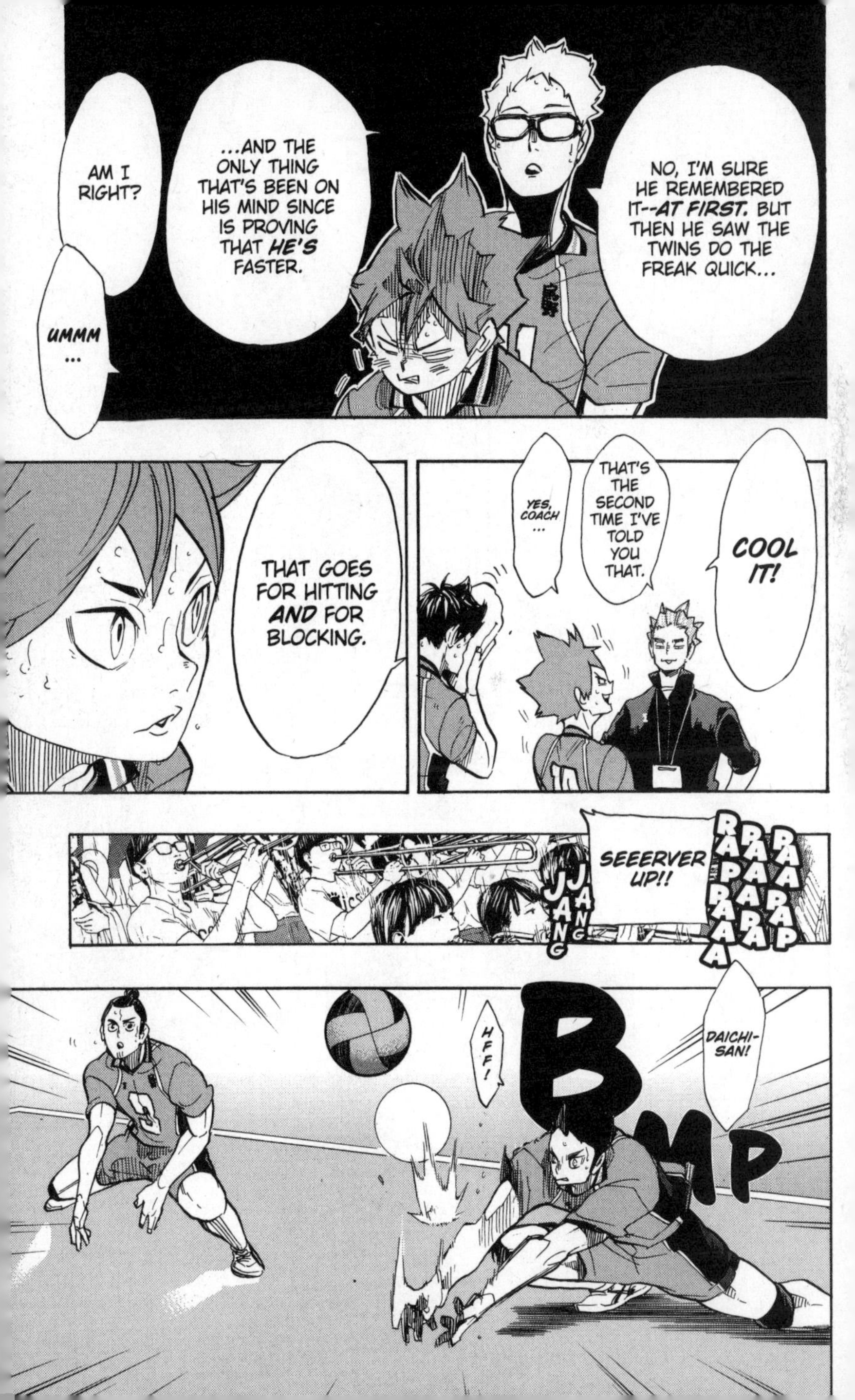
NO, I'M SURE HE REMEMBERED IT--*AT FIRST.* BUT THEN HE SAW THE TWINS DO THE FREAK QUICK...
...AND THE ONLY THING THAT'S BEEN ON HIS MIND SINCE IS PROVING THAT *HE'S* FASTER.
AM I RIGHT?
UMMM...
COOL IT!
THAT'S THE SECOND TIME I'VE TOLD YOU THAT.
YES, COACH...
THAT GOES FOR HITTING *AND* FOR BLOCKING.
PAAPAP
PAAAPAA
RAPAAAA
SEEERVER UP!!
JANG
JANG
DAICHI-SAN!
BMP
HFF!

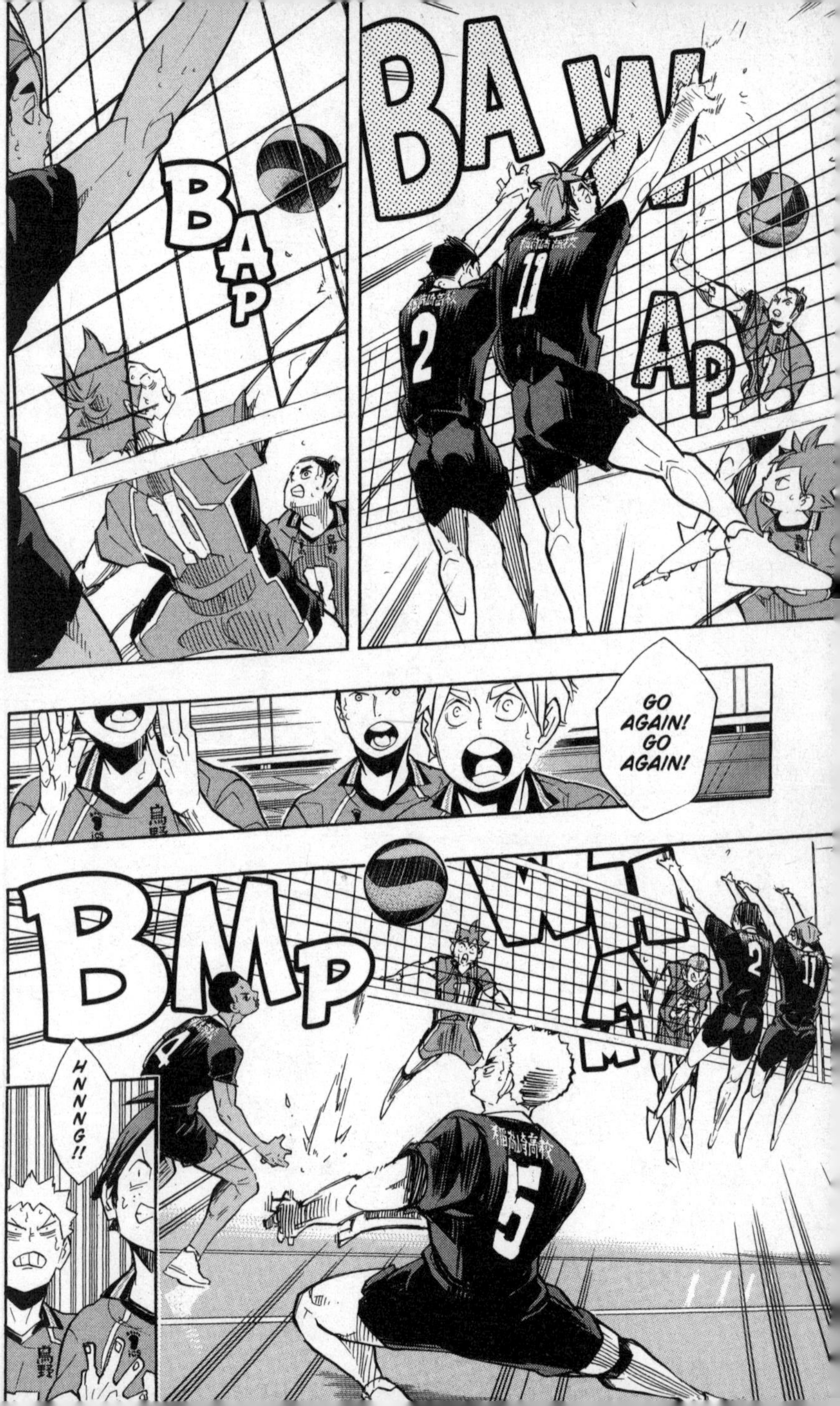
BAW
AP
BAP
GO AGAIN! GO AGAIN!
BMP
HNNNG!!

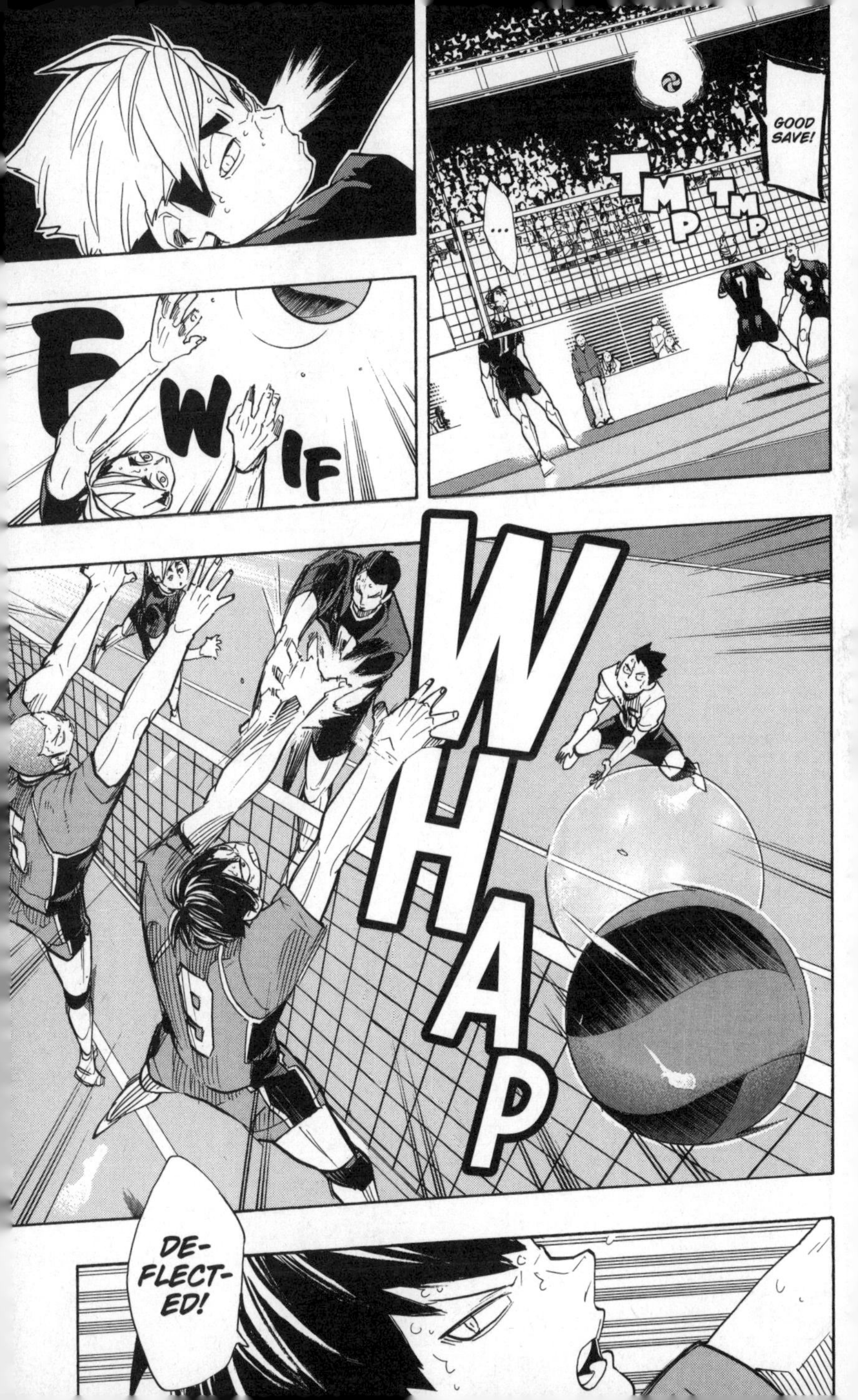
GOOD SAVE!
TMP TMP
...
FWIF
WHAP
DE-FLECT-ED!

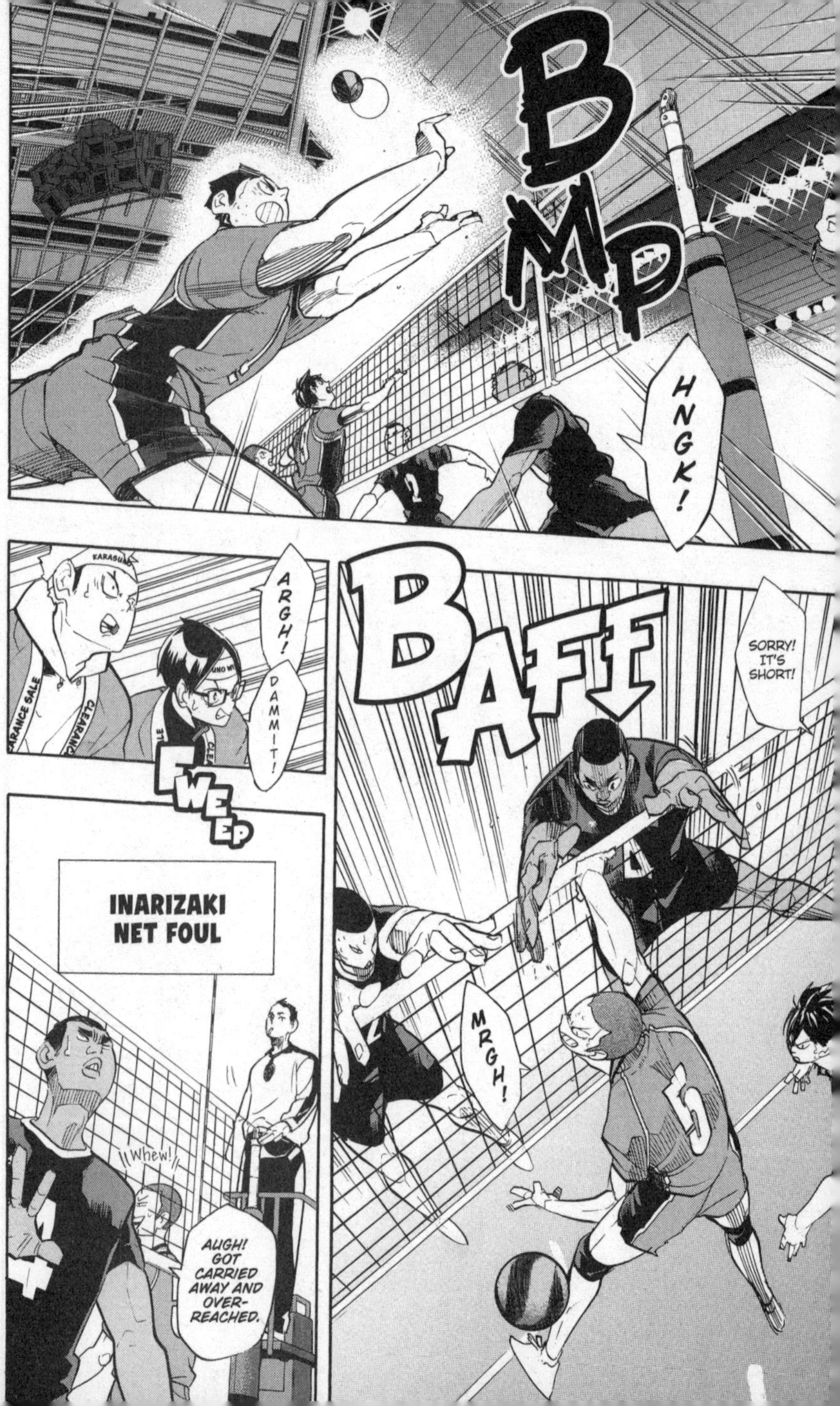
BMP
HNGK!
SORRY! IT'S SHORT!
BAFF
MRGH!
ARGH!
DAMMIT!
FWEEP
INARIZAKI NET FOUL
Whew!
AUGH! GOT CARRIED AWAY AND OVER-REACHED.

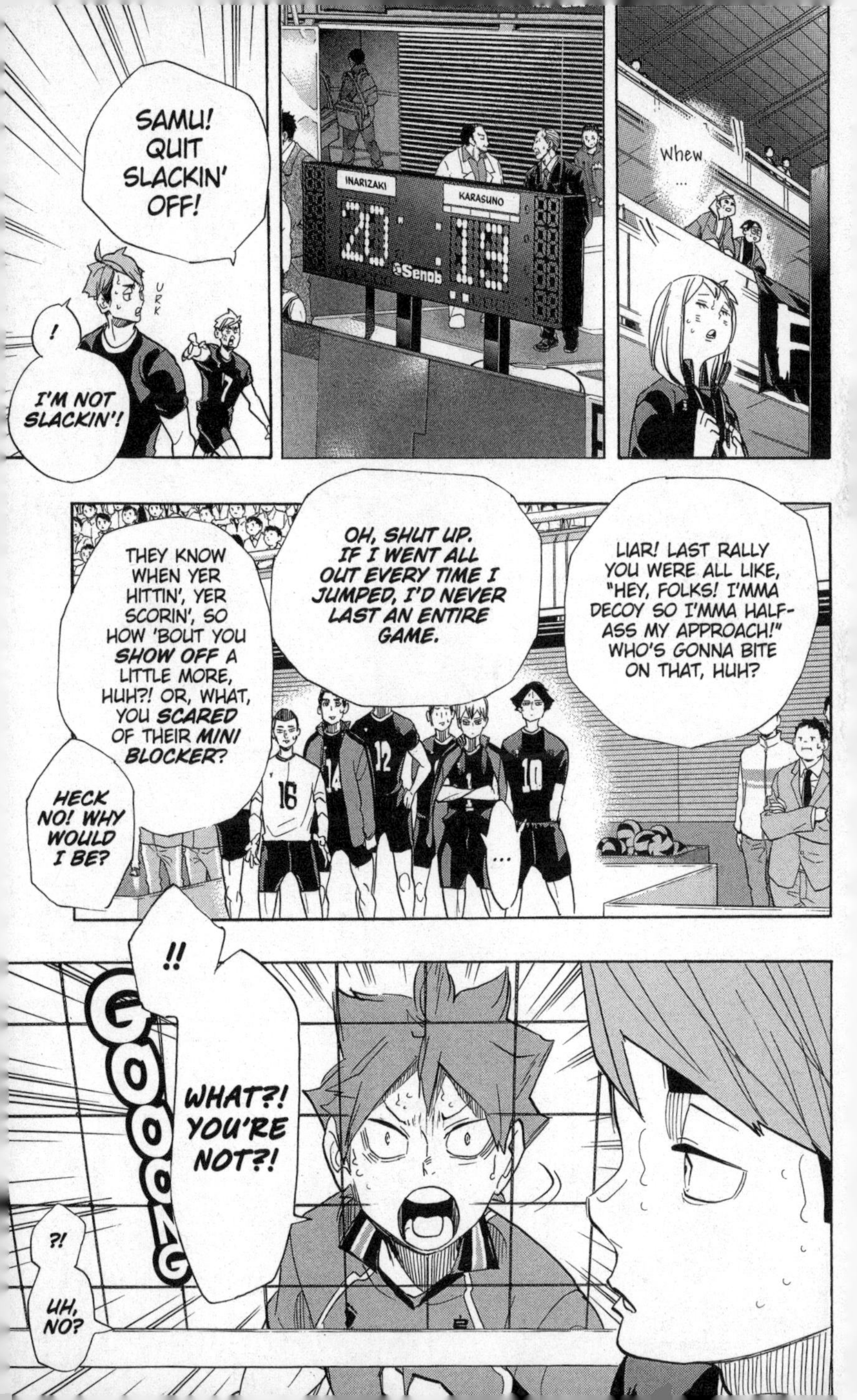
Whew
...
INARIZAKI
KARASUNO
20
19
Senob
SAMU! QUIT SLACKIN' OFF!
URK
!
I'M NOT SLACKIN'!
LIAR! LAST RALLY YOU WERE ALL LIKE, "HEY, FOLKS! I'MMA DECOY SO I'MMA HALF-ASS MY APPROACH!" WHO'S GONNA BITE ON THAT, HUH?
OH, SHUT UP. IF I WENT ALL OUT EVERY TIME I JUMPED, I'D NEVER LAST AN ENTIRE GAME.
THEY KNOW WHEN YER HITTIN', YER SCORIN', SO HOW 'BOUT YOU SHOW OFF A LITTLE MORE, HUH?! OR, WHAT, YOU SCARED OF THEIR MINI BLOCKER?
HECK NO! WHY WOULD I BE?
...
!!
WHAT?! YOU'RE NOT?!
GOOOONG
?!
UH, NO?

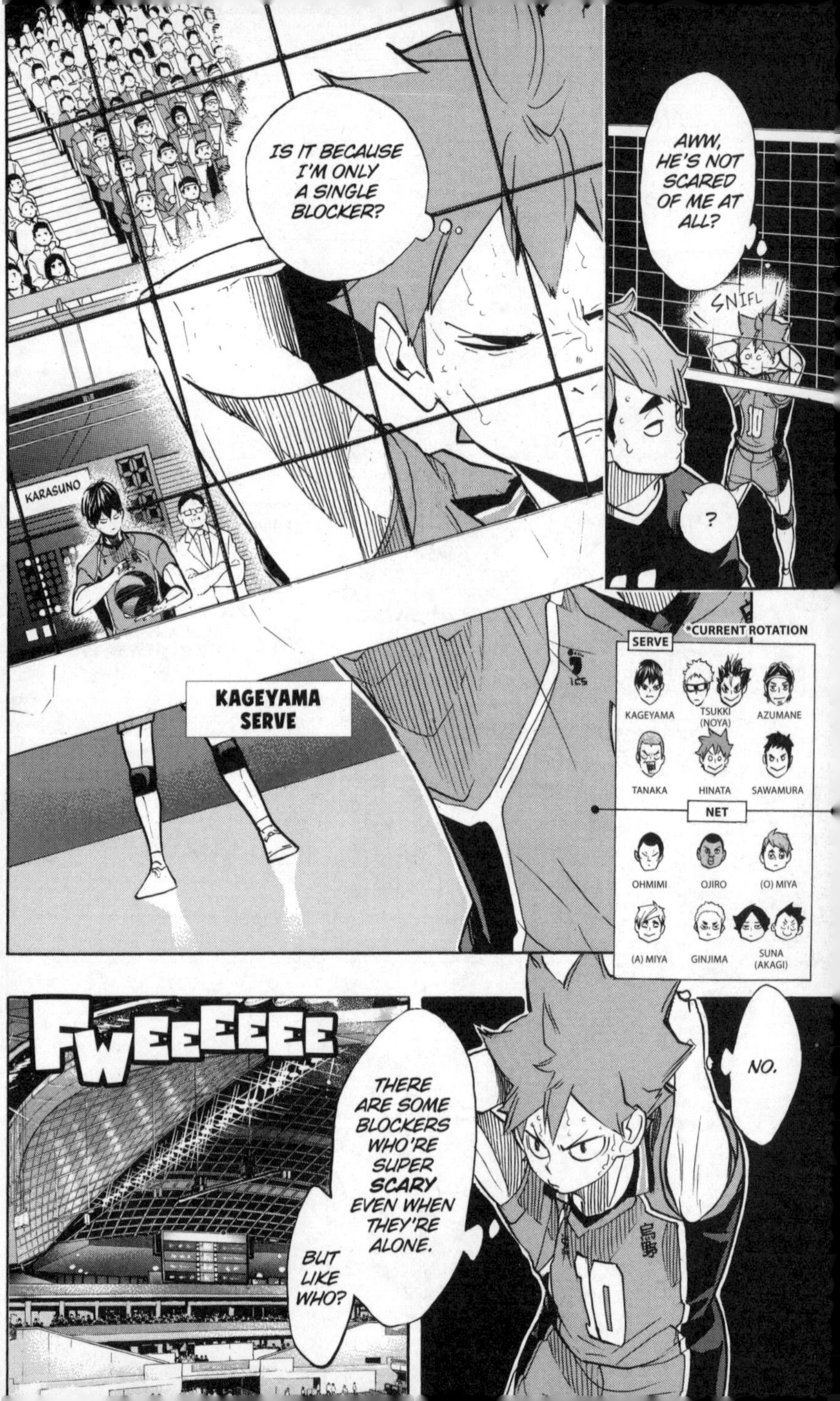
AWW, HE'S NOT SCARED OF ME AT ALL?
SNIFL
?
IS IT BECAUSE I'M ONLY A SINGLE BLOCKER?
KARASUNO
KAGEYAMA SERVE
*CURRENT ROTATION
SERVE
KAGEYAMA
TSUKKI (NOYA)
AZUMANE
TANAKA
HINATA
SAWAMURA
NET
OHMIMI
OJIRO
(O) MIYA
(A) MIYA
GINJIMA
SUNA (AKAGI)
NO.
THERE ARE SOME BLOCKERS WHO'RE SUPER SCARY EVEN WHEN THEY'RE ALONE.
BUT LIKE WHO?
FWEEEEEE

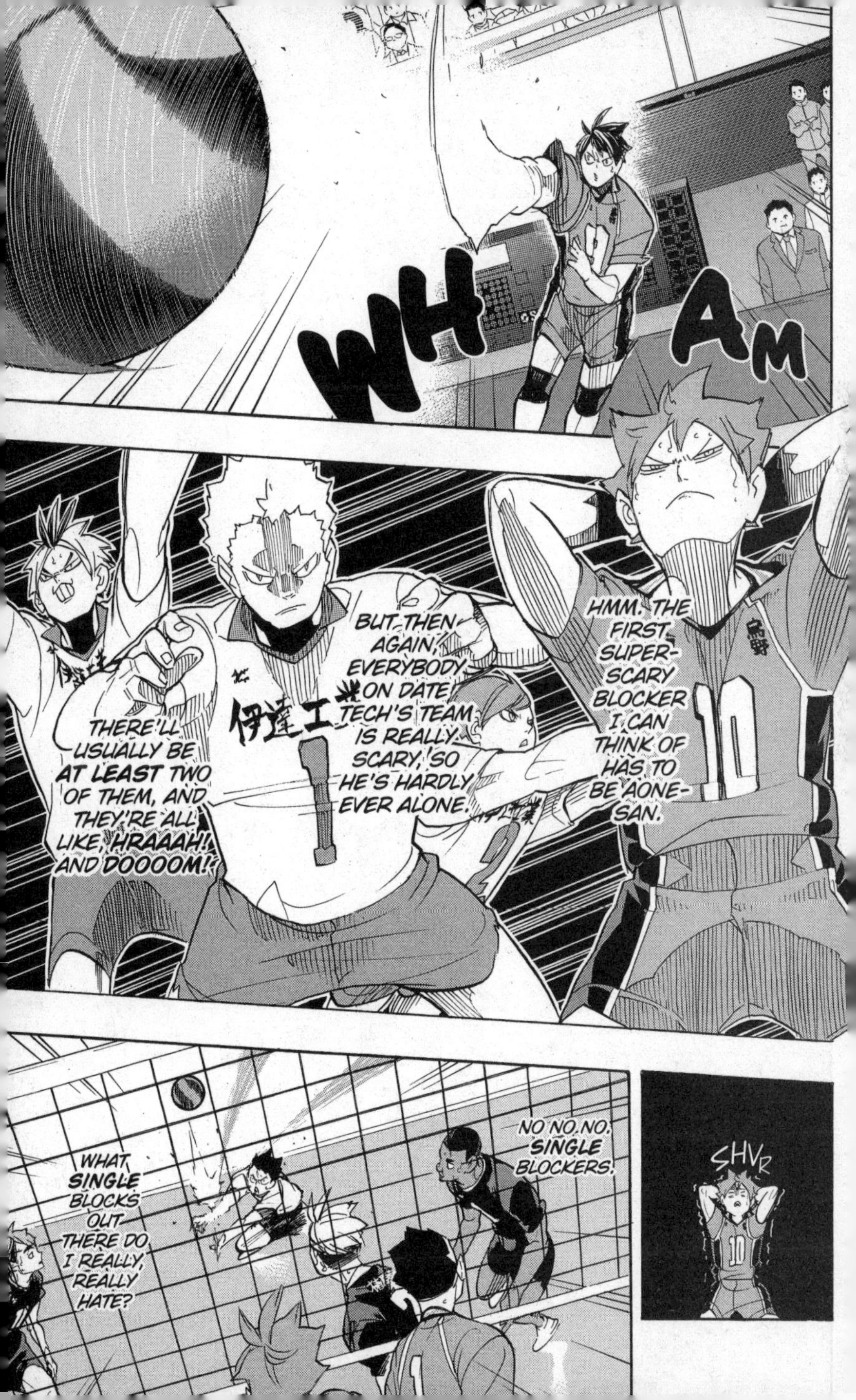
WHAM
HMM. THE FIRST SUPER-SCARY BLOCKER I CAN THINK OF HAS TO BE AONE-SAN.
BUT THEN AGAIN, EVERYBODY ON DATE TECH'S TEAM IS REALLY SCARY, SO HE'S HARDLY EVER ALONE.
THERE'LL USUALLY BE **AT LEAST** TWO OF THEM, AND THEY'RE ALL LIKE, **HRAAAH!** AND **DOOOOM!**
SHVR
NO NO NO. **SINGLE** BLOCKERS.
WHAT **SINGLE** BLOCKS OUT THERE DO I REALLY, REALLY HATE?

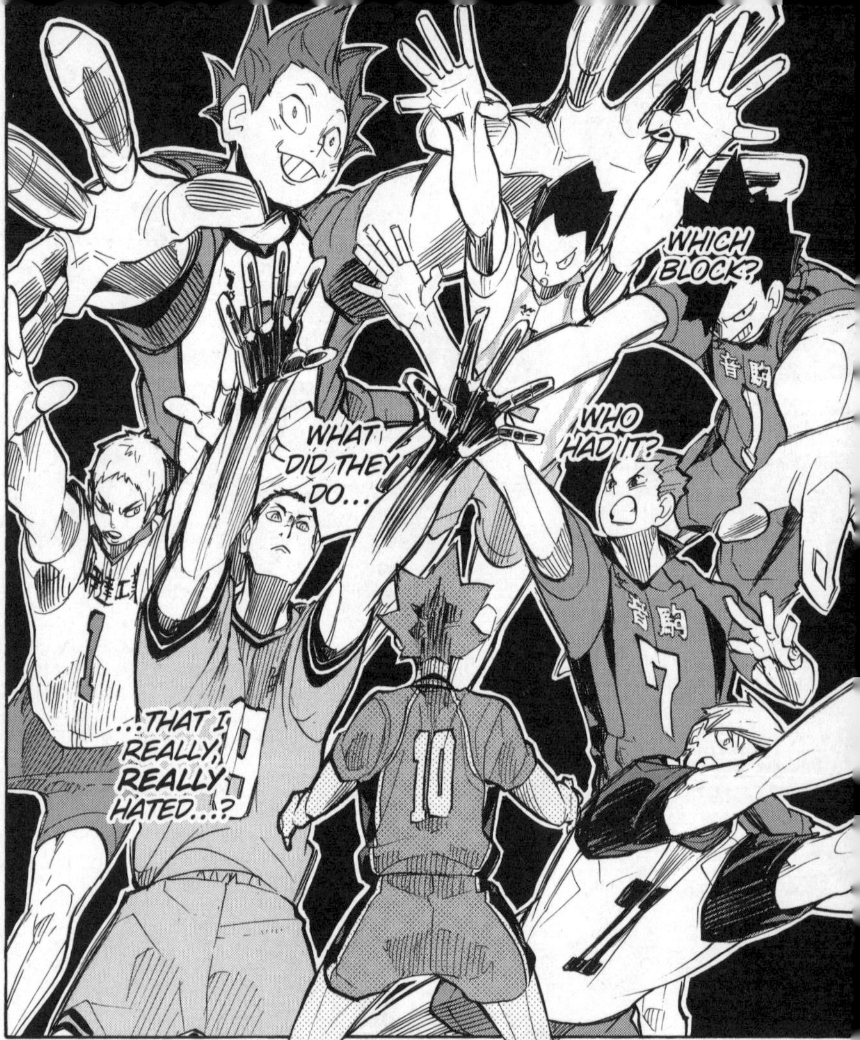
WHICH BLOCK?
WHO HAD IT?
WHAT DID THEY DO...
...THAT I REALLY, REALLY HATED...?

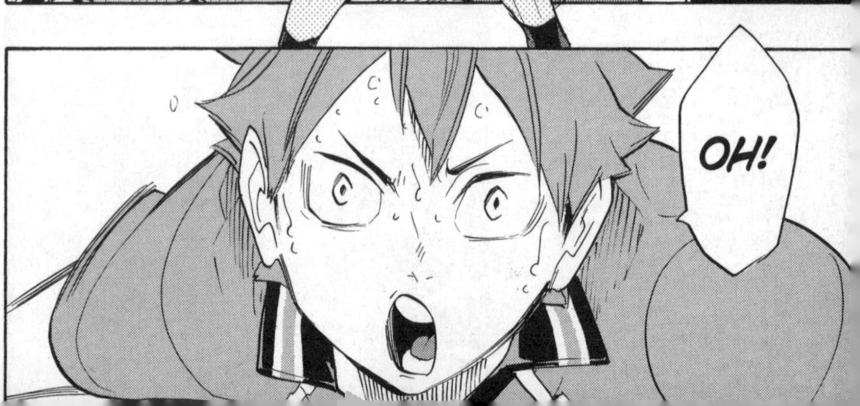
OH!

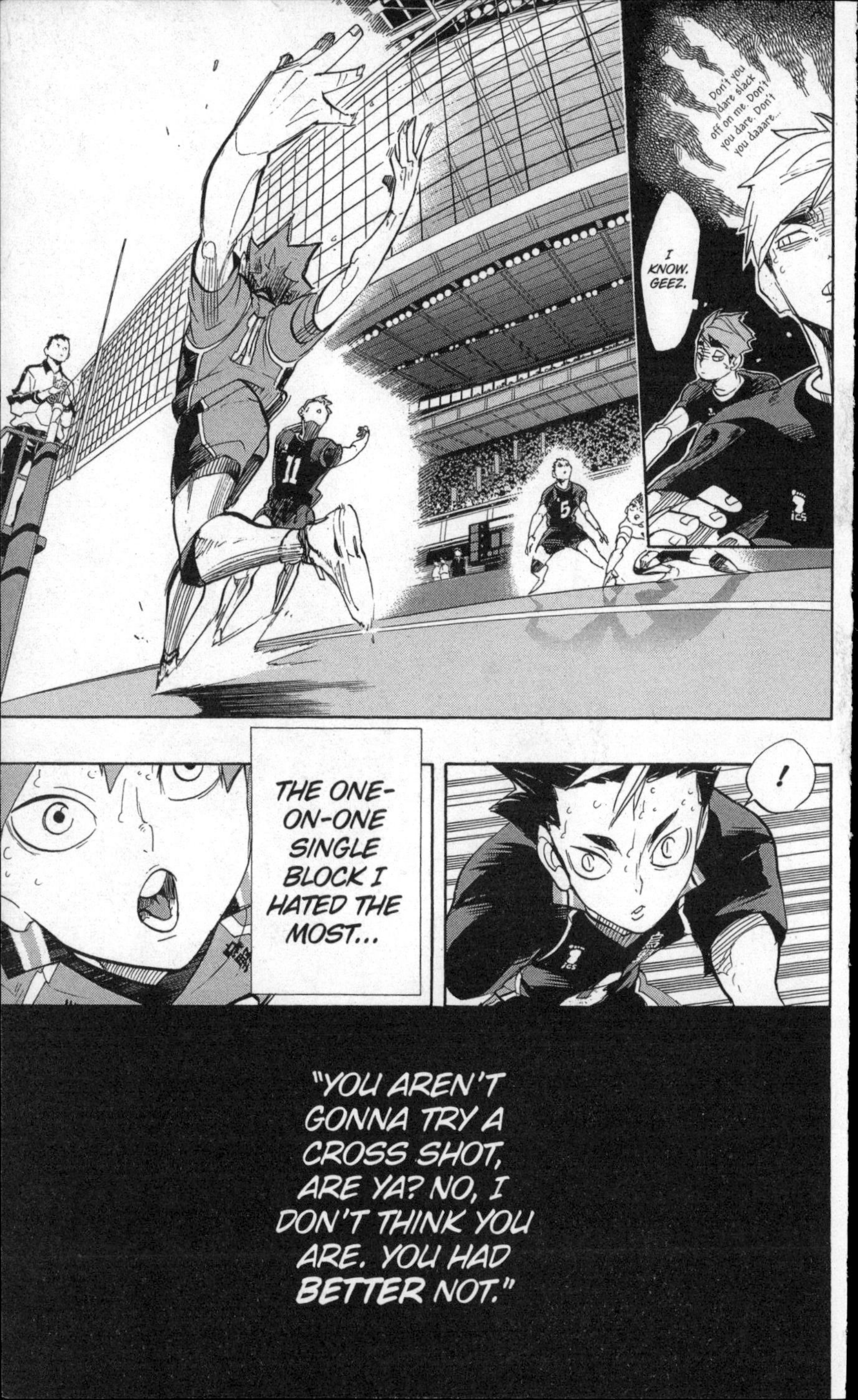
Don't you dare slack off on me. Don't you dare. Don't you daaare...
I KNOW. GEEZ.
!
THE ONE-ON-ONE SINGLE BLOCK I HATED THE MOST...
"YOU AREN'T GONNA TRY A CROSS SHOT, ARE YA? NO, I DON'T THINK YOU ARE. YOU HAD BETTER NOT."

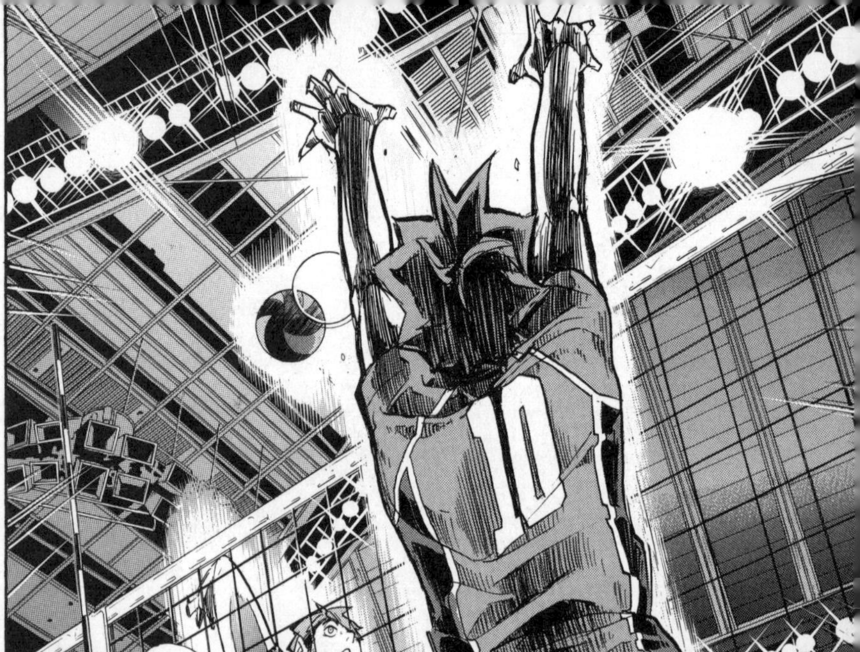
!
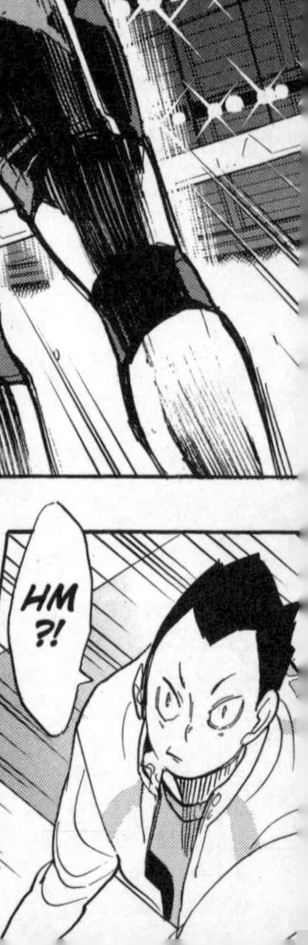
HM ?!
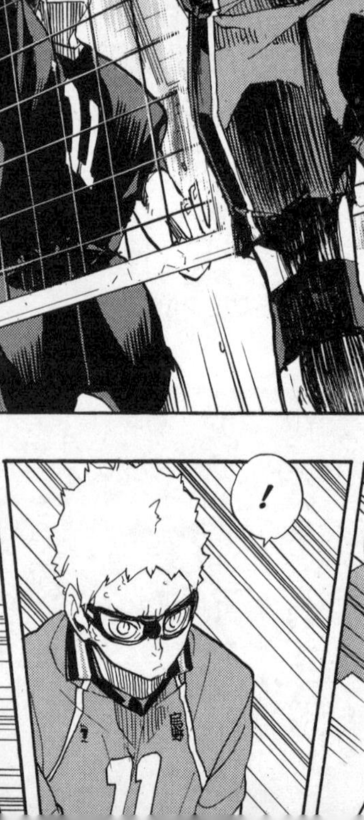
!
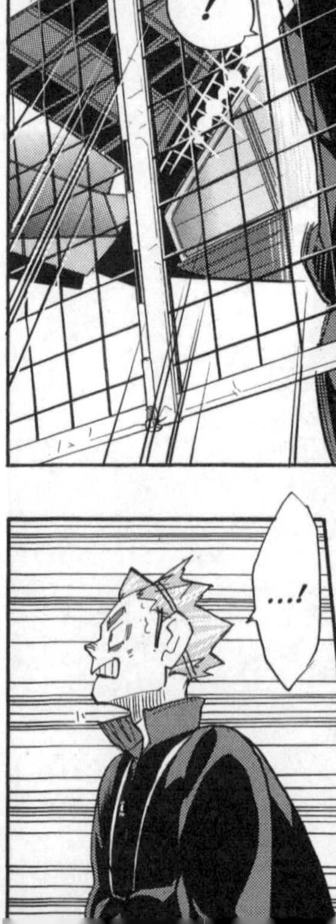
...!

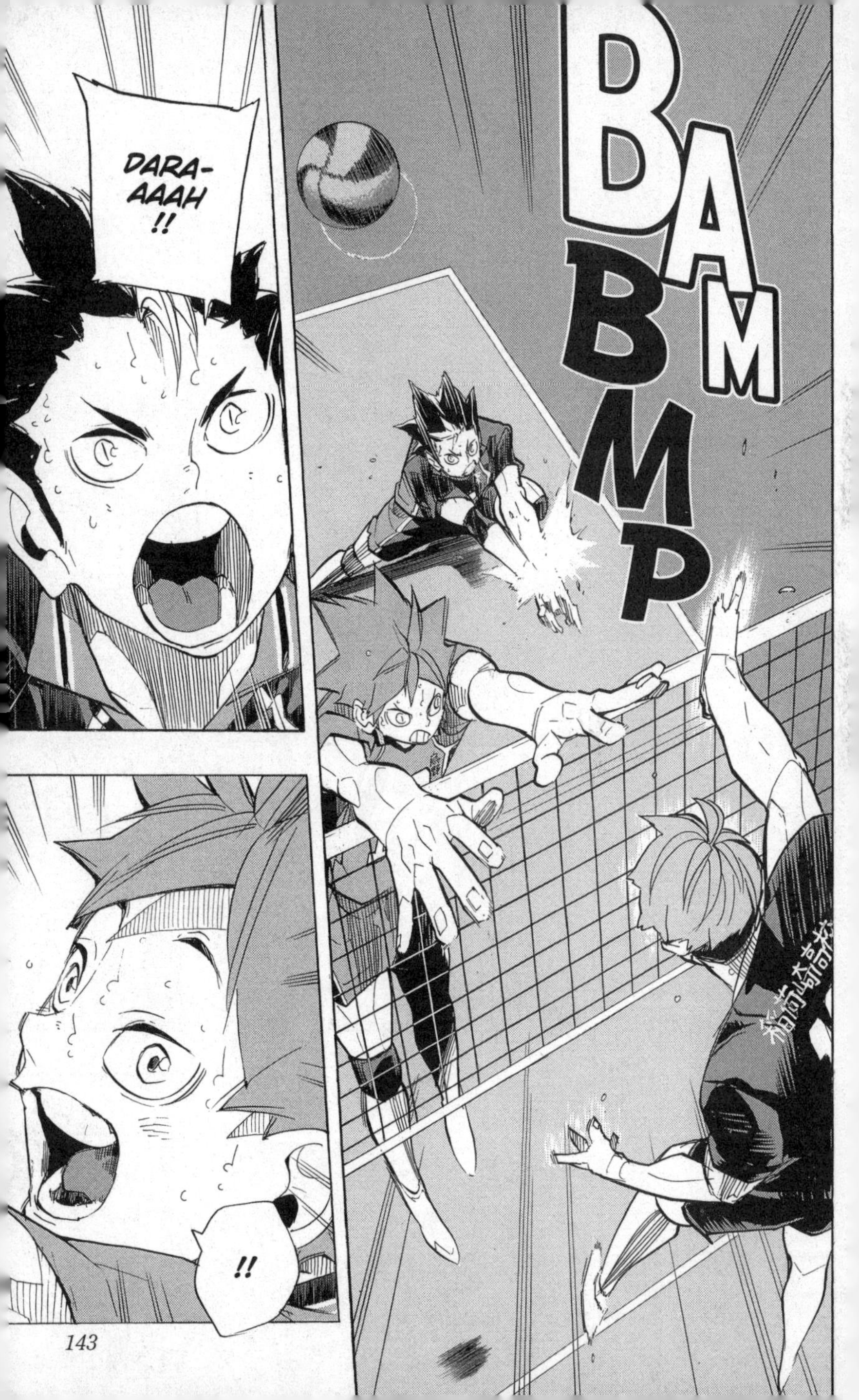
BAM
BMP
DARA-
AAAH
!!
!!

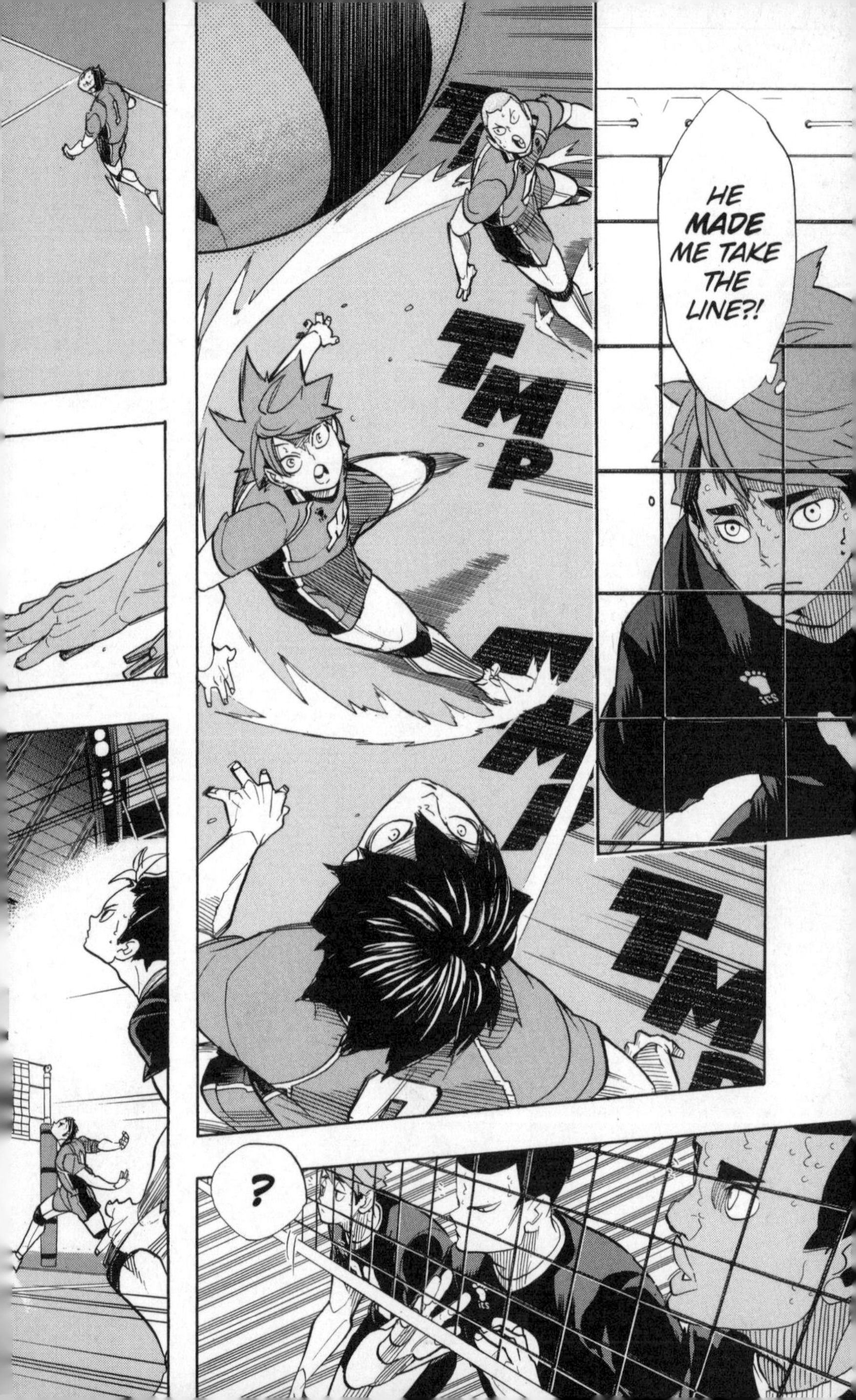
HE MADE ME TAKE THE LINE?!
TMP
TMP
TMP
?

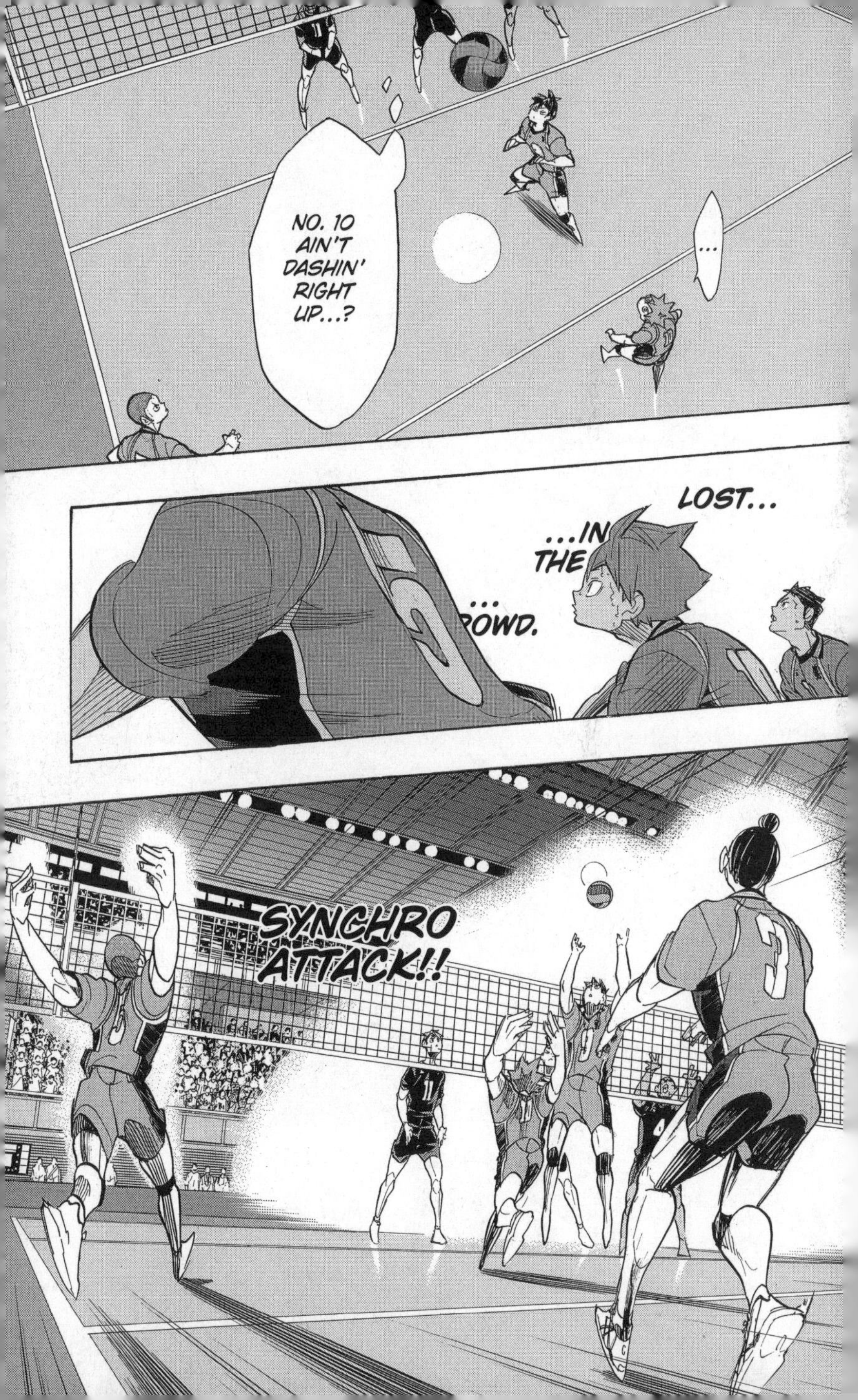
NO. 10 AIN'T DASHIN' RIGHT UP...?
...
LOST...
...IN THE
... ROWD.
SYNCHRO ATTACK!!

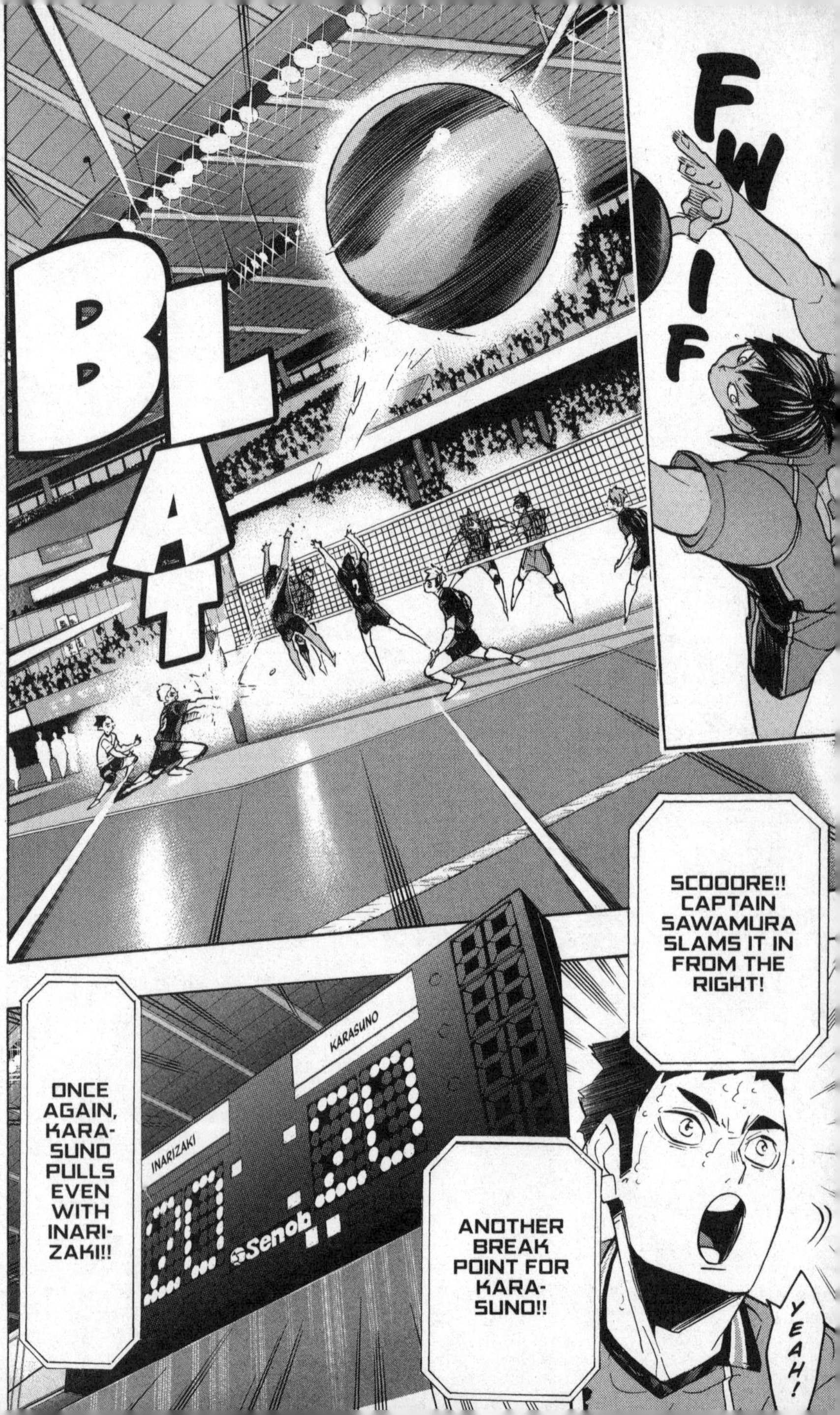
FWIF
BLAT
SCOOORE!! CAPTAIN SAWAMURA SLAMS IT IN FROM THE RIGHT!
ANOTHER BREAK POINT FOR KARA-SUNO!!
YEAH!
KARASUNO
INARIZAKI
Senob
ONCE AGAIN, KARA-SUNO PULLS EVEN WITH INARI-ZAKI!!

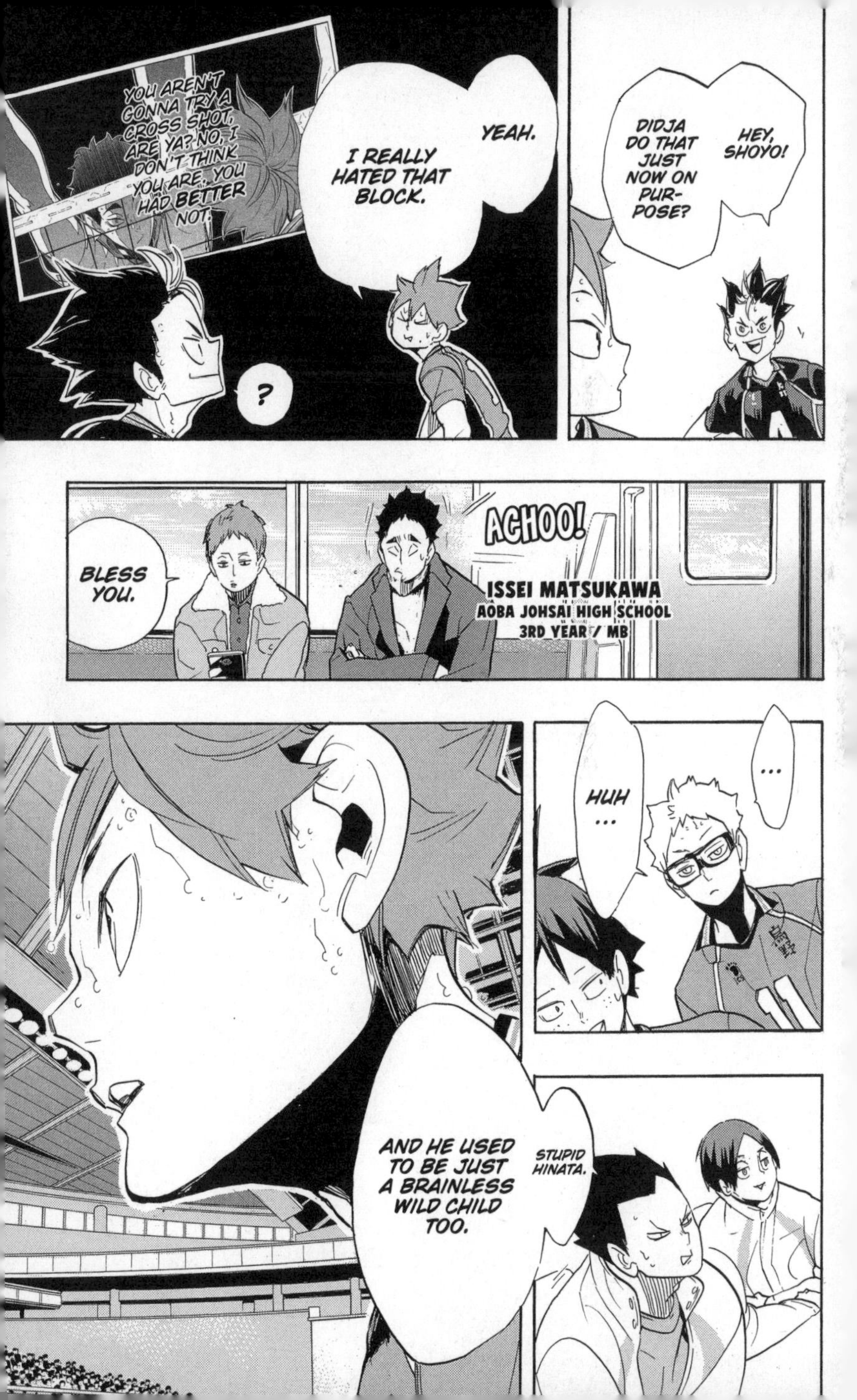
HEY, SHOYO!
DIDJA DO THAT JUST NOW ON PURPOSE?
YEAH.
I REALLY HATED THAT BLOCK.
YOU AREN'T GONNA TRY A CROSS SHOT, ARE YA? NO, I DON'T THINK YOU ARE. YOU HAD BETTER NOT.
?
ACHOO!
ISSEI MATSUKAWA
AOBA JOHSAI HIGH SCHOOL
3RD YEAR / MB
BLESS YOU.
...
HUH ...
STUPID HINATA.
AND HE USED TO BE JUST A BRAINLESS WILD CHILD TOO.

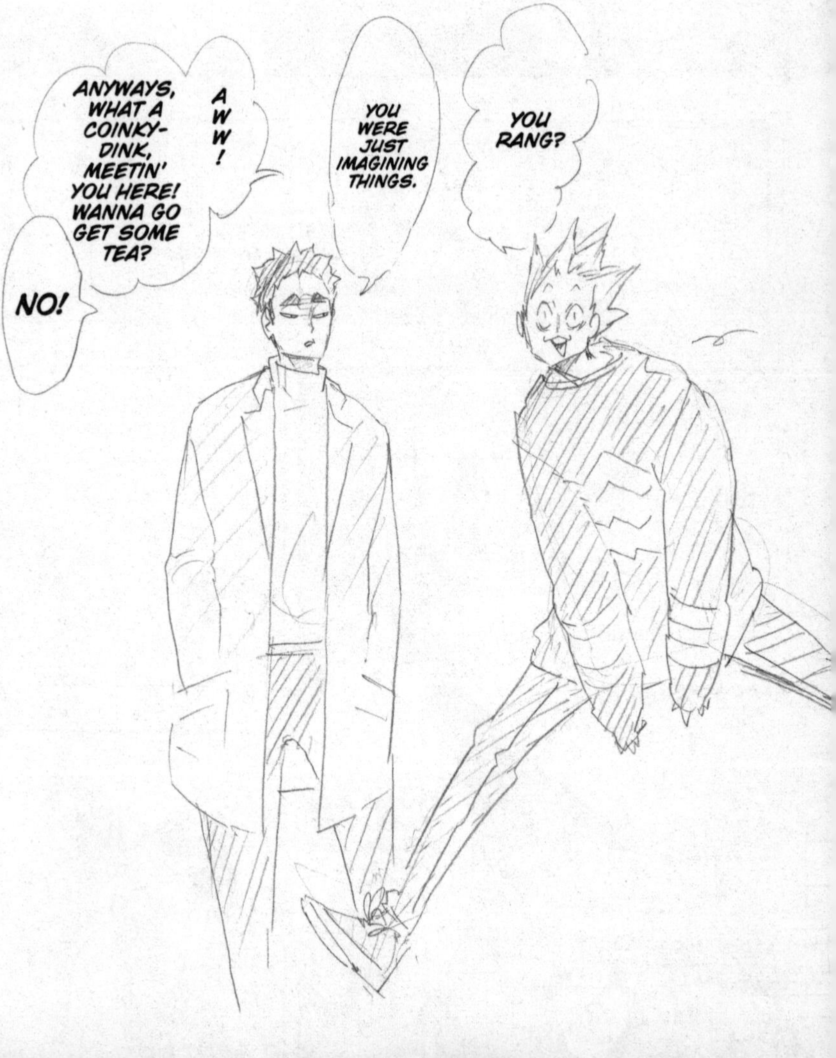
YOU RANG?
YOU WERE JUST IMAGINING THINGS.
AWW!
ANYWAYS, WHAT A COINKY-DINK, MEETIN' YOU HERE! WANNA GO GET SOME TEA?
NO!

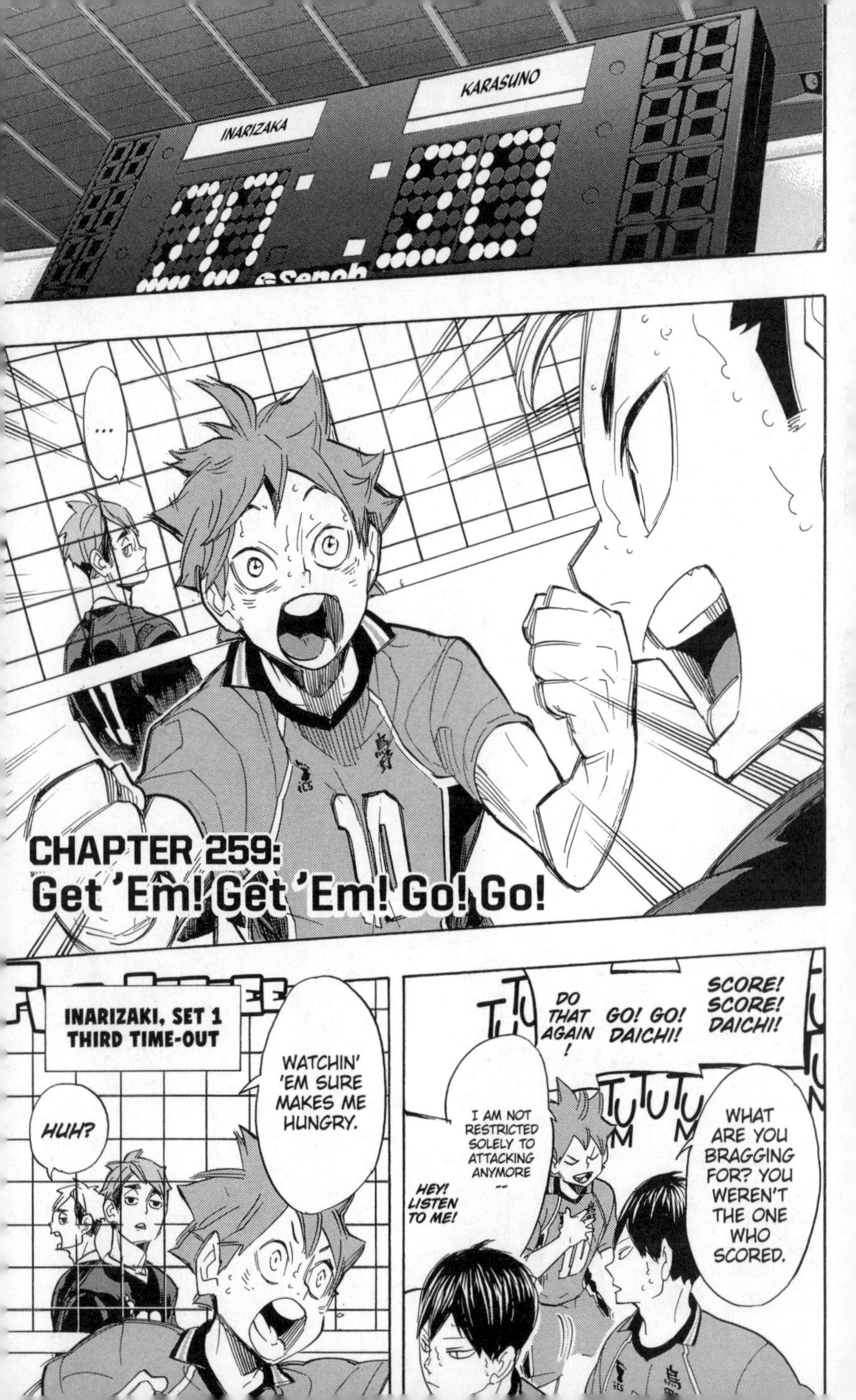
KARASUNO
INARIZAKA
...
CHAPTER 259:
Get 'Em! Get 'Em! Go! Go!
SCORE! SCORE! DAICHI!
GO! GO! DAICHI!
DO THAT AGAIN!
TUTUTUM
WHAT ARE YOU BRAGGING FOR? YOU WEREN'T THE ONE WHO SCORED.
I AM NOT RESTRICTED SOLELY TO ATTACKING ANYMORE--
HEY! LISTEN TO ME!
INARIZAKI, SET 1 THIRD TIME-OUT
WATCHIN' 'EM SURE MAKES ME HUNGRY.
HUH?

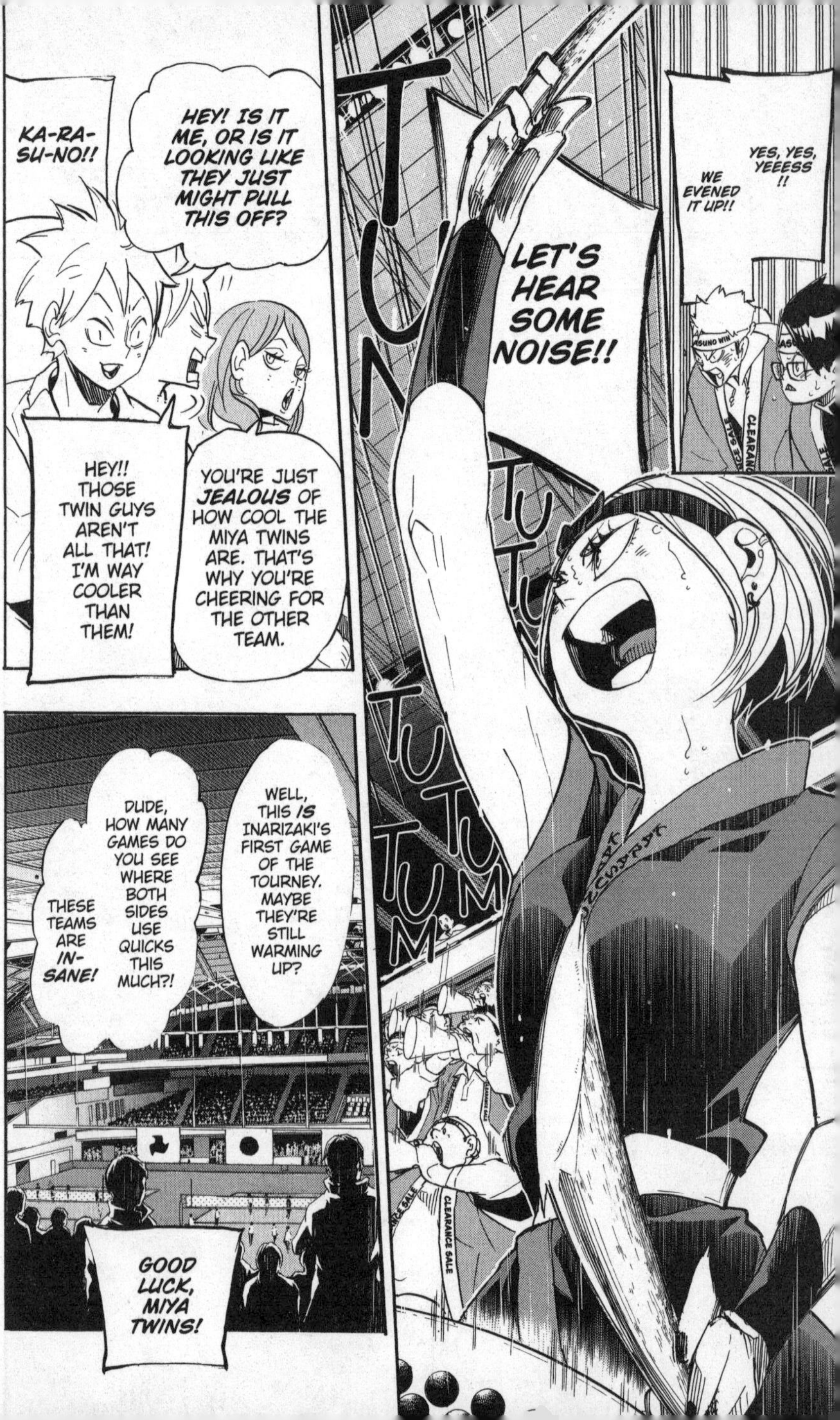

YES, YES, YEEESS !!
WE EVENED IT UP!!
LET'S HEAR SOME NOISE!!
TUM
TUTUTUM
TUTUM
TUM
HEY! IS IT ME, OR IS IT LOOKING LIKE THEY JUST MIGHT PULL THIS OFF?
KA-RA-SU-NO!!
YOU'RE JUST JEALOUS OF HOW COOL THE MIYA TWINS ARE. THAT'S WHY YOU'RE CHEERING FOR THE OTHER TEAM.
HEY!! THOSE TWIN GUYS AREN'T ALL THAT! I'M WAY COOLER THAN THEM!
WELL, THIS IS INARIZAKI'S FIRST GAME OF THE TOURNEY. MAYBE THEY'RE STILL WARMING UP?
DUDE, HOW MANY GAMES DO YOU SEE WHERE BOTH SIDES USE QUICKS THIS MUCH?!
THESE TEAMS ARE IN-SANE!
GOOD LUCK, MIYA TWINS!

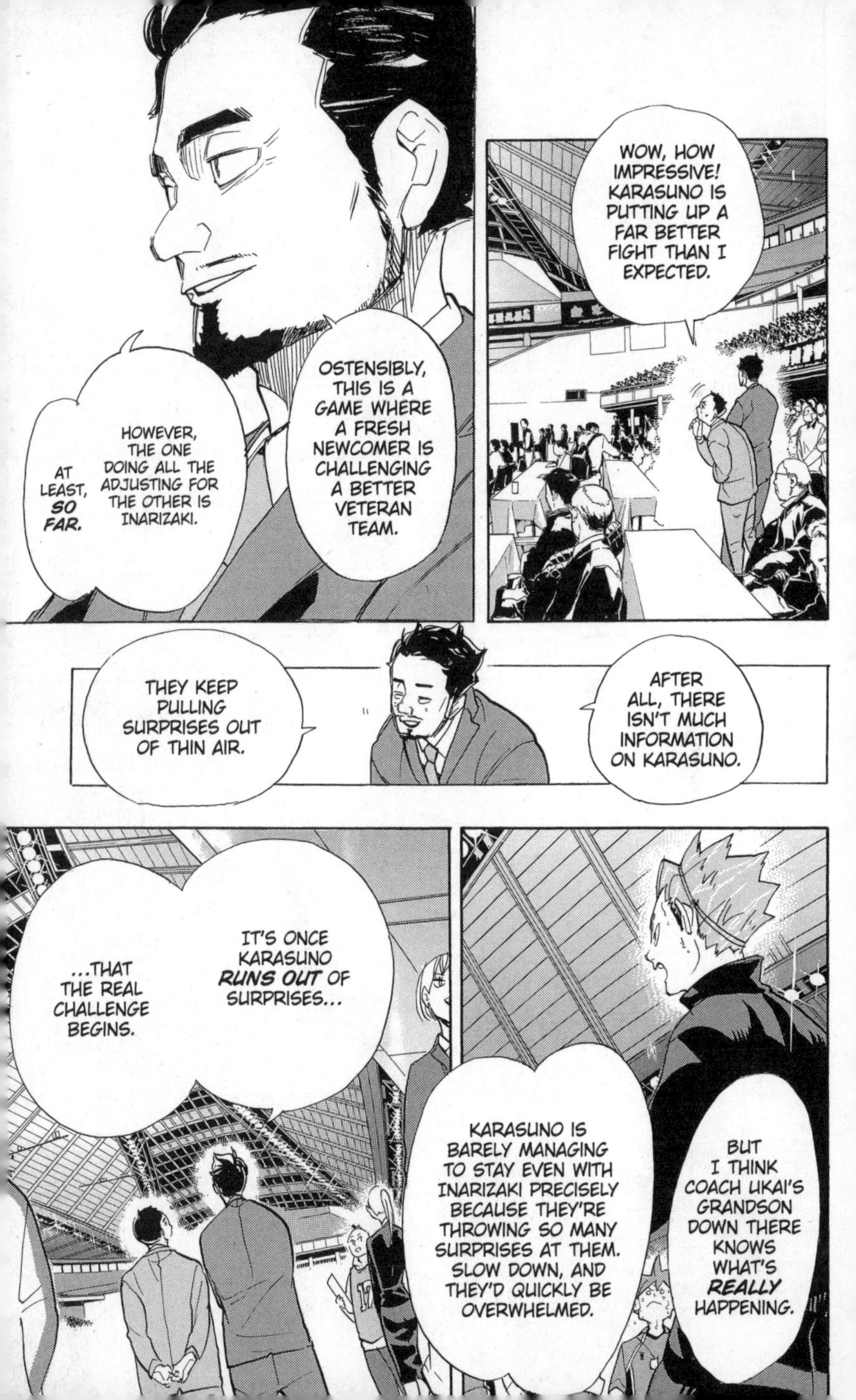
WOW, HOW IMPRESSIVE! KARASUNO IS PUTTING UP A FAR BETTER FIGHT THAN I EXPECTED.
OSTENSIBLY, THIS IS A GAME WHERE A FRESH NEWCOMER IS CHALLENGING A BETTER VETERAN TEAM.
HOWEVER, THE ONE DOING ALL THE ADJUSTING FOR THE OTHER IS INARIZAKI.
AT LEAST, **SO FAR.**
AFTER ALL, THERE ISN'T MUCH INFORMATION ON KARASUNO.
THEY KEEP PULLING SURPRISES OUT OF THIN AIR.
BUT I THINK COACH UKAI'S GRANDSON DOWN THERE KNOWS WHAT'S **REALLY** HAPPENING.
KARASUNO IS BARELY MANAGING TO STAY EVEN WITH INARIZAKI PRECISELY BECAUSE THEY'RE THROWING SO MANY SURPRISES AT THEM. SLOW DOWN, AND THEY'D QUICKLY BE OVERWHELMED.
IT'S ONCE KARASUNO **RUNS OUT** OF SURPRISES...
...THAT THE REAL CHALLENGE BEGINS.

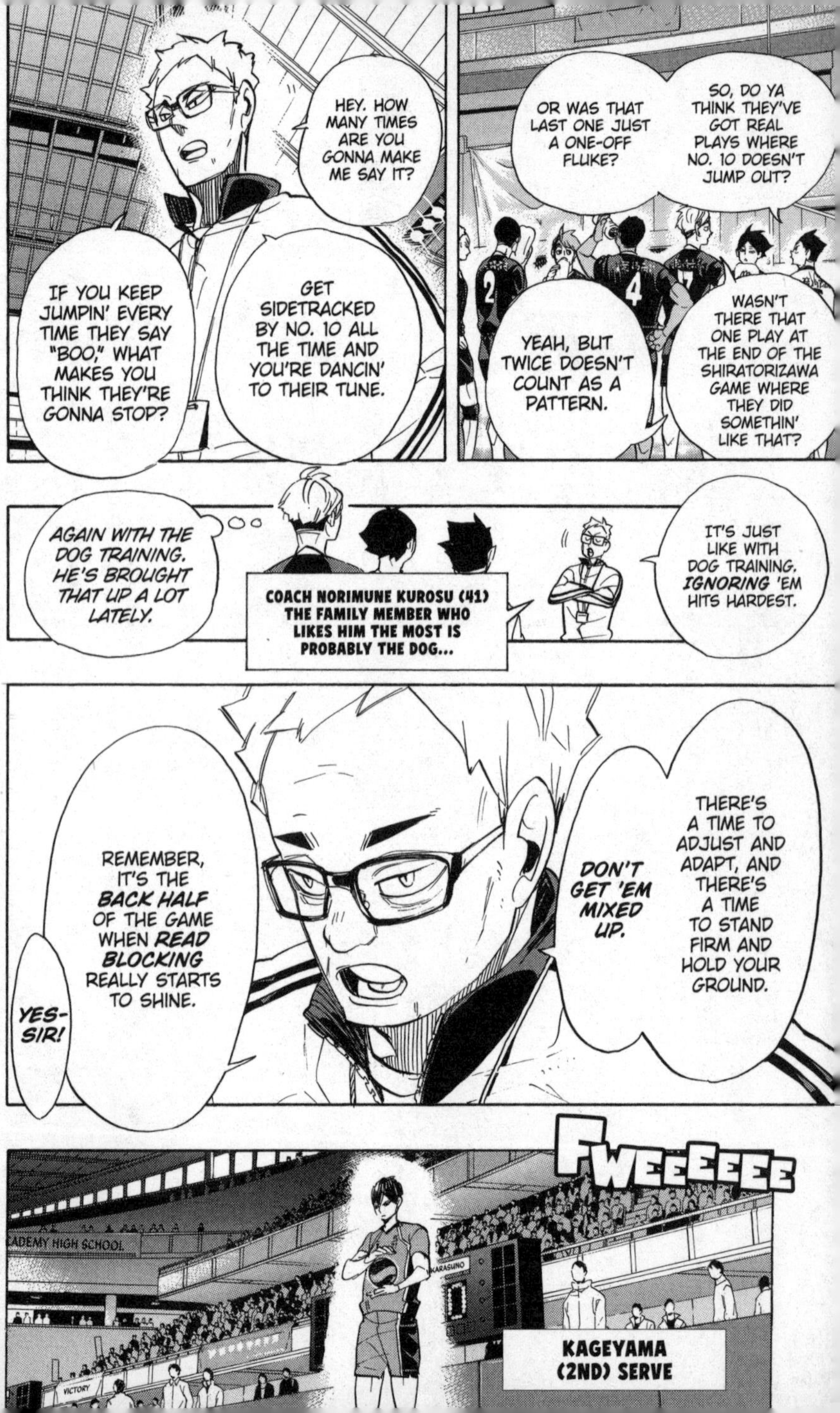
SO, DO YA THINK THEY'VE GOT REAL PLAYS WHERE NO. 10 DOESN'T JUMP OUT?
OR WAS THAT LAST ONE JUST A ONE-OFF FLUKE?
WASN'T THERE THAT ONE PLAY AT THE END OF THE SHIRATORIZAWA GAME WHERE THEY DID SOMETHIN' LIKE THAT?
YEAH, BUT TWICE DOESN'T COUNT AS A PATTERN.
HEY. HOW MANY TIMES ARE YOU GONNA MAKE ME SAY IT?
GET SIDETRACKED BY NO. 10 ALL THE TIME AND YOU'RE DANCIN' TO THEIR TUNE.
IF YOU KEEP JUMPIN' EVERY TIME THEY SAY "BOO," WHAT MAKES YOU THINK THEY'RE GONNA STOP?
IT'S JUST LIKE WITH DOG TRAINING. IGNORING 'EM HITS HARDEST.
COACH NORIMUNE KUROSU (41) THE FAMILY MEMBER WHO LIKES HIM THE MOST IS PROBABLY THE DOG...
AGAIN WITH THE DOG TRAINING. HE'S BROUGHT THAT UP A LOT LATELY.
THERE'S A TIME TO ADJUST AND ADAPT, AND THERE'S A TIME TO STAND FIRM AND HOLD YOUR GROUND.
DON'T GET 'EM MIXED UP.
REMEMBER, IT'S THE BACK HALF OF THE GAME WHEN READ BLOCKING REALLY STARTS TO SHINE.
YES-SIR!
FWEEEEEE
KARASUNO
VICTORY
KAGEYAMA (2ND) SERVE

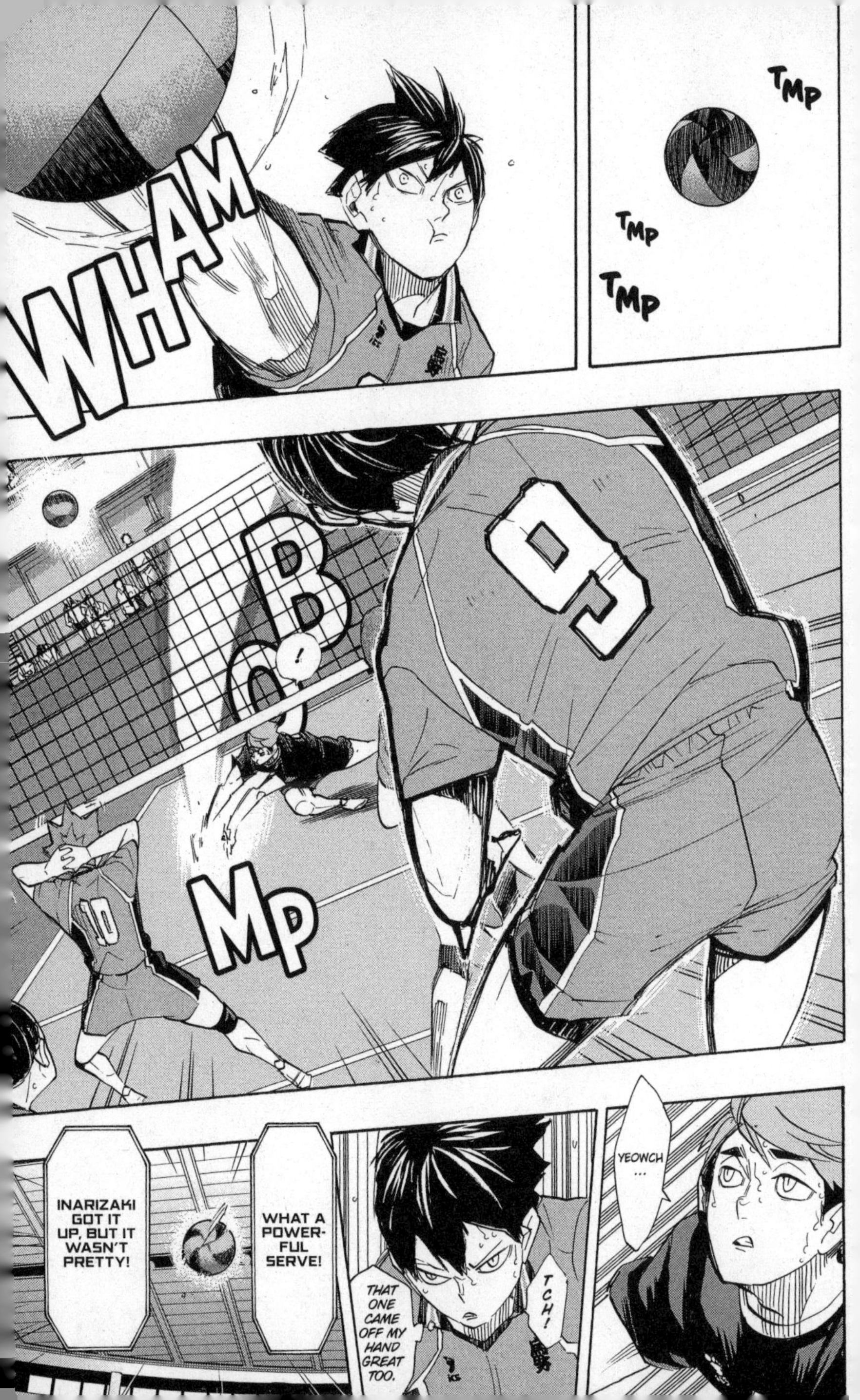
TMP
TMP
TMP
WHAM
BOMP
!
YEOWCH...
TCH!
THAT ONE CAME OFF MY HAND GREAT TOO.
WHAT A POWER-FUL SERVE!
INARIZAKI GOT IT UP, BUT IT WASN'T PRETTY!

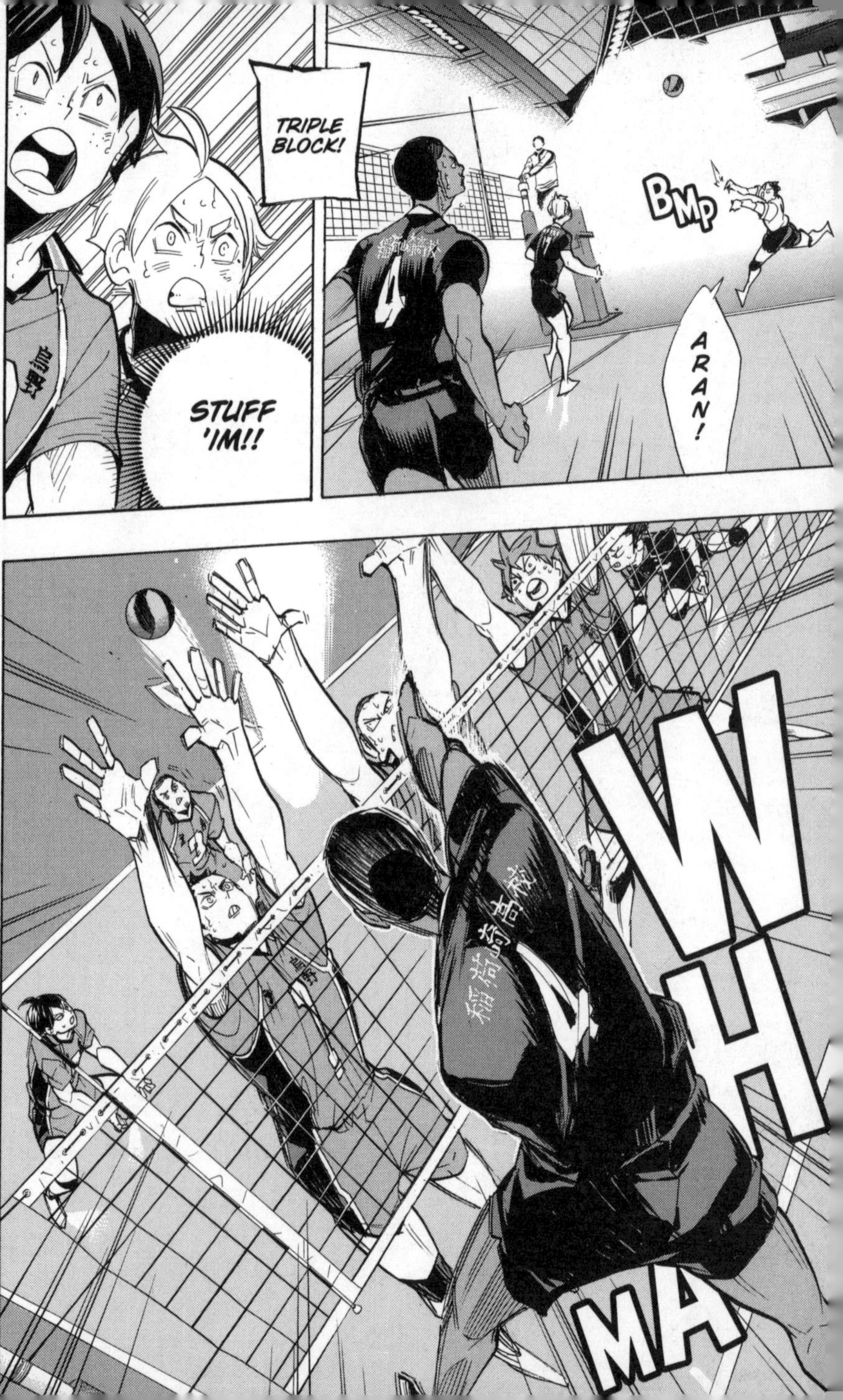
BMP
ARAN!
TRIPLE BLOCK!
STUFF 'IM!!
WHAM

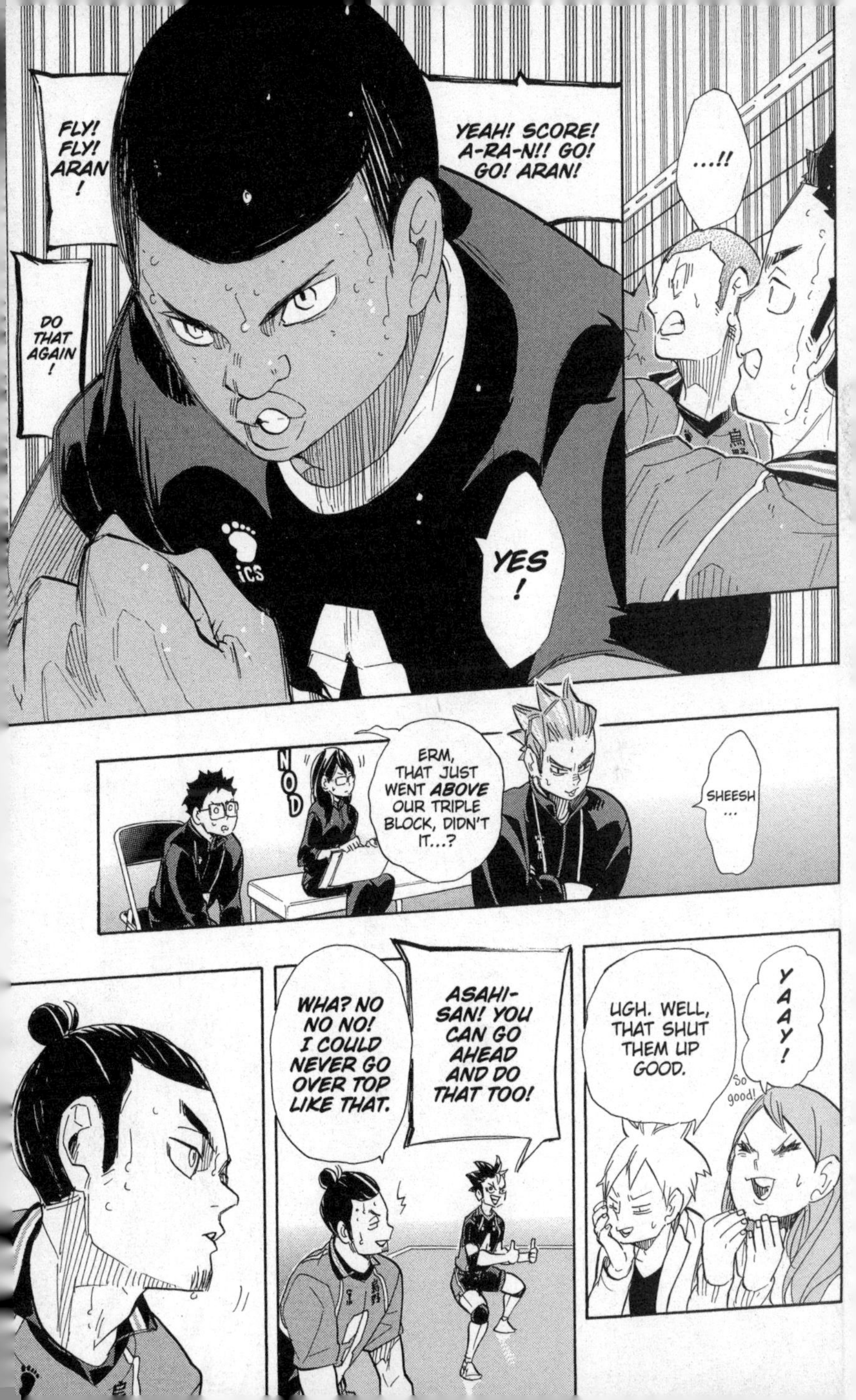
...!!
YEAH! SCORE! A-RA-N!! GO! GO! ARAN!
FLY! FLY! ARAN!
DO THAT AGAIN!
YES!
SHEESH...
ERM, THAT JUST WENT *ABOVE* OUR TRIPLE BLOCK, DIDN'T IT...?
NOD
YAAY!
UGH. WELL, THAT SHUT THEM UP GOOD.
So good!
ASAHI-SAN! YOU CAN GO AHEAD AND DO THAT TOO!
WHA? NO NO NO! I COULD NEVER GO OVER TOP LIKE THAT.

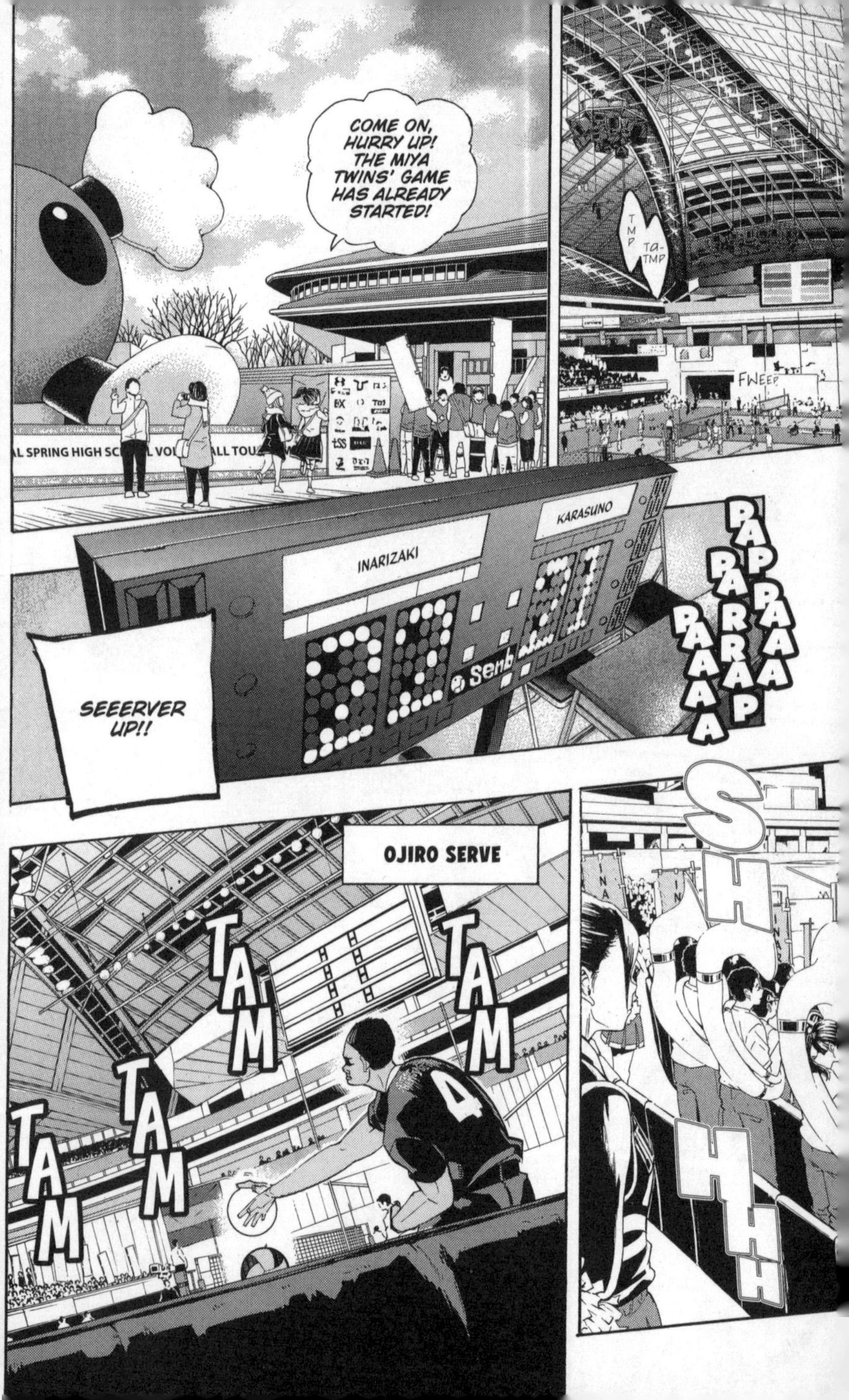

TMP
Ta-TMP
FWEEP
COME ON, HURRY UP! THE MIYA TWINS' GAME HAS ALREADY STARTED!
PAPPAAAA
PARARAP
PAAAAA
KARASUNO
INARIZAKI
SEEERVER UP!!
SHHHHHH
OJIRO SERVE
TAM
TAM
TAM
TAM

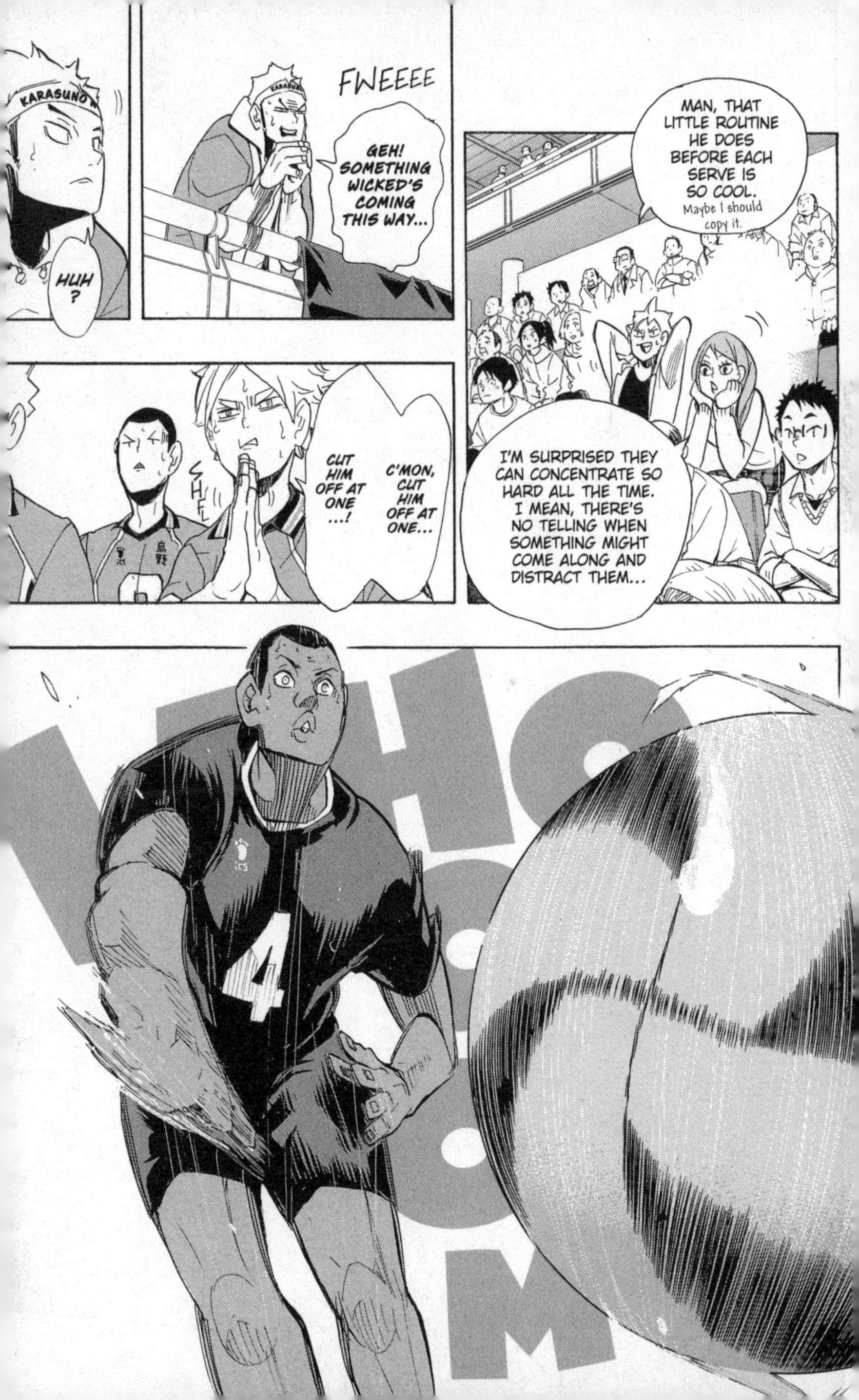
MAN, THAT LITTLE ROUTINE HE DOES BEFORE EACH SERVE IS SO COOL.
Maybe I should copy it.
I'M SURPRISED THEY CAN CONCENTRATE SO HARD ALL THE TIME. I MEAN, THERE'S NO TELLING WHEN SOMETHING MIGHT COME ALONG AND DISTRACT THEM...
FWEEEEE
GEH! SOMETHING WICKED'S COMING THIS WAY...
KARASUNO
HUH?
C'MON, CUT HIM OFF AT ONE...
CUT HIM OFF AT ONE...!
SHFL

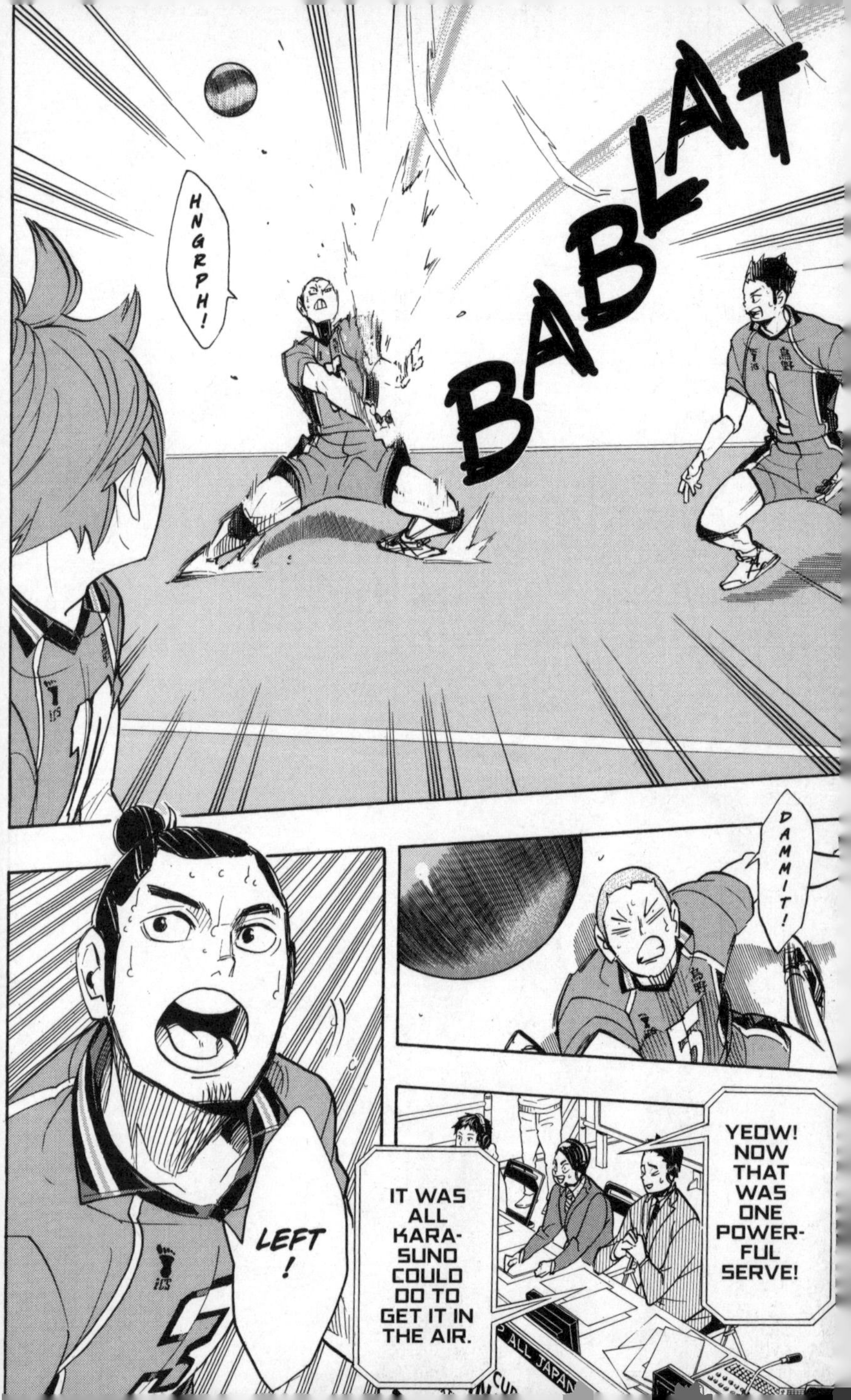
BABLAT
HNGRPH!
DAMMIT!
LEFT!
YEOW! NOW THAT WAS ONE POWER-FUL SERVE!
IT WAS ALL KARA-SUNO COULD DO TO GET IT IN THE AIR.

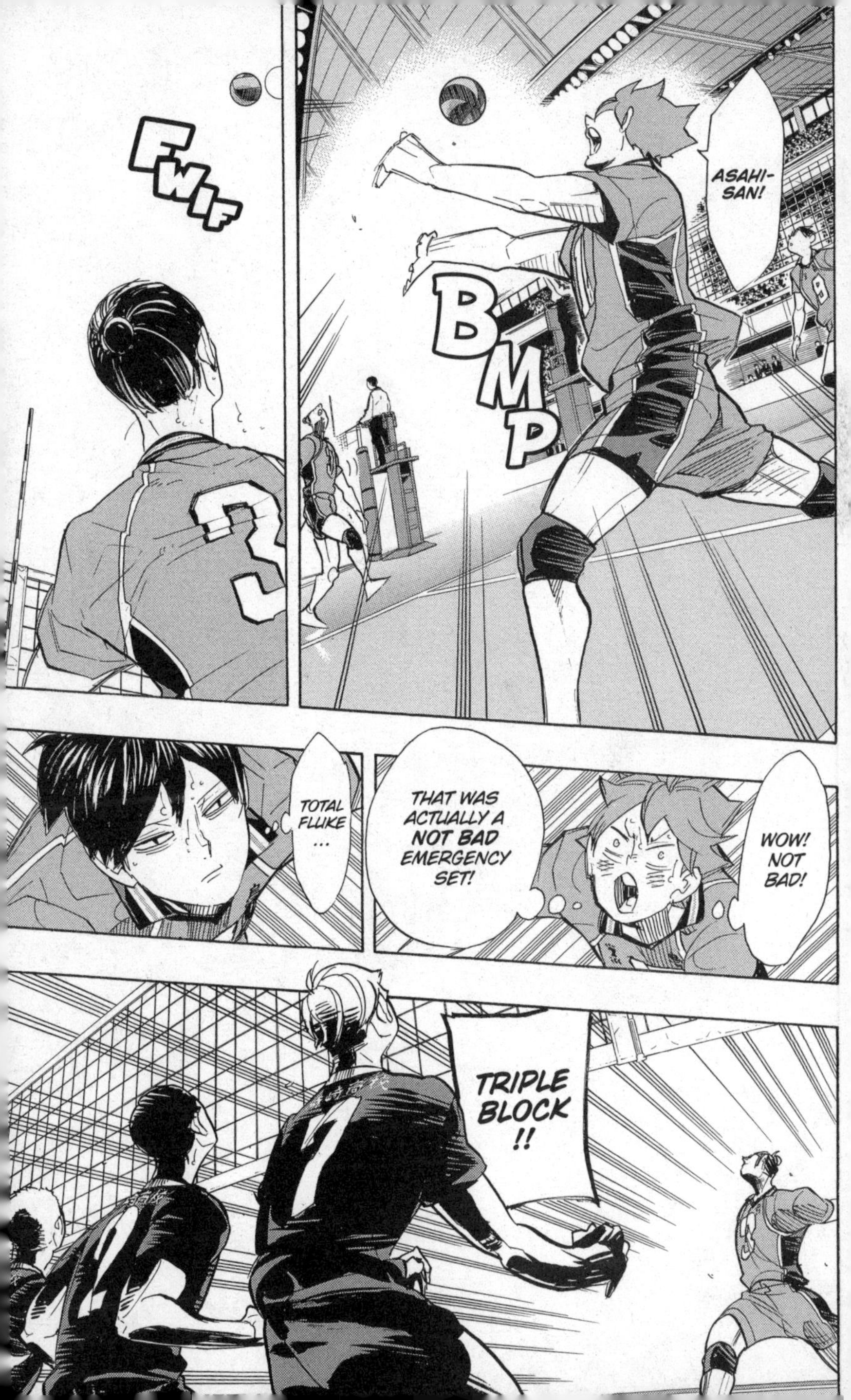
ASAHI-SAN!
BMP
FWIF
WOW! NOT BAD!
THAT WAS ACTUALLY A NOT BAD EMERGENCY SET!
TOTAL FLUKE ...
TRIPLE BLOCK !!

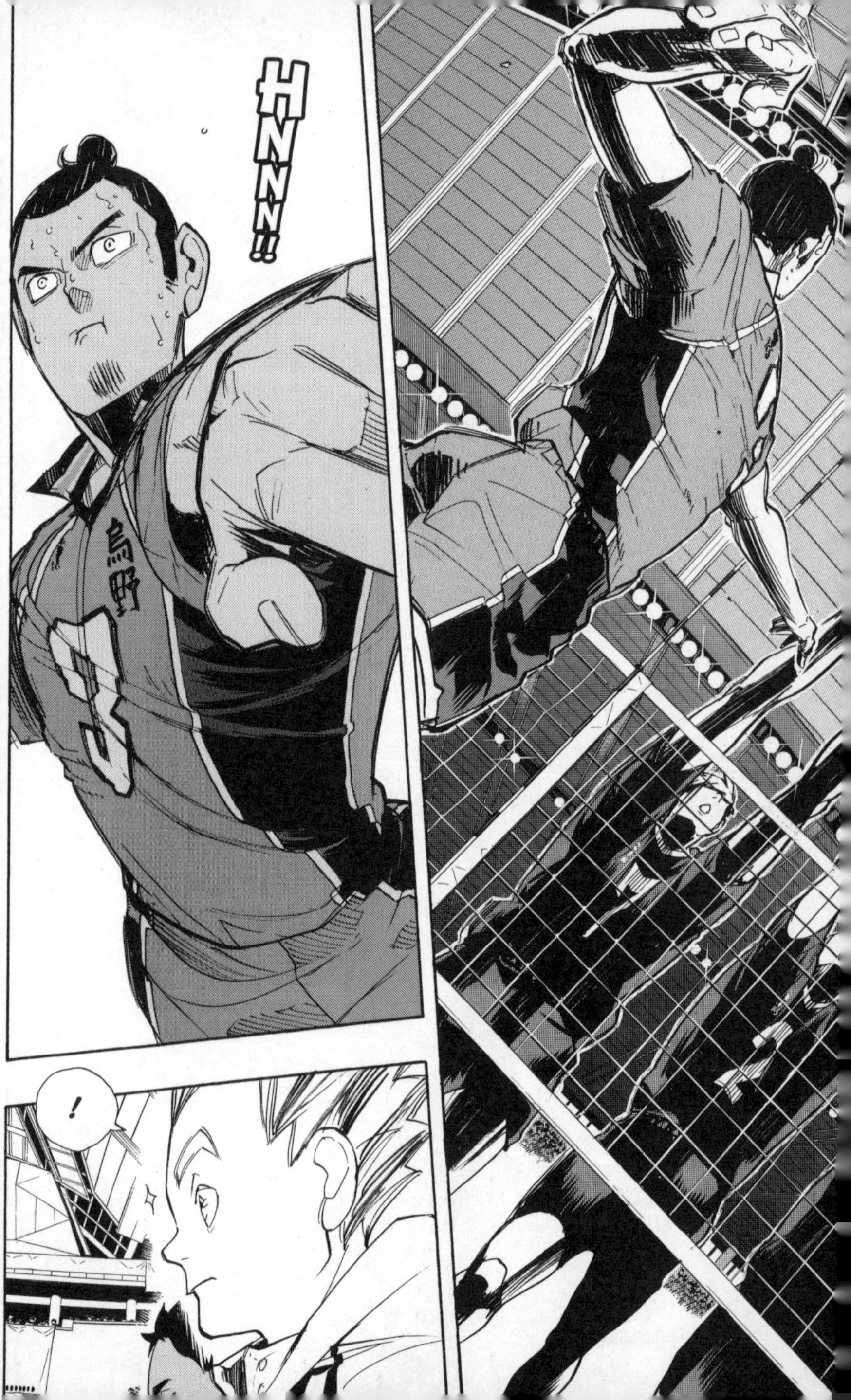
HNNNN!!
!

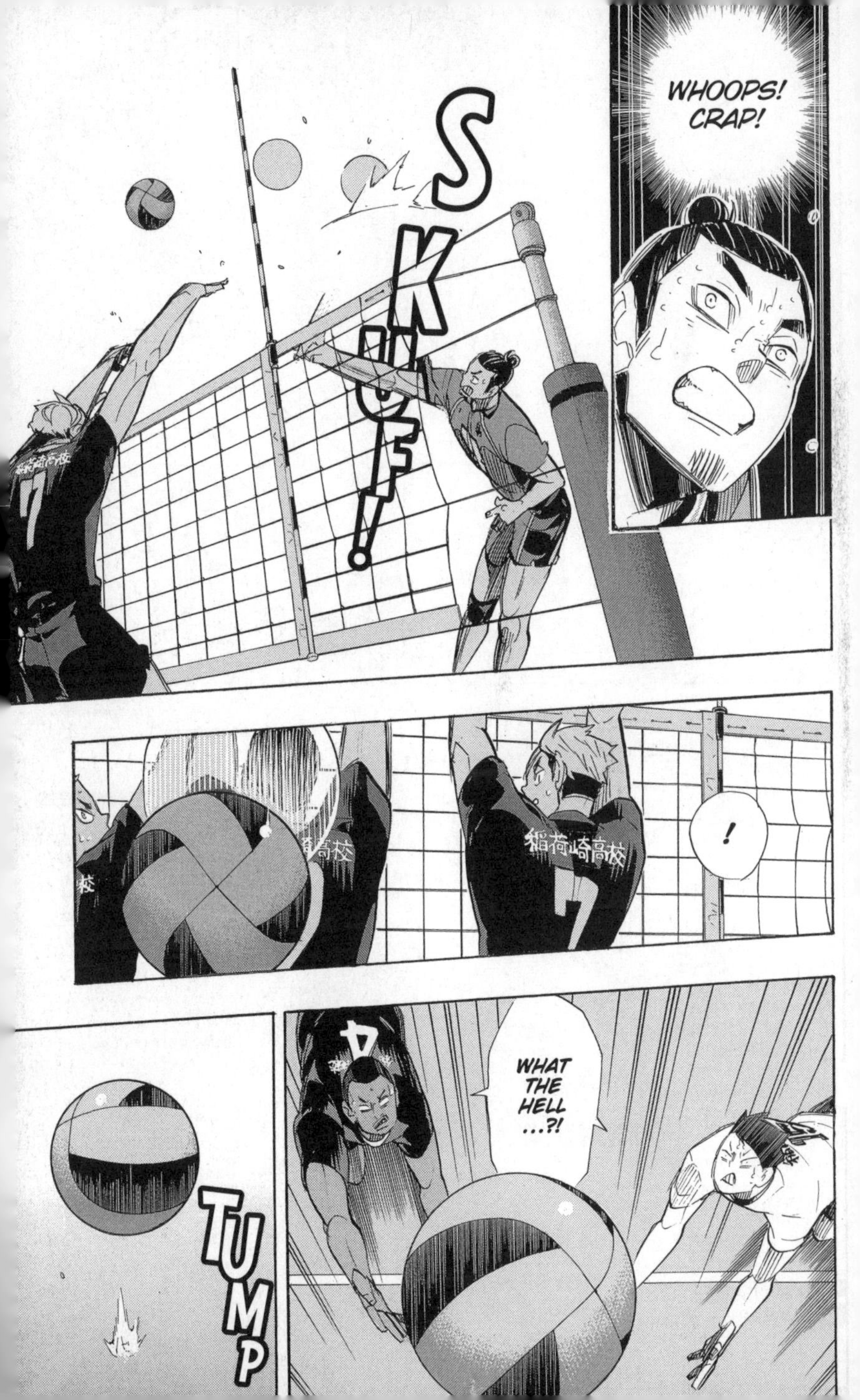
WHOOPS! CRAP!
SKUFF!
!
WHAT THE HELL ...?!
TUMP

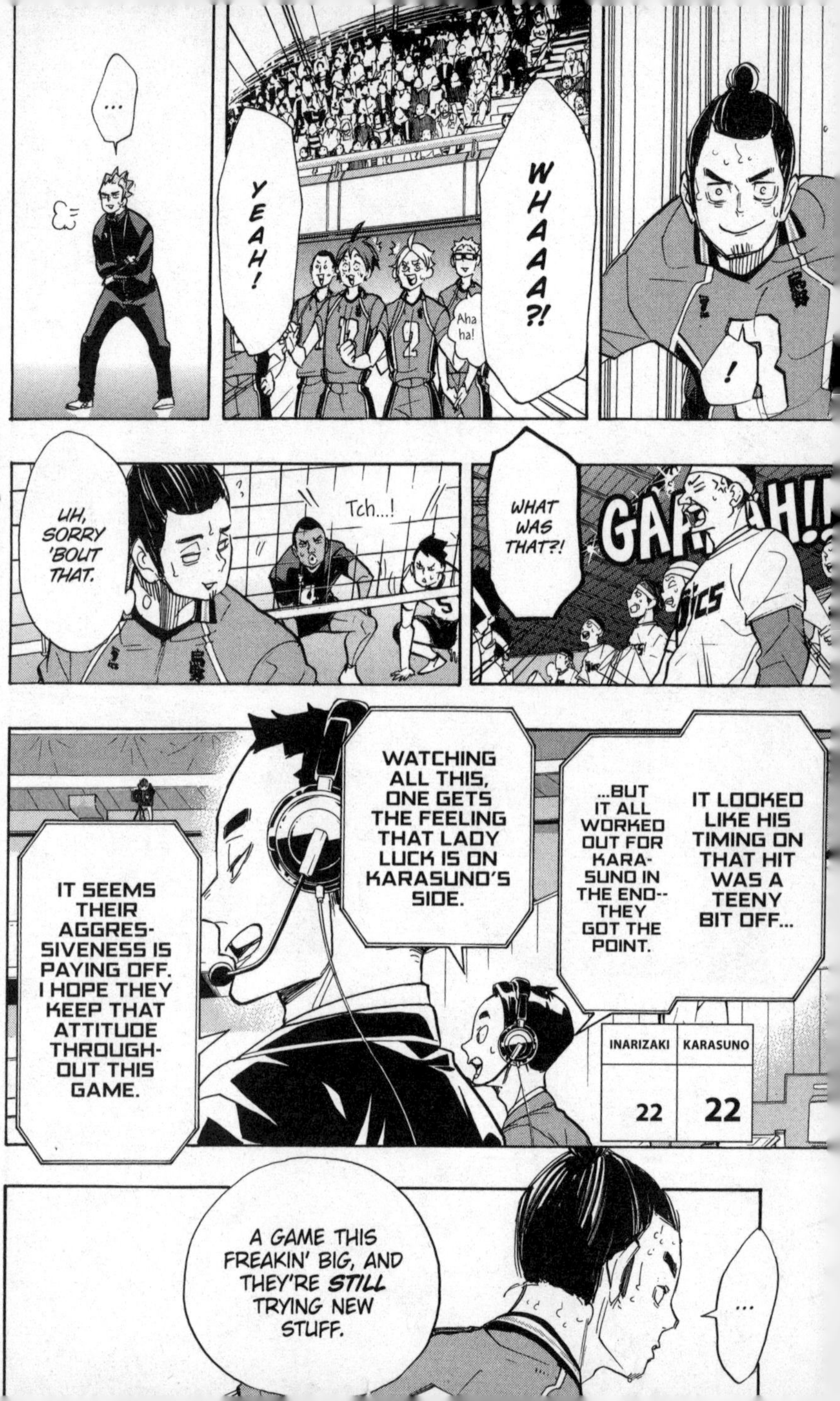
!
WHAAAA?!
YEAH!
Aha ha!
...
WHAT WAS THAT?!
Tch...!
UH, SORRY 'BOUT THAT.
IT LOOKED LIKE HIS TIMING ON THAT HIT WAS A TEENY BIT OFF...
...BUT IT ALL WORKED OUT FOR KARASUNO IN THE END--THEY GOT THE POINT.
WATCHING ALL THIS, ONE GETS THE FEELING THAT LADY LUCK IS ON KARASUNO'S SIDE.
IT SEEMS THEIR AGGRESSIVENESS IS PAYING OFF. I HOPE THEY KEEP THAT ATTITUDE THROUGHOUT THIS GAME.
INARIZAKI
KARASUNO
22
22
...
A GAME THIS FREAKIN' BIG, AND THEY'RE STILL TRYING NEW STUFF.

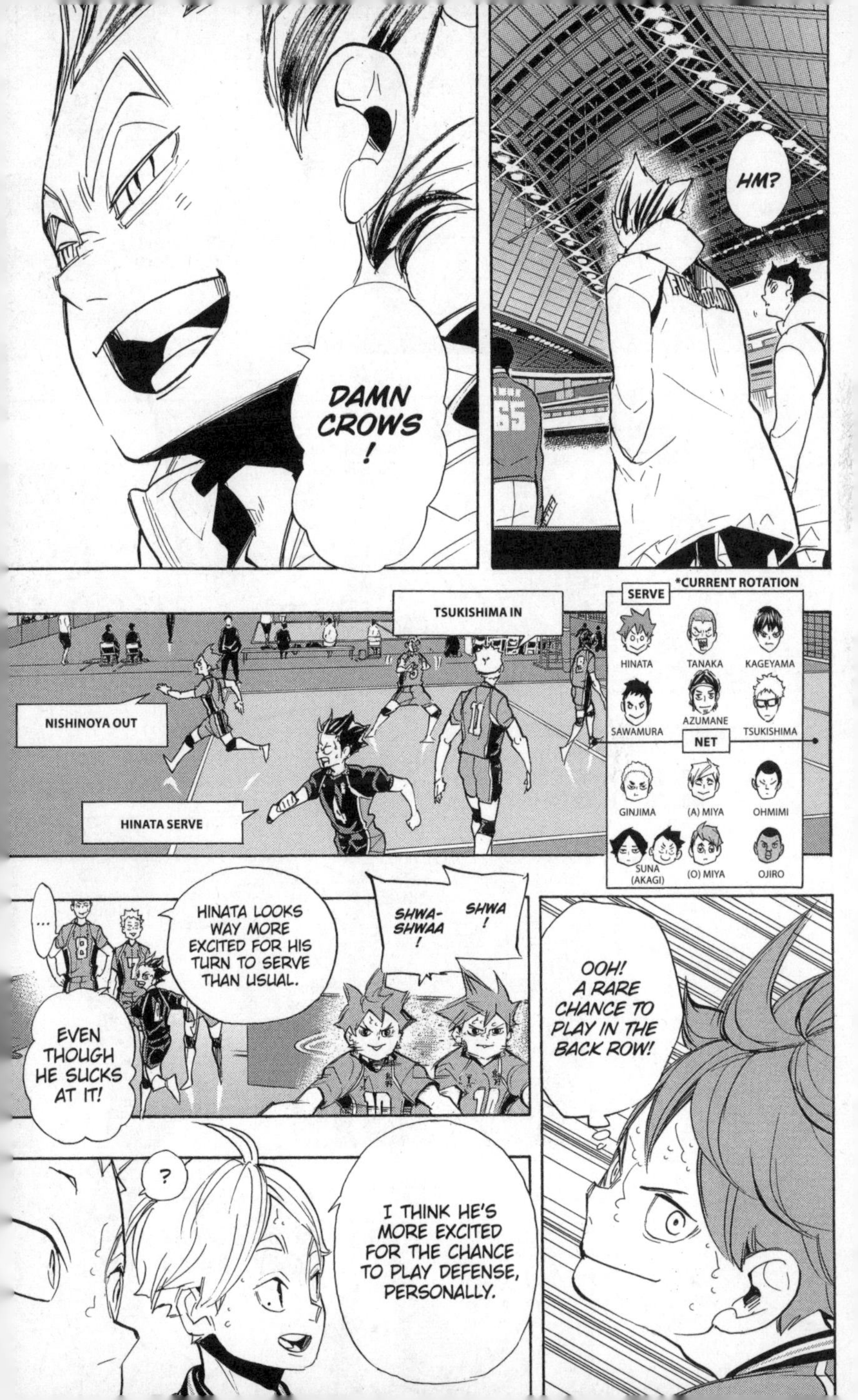
HM?
DAMN CROWS!
*CURRENT ROTATION
SERVE
HINATA
TANAKA
KAGEYAMA
SAWAMURA
AZUMANE
TSUKISHIMA
NET
GINJIMA
(A) MIYA
OHMIMI
SUNA (AKAGI)
(O) MIYA
OJIRO
TSUKISHIMA IN
NISHINOYA OUT
HINATA SERVE
OOH! A RARE CHANCE TO PLAY IN THE BACK ROW!
SHWA!
SHWA-SHWAA!
HINATA LOOKS WAY MORE EXCITED FOR HIS TURN TO SERVE THAN USUAL.
...
EVEN THOUGH HE SUCKS AT IT!
I THINK HE'S MORE EXCITED FOR THE CHANCE TO PLAY DEFENSE, PERSONALLY.
?

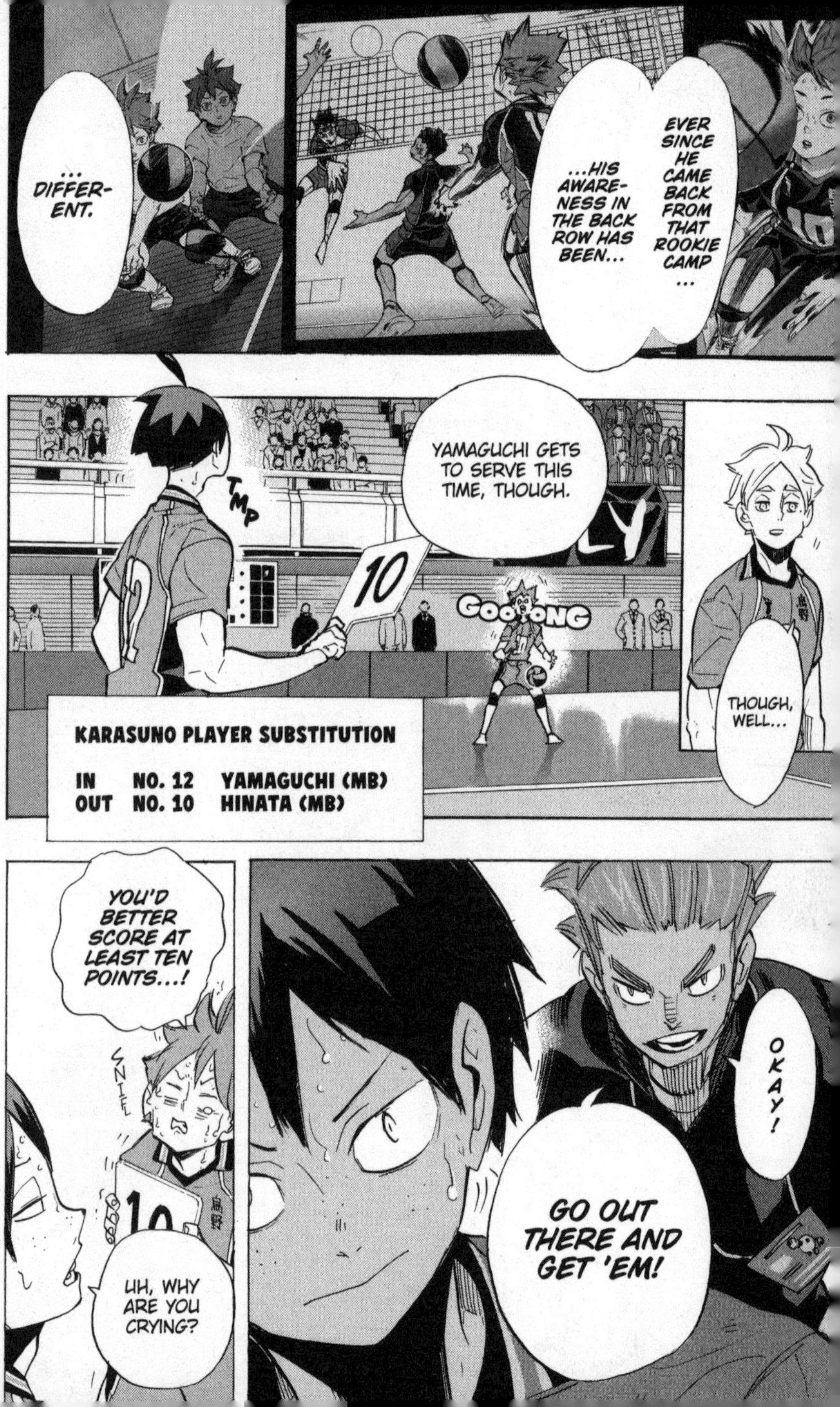
EVER SINCE HE CAME BACK FROM THAT ROOKIE CAMP...
...HIS AWARENESS IN THE BACK ROW HAS BEEN...
...DIFFERENT.
THOUGH, WELL...
YAMAGUCHI GETS TO SERVE THIS TIME, THOUGH.
TMP
10
KARASUNO PLAYER SUBSTITUTION
IN NO. 12 YAMAGUCHI (MB)
OUT NO. 10 HINATA (MB)
OKAY!
GO OUT THERE AND GET 'EM!
YOU'D BETTER SCORE AT LEAST TEN POINTS...!
UH, WHY ARE YOU CRYING?

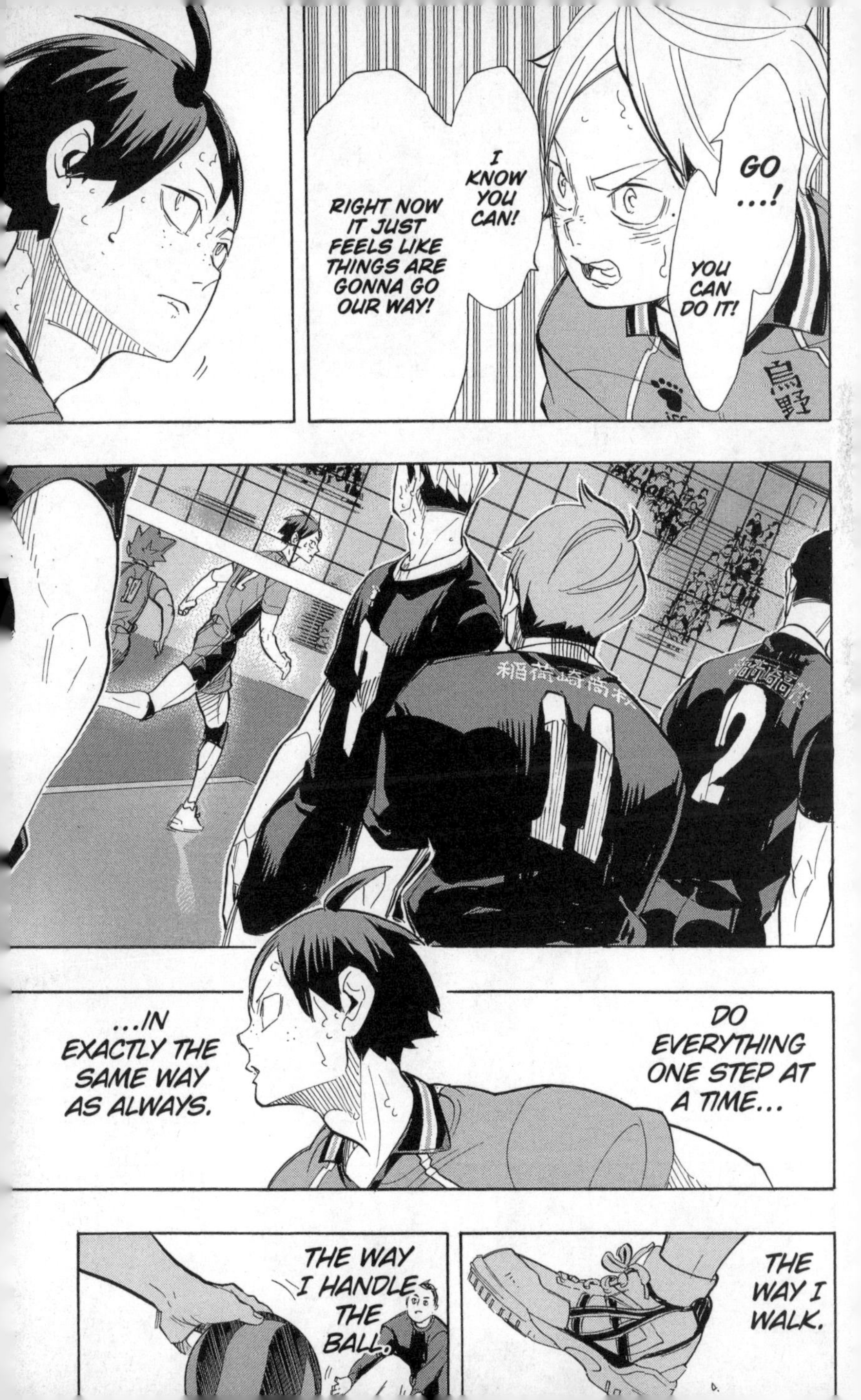
GO ...!
YOU CAN DO IT!
I KNOW YOU CAN!
RIGHT NOW IT JUST FEELS LIKE THINGS ARE GONNA GO OUR WAY!
DO EVERYTHING ONE STEP AT A TIME...
...IN EXACTLY THE SAME WAY AS ALWAYS.
THE WAY I WALK.
THE WAY I HANDLE THE BALL.

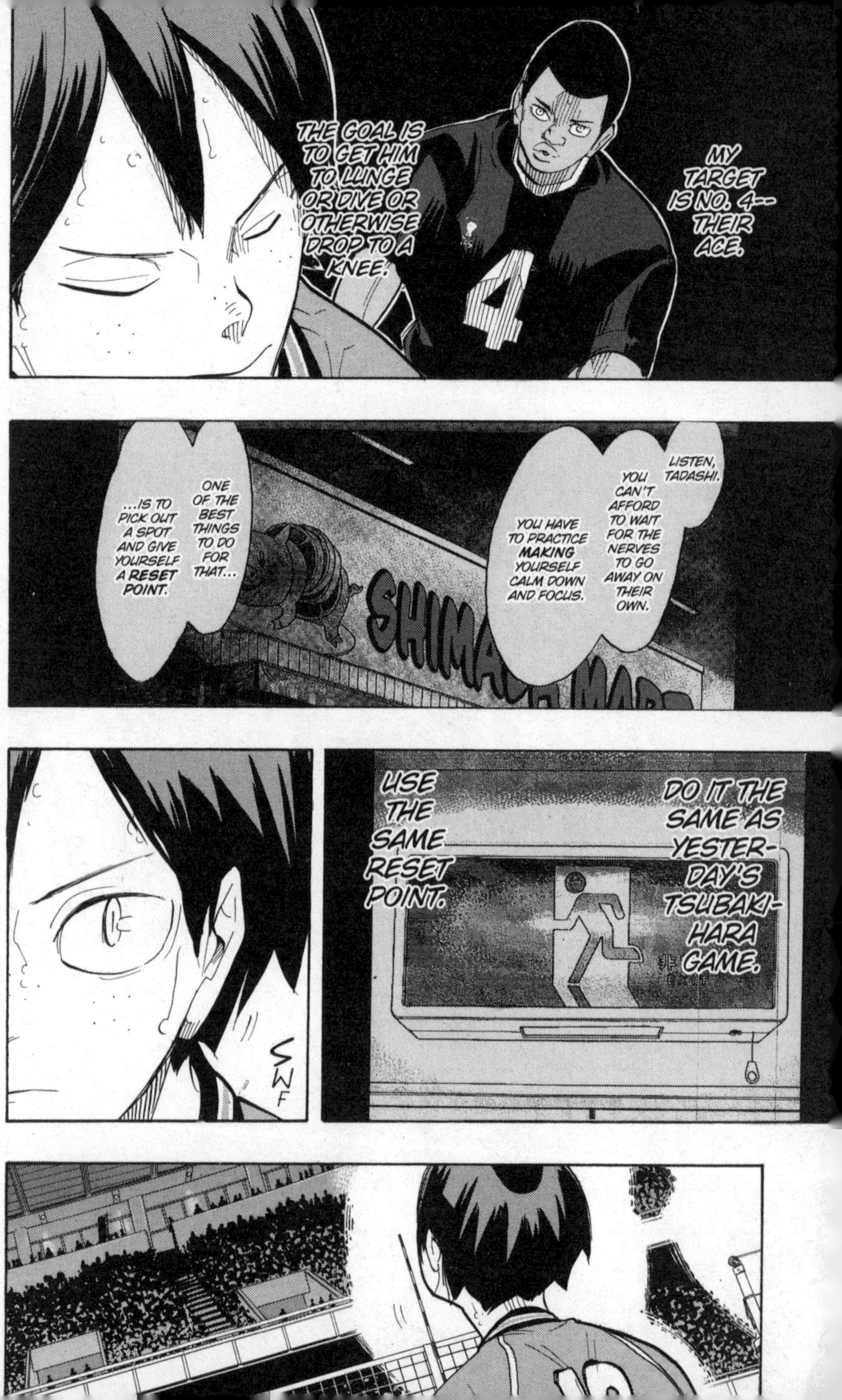
MY TARGET IS NO. 4-- THEIR ACE.
THE GOAL IS TO GET HIM TO LUNGE OR DIVE OR OTHERWISE DROP TO A KNEE.
LISTEN, TADASHI.
YOU CAN'T AFFORD TO WAIT FOR THE NERVES TO GO AWAY ON THEIR OWN.
YOU HAVE TO PRACTICE MAKING YOURSELF CALM DOWN AND FOCUS.
ONE OF THE BEST THINGS TO DO FOR THAT...
...IS TO PICK OUT A SPOT AND GIVE YOURSELF A RESET POINT.
DO IT THE SAME AS YESTER-DAY'S TSUBAKI-HARA GAME.
USE THE SAME RESET POINT.
SWF

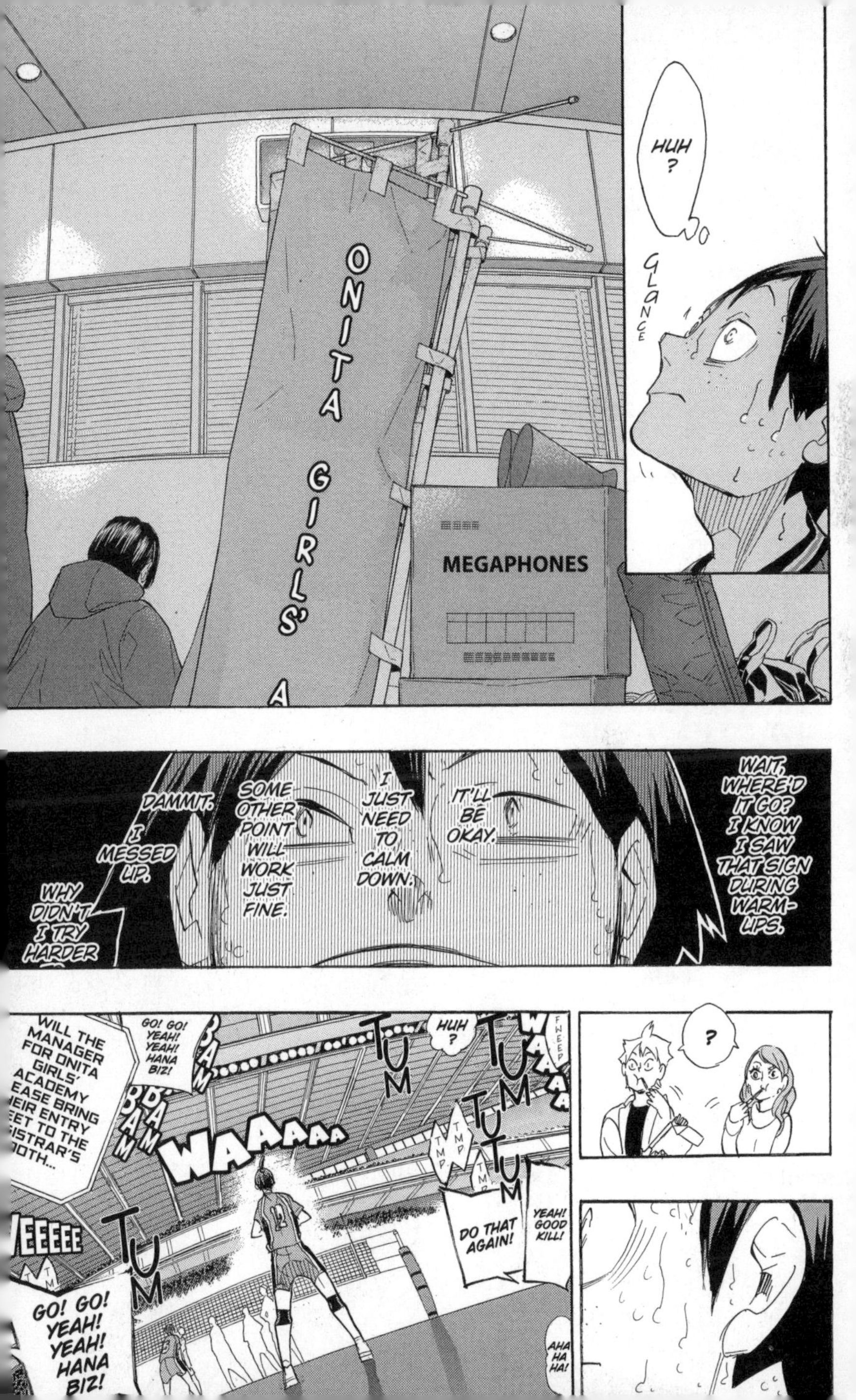
HUH?
GLANCE
ONITA GIRLS' A
MEGAPHONES
WAIT, WHERE'D IT GO? I KNOW I SAW THAT SIGN DURING WARM-UPS.
IT'LL BE OKAY.
I JUST NEED TO CALM DOWN.
SOME OTHER POINT WILL WORK JUST FINE.
DAMMIT.
I MESSED UP.
WHY DIDN'T I TRY HARDER
?
FWEEP
WAAAA
TUM TUM
HUH?
TUM
GO! GO! YEAH! YEAH! HANA BIZ!
BAM
BAM BAM
WILL THE MANAGER FOR ONITA GIRLS' ACADEMY EASE BRING HEIR ENTRY EET TO THE GISTRAR'S OOTH...
WAAAAAA
TMP TMP TMP
TUTUM
YEAH! GOOD KILL!
DO THAT AGAIN!
EEEEEE
TM
TUM
GO! GO! YEAH! YEAH! HANA BIZ!
AHA HA HA!

ARAN OJIRO

INARIZAKI HIGH SCHOOL
CLASS 3-5

POSITION:
WING SPIKER

HEIGHT: 6'1"

WEIGHT: 177 LBS.
(AS OF JANUARY, 3RD YEAR
OF HIGH SCHOOL)

BIRTHDAY: APRIL 4

FAVORITE FOOD:
RITZ CRACKERS

CURRENT WORRY:
HE TOLD HIMSELF HE'D
ONLY WEAR THAT PAIR
OF UNDERWEAR WITH A
HOLE IN IT ONE MORE TIME
BEFORE THROWING THEM
OUT, BUT IT'S BEEN THREE
TIMES SINCE THEN...

ABILITY PARAMETERS
(5-POINT SCALE)

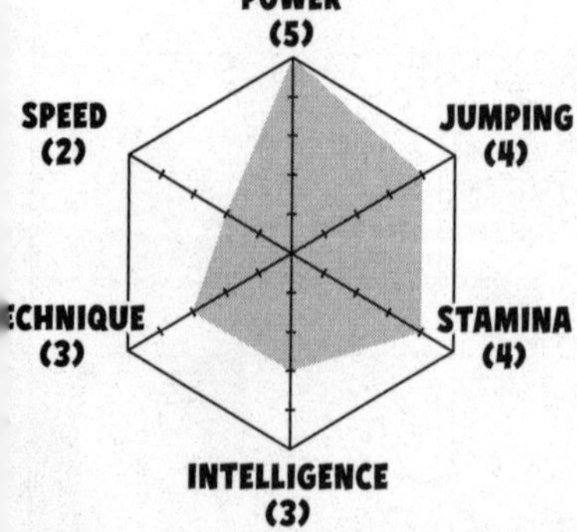
POWER
(5)
SPEED
(2)
JUMPING
(4)
ECHNIQUE
(3)
STAMINA
(4)
INTELLIGENCE
(3)

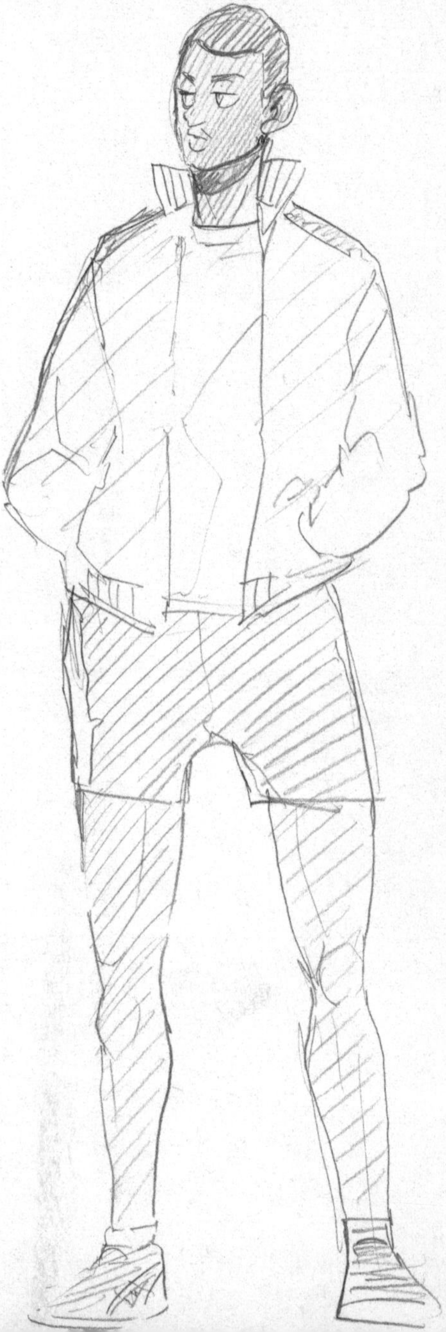

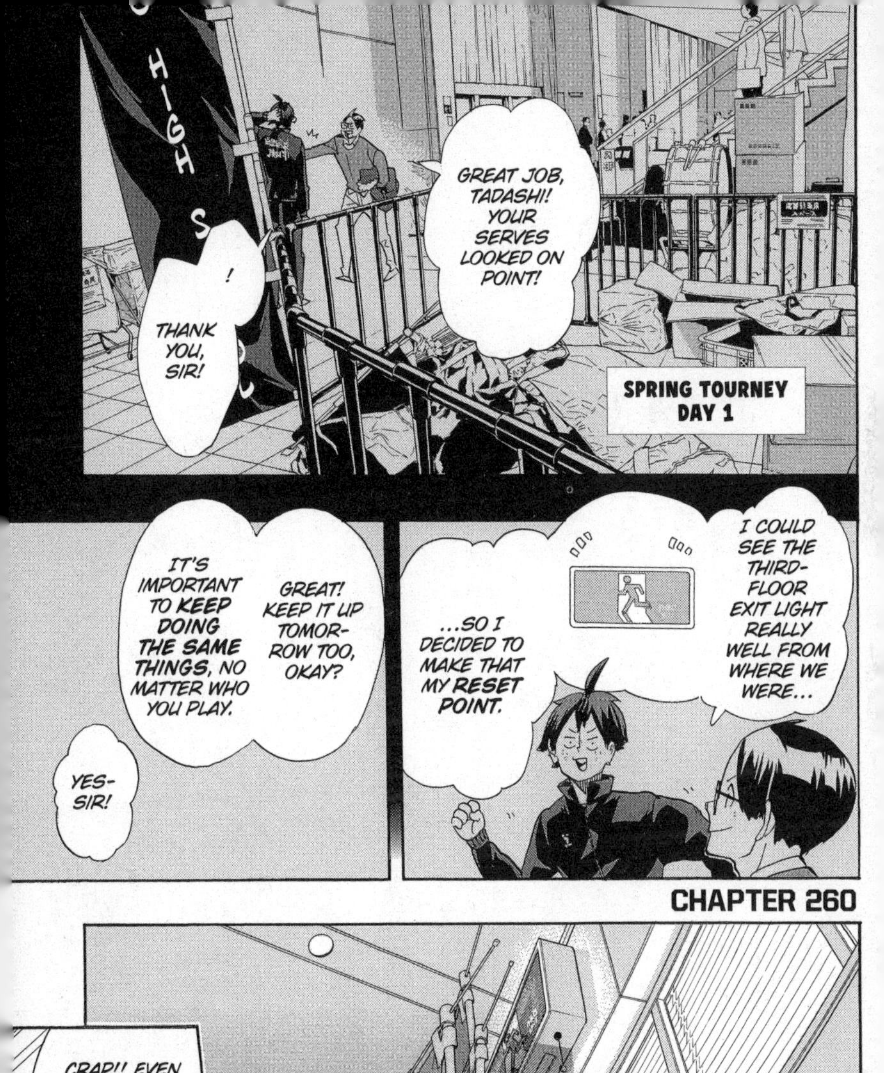
GREAT JOB, TADASHI! YOUR SERVES LOOKED ON POINT!
!
THANK YOU, SIR!
SPRING TOURNEY DAY 1
I COULD SEE THE THIRD-FLOOR EXIT LIGHT REALLY WELL FROM WHERE WE WERE...
...SO I DECIDED TO MAKE THAT MY RESET POINT.
GREAT! KEEP IT UP TOMOR-ROW TOO, OKAY?
IT'S IMPORTANT TO KEEP DOING THE SAME THINGS, NO MATTER WHO YOU PLAY.
YES-SIR!

CHAPTER 260

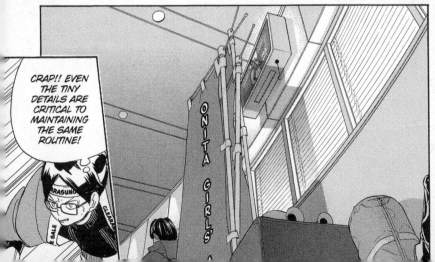

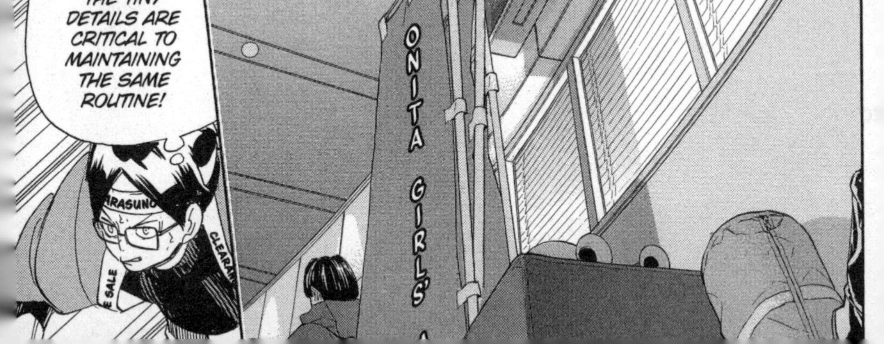
CRAP!! EVEN THE TINY DETAILS ARE CRITICAL TO MAINTAINING THE SAME ROUTINE!
ONITA GIRLS'

CHAPTER 260: Desperation

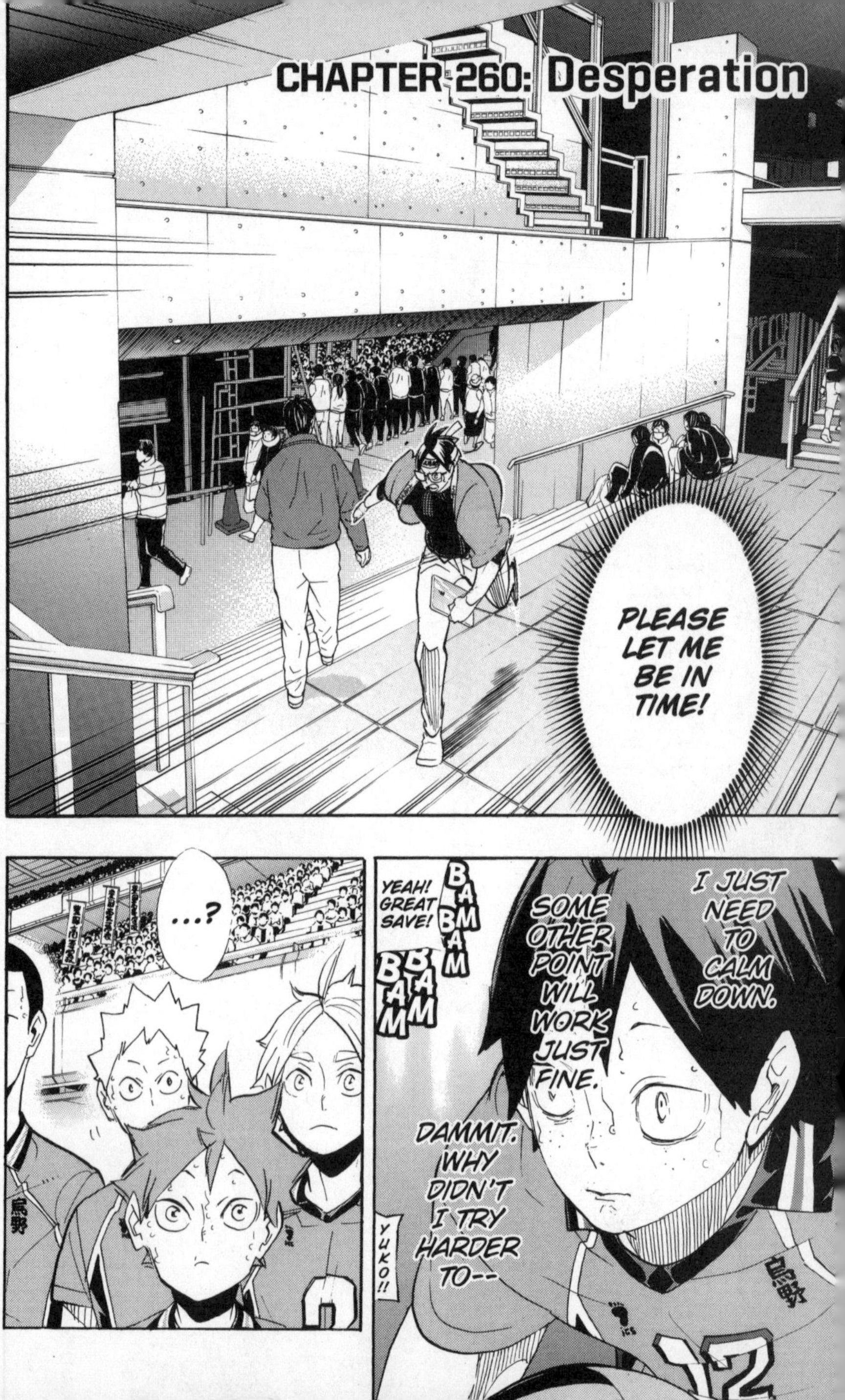
PLEASE LET ME BE IN TIME!
I JUST NEED TO CALM DOWN.
SOME OTHER POINT WILL WORK JUST FINE.
DAMMIT. WHY DIDN'T I TRY HARDER TO--
YUKO!!
BAM BAM
YEAH! GREAT SAVE!
BAM BAM
...?

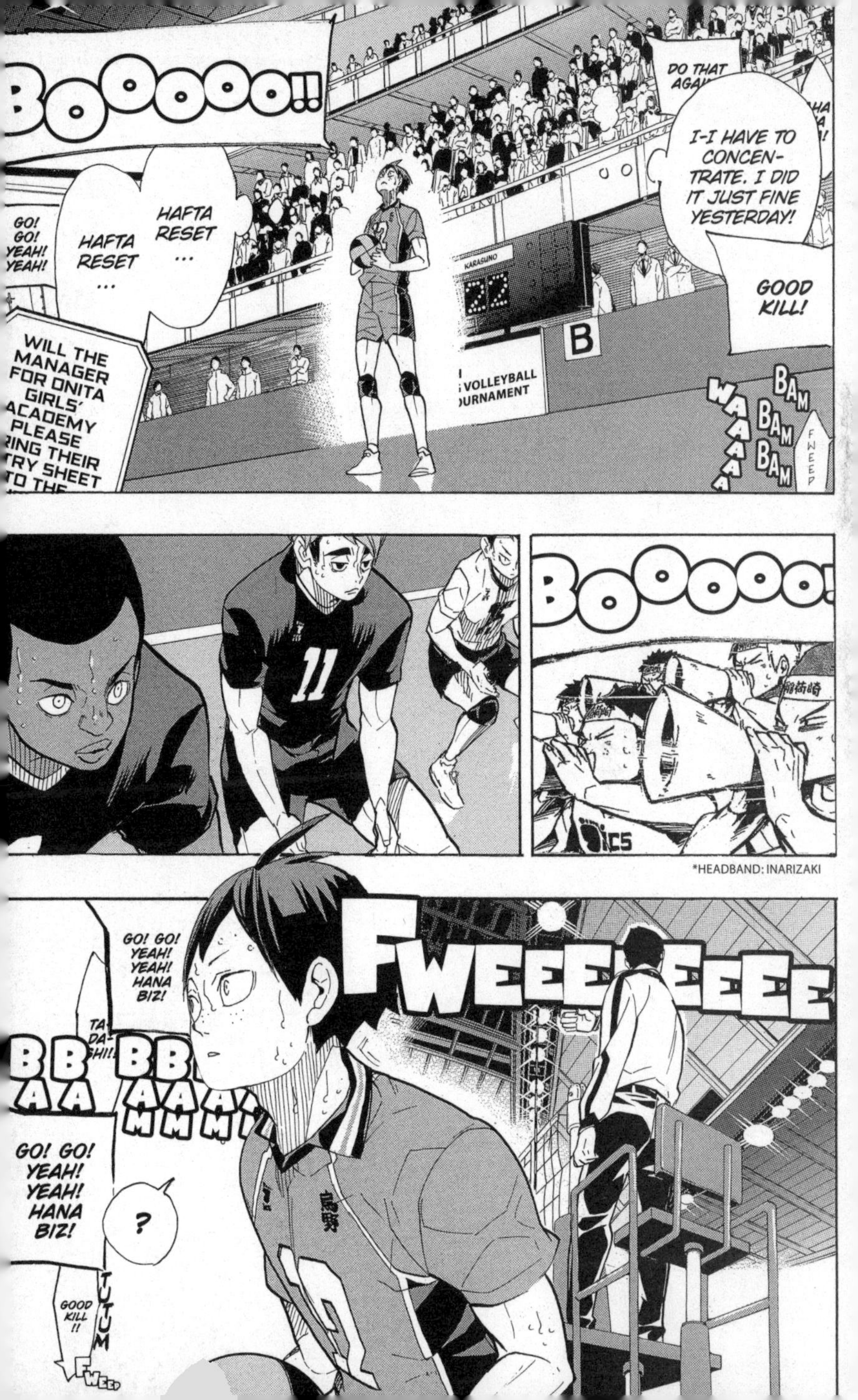
DO THAT AGAI
I-I HAVE TO CONCEN-TRATE. I DID IT JUST FINE YESTERDAY!
GOOD KILL!
BAM BAM BAM
FWEEP
WAAAAAA
KARASUNO
VOLLEYBALL OURNAMENT
HAFTA RESET ...
HAFTA RESET ...
BOOOOO!!
GO! GO! YEAH! YEAH!
WILL THE MANAGER FOR ONITA GIRLS' ACADEMY PLEASE RING THEIR TRY SHEET TO THE
BOOOOO!
*HEADBAND: INARIZAKI
FWEEEEEEEE
GO! GO! YEAH! YEAH! HANA BIZ!
TA-DASHI!!
BBB AAA MMM
BB AA
GO! GO! YEAH! YEAH! HANA BIZ!
?
TUTUM
GOOD KILL!!
FWEEP

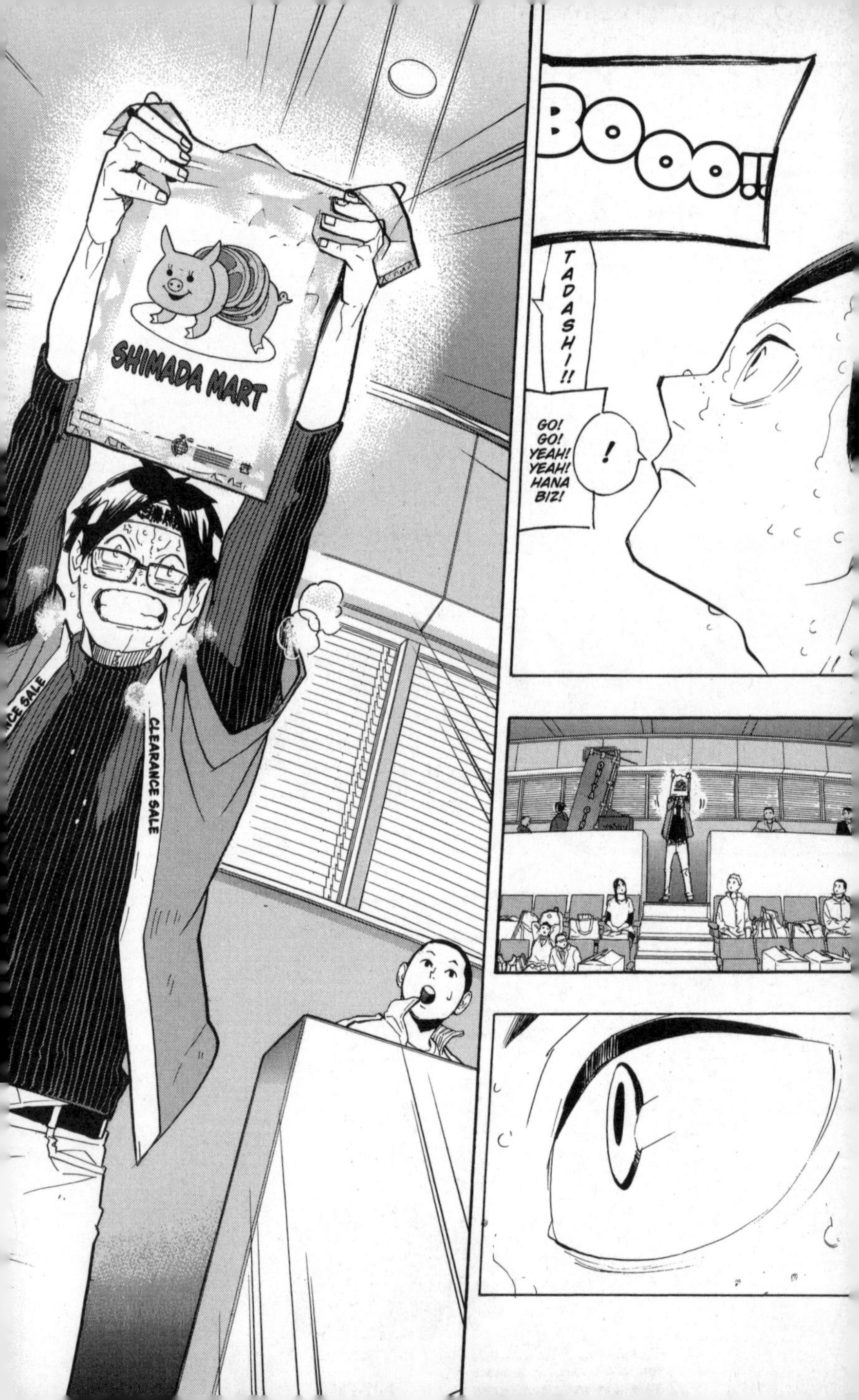
BOOO!!
TADASHI!!
GO! GO! YEAH! YEAH! HANA BIZ!
!
SHIMADA MART
CLEARANCE SALE

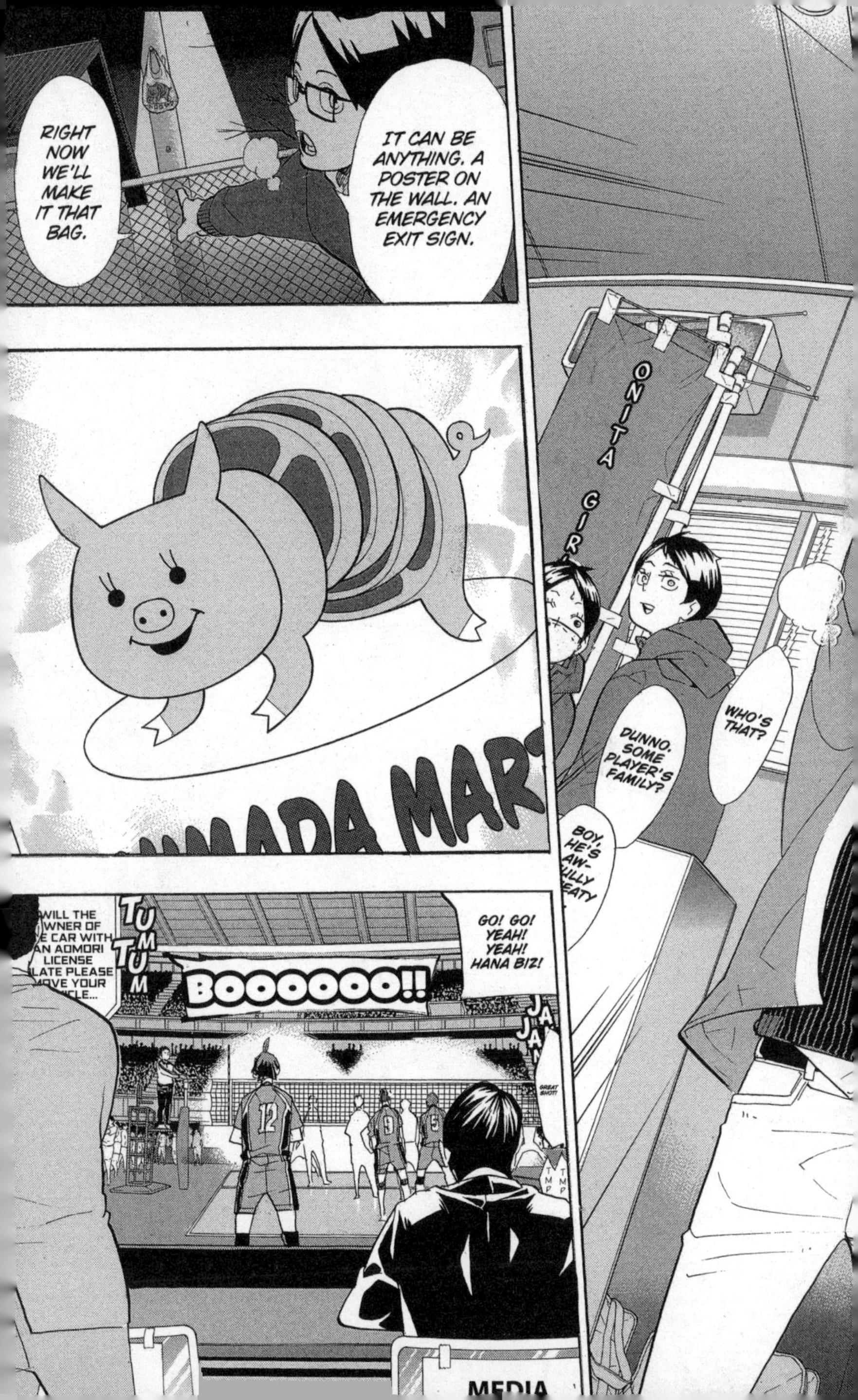
IT CAN BE ANYTHING. A POSTER ON THE WALL. AN EMERGENCY EXIT SIGN.
RIGHT NOW WE'LL MAKE IT THAT BAG.
ONITA GIR
WHO'S THAT?
DUNNO. SOME PLAYER'S FAMILY?
BOY, HE'S AW- ULLY EATY
MADA MAR
TUM TUM
WILL THE WNER OF E CAR WITH AN AOMORI LICENSE LATE PLEASE OVE YOUR ICLE...
BOOOOOOO!!
GO! GO! YEAH! YEAH! HANA BIZ!
JA JA
GREAT SHOT!
TMP TMP
MEDIA

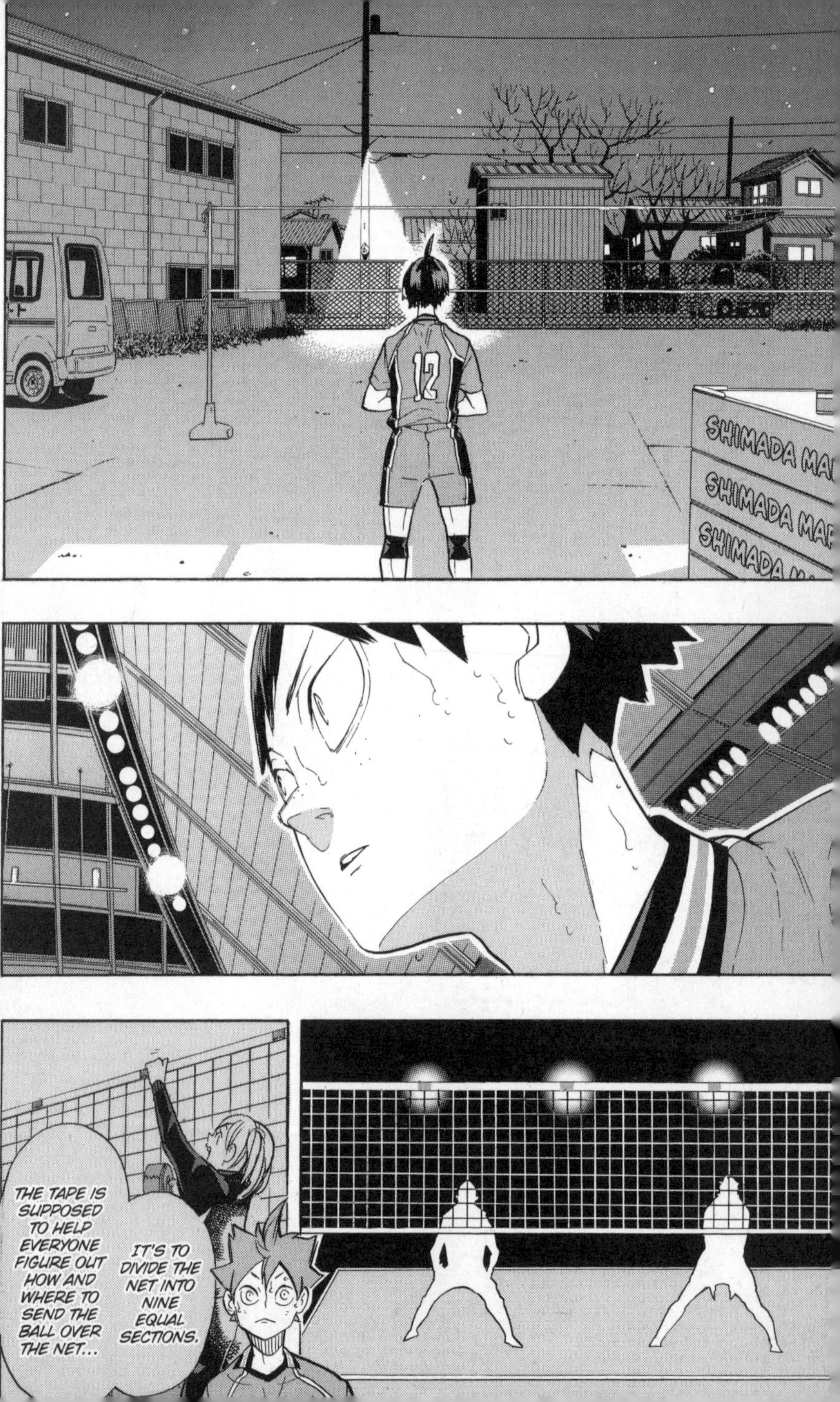
SHIMADA MAR
SHIMADA MAR
SHIMADA MA
IT'S TO DIVIDE THE NET INTO NINE EQUAL SECTIONS.
THE TAPE IS SUPPOSED TO HELP EVERYONE FIGURE OUT HOW AND WHERE TO SEND THE BALL OVER THE NET...

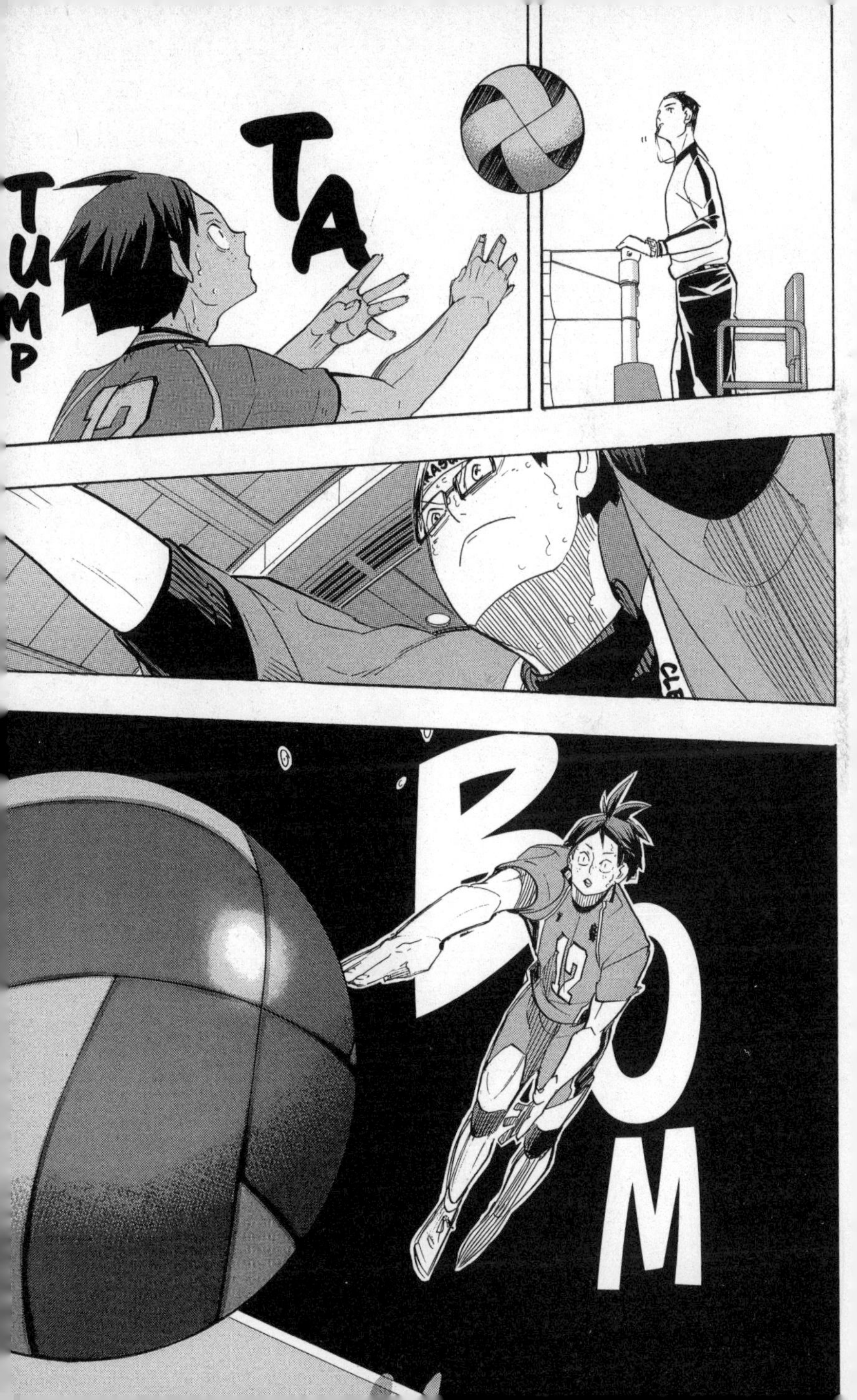
TA
TUMP
BOOM

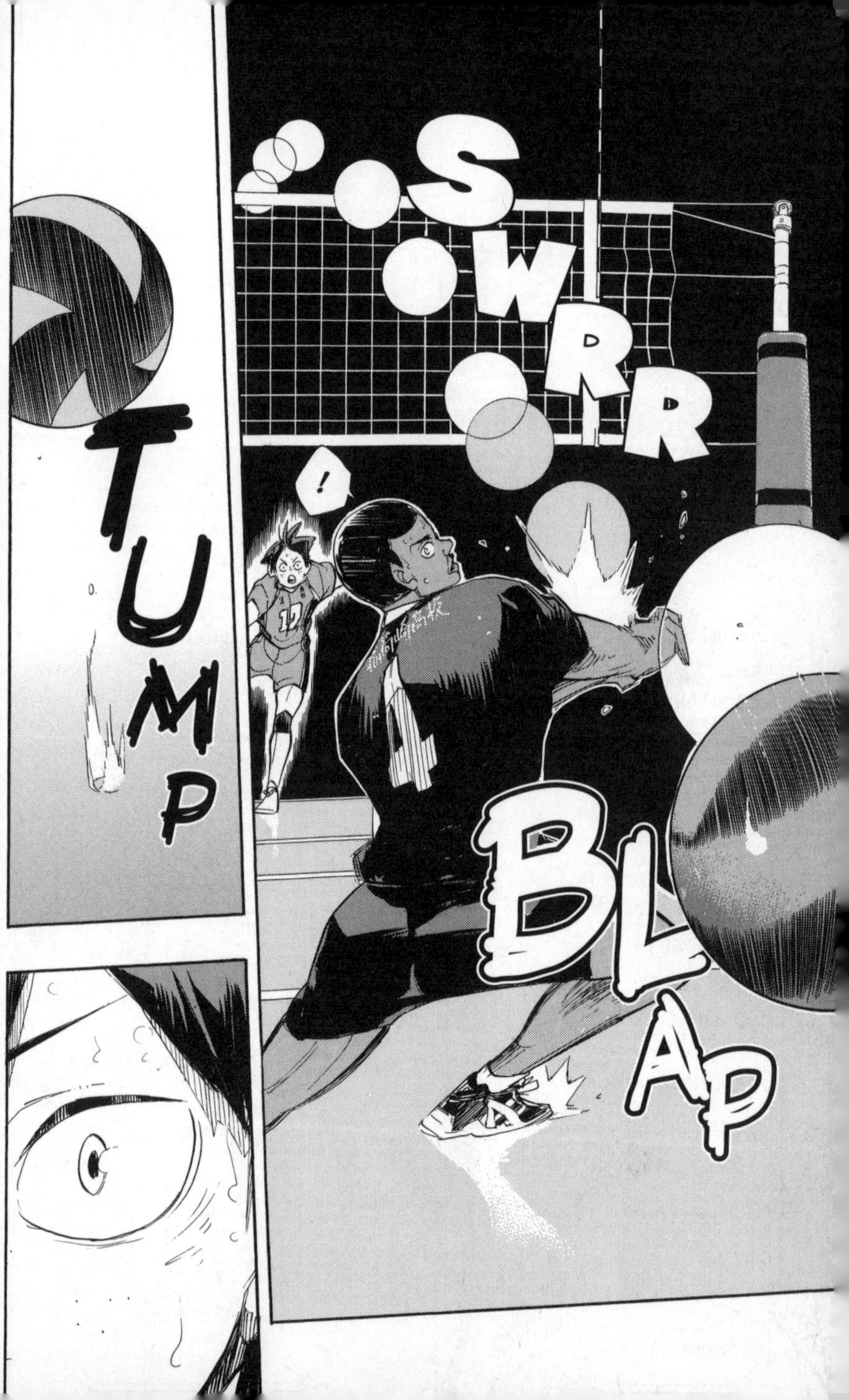
SWRR
!
BLAP
TUMP

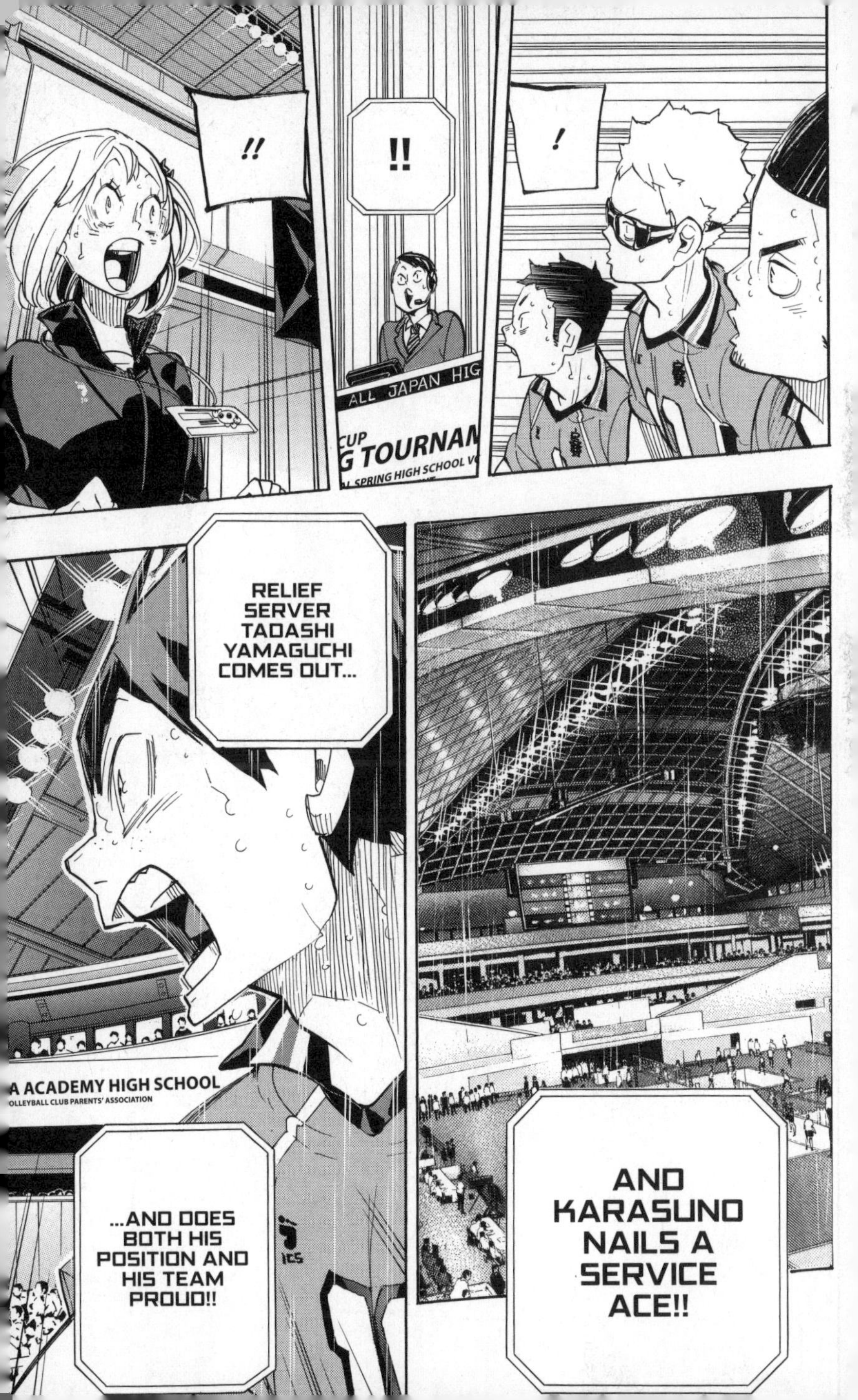

!
!!
ALL JAPAN HIG
G TOURNAM
!!
AND KARASUNO NAILS A SERVICE ACE!!
RELIEF SERVER TADASHI YAMAGUCHI COMES OUT...
A ACADEMY HIGH SCHOOL
...AND DOES BOTH HIS POSITION AND HIS TEAM PROUD!!

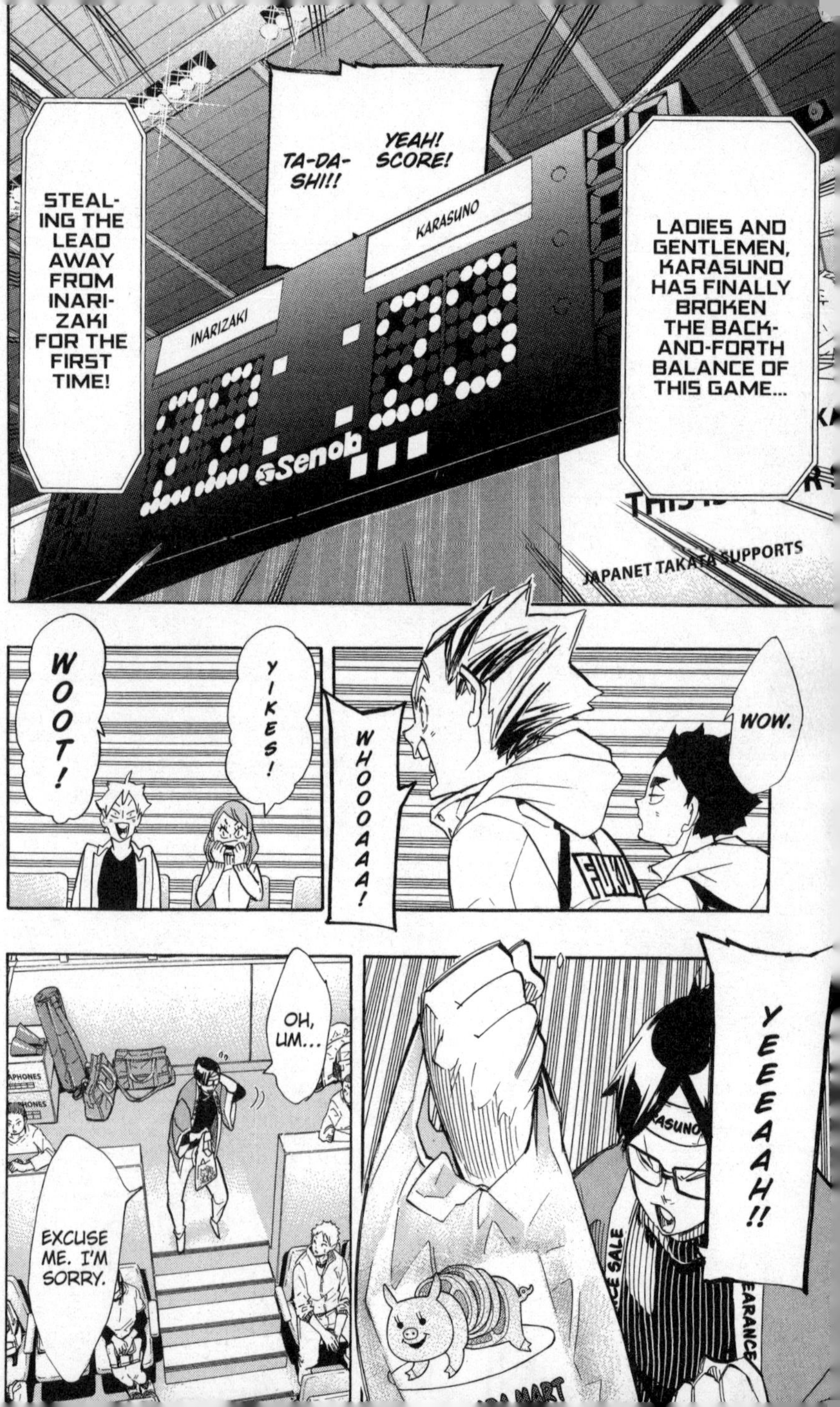
LADIES AND GENTLEMEN, KARASUNO HAS FINALLY BROKEN THE BACK-AND-FORTH BALANCE OF THIS GAME...
YEAH! SCORE!
TA-DA-SHI!!
KARASUNO
INARIZAKI
Senob
JAPANET TAKATA SUPPORTS
STEALING THE LEAD AWAY FROM INARIZAKI FOR THE FIRST TIME!
WOW.
WHOOOOAAA!
YIKES!
WOOT!
YEEEAAAH!!
OH, UM...
EXCUSE ME. I'M SORRY.

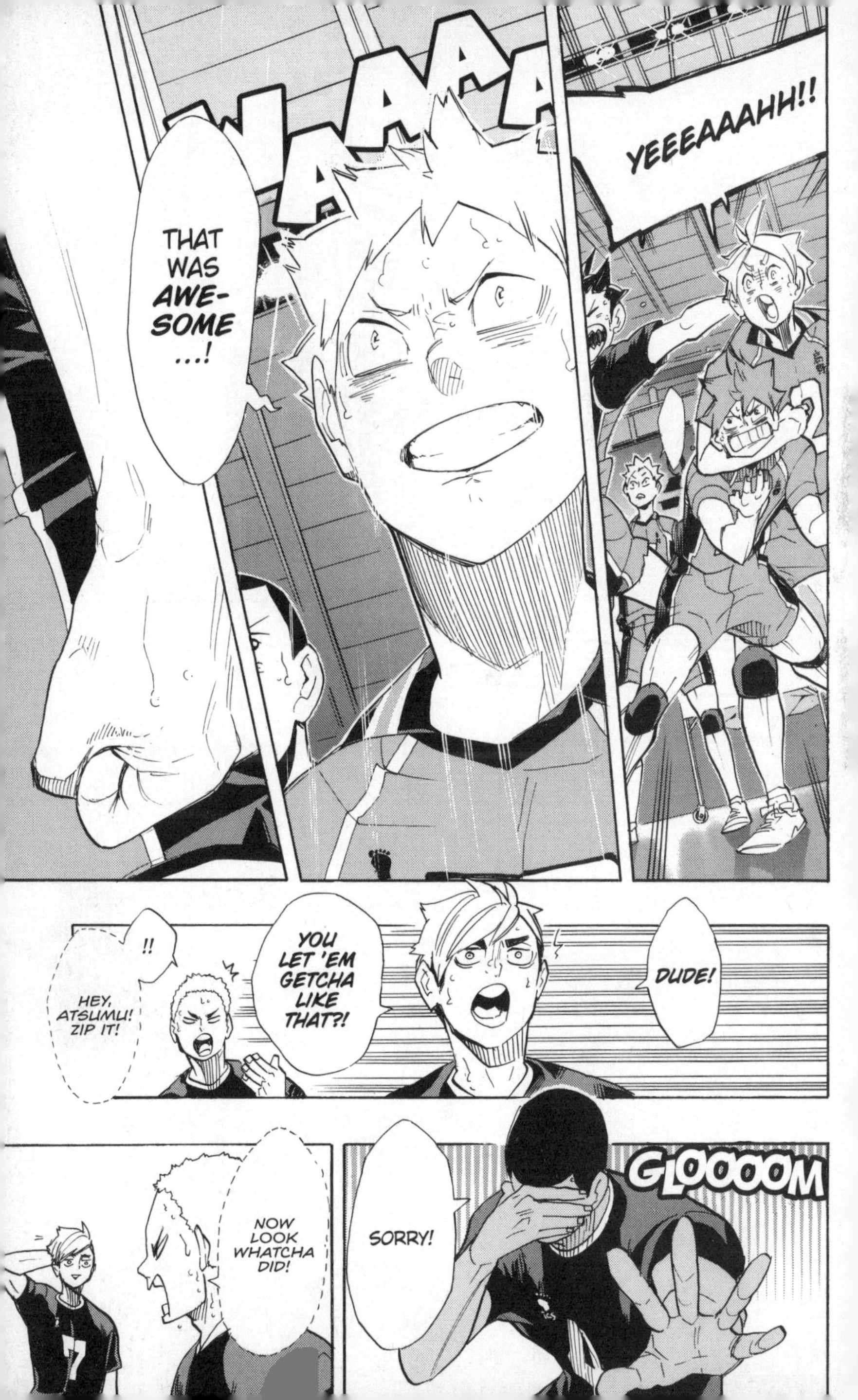
YEEEAAAHH!!
THAT WAS AWESOME...!
DUDE!
YOU LET 'EM GETCHA LIKE THAT?!
!!
HEY, ATSUMU! ZIP IT!
GLOOOOM
SORRY!
NOW LOOK WHATCHA DID!

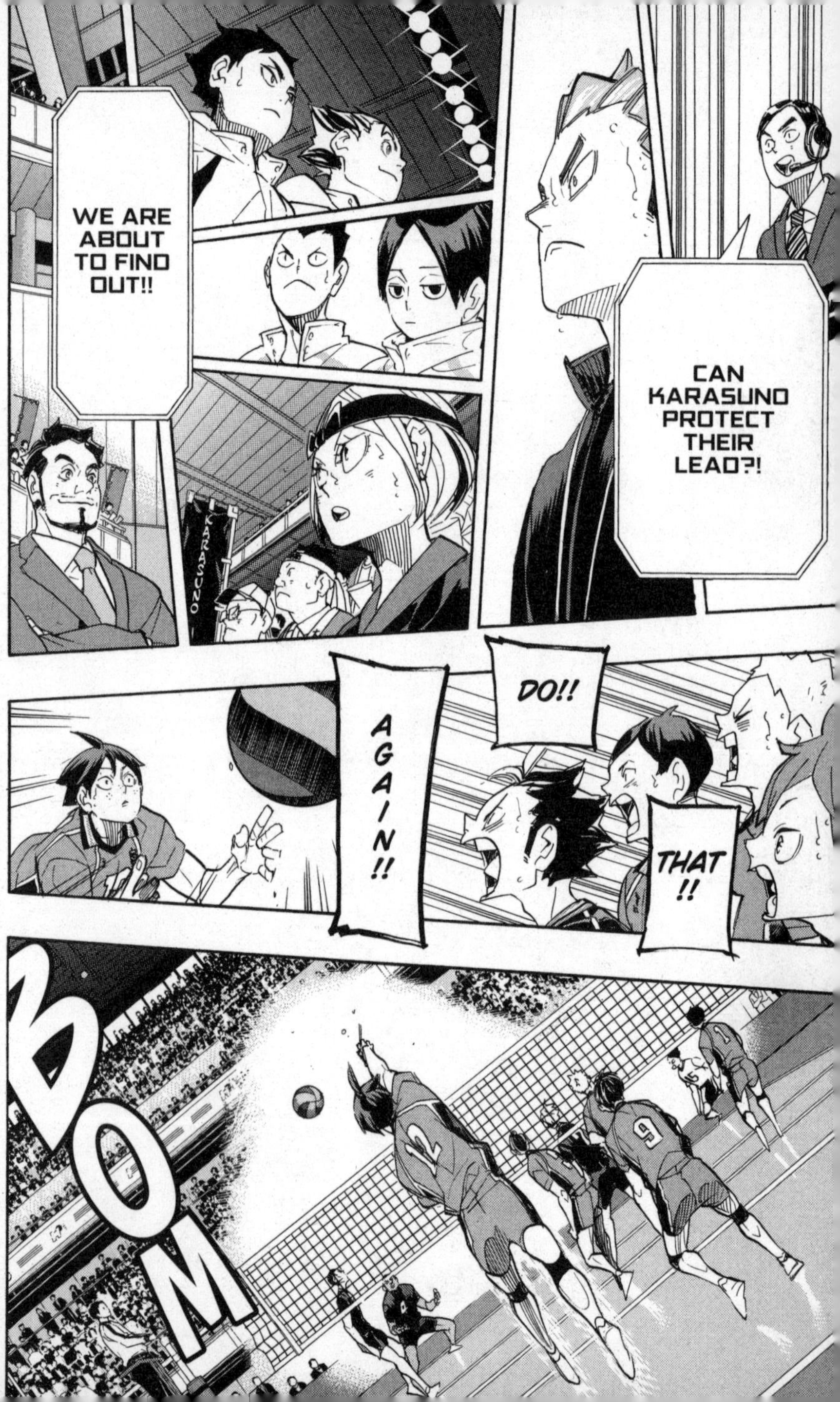
CAN KARASUNO PROTECT THEIR LEAD?!
WE ARE ABOUT TO FIND OUT!!
DO!!
THAT !!
AGAIN!!
BOOM

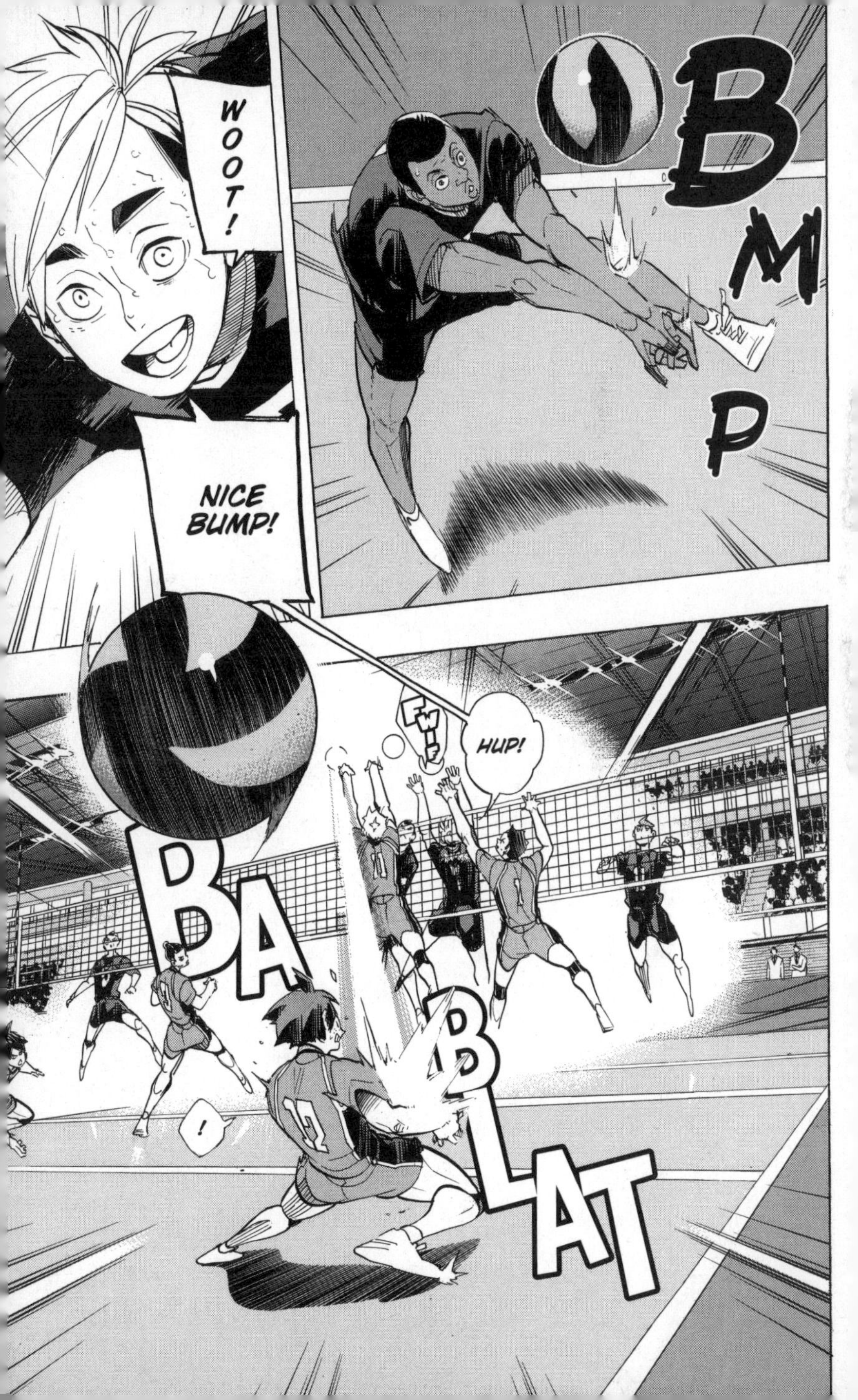
BMP
WOOT!
NICE BUMP!
FWIF
HUP!
BABLAT
!

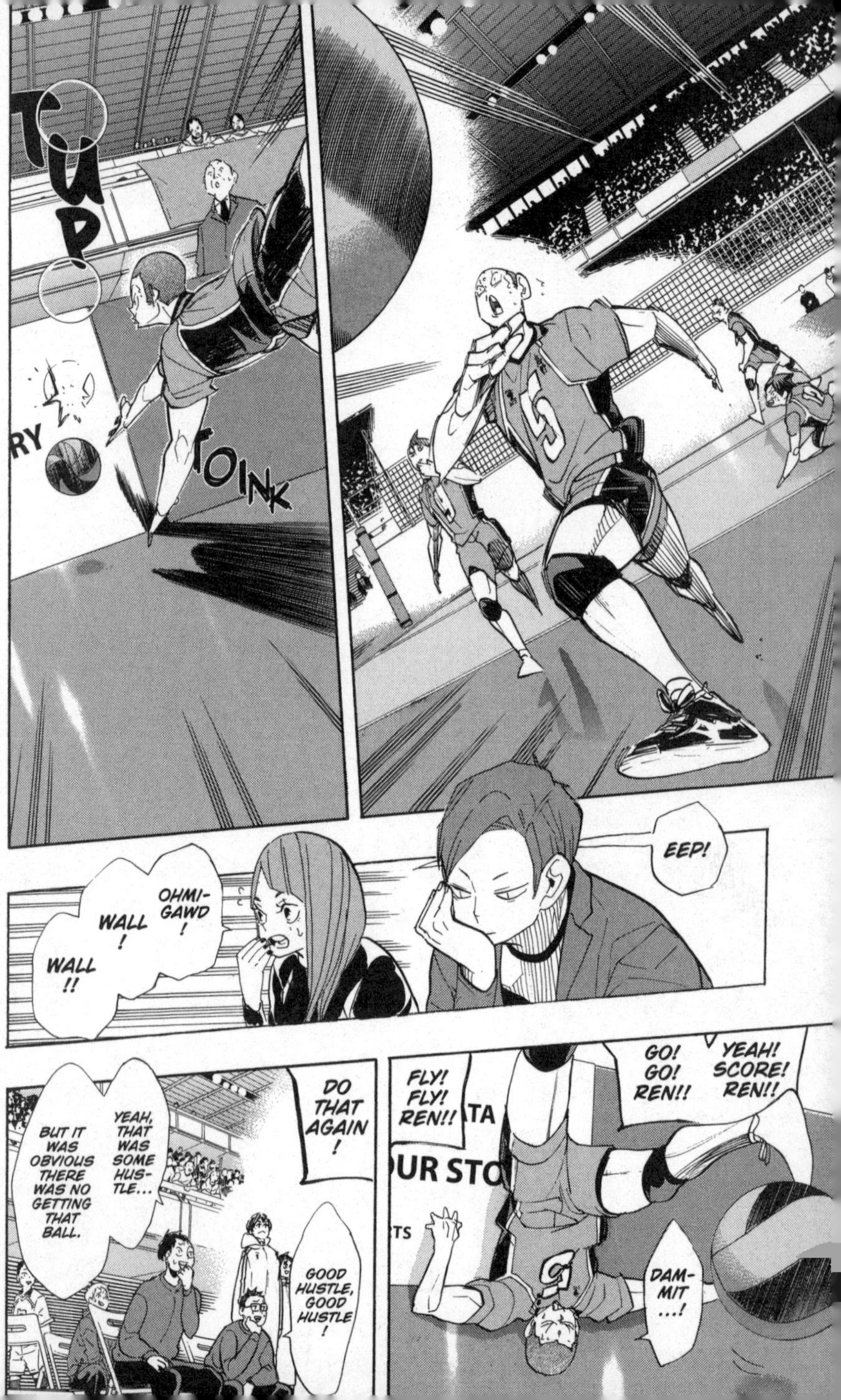

TUP
TOINK
EEP!
OHMI-GAWD!
WALL!
WALL!!
YEAH! SCORE! REN!!
GO! GO! REN!!
FLY! FLY! REN!!
DAM-MIT...!
DO THAT AGAIN!
YEAH, THAT WAS SOME HUS-TLE...
BUT IT WAS OBVIOUS THERE WAS NO GETTING THAT BALL.
GOOD HUSTLE, GOOD HUSTLE!

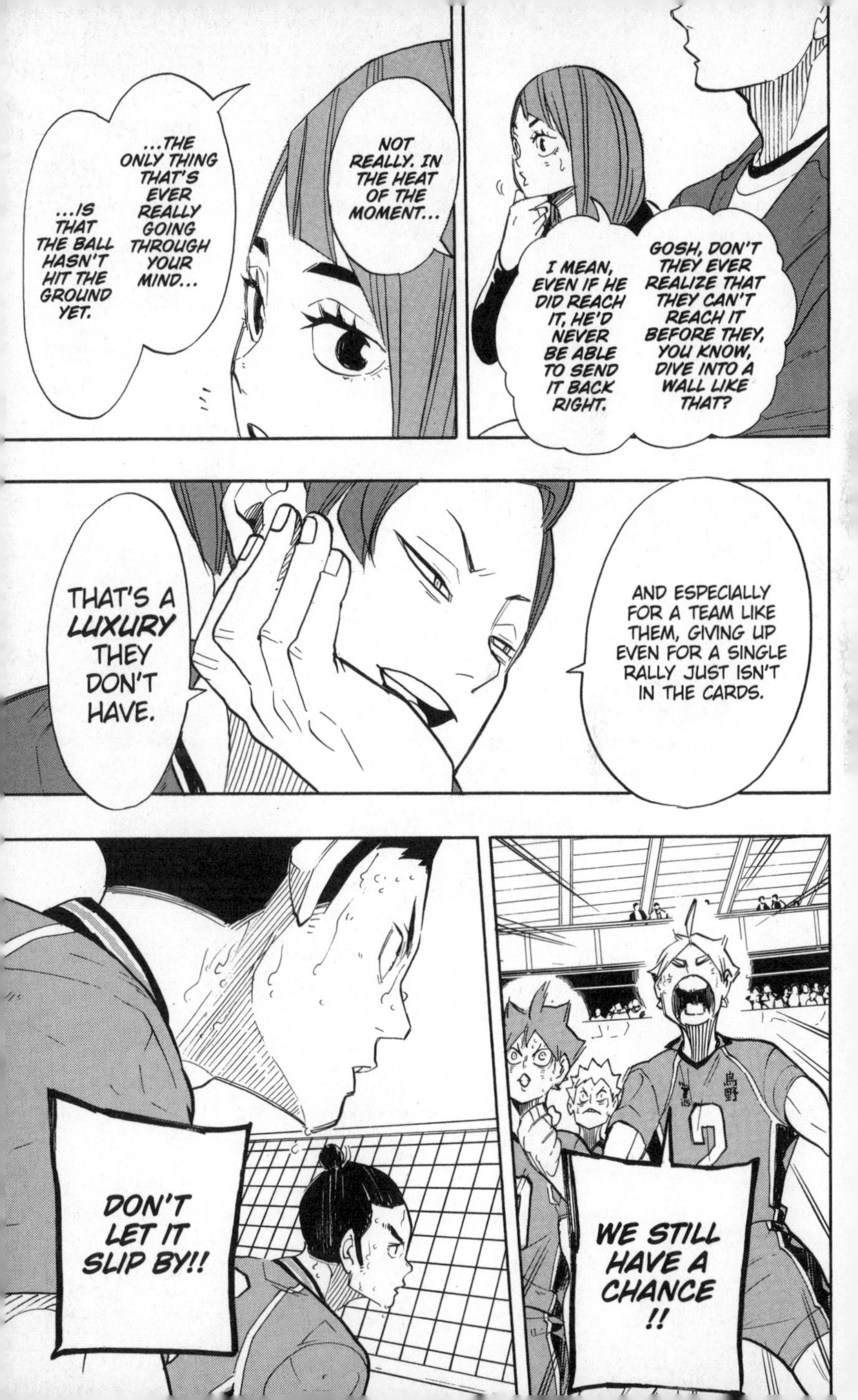
GOSH, DON'T THEY EVER REALIZE THAT THEY CAN'T REACH IT BEFORE THEY, YOU KNOW, DIVE INTO A WALL LIKE THAT?
I MEAN, EVEN IF HE DID REACH IT, HE'D NEVER BE ABLE TO SEND IT BACK RIGHT.
NOT REALLY. IN THE HEAT OF THE MOMENT...
...THE ONLY THING THAT'S EVER REALLY GOING THROUGH YOUR MIND...
...IS THAT THE BALL HASN'T HIT THE GROUND YET.
AND ESPECIALLY FOR A TEAM LIKE THEM, GIVING UP EVEN FOR A SINGLE RALLY JUST ISN'T IN THE CARDS.
THAT'S A LUXURY THEY DON'T HAVE.
WE STILL HAVE A CHANCE!!
DON'T LET IT SLIP BY!!

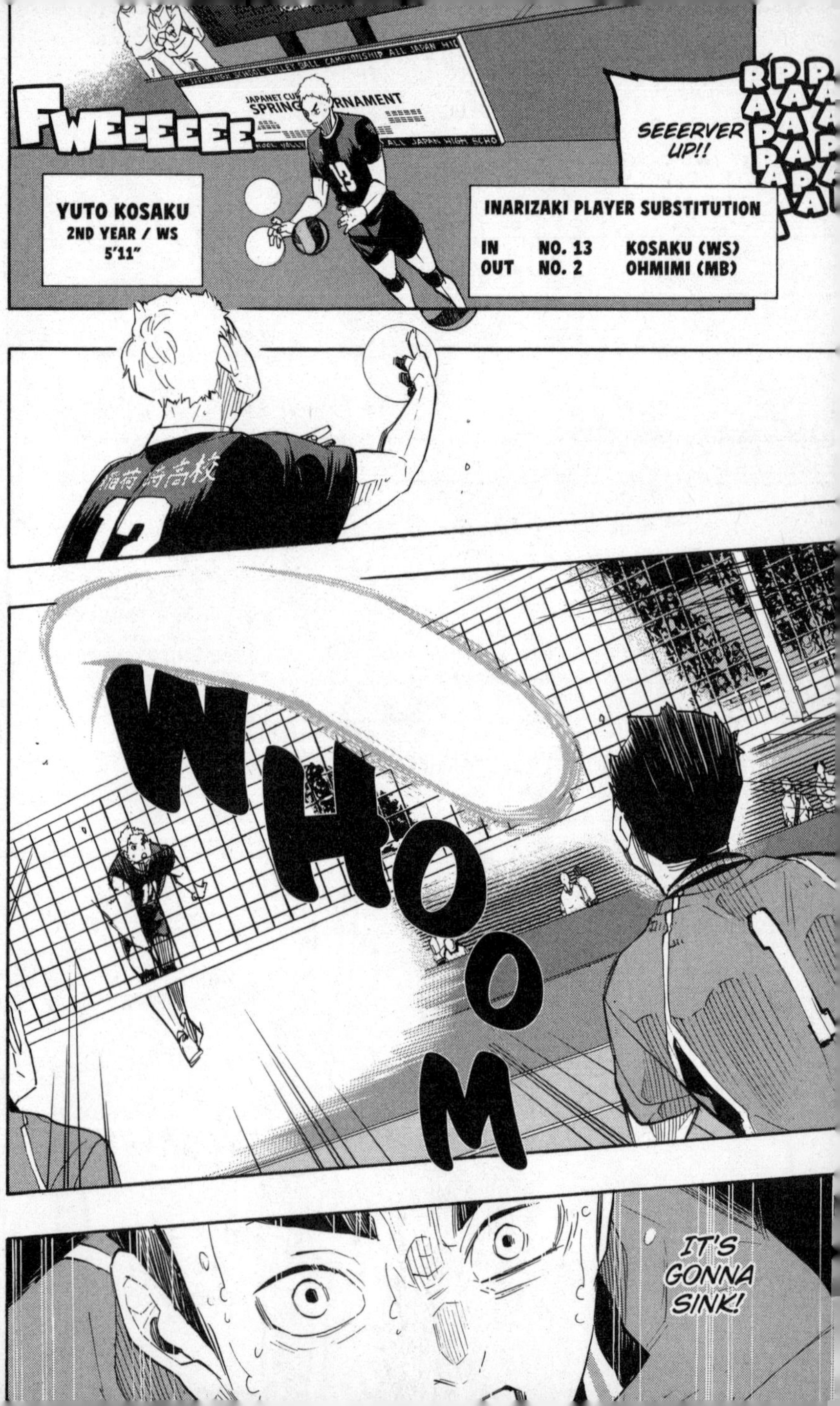
RAPAPAPA
SEEERVER UP!!
INARIZAKI PLAYER SUBSTITUTION
IN NO. 13 KOSAKU (WS)
OUT NO. 2 OHMIMI (MB)
YUTO KOSAKU
2ND YEAR / WS
5'11"
FWEEEEEE
WHOOOM
IT'S GONNA SINK!

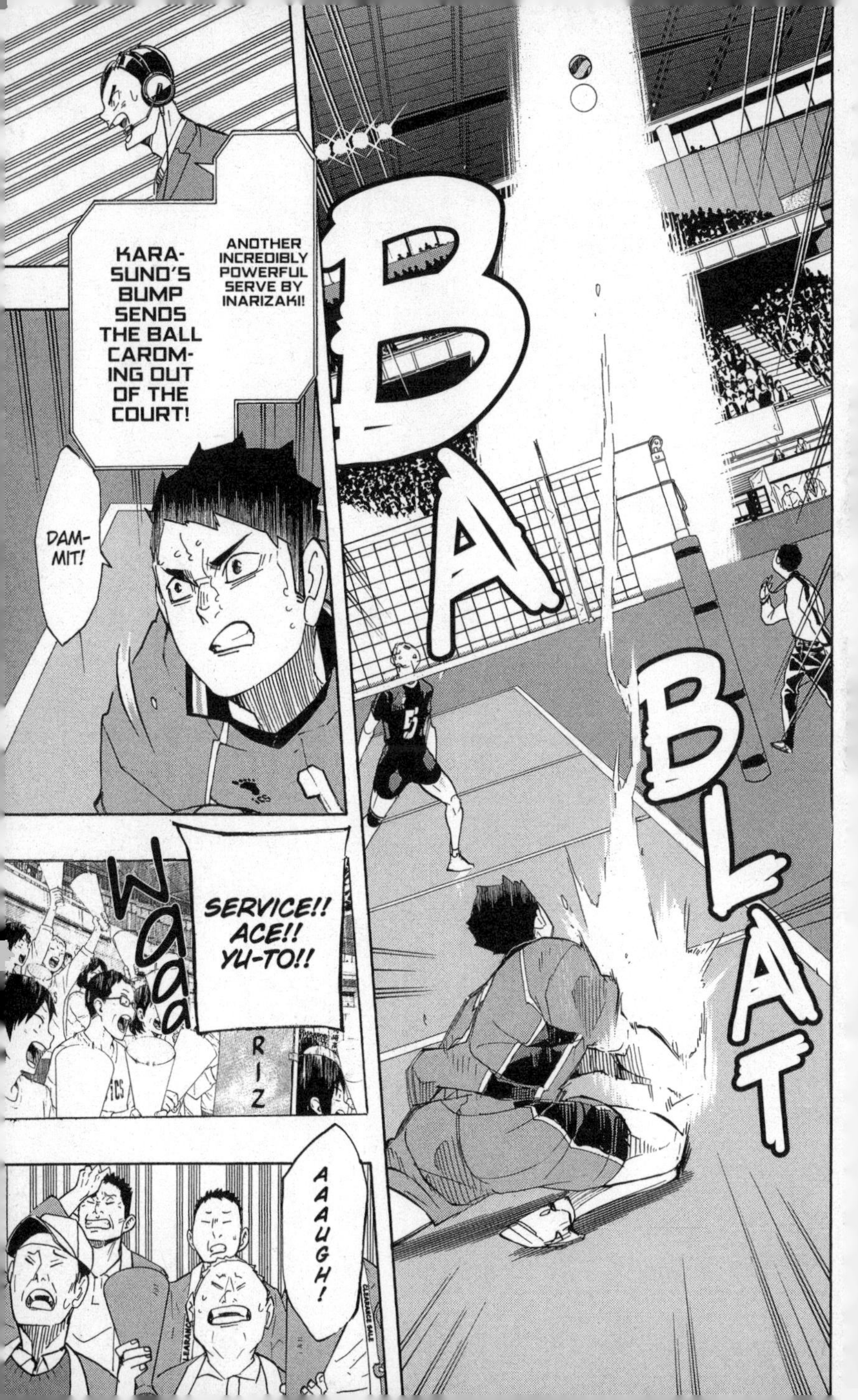
BA
BLAT
ANOTHER INCREDIBLY POWERFUL SERVE BY INARIZAKI!
KARASUNO'S BUMP SENDS THE BALL CAROMING OUT OF THE COURT!
DAMMIT!
SERVICE!! ACE!! YU-TO!!
WAAA
AAAAUGH!

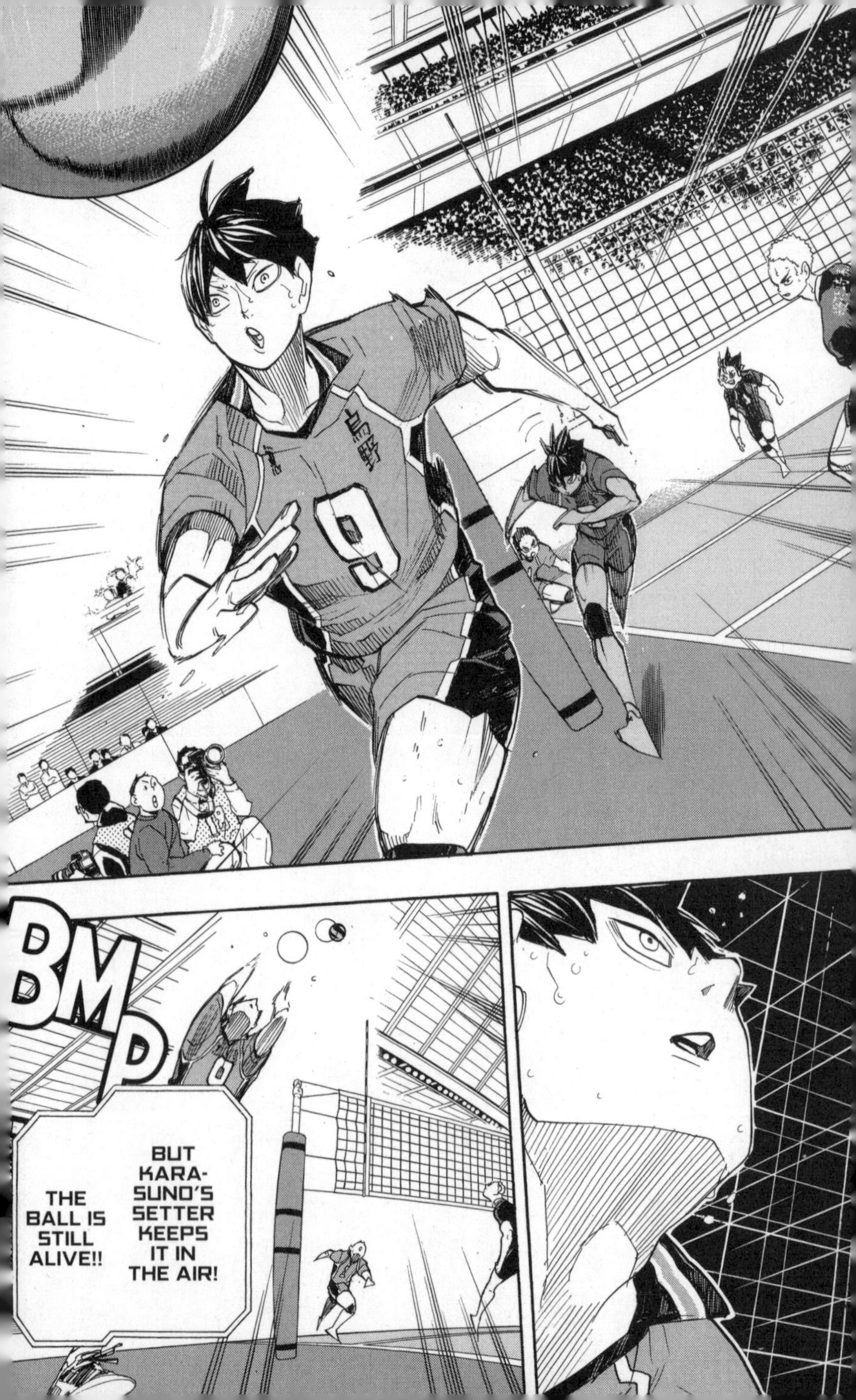
BMP
BUT KARA-SUNO'S SETTER KEEPS IT IN THE AIR!
THE BALL IS STILL ALIVE!!

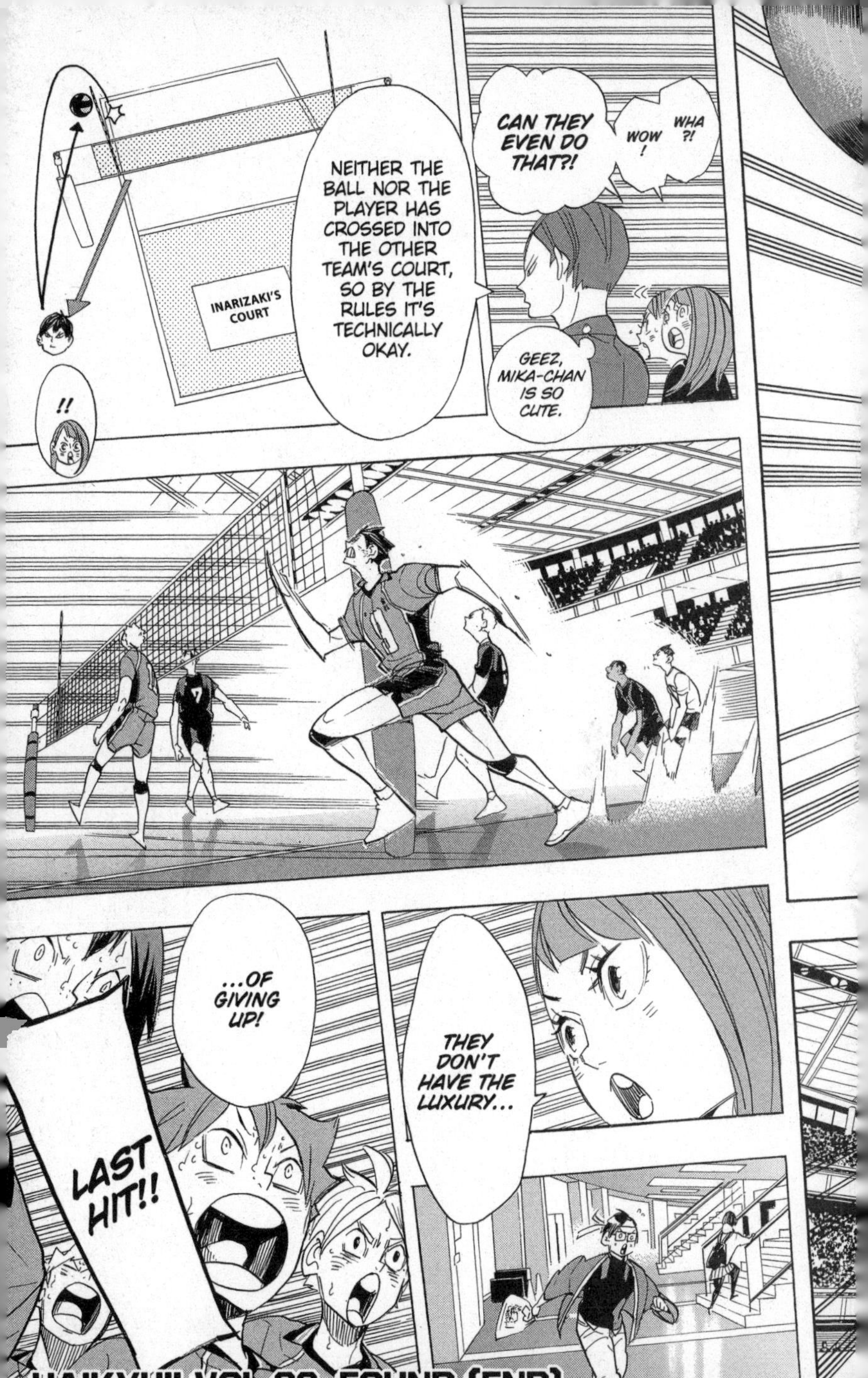
WHA?!
WOW!
CAN THEY EVEN DO THAT?!
GEEZ, MIKA-CHAN IS SO CUTE.
NEITHER THE BALL NOR THE PLAYER HAS CROSSED INTO THE OTHER TEAM'S COURT, SO BY THE RULES IT'S TECHNICALLY OKAY.
INARIZAKI'S COURT
!!
THEY DON'T HAVE THE LUXURY...
...OF GIVING UP!
LAST HIT!!

HAIKYU!! VOL 29: FOUND (END)

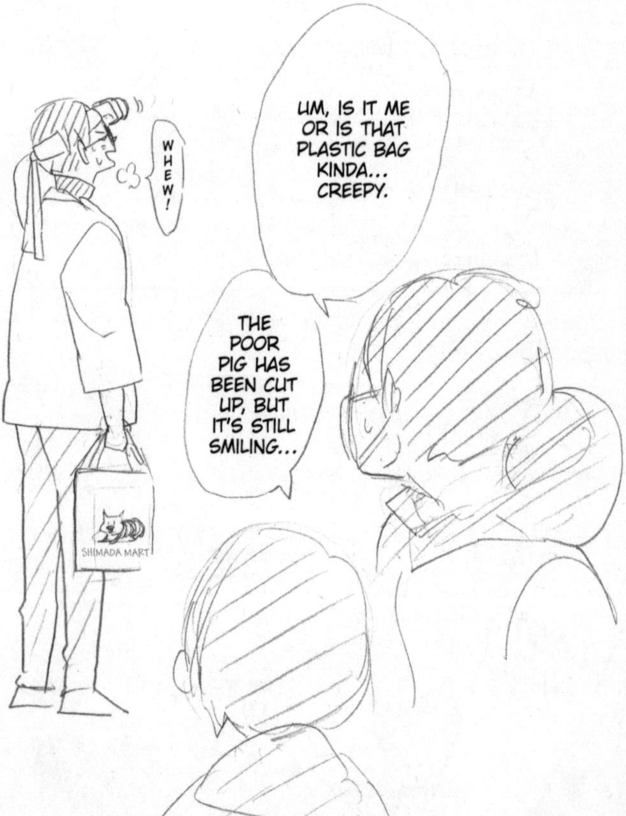
UM, IS IT ME OR IS THAT PLASTIC BAG KINDA... CREEPY.
WHEW!
THE POOR PIG HAS BEEN CUT UP, BUT IT'S STILL SMILING...
SHIMADA MART

MIKA YAMAKA

**NOHEBI ACADEMY
CLASS 3-4**

**POSITION:
WING SPIKER**

HEIGHT: 5'2"

**WEIGHT: 98 LBS.
(AS OF JANUARY, 3RD YEAR
OF HIGH SCHOOL)**

BIRTHDAY: DECEMBER 19

**FAVORITE FOOD:
PRETZ CRACKERS
(TOASTED FLAVOR)**

**CURRENT WORRY:
SHE'S HAVING TROUBLE
KEEPING UP WITH WHAT'S
TRENDING ON INSTAGRAM.**

**ABILITY PARAMETERS
(5-POINT SCALE)**

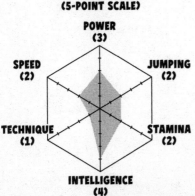

POWER
(3)

SPEED
(2)

JUMPING
(2)

TECHNIQUE
(1)

STAMINA
(2)

INTELLIGENCE
(4)

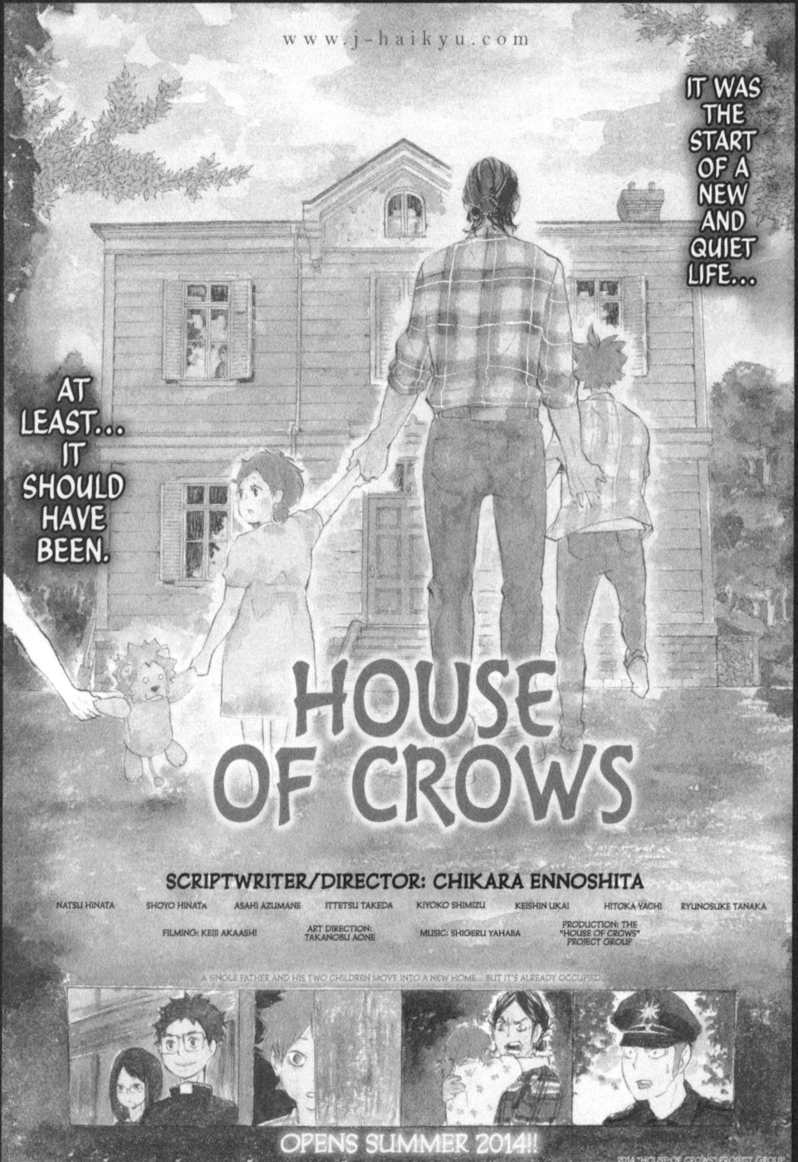
www.j-haikyu.com
IT WAS THE START OF A NEW AND QUIET LIFE...
AT LEAST... IT SHOULD HAVE BEEN.
HOUSE OF CROWS
SCRIPTWRITER/DIRECTOR: CHIKARA ENNOSHITA
NATSU HINATA
SHOYO HINATA
ASAHI AZUMANE
ITTETSU TAKEDA
KIYOKO SHIMIZU
KEISHIN UKAI
HITOKA YACHI
RYUNOSUKE TANAKA
FILMING: KEIJI AKAASHI
ART DIRECTION: TAKANOBU AONE
MUSIC: SHIGERU YAHABA
PRODUCTION: THE "HOUSE OF CROWS" PROJECT GROUP
A SINGLE FATHER AND HIS TWO CHILDREN MOVE INTO A NEW HOME... BUT IT'S ALREADY OCCUPIED...
OPENS SUMMER 2014!!
2014 "HOUSE OF CROWS" PROJECT GROUP

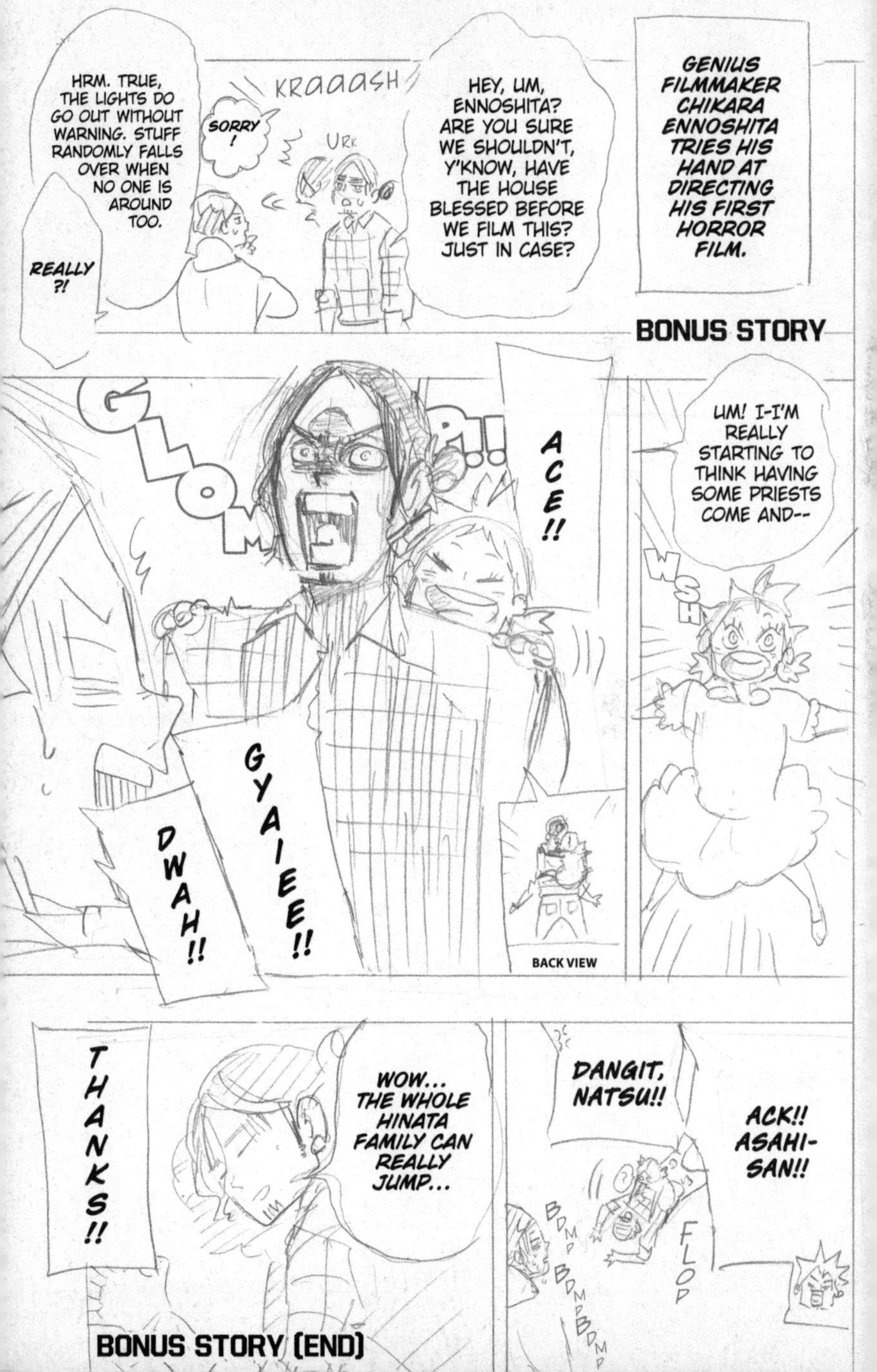
BONUS STORY
GENIUS FILMMAKER CHIKARA ENNOSHITA TRIES HIS HAND AT DIRECTING HIS FIRST HORROR FILM.
HEY, UM, ENNOSHITA? ARE YOU SURE WE SHOULDN'T, Y'KNOW, HAVE THE HOUSE BLESSED BEFORE WE FILM THIS? JUST IN CASE?
KRAAASH
URK
SORRY!
HRM. TRUE, THE LIGHTS DO GO OUT WITHOUT WARNING. STUFF RANDOMLY FALLS OVER WHEN NO ONE IS AROUND TOO.
REALLY?!
UM! I-I'M REALLY STARTING TO THINK HAVING SOME PRIESTS COME AND--
WSH
ACE!!
GLOMP!!
BACK VIEW
GYAIEE!!
DWAH!!
DANGIT, NATSU!!
ACK!! ASAHI-SAN!!
FLOP
BDMP BDMP BDMP BDMP
WOW... THE WHOLE HINATA FAMILY CAN REALLY JUMP...
THANKS!!
BONUS STORY (END)

EDITOR'S NOTES

The English edition of Haikyu!! maintains the honorifics used in the original Japanese version. For those of you who are new to these terms, here's a brief explanation to help with your reading experience!

When saying someone's name in Japanese, a suffix is often attached to indicate how familiar the speaker is with the person. Some are more polite and respectful, while others are endearing.

1 *-kun* is often used for young men or boys, usually someone you are familiar with.

2 *-chan* is used for young children and can be used as a term of endearment.

3 *-san* is used for someone you respect or are not close to, or to be polite.

4 *Senpai* is used for someone who is older than you or in a higher position or grade in school.

5 *Kohai* is used for someone who is younger than you or in a lower position or grade in school.

6 *Sensei* means teacher.

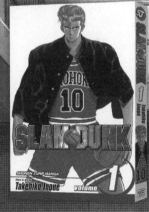

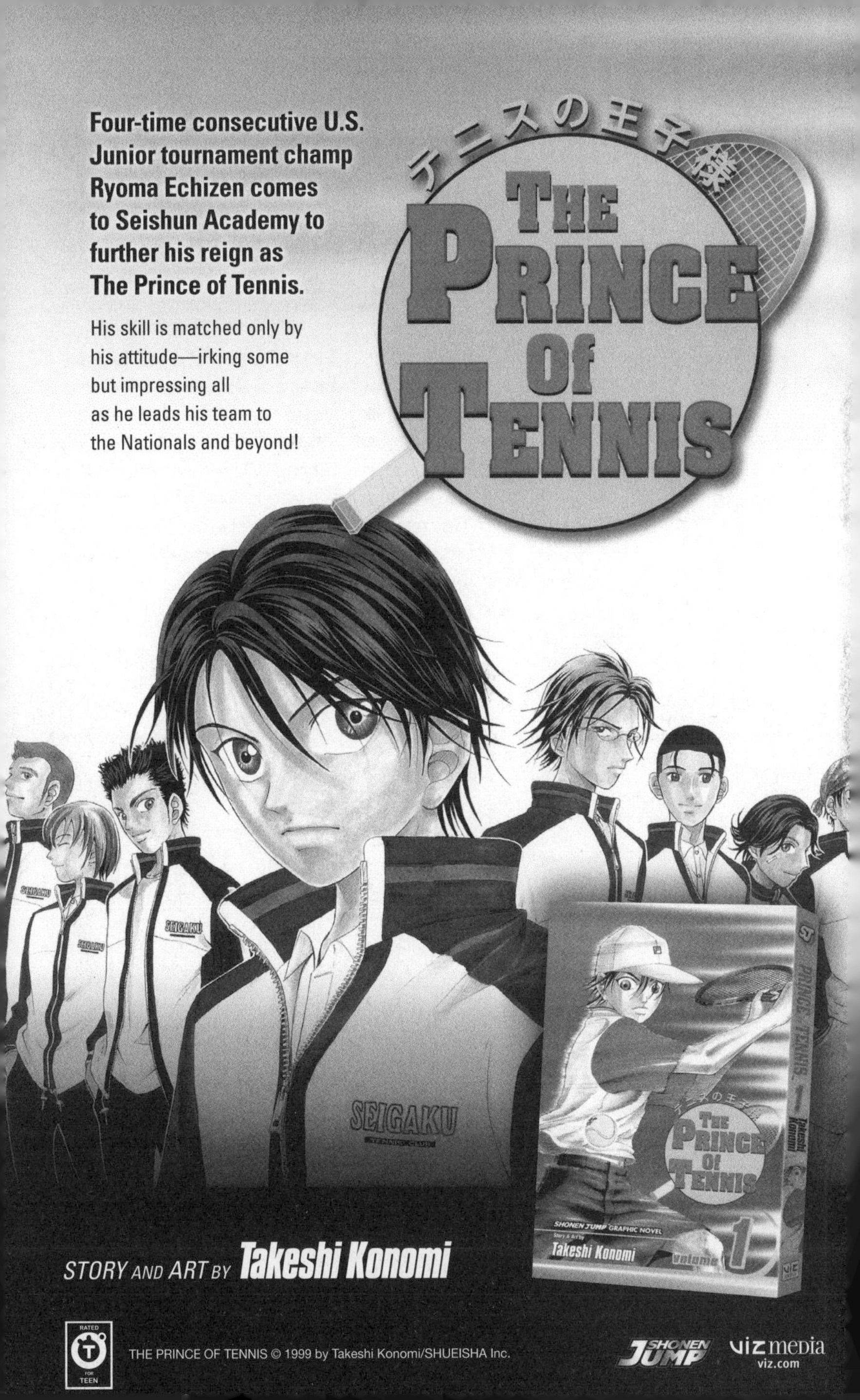

Four-time consecutive U.S. Junior tournament champ Ryoma Echizen comes to Seishun Academy to further his reign as The Prince of Tennis.

His skill is matched only by his attitude—irking some but impressing all as he leads his team to the Nationals and beyond!

THE PRINCE OF TENNIS

STORY AND ART BY **Takeshi Konomi**

SHONEN JUMP

viz media
viz.com

ON SALE NOW
YU-GI-OH!
ARC-V

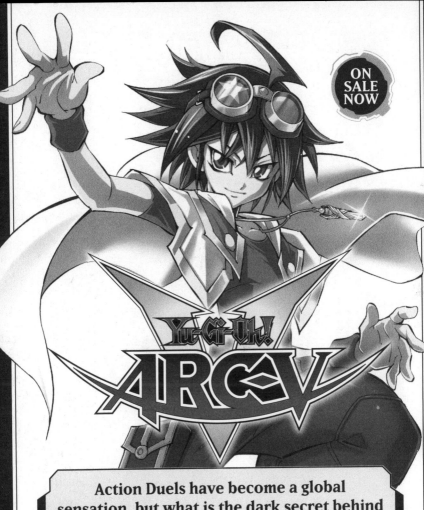

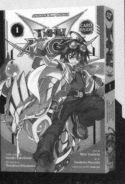

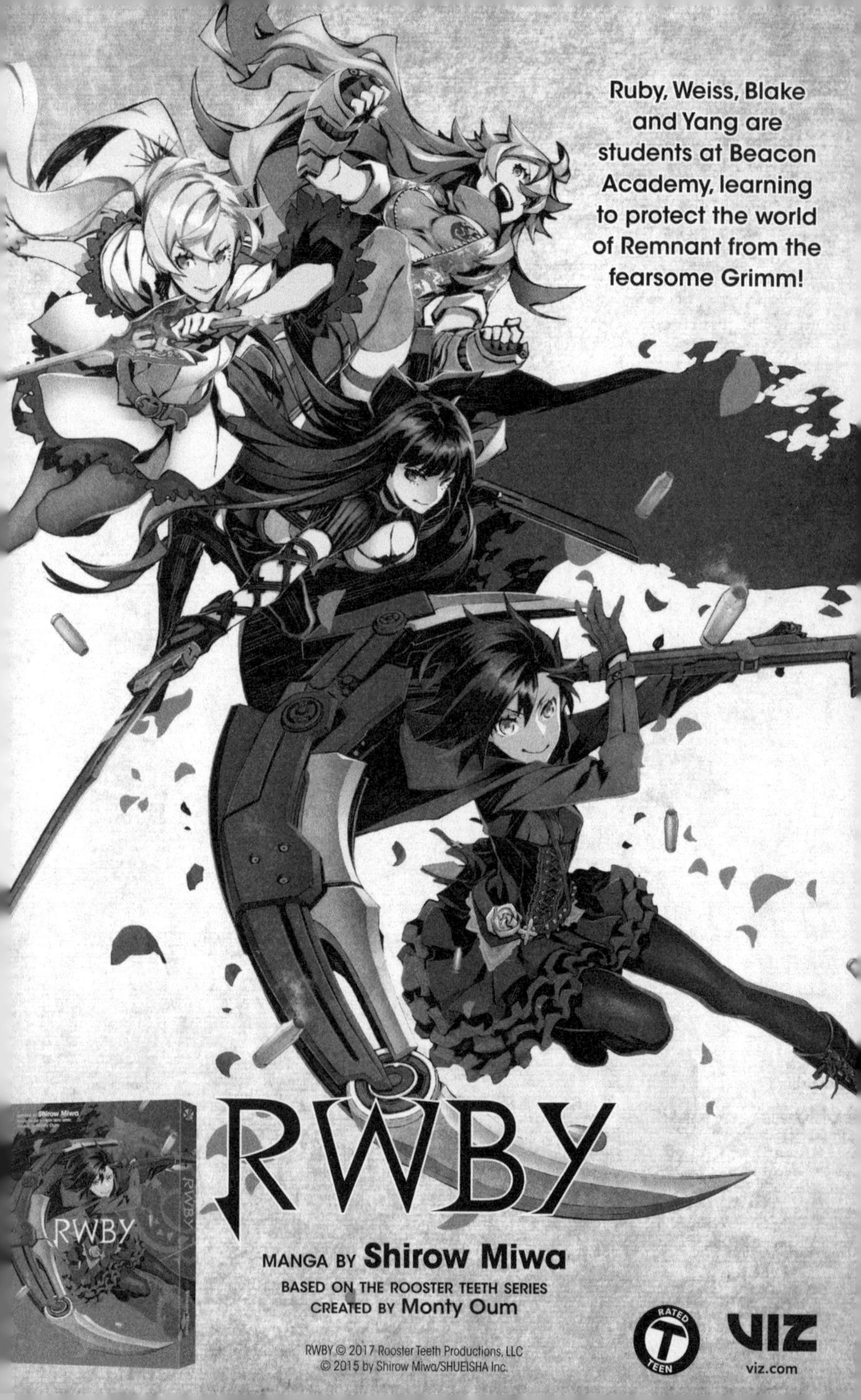
Ruby, Weiss, Blake and Yang are students at Beacon Academy, learning to protect the world of Remnant from the fearsome Grimm!
RWBY
MANGA BY Shirow Miwa
BASED ON THE ROOSTER TEETH SERIES
CREATED BY Monty Oum
RWBY © 2017 Rooster Teeth Productions, LLC
© 2015 by Shirow Miwa/SHUEISHA Inc.
RATED T TEEN
VIZ
viz.com

You're Reading the
WRONG WAY!

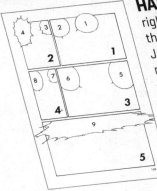

HAIKYU!! reads from right to left, starting in the upper-right corner. Japanese is read from right to left, meaning that action, sound effects and word-balloon order are completely reversed from English order.